The Living Language
A Reader

The Living Language
A Reader

Linda A. Morris
University of California, Davis

Hans A. Ostrom
University of Puget Sound

Linda P. Young
California State University, Sacramento

HARCOURT BRACE JOVANOVICH, PUBLISHERS
San Diego   New York   Chicago   Washington, D.C.   Atlanta
London   Sydney   Toronto

COVER: *Below the Towers of Tower Falls, Yellowstone Park* by Thomas Moran (1909). Courtesy San Diego Museum of Art

Copyright © 1984 by Harcourt Brace Jovanovich, Inc.

All rights reserved. No part of this publication may be reproduced or transmitted in any form or by any means, electronic or mechanical, including photocopy, recording, or any information storage and retrieval system, without permission in writing from the publisher.

Requests for permission to make copies of any part of the work should be mailed to: Permissions, Harcourt Brace Jovanovich, Publishers, Orlando, Florida 32887.

ISBN: 0-15-551127-0
Printed in the United States of America
Library of Congress Catalog Card Number: 83-081789

Copyrights and acknowledgments appear on pages 421–24, which constitute a continuation of the copyright page.

Preface

In offering a new language reader, we are reaffirming the conviction that an increased awareness of language and the goals of college-level composition courses go hand in hand. Students who become increasingly conscious of the power that language asserts over us—and who learn in turn to exert more control over their own use of language—will ultimately become more confident and competent writers. Our own experience as composition instructors, and the experience of our colleagues, has borne out this conviction.

Our dissatisfaction with most of the language readers currently available, however, has prompted us to be governed by three main principles in editing this reader. First of all, we wanted to include essays that emphasize the changing, dynamic nature of language, and that emphasize the positive potential inherent in our use of language. We have therefore attempted to avoid the tendency to include essays that stress unduly what has gone wrong with language; one need only peruse the table of contents of other readers to discover entire sections of books devoted to language misuse, to euphemisms, to clichés, to the "decline" of language. Without necessarily intending to do so, such readers give students the impression that our language, rather than offering exciting new horizons, represents a veritable mine-field of problems to avoid. We do not mean to suggest that we believe current language usage is without serious problems or that clichéd writing, for example, is desirable; rather, we have chosen to emphasize the more positive vistas that an increased awareness of language can offer our students.

Second, we have included only those essays that are in themselves models of good writing, that succeed as essays, *per se*. Accordingly, we have resisted the temptation to include a piece of writing just because it would illustrate a particular point or fit a particular category. In several instances, in fact, we have included essays that are not concerned with language as a subject matter but are instead excellent examples of writing within the field under consideration—essays, that is, that use language to advantage.

Third, as the table of contents of this reader suggests, we have organized the essays to illustrate how language functions within a variety of occupations, disciplines, or subject areas. One way to interest beginning writers in the topic of language, we believe, is to interest them in the function of language within particular areas that have already captured their attention. Science students, for example, may learn that written language plays a more central role in the sciences in general than they might have supposed. When a practicing surgeon or a recognized scientific scholar takes the time to write about the particular significance of language to the scientist, we trust our students will become more receptive to issues of language in general.

We have integrated reading assignments and discussions with the rhetorical and mechanical concerns commonly associated with composition courses. The discussion questions that follow each essay address issues relevant to the essay's content, its rhetorical strategies, the author's use of language, and suggestions for writing assignments. The headnotes to each essay provide, in addition to pertinent biographical information, a brief introduction to the author's rhetorical strategies; an alternate table of contents organizes the essays according to the chief rhetorical modes they demonstrate. Finally, we have written brief introductory essays for each chapter that, while discussing the particular perspective on language offered within the section, attempt to conform to the principles of good essay writing.

Although many universities use language readers primarily in entrance-level composition courses, we have prepared this reader with the thought that the variety and scope of the essays included will appeal to, and be useful to, students at all levels of accomplishment. We are confident, moreover, that our discussions of rhetorical concerns and our commitment to selecting essays of high quality will make this volume suitable for any college course in composition.

Preface

In preparing this text we were aided by a number of people who offered us helpful suggestions and/or moral support. Our thanks, therefore, go to Jackie Bacon, Ken DeBow, Nori Hirasuna, and Tom Venturino. We also wish to thank Matt Milan and Jack Thomas from Harcourt Brace Jovanovich, whose assistance and encouragement have been invaluable. Most especially, however, we wish to thank Evelyn Kasmire, Carol McConnell, and Susan Voss, whose patience and assistance were crucial throughout this entire endeavor.

LINDA A. MORRIS
HANS A. OSTROM
LINDA B. YOUNG

Table of Contents

Preface v

The Varieties of English 1
Peter Farb, "Man the Talker" 4
Helen Keller, "Everything Has a Name" 12
Richard Mitchell, "The Worm in the Brain" 17
William F. Buckley, "The Hysteria About Words" 28
Norman Cousins, "A Growing Wealth of Words" 32
Lewis Carroll, "Humpty Dumpty" 36
Lewis Thomas, "Notes on Punctuation" 46

Language and the Community 52
Diane Johnson, "Doctor Talk" 55
Burton Bernstein, "Rybernian" 61
Joan Didion, "On Going Home" 67
Maxine Hong Kingston, "A Visit to My Aunt" 72
Alleen Pace Nilsen, "Sexism in the Language of Marriage" 77
Daniel Yankelovich, "Lying Well Is the Best Revenge" 88
Martin Luther King, Jr., "Letter from Birmingham Jail" 95

Language and the Media 114
Tony Schwartz, "The Second God" 118
Joshua Meyrowitz, "Where Have the Children Gone?" 124

Tom Wolfe, "Porno-violence" 129
Norman Cousins, "An Epitaph for the *Saturday Review*—and Culture, Too" 137
M. F. K. Fisher, "As the Lingo Languishes" 142
Consumers Union, "It's Natural! It's Organic! Or Is It?" 154
Stanley Kauffmann, "Why I'm Not Bored" 162

Language and Politics 170

George Orwell, "Politics and the English Language" 173
Walter Lippmann, "The Indispensable Opposition" 188
Lewis H. Lapham, "Confusion Worse Confounded" 196
Edmund White, "The Political Vocabulary of Homosexuality" 203
Richard Rodriguez, "Aria" 217

Language and Sports 241

Francine Hardaway, "Foul Play: Sports Metaphors as Public Doublespeak" 243
Joseph Durso, "You Could Look It Up" 252
A. B. Giamatti, "Hyperbole's Child" 267
William Zinsser, "Sports" 276
Roger Angell, "Stories for a Rainy Afternoon" 286
Red Smith, "Unconquerable" 296

Language in Science and Technology 301

Albert Einstein, "The Common Language of Science" 304
Lewis Thomas, "Social Talk" 308
Francine Patterson and Eugene Linden, "Koko's First Words" 313
Ruth Nelson, "The First Literate Computers?" 324
Susan Sontag, "A Rhetoric of Disease" 333

Language and the Arts 343

Edward Weston, "Things Seen into Things Known" 345
Ingmar Bergman, "Film-making" 351
Agnes de Mille, "To Make Up a Dance" 361

Aaron Copland, "How We Listen" 365
Simone Signoret, "A Flying Leap into the Unknown" 372

Writers on Writing 380
Virginia Woolf, "A Writer's Diary" 381
Anne Frank, "I Want to Write" 386
Dylan Thomas, "The Colours of Words" 389
William Stafford, "Writing" 393
Joan Didion, "Why I Write" 397
Richard Selzer, "Why a Surgeon Would Write" 405
Robert Day, "What Is a Scientific Paper?" 412

Rhetorical Table of Contents

Fiction
Lewis Carroll, "Humpty Dumpty" 36

Diary
Anne Frank, "I Want to Write" 386
Virginia Woolf, "A Writer's Diary" 381

Narrative
Roger Angell, "Stories for a Rainy Afternoon" 286
Burton Bernstein, "Rybernian" 61
Joan Didion, "On Going Home" 67
Joseph Durso, "You Could Look It Up" 252
Helen Keller, "Everything Has a Name" 12
Maxine Hong Kingston, "A Visit to My Aunt" 72
Francine Patterson and Eugene Linden, "Koko's First Words" 313
Richard Rodriguez, "Aria" 217
Red Smith, "Unconquerable" 296
Dylan Thomas, "The Colours of Words" 389

Description
Burton Bernstein, "Rybernian" 61

Joseph Durso, "You Could Look It Up" 252
Francine Patterson and Eugene Linden, "Koko's First Words" 313
Simone Signoret, "A Flying Leap into the Unknown" 372

Definition

Burton Bernstein, "Rybernian" 61
Robert Day, "What Is a Scientific Paper?" 412
Albert Einstein, "The Common Language of Science" 304
Peter Farb, "Man the Talker" 4
M. F. K. Fisher, "As the Lingo Languishes" 142
Martin Luther King, Jr., "Letter from Birmingham Jail" 95
Ruth Nelson, "The First Literate Computers?" 324
Susan Sontag, "A Rhetoric of Disease" 333
William Stafford, "Writing" 393
Dylan Thomas, "The Colours of Words" 389
Edward Weston, "Things Seen into Things Known" 345
Tom Wolfe, "Porno-violence" 129

Example

Joseph Durso, "You Could Look It Up" 252
M. F. K. Fisher, "As the Lingo Languishes" 142
Diane Johnson, "Doctor Talk" 55
Walter Lippmann, "The Indispensable Opposition" 188
Ruth Nelson, "The First Literate Computers?" 324
Alleen Pace Nilsen, "Sexism in the Language of Marriage" 77
George Orwell, "Politics and the English Language" 173
Richard Rodriguez, "Aria" 217
Tony Schwartz, "The Second God" 118
Lewis Thomas, "Social Talk" 308
William Zinsser, "Sports" 276

Process Analysis

Ingmar Bergman, "Film-making" 351
Aaron Copland, "How to Listen to Music" 365
Agnes de Mille, "To Make Up a Dance" 361
Joan Didion, "Why I Write" 397

M. F. K. Fisher, "As the Lingo Languishes" 142
William Stafford, "Writing" 393
Edward Weston, "Things Seen into Things Known" 345
Tom Wolfe, "Porno-violence" 129
Virginia Woolf, "A Writer's Diary" 381

Classification
Aaron Copland, "How to Listen to Music" 365
Norman Cousins, "A Growing Wealth of Words" 32

Comparison/Contrast
Ingmar Bergman, "Film-making" 351
Norman Cousins, "Epitaph for the *Saturday Review*—and Culture Too" 137
Peter Farb, "Man the Talker" 4
Stanley Kauffmann, "Why I'm Not Bored" 162
Joshua Meyrowitz, "Where Have the Children Gone?" 124
Susan Sontag, "A Rhetoric of Disease" 333
Lewis Thomas, "Social Talk" 308

Cause/Effect
Richard Mitchell, "The Worm in the Brain" 17
Susan Sontag, "A Rhetoric of Disease" 333
Daniel Yankelovich, "Lying Well Is the Best Revenge" 88

Analogy
William F. Buckley, "The Hysteria About Words" 28
A. B. Giamatti, "Hyperbole's Child" 267
Walter Lippmann, "The Indispensable Opposition" 188
Tony Schwartz, "The Second God" 118
Simone Signoret, "A Flying Leap into the Unknown" 372

Analysis
Joan Didion, "On Going Home" 67
Peter Farb, "Man the Talker" 4

Diane Johnson, "Doctor Talk" 55
Joshua Meyrowitz, "Where Have the Children Gone?" 124
Ruth Nelson, "The First Literate Computers?" 324
Lewis Thomas, "Notes on Punctuation" 46
Edmund White, "The Political Vocabulary of
  Homosexuality" 203
Daniel Yankelovich, "Lying Well Is the Best Revenge" 88

Argument
William F. Buckley, "The Hysteria About Words" 28
Consumer's Union, "It's Natural! It's Organic! Or Is It?" 154
Norman Cousins, "Epitaph for the *Saturday Review*—and
  Culture, Too" 137
Francine Hardaway, "Foul Play: Sports Metaphors as Public
  Doublespeak" 243
Stanley Kauffmann, "Why I'm Not Bored" 162
Martin Luther King, Jr., "Letter from Birmingham Jail" 95
Lewis Lapham, "Confusion Worse Confounded" 196
Walter Lippmann, "The Indispensable Opposition" 188
George Orwell, "Politics and the English Language" 173
Richard Rodriguez, "Aria" 217
Richard Selzer, "Why a Surgeon Would Write" 405
Edmund White, "The Political Vocabulary of
  Homosexuality" 203
Daniel Yankelovitch, "Lying Well is the Best Revenge" 88

The Living Language
A Reader

The Varieties of English

1

The English language is the native tongue of more than a quarter billion people; in the United States alone, more than a dozen different dialects of English are spoken. In everyday situations we use words that originated in the age when Anglo-Saxon kings ruled the British Isles, yet in the same sentence we might use a word that did not even exist before we launched our first space ship. Like all modern languages, English is a dynamic entity capable of changes that are at once predictable and nearly limitless in scope. Even if our language were suddenly frozen in time, with no further possibilities for change, we could still use it to express almost every nuance of thought anyone is ever likely to think.

"Linguistic creativity" is the term our first essayist, Peter Farb, uses to describe the almost limitless possibilities inherent in every native speaker's use of his or her own language. Every time we speak or write a sentence, Farb's essay shows, we are selecting from among an almost infinite variety of words and grammatical constructions; that ability to choose separates human language from all forms of animal communication. Even animals—such as parrots and mynah birds—that have been taught to imitate human languages are incapable of using their vocabularies to form new phrases or sentences of their own devising. That ability remains solely the province of humans; if we think about the implications of this fact, we will begin to understand how unique a role language plays in human interactions.

The Living Language

The second essay in this chapter, written by the remarkable Helen Keller, records the story of her childhood struggle to break through the double barriers of deafness and blindness, aided by the patient instruction of her teacher, Anne Sullivan. But before she could begin to understand the significance of the letters Miss Sullivan spelled into her hand, Helen Keller had first to discover the simple truth that we all take for granted—that "everything has a name." Few people could recount with much accuracy the point when they first began to associate individual words with specific objects, but for Helen Keller that moment is recalled in vivid detail and with strong emotions. It made the world for her seem to blossom, "like Aaron's rod, with flowers."

In sharp contrast to Helen Keller's serious narration, Richard Mitchell's essay, "The Worm in the Brain," light-heartedly attacks administrative language, with all its passive constructions and misplaced modifiers. Taking his cue from a statement by Carl Sagan, Mitchell proposes that some literal "trouble in the brain" causes once ordinary people to begin to write like administrators. In calling such language the product of a disease, Mitchell suggests that "official" language need not be the way it is; his metaphor of disease even holds out the implicit promise of a cure. But Mitchell doesn't moralize in his essay, nor does he adopt the stance of a language purist resistant to change. Instead, he is content to maintain a playful tone throughout his essay, nonetheless making the point that language may reveal as much about the speaker as it does about the concepts the speaker articulates.

In "The Hysteria About Words," the political columinst William F. Buckley defends himself against the frequent charge that he uses "unusual" and unfamiliar words in an affected way. Anyone who has heard Buckley on television or read his articles in magazines will know immediately why such a charge might have been leveled against him: His vocabulary is extraordinary, and he is among the most erudite and articulate television personalities in America. In the essay reprinted here, Buckley does not defend his vocabulary on the grounds that it can in fact be understood by those with whom he seeks to communicate; rather, he argues that we have fallen prey to a "phony democratic bias against the use of unusual words." This is unfortunate, Buckley insists, because such words are "as necessary to philosophy, economics, esthetics, and political science as they are necessary in the world of higher mathematics. . . ."

Whether or not we ultimately agree with Buckley's conclusion, we are likely to find his defense of unusual words spirited and provocative.

Norman Cousins, in his brief essay, "A Growing Wealth of Words," focuses on the wide array of words that have been added to the English language in the last 80 years—all, he says, the "products of 20th-century civilization." He cites examples from space-age activities, the Psychological Revolution, modern medicine, and public communication. Like Buckley, although from an entirely different point of view, Cousins takes great delight in our ever-expanding vocabulary. Acknowledging that "we have seen the growth of the cult of incoherence," Cousins is nonetheless optimistic about the health of the English language. It "has never been richer than it is today and it will become richer still."

The sixth essay in this chapter is altogether different than the others. Technically speaking, it is not an essay at all, but a chapter from Lewis Carroll's nineteenth-century classic work *Through the Looking Glass*. In it, Alice encounters the moody and unpredictable Humpty Dumpty, first memorialized in the Mother Goose rhyme by the same name. Alice finds Humpty Dumpty a particularly difficult conversationalist not only because he is irascible but because, as he says, he makes words mean whatever he wants them to mean. We include this excerpt here in part because it is a classic piece about language, but primarily because it is a delightful tribute to the inventive possibilities involved in word play.

The final essay in this chapter was written by Lewis Thomas, essayist and physician of national renown. Thomas concerns himself here with a topic that is important to language only in its written form—punctuation. His concern, however, is not the correctness or the incorrectness of a given mark of punctuation; rather, he devotes at least one paragraph to the qualities inherent in each major mark of punctuation, and he does so in a way that playfully attempts to capture the essence of each. Thomas shares with the other writers represented in this section a firm sense of the richness inherent in the human use of language.

Underlying all these essays is the notion that whenever we speak or write we make myriad choices, whether consciously or unconsciously. The essays all imply that rather than be intimidated by these choices, we should welcome them and enjoy them for their limitless potential to enrich human communication.

Man the Talker

Peter Farb

Peter Farb (1929–1980), a free-lance writer and researcher in the science and natural history of North America, was a feature editor for Argosy magazine. He wrote and edited dozens of books, including The Insects *(1962),* The Atlantic Shore *(1966), and* Wordplay: What Happens When People Talk *(1974). "Man The Talker" celebrates the dazzling complexity and spontaneity of human language, particularly English, which Farb compares and contrasts to other human and non-human languages.*

Some twenty-five hundred years ago, Psamtik, an Egyptian pharaoh, desired to discover man's primordial tongue. He entrusted two infants to an isolated shepherd and ordered that they should never hear a word spoken in any language. When the children were returned to the pharaoh several years later, he thought he heard them utter *bekos*, which means "bread" in Phrygian, a language of Asia Minor. And so he honored Phrygian as man's "natural" language. Linguists today know that the story of the pharaoh's experiment must be apocryphal. No child is capable of speech until he has heard other human beings speak, and even two infants reared together cannot develop a language from scratch. Nor does any single "natural" language exist. A child growing up anywhere on earth will speak the tongue he hears in his speech community, regardless of the race, nationality, or language of his parents.

Every native speaker is amazingly creative in the various strategies of speech interaction, in word play and verbal dueling, in exploiting a language's total resources to create poetry and literature. Even a monosyllabic *yes*—spoken in a particular speech situation, with a certain tone of voice, and accompanied by an appropriate gesture—might constitute an original use of English. This sort of linguistic creativity is the birthright of every human being on earth, no matter what language he speaks, the kind of community he lives in, or his degree of intelligence. As Edward Sapir pointed out, when it comes to language "Plato walks with the Macedonian swineherd, Confucius with the head-hunting savage of Assam."

And at a strictly grammatical level also, native speakers are unbelievably creative in language. Not every human being can play the violin, do calculus or jump high hurdles, no matter how excellent his teachers or how arduous his training—but every person constantly creates utterances never before spoken on earth. Incredible as it may seem at first thought, the sentence you just read possibly appeared in exactly this form for the first time in the history of the English language—and the same thing might be said about the sentence you are reading now. In fact, if conventional remarks—such as greetings, farewells, stock phrases like *thank you*, proverbs, clichés, and so forth—are disregarded, in theory all of a person's speech consists of sentences never before uttered.

A moment's reflection reveals why that may be so. Every language groups its vocabulary into a number of different classes such as nouns, verbs, adjectives, and so on. If English possessed a mere 1,000 nouns (such as *trees, children, horses*), and only 1,000 verbs (*grow, die, change*), the number of possible two-word sentences therefore would be 1,000 × 1,000, or one million. Of course, most of these sentences will be meaningless to a speaker today—yet at one time people thought *atoms split* was a meaningless utterance. The nouns, however, might also serve as the objects of these same verbs in three-word sentences. So with the same meager repertory of 1,000 nouns and 1,000 verbs capable of taking an object, the number of possible three-word sentences increases to 1,000 × 1,000 × 1000, or one billion. These calculations, of course, are just for minimal sentences and an impoverished vocabulary. Most languages offer their speakers many times a thousand nouns and a thousand verbs, and in addition they possess other classes of words that function as adverbs, adjectives, articles, prepositions, and so on. Think, too, in terms of four-word, ten-word, even fifty-word sentences—and the number of possible grammatical combinations becomes astronomical. One linguist calculated that it would take 10,000,000,000,000 years (two thousand times the estimated age of the earth) to utter all the possible English sentences that use exactly twenty words. Therefore, it is improbable that any twenty-word sentence a person speaks was ever spoken previously—and the same thing would hold true, of course, for sentences of greater length, and for most shorter ones as well.

For a demonstration of just why the number of sentences that can be constructed in a language is, at least in theory, infinite, show twenty-five speakers of English a cartoon and ask them to describe in a single sentence what they see. Each of the twenty-five speakers will come up with a different sentence, perhaps examples similar to these:

> I see a little boy entering a magic and practical-joke shop to buy something and not noticing that the owner, a practical joker himself, has laid a booby trap for him.

> The cartoon shows an innocent little kid, who I guess is entering a magic shop because he wants to buy something, about to be captured in a trap by the owner of the shop, who has a diabolical expression on his face.

It has been calculated that the vocabulary and the grammatical structures used in only twenty-five such sentences about this cartoon might provide the raw material for nearly twenty *billion* grammatical sentences—a number so great that about forty human life spans would be needed to speak them, even at high speed. Obviously, no one could ever speak, read, or hear in his lifetime more than the tiniest fraction of the possible sentences in his language. That is why almost every sentence in this book—as well as in all the books ever written or to be written—is possibly expressed in its exact form for the first time.

This view of creativity in the grammatical aspects of language is a very recent one. It is part of the revolution in ideas about the structure of language that has taken place since 1957, when Noam Chomsky, of the Massachusetts Institute of Technology, published his *Syntactic Structures*. Since then Chomsky and others have put forth a theory of language that bears little resemblance to the grammar most people learned in "grammar" school. Not all linguists accept Chomsky's theories. But his position, whether it is ultimately shown to be right or wrong, represents an influential school in theoretical linguistics today, one that other schools often measure themselves against.

Chomsky believes that all human beings possess at birth an innate capacity to acquire language. Such a capacity is biologically determined—that is, it belongs to what is usually termed "human nature"—and it is passed from parents to children as part of the offspring's biological inheritance. The innate capacity endows speakers with the general shape of human language, but it is not detailed enough to dictate the precise tongue each child will speak—which accounts for why different languages are spoken in the world. Chomsky states that no one learns a language by learning all of its possible sentences, since obviously that would require countless lifetimes. For example, it is unlikely that any of the speakers who saw the cartoon of the child entering the magic store encountered such a bizarre situation before—yet none of the speakers had any difficulty in constructing sentences about it. Nor would a linguist who wrote down these twenty-five sentences ever have heard them previously—yet he had no difficulty understanding them. So, instead of learning billions of sentences, a person unconsciously acquires a grammar that can generate an infinite number of new sentences in his language.

Such a grammar is innately within the competence of any native speaker of a language. However, no speaker—not even Shakespeare, Dante, Plato, or the David of the Psalms—lives up to his theoretical competence. His actual performance in speaking a language is considerably different, and it consists of numerous errors, hesitations, repetitions, and so forth. Despite these very uneven performances that a child hears all around him, in only a few years—and before he even receives instruction in reading and writing in "grammar" school—he puts together for himself the theoretical rules for the language spoken in his community. Since most sentences that a child hears are not only unique but also filled with errors, how can he ever learn the grammar of his language? Chomsky's answer is that children are born with the capacity to learn only grammars that accord with the innate human blueprint. Children disregard performance errors because such errors result in sentences that could not be described by such a grammar. Strong evidence exists that native speakers of a language know intuitively whether a sentence is grammatical or not. They usually cannot specify exactly what is wrong, and very possibly they make the same mistakes in their own speech, but they know—unconsciously, not as a set of rules they learned in school—when a sentence is incorrect.

The human speaker—born with a capacity for language, infinitely creative in its use, capable of constructing novel utterances in unfamiliar speech situations—shares the globe with a variety of animals that whistle, shriek, squeak, bleat, hoot, coo, call, and howl. And so it has been assumed, ever since Aristotle first speculated about the matter, that human speech is only some superior kind of animal language. Alexander Graham Bell saw nothing odd about his attempts to teach a dog to speak by training it to growl at a steady rate while he manipulated its throat and jaws. The dog finally managed to produce a sequence of syllables which sounded somewhat like *ow ah oo gwah mah*—the closest it could come to "How are you, Grandma?" And Samuel Pepys, in his *Diary* entry for August 24, 1661, noted:

> by and by we are called to Sir W. Batten's to see the strange creature that Captain Holmes hath brought with him from Guiny; it is a great baboon [apparently not a baboon at all but rather a chimpanzee], but so much like a man in most things, that though they say there is a species of them, yet I cannot believe but that it is a monster got of a man and a she-baboon. I do believe that it already understands much English, and I am of the mind it might be taught to speak or make signs.

Other experimenters concluded that animals could not be taught human languages, but they saw no reason why they themselves should not learn to speak the way animals do. A few enthusiasts have even published dictionaries for various bird and animal languages—among them E. I. Du Pont de Nemours, the French-born founder of the American chemical firm, who in 1807 compiled dictionaries for the languages of such birds as crows and nightingales. These efforts are ludicrous because human speech is quite different from most animal communication. Between the bird's call to its mate and the human utterance *I love you* lie a few hundred million years of evolution, at least one whole day of Biblical Creation. St. Francis of Assisi, talking to the birds, may have had much to say to them, but they had nothing to discuss with him.

Human speech seemingly resembles animal calls in that it employs a small number of sounds, often no more than the number emitted by many species of birds and mammals. But, unlike animal calls, human sounds are combined to form a vast vocabulary, which in turn is structured into an infinite number of utterances. The number of different units of sound in each human language, such as the *m* in *man* or the *ou* in *house*, varies between about a dozen and a little more than five dozen. English recognizes about 45 units, Italian 27, Hawaiian 13. This range is not notably different from the separate units of sound emitted by many kinds of animals: prairie dog, 10; various species of monkeys, about 20; domestic chicken, 25; chimpanzee, 25; bottle-nosed dolphin, 28; fox, 36.

Chimpanzees, with their 25 units of sound, are incapable of speech, while Hawaiians, with only 13 units, possess a very expressive language. That is because the chimpanzee employs one unit of sound in social play, another when a juvenile is lost, a third when attacked, and so on—but two or more calls cannot be combined to generate additional messages. In contrast, the 13 sounds of Hawaiian can be combined to form 2,197 potential three-sound words, nearly five million six-sound words—and an astronomical number if the full repertory of 13 sounds is used to form longer words. In the same way, a speaker of English can select three units of sound out of his store of 45, such as the sounds represented in writing by *e, n,* and *d*—and then combine them into such meaningful words as *end, den,* and *Ned.* But the chimpanzee cannot combine the three units of sound that mean play, lost juvenile, and threat of attack to form some other message. Nor can the chimpanzee's call that means "Here is food" ever be changed to talk about the delicacies it consumed yesterday or its expectations about finding certain fruits tomorrow. Generation after generation, as far into the future as the chimpanzee survives as a species, it will use that call solely to indicate the immediate presence of food.

Certain animals—most notably parrots, mynahs, and other mimicking birds—can emit a wide repertory of sounds, and they also have an uncanny ability to combine them into longer utterances. Nevertheless, they do not exploit their abilities the way human beings do. A trained mynah bird can so unerringly repeat an English sentence that it is scarcely distinguishable on a tape recording from the same sentence spoken by a human being. Parrots also can duplicate human speech with awesome fidelity, and they have been taught vocabularies of more than a hundred words. A parrot can easily enough be trained to mimic the utterance *a pail of water* and also to mimic a variety of nouns such as *sand* and *milk*. But, for all its skill, the parrot will never substitute nouns for each other and on its own say *a pail of sand* or *a pail of milk*.

Even the most vocal animals are utterly monotonous in what they say in a given situation. The well-known nursery rhyme does not reveal what Jack said to Jill when they went up the hill to fetch a pail of water, and in fact no way exists to predict which of the tremendous strategies two people will select in such a speech situation. But everyone knows what a male songbird will say when another male enters its territory during the breeding season. It will emit a distinctive series of sounds that signify "Go away!" It cannot negotiate with the intruder, nor can it say "I'm sorry that I must ask you to depart now, but I will be happy to make your acquaintance after the breeding season is concluded." The male defender of the territory is simply responding to the stimulus of an intruder at a certain time of the year by uttering a general statement about the existence of such a stimulus.

Specialists in animal behavior infer the "meaning" of animal sounds from the behavior of the animals at the time they emit sounds, but it is safe to conclude that the sounds express only indefinable emotions. Individuals belonging to the same animal species emit approximately the same sounds to convey the same emotions. All expressions of pain uttered by any individuals of a monkey species are very much the same, but in the human species the sounds that a speaker uses to communicate his pain are quite arbitrary. A speaker of English says *ouch*, but a Spaniard says *ay* and a Nootka Indian *ishkatakh*. Jill might have emitted an animal-like cry of pain as she came tumbling down the hill—but, as a speaker of English, she also had the choice of saying *I hurt my head* or *Please take me to a doctor*. Even if Jill merely uttered the conventional word, *ouch*, which signifies pain in English, this sound is nevertheless considerably different from an animal's cry of pain. An animal's cry cannot be removed from its immediate context, but Jill's *ouch* can. She could, for example, tell someone the next day about her accident by saying *When I fell down the hill, I cried "ouch."* Or she could utter *ouch* in a completely different context, as when someone makes a feeble pun and she wishes to convey that her sensibilities, not her bones, have been wounded.

An animal, though, has no such choices. As Bertrand Russell remarked about a dog's ability to communicate, "No matter how eloquently a dog may bark, he cannot tell you that his parents were poor but honest." Despite the variety of sounds in the babel of the animal world, nonhuman calls are emotional responses to a very limited number of immediate stimuli. Every other kind of sound made by living things on the planet belongs to human speech alone.

Content

1. What does Farb seem to mean by "linguistic creativity"? What example best illustrates its meaning, from your point of view? Explain.
2. Farb summarizes Noam Chomsky's theory in the first half of the essay;

paraphrase, in your own words, the main points of Chomsky's theory about humans' "innate capacity to acquire language" as it is presented in this essay.
3. At one point, Farb asserts that not even Shakespeare, for example, lived up to his "theoretical competence" as a speaker of English. What do you understand him to mean by this point?
4. The second half of this essay focuses on the differences between human and animal "language." What does Farb say are the primary differences? What other differences does he cite?
5. Why, according to Farb, are animal "dictionaries" ludicrous?

Technique

1. Farb begins this essay with a brief story. How does this story fit into his argument as a whole? How effective an opening strategy is it?
2. Farb follows his examples of our linguistic creativity with an explanation of Chomsky's theory of language. How might you have reacted, as a reader, if he had presented the information the other way around? Explain.
3. Farb makes several references to famous people, not necessarily experts on the subject of human speech. What advantage does he gain by referring to these people? Does he manage to go beyond mere name-dropping, in your opinion?
4. Farb ends this selection with an extended section on animal language. How does this section support his basic thesis about human language, about "man the talker"?

Language

1. Farb uses the term "linguistics" in this essay; consult the dictionary and an encyclopedia to determine more about the field of linguistics. If your college or university has courses in linguistics, or a separate department or major, where does it appear—in the sciences, in the humanities, in the social sciences?
2. To what extent is Farb's idea about linguistic creativity continued in the section about animal language? What seems to you to be his purpose in giving so much attention to animal language in an essay about human speech?
3. What definition of language is Farb using that would exclude animal communication as a language? Do you agree with his exclusion? Why or why not?

Vocabulary

primordial	arduous	linguistics
apocryphal	repertory	innate
strategies	improbably	bizarre

Writing Suggestions

1. With the aid of five of your friends, duplicate for yourself Farb's "experiment" about describing a cartoon. Based on the responses you get, write a brief paper in which you analyze the different descriptions you receive. Are there any basic similarities in the way people described the cartoon? How many different words, for example, did the five friends use, combined? Use these questions to begin to formulate a thesis and structure for your essay.
2. If possible, visit a neighborhood nursery school or play group and record the kinds of "mistakes" pre-school children make in their speech. Classify the errors by a scheme of your own devising, and write a paper based on your observations.
3. Some people claim that their pets "communicate" with them clearly. Write a paragraph in which you list the various ways your pet has made you "understand" something. Would you call any of these forms of communication "language"? Why or why not?

Everything Has a Name
Helen Keller

Helen Keller (1880–1968) became blind and deaf after a childhood illness. The story of her courageous struggle with such disabilities has made her an enduring figure of inspiration. Her childhood training with Anne Sullivan, touched on in the essay here, was the subject of William Gibson's Pulitzer Prize-winning play, The Miracle Worker; *her own books include* The Story of My Life *(1902),* Out of the Dark *(1913), and* Helen Keller's Journal *(1938). "Everything Has a Name" recounts her meeting with Sullivan and the beginning of her emergence into the world of language.*

The most important day I remember in all my life is the one on which my teacher, Anne Mansfield Sullivan, came to me. I am filled with wonder when I consider the immeasurable contrast between the two lives which it connects. It was the third of March, 1887, three months before I was seven years old.

On the afternoon of that eventful day, I stood on the porch, dumb, expectant. I guessed vaguely from my mother's signs and from the hurrying to and fro in the house that something unusual was about to happen, so I went to the door and waited on the steps. The afternoon sun penetrated the mass of honeysuckle that covered the porch, and fell on my upturned face. My fingers lingered almost unconsciously on the familiar leaves and blossoms which had just come forth to greet the sweet southern spring. I did not know what the future held of marvel or surprise for me. Anger and bitterness had preyed upon me continually for weeks and a deep languor had succeeded this passionate struggle.

Have you ever been at sea in a dense fog, when it seemed as if a tangible white darkness shut you in, and the great ship, tense and anxious, groped her way toward the shore with plummet and sounding-line, and you waited with beating heart for something to happen? I was like that ship before my education began, only I was without compass or sounding-line, and had no way of knowing how near the harbour was. "Light! give me light!" was the wordless cry of my soul, and the light of love shone on me in that very hour.

I felt approaching footsteps. I stretched out my hand as I supposed to my mother. Someone took it, and I was caught and held close in the arms of her who had come to reveal all things to me, and, more than all things else, to love me.

The morning after my teacher came she led me into her room and gave me a doll. The little blind children at the Perkins Institution had sent it and Laura Bridgman had dressed it; but I did not know this until afterward. When I had played with it a little while, Miss Sullivan slowly spelled into my hand the word "d-o-l-l." I was at once interested in this finger play and tried to imitate it. When I finally succeeded in making the letters correctly I was flushed with childish pleasure and pride. Running downstairs to my mother I held up my hand and made the letters for doll. I did not know that I was spelling a word or even that words existed; I was simply making my fingers go in monkey-like imitation. In the days that followed I learned to spell in this uncomprehending way a great many words, among them *pin*, *hat*, *cup* and a few verbs like *sit*, *stand* and *walk*. But my teacher had been with me several weeks before I understood that everything has a name.

One day, while I was playing with my new doll, Miss Sullivan put my big rag doll into my lap also, spelled "d-o-l-l" and tried to make me understand that "d-o-l-l" applied to both. Earlier in the day we had had a tussle over the words "m-u-g" and "w-a-t-e-r." Miss Sullivan had tried to impress it upon me that "m-u-g" is *mug* and that "w-a-t-e-r" is *water*, but I persisted in confounding the two. In despair she had dropped the subject for the time, only to renew it at the first opportunity. I became impatient at her repeated attempts and seizing the new doll, I dashed it upon the floor. I was keenly delighted when I felt the fragments of the broken doll at my feet. Neither sorrow nor regret followed my passionate outburst. I had not loved the doll. In the still, dark world in which I lived there was no strong sentiment or tenderness. I felt my teacher sweep the fragments to one side of the hearth, and I had a sense of satisfaction that the cause of my discomfort was removed. She brought me my hat, and I knew I was going out into the warm sunshine. This thought, if a wordless sensation may be called a thought, made me hop and skip with pleasure.

We walked down the path to the well-house, attracted by the fragrance of the honeysuckle with which it was covered. Someone was drawing water and my teacher placed my hand under the spout. As the cool stream gushed over one hand she spelled into the other the word *water*, first slowly, then rapidly. I stood still, my whole attention fixed upon the motions of her fingers. Suddenly I felt a misty consciousness as of something forgotten—a thrill of returning thought; and somehow the mystery of language was revealed to me. I knew then that "w-a-t-e-r" meant the wonderful cool something that was flowing over my hand. That living word awakened my soul, gave it light, hope, joy, set it free! There were barriers still, it is true, but barriers that could in time be swept away.

I left the well-house eager to learn. Everything had a name, and each name gave birth to a new thought. As we returned to the house every object which I touched seemed to quiver with life. That was because I saw everything with the strange, new sight that had come to me. On entering the door I remembered the doll I had broken. I felt my way to the hearth and picked up the pieces. I tried vainly to put them together. Then my eyes filled with tears; for I realized what I had done, and for the first time I felt repentance and sorrow.

I learned a great many words that day. I do not remember what they all were; but I do know that *mother, father, sister, teacher* were among them—words that were to make the world blossom for me, "like Aaron's rod, with flowers." It would have been difficult to find a happier child than I was as I lay in my crib at the close of that eventful day and lived over the joys it had brought me, and for the first time longed for a new day to come.

Content

1. Explain, in your own words, why the words that Anne Sullivan "spelled out" for the young Helen Keller were mere "finger play" until Keller understood the relationship between "w-a-t-e-r-" and the actual substance that poured over her hand.

2. At one point in this chapter, Keller tells about her pleasure at anticipating going outside into the warm sunshine. She says, "This thought, if a wordless sensation may be called a thought, made me hop and skip with pleasure." Why might a "wordless sensation" not qualify as a "thought"? Do you agree or disagree? Explain.

3. Why do you suppose that Helen Keller felt remorse for breaking her doll only after she discovered that "everything has a name"? What is the connection between naming and the potential for strong feelings?

4. Helen Keller narrates the single moment when "the mystery of language" was revealed to her. In your own words, describe what you understand that "mystery" to be, specifically for Keller and generally for all people.

Technique

1. This chapter opens with a simple but eloquent statement about Keller's teacher, Anne Sullivan. To what extent is this statement born out in this chapter alone? Is it an effective opening statement? Why or why not?

2. In the third paragraph, Keller develops an extended analogy, comparing herself before her "education" began to a ship at sea in the fog. What sense is she trying to convey to her readers through this analogy? Is it an effective way to make the point?

3. The fact that Anne Sullivan first came to live with Helen Keller in the springtime is, of course, an accident of biography. How does Keller weave this fact into her story? In what sense is it an appropriate metaphor for the narration that follows?

4. The chapter reprinted here is one that appears early in Keller's autobiography. What hints are there that particular themes will be developed later in the book? What must have come before this chapter that would make the "miracle" presented here all the more powerful?

Language

1. Several words Keller uses to describe herself as a child emphasize her sightlessness and deafness. What are those words? Did they seem unusual to you when you first came across them? Explain.
2. In the first sentence of the second paragraph, Keller describes herself as "dumb, expectant." What precisely does she mean by dumb? How might we misunderstand her?
3. In the final paragraph of the chapter, Keller says that words began to "blossom for me, 'like Aaron's rod, with flowers.'" Look up Aaron's rod in several reference books. What, literally, does it refer to? Is it, in your opinion, an apt image as it is used here?
4. Keller says that "every name gave birth to a new thought." What is the relationship between thinking and naming, between thoughts and words?

Vocabulary

languor
plummet
sounding-line
tangible
confounding

Writing Suggestions

1. Consult the *OED (Oxford English Dictionary)* in the library to determine the various meanings of the word "dumb." Write a paragraph in which you explain how you imagine it came to be a synonym for "stupid" in colloquial English.
2. Write an essay in which you explore the relationship between naming and thinking. You might consider, for example, how knowing the name for a particular bird, tree, or flower might actually help us "see" it more clearly. If you can "name" a feeling you are having, does it help you understand that feeling better?
3. Write an autobiographical essay in which you show how one person who was not a member of your family made a significant change in your life.

The Worm In the Brain
Richard Mitchell

Richard Mitchell (b. 1929) received a Ph.D. from Syracuse University in 1963. Since then, he has taught English at several colleges, including Glassboro State College, where he is now Professor of English. He is the editor of The Underground Grammarian *and has written two books,* Less Than Words Can Say *(1979) and* The Graves of Academe *(1981). "The Worm In the Brain" details the drastic changes that one man's language underwent when he became an administrator. Mitchell examines several symptoms and the significance of his friend's new "official" style.*

There's an outrageous but entertaining assertion about language and the human brain in Carl Sagan's *Dragons of Eden*. It is possible, Sagan says, to damage the brain in precisely such a way that the victim will lose the ability to understand the passive or to devise prepositional phrases or something like that. No cases are cited, unfortunately—it would be fun to chat with some victim—but the whole idea is attractive, because if it were true it would explain many things. In fact, I can think of no better way to account for something had happened to a friend of mine—and probably to one of yours too.

He was an engaging chap, albeit serious. We did some work together—well, not exactly work, committee stuff—and he used to send me a note whenever there was to be a meeting. Something like this: "Let's meet next Monday at two o'clock, OK?" I was always delighted to read such perfect prose.

Unbeknownst to us all, however, something was happening in that man's brain. Who can say what? Perhaps a sleeping genetic defect was stirring, perhaps some tiny creature had entered in the porches of his ear and was gnawing out a home in his cranium. We'll never know. Whatever it was, it had, little by little, two effects. At one and the same time, he discovered in himself the yearning to be an assistant dean pro tem, and he began to lose the power of his prose. Ordinary opinion, up to now, has always held that one of these things, either one, was the cause of the other. Now we can at last guess the full horror of the truth. *Both* are symptoms of serious trouble in the brain.

Like one of these Poe characters whose friends are all doomed, I watched, helpless, the inexorable progress of the disease. Gradually but inevitably my friend was being eaten from within. In the same week that saw his application for the newly created post of assistant dean pro tem, he sent me the following message: "This is to inform you that there'll be a meeting next Monday at 2:00." Even worse, much worse, was to come.

A week or so later it was noised about that he would indeed take up next semester a new career as a high-ranking dean pro tem. I was actually writing him a note of congratulation when the campus mail brought me what was to be his last announcement of a meeting of our committee. Hereafter he would be frying fatter fish, but he wanted to finish the business at hand. His note read: "Please be informed that the Committee on Memorial Plaques will meet on Monday at 2:00."

I walked slowly to the window, his note in my hand, and stared for a while at the quad. The oak trees there had been decimated not long before by a leak in an underground gas line. The seeping poison had killed their very roots, but they had at least ended up as free firewood for the faculty. Pangloss might have been right, after all, and, calamity that it was, this latest message spared me the trouble of writing the congratulatory note and even afforded me a glimpse of a remarkably attractive young lady straying dryad-fashion through the surviving oaks. Things balance out.

You would think, wouldn't you, that the worm or whatever had at last done its work, that the poor fellow's Hydification was complete and his destruction assured. No. It is a happy mercy that most of us cannot begin to imagine the full horror of these ravaging disorders. To this day that man still sends out little announcements and memos about this and that. They begin like this: "You are hereby informed . . ." Of what, I cannot say, since a combination of delicacy and my respect for his memory forbid that I read further.

It's always a mistake to forget William of Occam and his razor. Look first for the simplest explanation that will handle the facts. I had always thought that perfectly normal human beings turned into bureaucrats and administrators and came to learn the language of that tribe through some exceedingly complicated combination of nature and nurture, through imitative osmosis and some flaw of character caused by inappropriate weaning. Piffle. These psychologists have captured our minds and led us into needless deviousness. The razor cuts to the heart of things and reveals the worm in the brain.

Admittedly, that may be a slight oversimplification. It may be that the decay of language and the desire to administrate are not merely concomitant symptoms of one and the same disease, but that *one* is a symptom and the other a symptom of the symptom. Let's imagine what deans, who like to imitate government functionaries, who, in their turn, like to imitate businessmen, who themselves seem to imitate show-business types, would call a "scenario."

There you sit, minding your own business and hurting no man. All at once, quite insensibly, the *thing* creeps into your brain. It might end up in the storage shelves of the subjunctive or the switchboard of the nonrestrictive clauses, of course, but in your case it heads for the cozy nook where the active and passive voices are balanced and adjusted. There it settles in and nibbles a bit here and a bit there. In our present state of knowledge, still dim, we have to guess that the active voice is tastier than the passive, since the destruction of the latter is very rare but of the former all too common.

So there you are with your active verbs being gnawed away. Little by little and only occasionally at first, you start saying things like: "I am told that . . ." and "This letter is being written because . . ." This habit has subtle effects. For one thing, since passives always require more words than actives, anything you may happen to write is longer than it would have been before the attack of the worm. You begin to suspect that you have a lot to say after all and that it's probably rather important. The suspicion is all the stronger because what you write has begun to sound—well, sort of "official." "Hmm," you say to yourself, "Fate may have cast my lot a bit below my proper station," or, more likely, "Hmm. My lot may have been cast by Fate a bit below my proper station."

Furthermore, the very way you consider the world, or the very way in which the world is considered by you, is subtly altered. You used to see a world in which birds ate worms and men made decisions. Now it looks more like a world in which worms are eaten by birds and decisions are made by men. It's almost a world in which victims are put forward by "doers" responsible for whatever may befall them and actions are almost unrelated to those who perform them. But only almost. The next step is not taken until you learn to see a world in which worms are eaten and decisions made and *all* responsible agency has disappeared. Now you are ready to be an administrator.

This is a condition necessary to successful administration of any sort and in any calling. Letters are written, reports are prepared, decisions made, actions taken, and consequences suffered. These things happen in the world where agents and doers, the responsible parties around whose throats we like our hands to be gotten, first retreat to the remoter portions of prepositional phrases and ultimately disappear entirely. A too-frequent use of the passive is not just a stylistic quirk; it is the outward and visible sign of a certain weltanschauung.

And now that it is *your* weltanschauung (remember the worm has been gnawing all this time), you discover that you are suited to the life of the administrator. You'll fit right in.

Therefore, we may say that it is not the worm in the skull that causes deans and managers and vice presidents, at least not directly. The worm merely causes the atrophy of the active and the compensatory dominance of the passive. (Through a similar compensatory mechanism, three-legged dogs manage to walk, and the language of the typical administrator is not very different from the gait of the three-legged dog, come to think of it.) The dominance of the passive causes in the victim an alteration of philosophy, which alteration is itself the thing that both beckons him to and suits him for the work of administration. And there you have it. Thanks to Carl Sagan and a little help from William of Occam, we understand how administrators come to be.

You may want to object that a whole view of the world and its meanings can hardly be importantly altered by a silly grammatical form. If so, you're just not thinking. Grammatical forms are *exactly* the things that make us understand the world the way we understand it. To understand the world, we make propositions about it, and those propositions are both formed and limited by the grammar of the language in which we propose.

To see how this works, let's imagine an extreme case. Suppose there *is* after all a place in the brain that controls the making and understanding of prepositional phrases. Suppose that Doctor Fu Manchu has let loose in the world the virus that eats that very place, so that in widening circles from Wimbledon mankind loses the power to make and understand prepositional phrases. Now the virus has gotten you, and to you prepositional phrases no longer make sense. You can't read them, you can't write them, you can't utter them, and when you hear them you can only ask "Wha?" Try it. Go read something, or look out the window and describe what you see. Tell the story of your day. Wait . . . you can't exactly do that . . . tell, instead, your day-story. Recite how you went working . . . how morning you went . . . no . . . morning not you . . . morning went . . . how you morning went . . . The rest will be silence.

Only through unspeakable exertion and even ad hoc invention of new grammatical arrangements can we get along at all without the prepositional phrase, as trivial as that little thing seems to be. It's more than that. Should we lose prepositional phrases, the loss of a certain arrangement of words would be only the visible sign of a stupendous unseen disorder. We would in fact have lost *prepositionalism*, so to speak, the whole concept of the kind of relationship that is signaled by the prepositional phrase. We'd probably be totally incapacitated.

Try now to imagine the history of mankind without the prepositional phrase, or, if you're tired of that, the relative clause or the distinction between subject and object. It would be absurd to think that lacking those and other such things the appearance and growth of human culture would have been merely hindered. It would have been impossible. *Everything* that we have done would have been simply impossible. The world out there is made of its own stuff, but the world that we can understand and manipulate and predict is made of discourse, and discourse is ruled by grammar. Without even so elementary a device as the prepositional phrase we'd be wandering around in herds right now, but we wouldn't know how to name what we were doing.

We're inclined to think of things like prepositional phrases as though they were optional extras in a language, something like whitewall tires. This is because we don't spend a lot of time dwelling on them except when we study a language not our own. We study German, and here comes a lesson on the prepositional phrase. Great, now we can *add* something to our German. That's the metaphor in our heads; we think—there *is* German, it exists, and when you get good at it you can add on the fancy stuff like prepositional phrases. All we have to do is memorize the prepositions and remember which ones take the dative and which ones take the accusative and which ones sometimes take the one and sometimes the other and when and why and which ones are the exceptions. Suddenly it becomes depressing. How about we forget the whole thing and settle for your stripped-down basic model German without any of the fancy stuff? If you do that, of course, you'll never find the *Bahnhof*. You'll be stymied in Stuttgart.

Like prepositional phrases, certain structural arrangements in English are much more important than the small bones of grammar in its most technical sense. It really wouldn't matter much if we started dropping the *s* from our plurals. Lots of words get along without it anyway, and in most cases context would be enough to indicate number. Even the distinction between singular and plural verb forms is just as much a polite convention as an essential element of meaning. But the structures, things like passives and prepositional phrases, constitute, among other things, an implicit system of moral philosophy, a view of the world *and* its presumed meanings, and their misuse therefore often betrays an attitude or value that the user might like to disavow.

Here's an example from the works of a lady who may also have a worm in her brain. She is "the chair" of the Equal Employment Opportunity Commission. It's very short and seems, to those willing to overlook a "small" grammatical flaw, almost too trivial to be worthy of comment. She writes: "Instead of accepting charges indiscriminately and giving them docket numbers, charging parties are counseled immediately."

"Charging parties" are probably faster than landing parties and larger than raiding parties, but no matter. She means, probably, people who are bringing charges of some sort, but there are many kinds of prose in which people become parties. It's not really meant to sound convivial, though; it's meant to sound "legal." What's important is that the structure of her sentence leads us to expect that the people (or parties) named first after that comma will also be the people (or parties) responsible for doing the "accepting." We expect something like: "Instead of doing *that*, we now do this." That's not because of some *rule*; it's just the way English works. It both reflects and generates the way the mind does its business in English. We, the readers, are disappointed and confused because somebody who ought to have shown up in this sentence has in fact not appeared. What has become of the *accepting* parties? Are they hanging around the water cooler? Do they refuse to accept? Are they at least hoping that no one will remember that they are *supposed* to accept? We can guess, of course, that they are the same people who make up the counseling parties, who have also disappeared into a little passive. It's as though we went charging down to the EEOC and found them all out to lunch.

Well, that could have been a slip of the mind, the mind of the chair, of course, but later we read: "Instead of dealing with charging parties and respondents through formalistic legal paper, the parties are called together within a few weeks . . ."

It's the same arrangement. Who does that dealing, or, since that's what they did before the "instead" who *did* that dealing through "formalistic" paper? Wouldn't they be the same parties who ought to do the calling together? Where have they all gone?

A schoolteacher would call those things examples of dangling modifiers and provide some rules about them, but that's not important. What's important is that those forms are evocations of that imagined world in which responsible agency is hardly ever visible, much to the comfort of responsible agency. Since that is the nature of the world already suggested by the passive voice, you would expect that this writer, or chair, would be addicted to the passive. You'd be right. Here are the bare skeletons of a few consecutive sentences:

. . . staff is assigned . . .
. . . cases are removed . . .
. . . parties are contacted . . .
. . . files are grouped . . . and prioritized . . .
. . . steps are delineated . . . and time frames established . . .
. . . discussions are encouraged . . .

You have to wonder how much of a discussion you could possibly have with these people. They're never around.

Admittedly, it does these bureaucrats some credit that in their hearts they are ashamed to say that they actually do those things that they do. After all, who would want to tell the world that he, himself, in his very flesh, goes around grouping and prioritizing?

The dangling modifiers go well with the passives, and, in suggesting the nature of the world as seen by bureaucrats, they even add something new. The passives are sort of neutral, verbal shoulder-shrugs—these things happen—what can I tell you? The danglers go the next obvious and ominous step and suggest subtly that those charging parties have caused a heap of trouble and really ought to be handed the job of sorting things out for themselves, which, grammatically, is exactly what happens. In the first example the people who do the accepting and the counseling ought to appear right after the comma, but they don't. In the second, the people who do the dealing and the calling ought to appear right after the comma, but they don't. In both cases the people who *do* appear are the clients on whose behalf someone is supposed to accept, counsel, deal, and call. Does that mean something about the way in which those clients are regarded by this agency? They seem to have been put in some kind of grammatical double jeopardy, which is probably unconstitutional.

The poor lady, or chair, has inadvertently said what she probably meant. Working for the government would be so pleasant if it weren't for those pesky citizens. A waspish psychiatrist might observe that she has taken those charging parties and has "put them in their place" with a twist of grammar, thus unconsciously expressing her wish that they ought to be responsible for all the tedious labor their charges will cost her and her friends. She herself, along with the whole blooming EEOC, has withdrawn behind a curtain of cloudy English from the clash of charging parties on the darkling plain. "Ach so, sehr interessant, nicht wahr, zat ze patzient ist immer py ze Wort 'inshtead' gonvused. Es gibt, vielleicht, a broplem of, how you zay, Inshteadness." And indeed, the result of the dangling modifiers is to put the charging parties forth *instead* of someone else, as though the word had been chosen to stand out in front of the sentence as a symbol of the latent meaning.

Surely this lady, or chair, is an educated person, or chair, perfectly able to see and fix dangling modifiers of the sort they used to deal with in the early grades. After all, she has been hired as a chair, and for such a position we can assume some pretty high standards and stringent requirements. All right, so she doesn't know the difference between "formal" and "formalistic"—big deal. When such a high-ranking official of our government apparatus makes a mistake in structure, and habitually at that, it's not much to the point to underline it and put an exclamation mark in the margin. In a small child these would be mistakes; in a chair they are accidental revelations of a condition in the mind. To put the name of the thing modified as close as possible to the modifier is not a "rule" of English; it is a sign of something the mind does in English. When the English doesn't do that thing, it's because the mind hasn't done it.

It would be fatuous for us to say that we don't understand those sentences because of the disappearance of the people who are supposed to do all those things. It is a schoolteacher's cheap trick to say that if you don't get your grammar right people won't understand you. It's almost impossible to mangle grammar to that point where you won't be understood. We understand those sentences. In fact, we understand them better than the writer; we understand both what she thought she was saying and something else that she didn't think she was saying.

Many readers, of course, would "understand" those sentences without even thinking of the problem they present, and they might think these comments pedantic and contentious. Oh, come on, what's all the fuss? A couple of little mistakes. What does it matter? We all know what she means, don't we?

Such objections come from the erroneous idea that the point of language is merely to communicate, "to get your ideas across," whatever that means. Furthermore, such objectors may think that they are defending a hard-working and well-meaning chair, but she is little likely to be grateful for their partisanship if she figures out what it means. They say, in effect, that her little mistakes are just that, little mistakes rather than inadvertent and revealing slips of the mind. In the latter case, however, we can conclude that she is merely a typical bureaucrat with an appropriately managerial twist in the brain; in the former we would simply have to conclude that she is not well enough educated to be allowed to write public documents. Which of these conclusions do you suppose she would prefer? It seems that we must choose one or the other. Those are either mistakes made in ignorance or mistakes made in something other than ignorance.

The mind, thinking in English, does indubitably push modifiers and things modified as close together as possible. Can there really be a place in the brain where that happens, a function that might be damaged or dulled? It doesn't matter, of course, because there is surely a "place" in the mind analogous to the imagined place in the brain.

Whether by worms or world-views, it does seem sometimes to be invaded and eaten away. The malfunctions we can see in this chair and in my erstwhile friend, now an assistant dean pro tem, are small inklings of a whole galaxy of disorders that has coalesced out of the complicated history of language, of our language in particular, and out of the political history of language in general.

Content

1. At the end of the first paragraph, Mitchell describes his friend's note as "perfect prose." In what sense do you think he means it is "perfect"? Would you have given it the same label? Why or why not?
2. What larger point does Mitchell make when he insists that the fact of becoming an administrator does not in itself cause a person to write like an administrator, or vice versa?
3. How would you describe Mitchell's attitude toward administrators or bureaucrats throughout this essay? What, specifically, in the essay leads you to your conclusion?
4. Mitchell's thesis might be paraphrased as follows: The specific way we write and speak (the grammatical forms we use) determines the way we view the world we live in. In your own words, summarize why Mitchell says that this is so. Is his argument convincing?

Technique

1. Mitchell begins his essay with a relatively long anecdote about a friend and his friend's "diseased" prose. How does this anecdote help establish the tone for the observations that follow? How does this anecdote help establish the content of what follows?
2. Although Mitchell pursues the metaphor of the "worm in the brain" throughout most of the essay, we still are not tempted to literally believe he thinks a brain disorder causes the problems he cites. How effective did you find this metaphor? What does it allow him to achieve in this essay that he otherwise might not have achieved?
3. Toward the end of the essay, Mitchell makes a number of assertions that he does not attempt to support. Identify several of these and discuss their validity in the context of Mitchell's argument.
4. In this essay, side by side with words such as "fatuous" and "indubitably," we find expressions such as these: "frying fatter fish," "piffle," "whitewall tires," "fancy stuff," and "three-legged dog." How would you describe these latter phrases? What level of diction do they represent? What is the effect of his use of these phrases?

Language

1. Like many who write about "official" or "administrative" prose, Mitchell focuses a good deal of attention on the passive voice rather than the active voice. What seems to be the major objection to the use of the passive voice? Do you find Mitchell's argument against it convincing?
2. What, according to Mitchell, is the relationship between the way we think and the grammatical constructions we use? Do you agree with him? Why or why not?
3. Mitchell says that we end up telling more about ourselves than we sometimes intend to when we use certain grammatical constructions, such as the passive voice. To what extent is this argument convincing?
4. At one point Mitchell disagrees with the notion that the point of language is to communicate, yet he does not say explicitly what the real point is. Given Mitchell's point of view, what might be the point of language?

Vocabulary

albeit	functionaries	evocations
inexorable	atrophy	fatuous
pro tem	ad hoc	indubitably
decimated	incapacitated	
concomitant	implicit	

Writing Suggestions

1. Drawing upon official publications, letters, notices, and the like from your college or university, write a paper in which you analyze the "unconscious" messages that the writing conveys.
2. Use Mitchell's image of the worm in the brain to explain another event or activity in an essay of your own. How could such an image change our thinking about certain political situations or speeches, the format of local TV news shows, or the like? In your essay, attempt to capture some of the same tone that pervades Mitchell's essay.
3. In a paragraph, describe how another group (other than administrators) talk or write. Be sure to include specific examples to illustrate the point you want to make about the group you choose.

The Hysteria About Words

William F. Buckley

William F. Buckley (b. 1925) has been a controversial conservative writer since he began editing the National Review *in 1955. He has been a nationally syndicated columnist since 1962 and the host of the interview program "Firing Line" on the Public Broadcasting System since 1966. He has written several novels (Saving The Queen; Marco Polo, If You Can) as well as books on politics and government. In the following essay, Buckley defends his use of unusual words and attacks those he terms "anti-intellectuals" who fear such words. Buckley uses analogy, logic, and personal experience to argue that unusual words broaden one's "conceptual and descriptive powers."*

Have you noticed that the use of an unusual word sometimes irritates the reader to such a point that he will accuse the user of affectation, than which there is no more heinous crime in the American republic? The distinguished political and social philosopher and columnist Russell Kirk used the word "energumen" to describe, in his Introduction to my book *Rumbles Left and Right*, whom it is I agitate against, and one reviewer fairly exploded with annoyance. Now the word in question means "someone possessed by an evil spirit" and fanatically addicted to a particular idea—can you think of a better word to describe certain kinds of people who seek to reorder public affairs according to their hypnotic visions? Should one refuse to use a venerable word for which there is no obvious synonym simply because it is a word that does not regularly appear in the diet of the average reader?

I raise the problem because I am often accused of an inordinate reliance on unusual words and desire—as would you in my shoes, I think—to defend myself against the insinuation that I write as I do simply to prove that I have returned recently from the bowels of a dictionary with a fish in my mouth, establishing my etymological dauntlessness. Surely one must distinguish between those who plunder old tomes to find words which, in someone's phrase, should never be let out, belonging strictly to the zoo sections of the dictionary, and such others as Russell Kirk, who use words because (a) the words signify just exactly what the user means and because (b) the user deems it right and proper to preserve in currency words which in the course of history were coined as the result of a felt need.

There is a sort of phony democratic bias against the use of unusual words. Recently I heard a young movie actress being interviewed on a radio station. She was asked by her interrogator what it meant to be an actress and replied that an actor's life was "multifaceted." "What are you trying to pull on me?" demanded the radio announcer. Sweetie pie ran, panicked, from the argument—what else, in the democratic age, when it is deemed an effrontery on the democratic ideal to use a word that is not used twice a week by Little Orphan Annie? "I'm sorry I used such a fancy word . . . I guess I don't really know what it means . . . I should have said, there are lots of aspects to being an actress." Democracy won the day, and the show droned on.

Awhile ago I was on Jack Paar's program, and he asked me a number of questions having to do with this and that, which I tried, vainly, to answer as best I knew how. I wrote about that experience in *Rumbles* and described the ensuing tantrum of Mr. Paar and his associates, who steamed on and on about my ideological vices, expressing special outrage at my unintelligibility.

It is a curious thing, this universal assumption by a number of prominently situated opinion, or rather mood, makers that the American people are either unaware of the unusual word or undisposed to hear it and find out what it means, thus broadening not merely their vocabulary—that isn't the important thing—but their conceptual and descriptive powers. Those who say that the average American is incapable of appreciating the meaning of the word "energumen" are, in my humble judgment, nuts. The average American is, in Franklin P. Adams' phrase, above average, and his intelligence is not tied umbilically to Jack Paar's antiintellectualist muse. It is curious that a man who is offended by the use of the word "multifaceted" or "energumen" is perfectly capable of expressing a sentence of death-defying mechanical complexity. I am, unfortunately, innocent in the world of science, and I wish I knew what in the world the TV hawker is talking about when he reels off something having to do with a "double action injector system in the valve mechanism," but it does not occur to me to suggest that he is putting on airs; it occurs to me to rue my patently inadequate knowledge of my mechanical *abc's*.

The point about unusual words is that they are as necessary to philosophy, economics, esthetics, and political science as they are necessary in the world of higher mechanics, in which so many people, displaying the natural American genius, are so much at home. It is possible, I suppose, to describe the refinements of an Astrojet fan-injection blah blah blah engine in words understandable to me, but the exercise is not often resorted to, because the manufacturers assume a certain level of mechanical literacy, as they assume that those who do not have it ought not to set the standards for those who do have it. So it is in other fields, which is why, in my judgment, when Mr. Russell Kirk uses the word "energumen," he should be allowed to use it, and the thing for book reviewers to do when they come upon it, if they are unfamiliar with it, is not to pout, but to open a dictionary and see if the word is one whose meaning they wish to learn. They must guard against going about like antiliterate energumens.

Content

1. Summarize, in your own words, Buckley's defense of unusual words. Are you persuaded by his argument? Why or why not?
2. In paragraph three, Buckley asserts that there is a "phony democratic bias against the use of unusual words." What do you understand him to mean by this phrase? What evidence in the rest of the essay supports your interpretation?
3. Buckley says that to broaden our vocabularies is to broaden our "conceptual and descriptive powers." What evidence could you offer from your own experience to support or refute this statement? Do you agree or disagree, on the whole, with his point?
4. In this essay, Buckley offers in passing a number of arguments in defense of unusual words. What appears to be his main argument? His secondary arguments?
5. Buckley says he does not expect mechanical or scientific experts to write or speak so he can understand them; how does this argument support his main argument? What do you understand him to mean by this statement?

The Hysteria About Words

Technique

1. Buckley begins the essay with an anecdote about another writer accused of affectation because of his use of the word "energumen." Yet it is Buckley himself who is usually accused of affectation; what advantage, if any, does he gain by focusing on someone other than himself? Explain.
2. To what extent is it ironic that a reviewer of Buckley's book is in turn the one that a second reviewer found annoying in his choice of language?
3. How does Buckley turn his own "innocence" about scientific terms to his advantage in this essay? Is his argument convincing to you?
4. The essayist begins and ends his article with reference to the term "energumen". What is his apparent purpose in using this term a second time? Is it an effective technique?
5. Describe Buckley's tone. Is he repentant? Ironic? Sarcastic? Flippant? Earnest? What words would you point to, or what phrases, to support your answer?
6. "Mixed diction" refers to the use of terms from different levels of usage, or difficult or obscure terms set side by side with terms from everyday speech. To what extent does Buckley use mixed diction in this essay? How effectively does he combine the different levels of diction here? Why do you suppose he does so?

Language

1. Does Buckley, in your opinion, use "unnecessary" words in this essay? Explain.
2. The term "democratic ideal" has a negative connotation as Buckley uses it here. How does he manage to make negative use of a term that is usually used positively? Why, specifically, does he object to a "democratic" notion of language use?
3. Look up the word "affectation" in the dictionary. To what extent does it apply to Buckley in this essay?
4. Is there any sign in the essay that the author is sincere in his statement that he "rues" his "patently inadequate knowledge of my mechanical *abc's*"? Explain.

Vocabulary

affectation   insinuation
heinous   effrontery
venerable   patently

Writing Suggestions

1. In the final paragraph of the essay, the author uses the word "antiliterate." Write a paragraph in which you distinguish between "antiliterate" and "illiterate." Show why this might be an important distinction.
2. Write an essay in which you defend the use of any specialized vocabulary with which you are familiar; feel free to draw from the worlds of sports, arts, crafts, an academic discipline, to name only a few. You might consider these questions in getting started: What advantages do specialized vocabularies offer? What audience does a specialized vocabulary include? Exclude? When, if ever, is it appropriate to "translate" that special vocabulary for a reader?
3. In a paragraph or two, explain a "technical" process in nontechnical terms. What special problems does such an exercise raise? To what extent does such an exercise lend strength to Buckley's argument?

A Growing Wealth of Words
Norman Cousins

Norman Cousins (b. 1915) served as editor for Saturday Review *from 1940 to 1971. He has long worked for the cause of peace, serving on a number of national committees and citizens' groups, and has won numerous awards for his journalism. Cousins has authored and edited more than a dozen books, including* The Democratic Chance *(1942),* Writing for Love or Money *(1949), and* Anatomy of an Illness *(1979). Currently he is an adjunct professor in the School of Medicine at UCLA. In the following essay, he shows, through example, how rapidly our language is acquiring new words, a process he actively endorses.*

Fair warning: I write here unashamedly about a book project with which I have been personally involved—*March's Thesaurus-Dictionary*. Originally published in 1902, it represented a significant advance over *Roget's*. It combined dictionary definitions with a wide array of synonyms and associative words. Perhaps its most unique feature was a special system of juxtapositions it employed to bring out the full flavor of a word. The work was the product of one of America's most gifted lexicographers, Francis A. March. It dropped out of print somewhere during the Thirties and quickly became a collector's item. I prized my copy, which became the single most useful reference work in my personal library, and called the book to the attention of Doubleday, which brought out a revised edition in 1958. After 20 years, that edition, too, dropped out of print. Then, in 1978, the late Harry Abrams brought out an updated edition under the imprint of his Abbeville Press.

What to me is the most fascinating of all about the new edition is a supplement by Stuart Berg Flexner and R. A. Goodwin containing words that have come into the language since the original edition 80 years ago. The new supplement, therefore, is a guide to the language of the 20th century. Thousands of words have come into the language in a comparatively short time. Most of these words are by now so commonplace that it is difficult to imagine how people ever got along without them. It hardly seems possible that words like *activate, displacement, empathy, documentary, heartland, escalate, defeatist, disposable, euphoria, decibel, deflate, demote, imbalance, immobilize, intelligentsia, inoperable, deadline, foolproof, editorialize, highlight, threshold, thumbnail, addict, bypass,* and *backlash* are all of comparatively recent origin.

Many words, of course, are the products of 20th-century civilization. The automobile alone is responsible for a vast addition to the language. Consider *backup, convertible, jalopy, hot rod, trailer, van, hit-and-run, back-seat driver,* etc. Similarly, the world of aviation has enriched the vocabulary with *airport, blimp, glider, helicopter, runway, tailspin, jet lag, skywriting,* etc. Hardly less enriching to the language is the vocabulary of the space age: *blast-off, countdown, launching pad, splashdown,* and *moonshot.* Immediately adjacent is the entire new world of atomic energy: *antigravity, chain reaction, electron, fission, fusion, isotope, nuclear, radioactivity, reactor,* and *SALT.*

The advent of the Psychological Revolution has not been without its effects on the language. Witness *catharsis, escapism, extrovert, introvert, fixation, hang-up, id, identity crisis, inferiority complex, superiority complex, crack-up, flip out, freak out, go haywire, batty, bananas, masochism, sadism, hallucination, inhibition, libido, narcissism, Oedipus complex, neurosis, overcompensation, stream of consciousness, trauma,* and *wishful thinking.*

Words like *burnout, psych-out, psych-up, rationalize,* and *maladjusted* are the product of an age that is trying to understand itself. Closely related, of course, is the medical vocabulary that has spilled over to the general language, where we freely use words like *allergy, blackout, shut-in, whiplash, blacklung, hormone,* and *holistic.*

As for uncomplimentary references, the 20th century is not lacking in derogation: *bonehead, boob, crackpot, dimwit, dumbbell, goof, kook, misfit, nitwit, punk, nut, rattlebrain, sad sack, screwball, zombie.*

Few developments in recent years have been more characteristic of American life than the arena of publicity and communications: *ballyhoo, blurb, buildup, centerfold, cheesecake, handout, hoopla, hype, plug, promo, public relations, sponsor, skywriting, throwaway, columnist, want ad.*

It is important to be reminded that the human species is in a constant condition of experimentation, adaptation, and adventure; and that language is a way of keeping astride change. It is also the currency of communication; we become richer in direct proportion to our linguistic capital. Progress for the individual or the group depends not just on purpose and action but the use of the right words. The greater the ability to express abstractions and nuances, the wider the thinking ability and the more effective the command of complex situations.

In recent years, we have seen the growth of the cult of incoherence; it is considered fashionable in some circles to grunt and stammer and to litter the language with stale expressions (you know, I mean, etc.). But the contraction of language is a temporary phenomenon. Far more significant and enduring is the infusion that comes from new ideas and new thrusts. The language has never been richer than it is today and it will become richer still.

Content

1. In what sense are the terms Cousins lists in the body of his essay "a guide to the language of the 20th century," as Cousins asserts they are?
2. Did any terms in Cousins' lists surprise you? That is to say, if you had been asked to guess how long particular terms have been in our vocabulary, are there any you would have placed prior to the beginning of the twentieth century? Why?
3. Cousins refers to "the cult of incoherence" at the end of the essay. What do you understand him to mean by this phrase? To what extent does "cult" seem an appropriate term in this context? Explain.
4. "Progress," Cousins asserts, "depends . . . on the use of right words." What do you think this statement means? Do you agree or disagree?

5. Cousins calls his thesaurus "the single most useful reference work in my personal library," but he does not elaborate upon this statement. How might one use a thesaurus? When might one misuse it? If you haven't done so before, be sure to examine a thesaurus carefully before attempting to answer this question.

Technique

1. An unusually large portion of this essay depends on lists; under what circumstances is such a technique appropriate? When is it inappropriate? Explain.
2. Cousins saves his main point, or thesis, for the end of the essay. This technique of building from the particular to the general is called "inductive reasoning." How well does it work for Cousins? Under what other circumstances do you think it would be an appropriate or effective essay technique?
3. Identify Cousins' thesis. To what extent is it supported by the detail of the rest of the essay? Explain.
4. Near the end of the essay Cousins refers to the "cult of incoherence." Why do you suppose he might have introduced this idea, which on the surface has no direct relevance to the terms added to English in this century?
5. Cousins gives no categorial label to the first set of terms he lists in paragraph 2. How would you distinguish the words in this list from those that follow? Is it useful, in your opinion, to make such a distinction? Why or why not?

Language

1. Cousins uses the term "linguistic capital" in the next-to-last paragraph of the essay. Explain what you think he means by this term.
2. Locate the OED (*Oxford English Dictionary*) in your library and skim through one or two of its volumes, looking for familiar words that date back to the 1500s or before. Make a list of several such words, noting how their meanings have changed over the centuries.
3. Following the directions in the preceding question, search for words that appear to have become extinct or obsolete. If scientific discoveries, for example, brought new words into our language, what seems to have caused other words to disappear from common usage?

4. Cousins assumes that readers will be familiar with the terms he lists under new words in the language. Were there any words in his lists that were new to you? Was there a single category of words more or less familiar? Be prepared to cite specific examples in responding to these questions.

Vocabulary

juxtaposition lexicographers
thesarus derogation
unashamedly nuances
synonyms infusion

Writing Suggestions

1. Make a list of words that because of some technological changes might become obsolete in the distant future—for example, "clockwise." Write a paragraph in which you explain why the words you identify might drop out of everyday vocabularies.
2. Write a brief narrative essay in which you show how you came to acquire a particular set or class of new words in your vocabulary.
3. Write two or three paragraphs in which you compare and contrast a thesaurus and a traditional dictionary. What are the advantages of each for a reader? The disadvantages?

Humpty Dumpty
Lewis Carroll

Lewis Carroll is the pseudonym of Charles Dodgson (1832–1898), a British logician, photographer, and mathematician. He was also the author of two children's books that adults have been reading ever since their publication in the nineteenth century: Alice in Wonderland *(1865) and* Through the Looking Glass and What Alice Found There *(1871). "Humpty Dumpty," featuring the irascible, if fragile, character who makes words mean precisely what he wants them to mean, is taken from the latter book.*

However, the egg only got larger and larger, and more and more human: when she had come within a few yards of it, she saw that it had eyes and a nose and mouth; and, when she had come close to it, she saw clearly that it was HUMPTY DUMPTY himself. "It can't be anybody else!" she said to herself. "I'm as certain of it, as if his name were written all over his face!"

It might have been written a hundred times, easily, on that enormous face. Humpty Dumpty was sitting, with his legs crossed like a Turk, on the top of a high wall—such a narrow one that Alice quite wondered how he could keep his balance—and, as his eyes were steadily fixed in the opposite direction, and he didn't take the least notice of her, she thought he must be a stuffed figure, after all.

"And how exactly like an egg he is!" she said aloud, standing with her hands ready to catch him, for she was every moment expecting him to fall.

"It's *very* provoking," Humpty Dumpty said after a long silence, looking away from Alice as he spoke, "to be called an egg—very!"

"I said you *looked* like an egg, Sir," Alice gently explained. "And some eggs are very pretty, you know," she added, hoping to turn her remark into a sort of compliment.

"Some people," said Humpty Dumpty, looking away from her as usual, "have no more sense than a baby!"

Alice didn't know what to say to this: it wasn't at all like conversation, she thought, as he never said anything to *her*; in fact, his last remark was evidently addressed to a tree—so she stood and softly repeated to herself:—

> *"Humpty Dumpty sat on a wall:*
> *Humpty Dumpty had a great fall.*
> *All the King's horses and all the King's men*
> *Couldn't put Humpty Dumpty in his place again.*

"That last line is much too long for the poetry," she added, almost out loud, forgetting that Humpty Dumpty would hear her.

"Don't stand chattering to yourself like that," Humpty Dumpty said, looking at her for the first time, "but tell me your name and your business."

"My *name* is Alice, but—"

"It's a stupid name enough!" Humpty Dumpty interrupted impatiently. "What does it mean?"

"*Must* a name mean something?" Alice asked doubtfully.

"Of course it must," Humpty Dumpty said with a short laugh: "*my* name means the shape I am—and a good handsome shape it is, too. With a name like yours, you might be any shape, almost."

"Why do you sit out here all alone?" said Alice, not wishing to begin an argument.

"Why, because there's nobody with me!" said Humpty Dumpty. "Did you think I didn't know the answer to *that*? Ask another."

"Don't you think you'd be safer down on the ground?" Alice went on, not with any idea of making another riddle, but simply in her good-natured anxiety for the queer creature. "That wall is so *very* narrow!"

"What tremendously easy riddles you ask!" Humpty Dumpty growled out. "Of course I don't think so! Why, if ever I *did* fall off—which there's no chance of—but *if* I did—" Here he pursed up his lips, and looked so solemn and grand that Alice could hardly help laughing. "*If* I *did* fall," he went on, "*the King has promised me*—ah, you may turn pale, if you like! You didn't think I was going to say that, did you? *The King has promised me*—with his very own mouth—to—to—"

"To send all his horses and all his men," Alice interrupted, rather unwisely.

"Now I declare that's too bad!" Humpty Dumpty cried, breaking into a sudden passion. "You've been listening at doors—and behind trees—and down chimneys—or you couldn't have known it!"

"I haven't indeed!" Alice said very gently. "It's in the book."

"Ah, well! They may write such things in a *book*," Humpty Dumpty said in a calmer tone. "That's what you call a History of England, that is. Now, take a good look at me! I'm one that has spoken to a King, *I* am: mayhap you'll never see such another: and, to show you I'm not proud, you may shake hands with me!" And he grinned almost from ear to ear, as he leant forwards (and as nearly as possible fell off the wall in doing so) and offered Alice his hand. She watched him a little anxiously as she took it. "If he smiled much more the ends of his mouth might meet behind," she thought: "And then I don't know *what* would happen to his head! I'm afraid it would come off!"

"Yes, all his horses and all his men," Humpty Dumpty went on. "They'd pick me up again in a minute, *they* would! However, this conversation is going on a little too fast: let's go back to the last remark but one."

"I'm afraid I ca'n't quite remember it," Alice said, very politely.

"In that case we start afresh," said Humpty Dumpty, "and it's my turn to choose a subject—" ("He talks about it just as if it was a game!" thought Alice.) "So here's a question for you. How old did you say you were?"

Alice made a short calculation, and said "Seven years and six months."

"Wrong!" Humpty Dumpty exclaimed triumphantly. "You never said a word like it!"

"I thought you meant 'How old *are* you?'" Alice explained.

"If I'd meant that, I'd have said it," said Humpty Dumpty.

Alice didn't want to begin another argument, so she said nothing.

"Seven years and six months!" Humpty Dumpty repeated thoughtfully. "An uncomfortable sort of age. Now if you'd asked *my* advice, I'd have said, 'Leave off at seven'—but it's too late now."

"I never ask advice about growing," Alice said indignantly.

"Too proud?" the other enquired.

Alice felt even more indignant at this suggestion. "I mean," she said, "that one ca'n't help growing older."

"*One* ca'n't, perhaps," said Humpty Dumpty; "but *two* can. With proper assistance, you might have left off at seven."

"What a beautiful belt you've got on!" Alice suddenly remarked. (They had had quite enough of the subject of age, she thought: and, if they really were to take turns in choosing subjects, it was *her* turn now.) "At least," she corrected herself on second thoughts, "a beautiful cravat, I should have said—no, a belt, I mean—I beg your pardon!" she added in dismay, for Humpty Dumpty looked thoroughly offended, and she began to wish she hadn't chosen that subject. "If only I knew," she thought to herself, "which was neck and which was waist!"

Evidently Humpty Dumpty was very angry, though he said nothing for a minute or two. When he *did* speak again, it was in a deep growl.

"It is a—most—provoking—thing," he said at last, "when a person doesn't know a cravat from a belt!"

"I know it's very ignorant of me," Alice said, in so humble a tone that Humpty Dumpty relented.

"It's a cravat, child, and a beautiful one, as you say. It's a present from the White King and Queen. There now!"

"Is it really?" said Alice, quite pleased to find that she *had* chosen a good subject after all.

"They gave it me," Humpty Dumpty continued thoughtfully as he crossed one knee over the other and clasped his hands round it, "they gave it me—for an unbirthday present."

"I beg your pardon?" Alice said with a puzzled air.

"I'm not offended," said Humpty Dumpty.

"I mean, what *is* an un-birthday present?"

"A present given when it isn't your birthday, of course."

Alice considered a little. "I like birthday presents best," she said at last.

"You don't know what you're talking about!" cried Humpty Dumpty. "How many days are there in a year?"

"Three hundred and sixty-five," said Alice.

"And how many birthdays have you?"

"One."

"And if you take one from three hundred and sixty-five what remains?"

"Three hundred and sixty-four, of course."

Humpty Dumpty looked doubtful. "I'd rather see that done on paper," he said.

Alice couldn't help smiling as she took out her memorandum-book, and worked the sum for him:

$$\begin{array}{r} 3\ 6\ 5 \\ \underline{1} \\ 3\ 6\ 4 \end{array}$$

Humpty Dumpty took the book and looked at it carefully. "That seems to be done right—" he began.

"You're holding it upside down!" Alice interrupted.

"To be sure I was!" Humpty Dumpty said gaily as she turned it round for him. "I thought it looked a little queer. As I was saying, that *seems* to be done right—though I haven't time to look it over thoroughly just now—and that shows that there are three hundred and sixty-four days when you might get un-birthday presents—"

"Certainly," said Alice.

"And only *one* for birthday presents, you know. There's glory for you!"

"I don't know what you mean by 'glory,'" Alice said.

Humpty Dumpty smiled contemptuously. "Of course you don't—till I tell you. I mean 'there's a nice knock-down argument for you!'"

"But 'glory' doesn't mean 'a nice knock-down argument,' " Alice objected.

"When *I* use a word," Humpty Dumpty said, in rather a scornful tone, "it means just what I choose it to mean—neither more nor less."

"The question is," said Alice, "whether you *can* make words mean so many different things."

"The question is," said Humpty Dumpty, "which is to be master—that's all."

Alice was too much puzzled to say anything; so after a minute Humpty Dumpty began again. "They've a temper, some of them—particularly verbs: they're the proudest—adjectives you can do anything with, but not verbs—however, *I* can manage the whole lot of them! Impenetrability! That's what *I* say!"

"Would you tell me please," said Alice, "what that means?"

"Now you talk like a reasonable child," said Humpty Dumpty, looking very much pleased. "I meant by 'impenetrability' that we've had enough of that subject, and it would be just as well if you'd mention what you mean to do next, as I suppose you don't mean to stop here all the rest of your life."

"That's a great deal to make one word mean," Alice said in a thoughtful tone.

"When I make a word do a lot of work like that," said Humpty Dumpty, "I always pay it extra."

"Oh!" said Alice. She was much too puzzled to make any other remark.

"Ah, you should see 'em come round me of a Saturday night," Humpty Dumpty went on, wagging his head gravely from side to side, "for to get their wages, you know."

(Alice didn't venture to ask what he paid them with; and so you see I ca'n't tell *you*.)

"You seem very clever at explaining words, Sir," said Alice. "Would you kindly tell me the meaning of the poem called 'Jabberwocky'?"

"Let's hear it," said Humpty Dumpty. "I can explain all the poems that ever were invented—and a good many that haven't been invented just yet."

This sounded very hopeful, so Alice repeated the first verse:—

" '*Twas brillig, and the slithy toves*
    Did gyre and gimble in the wabe:

All mimsy were the borogoves,
    And the mome raths outgrabe."

"That's enough to begin with," Humpty Dumpty interrupted: "there are plenty of hard words there. 'Brillig' means four o'clock in the afternoon—the time when you begin *broiling* things for dinner."

"That'll do very well," said Alice: "and '*slithy*'?"

"Well, '*slithy*' means 'lithe and slimy.' 'Lithe' is the same as 'active.' You see it's like a portmanteau—there are two meanings packed up into one word."

"I see it now," Alice remarked thoughtfully: "and what are '*toves*'?"

"Well, '*toves*' are something like badgers—they're something like lizards—and they're something like corkscrews."

"They must be very curious-looking creatures."

"They are that," said Humpty Dumpty; "also they make their nests under sun-dials—also they live on cheese."

"And what's to '*gyre*' and to '*gimble*'?"

"To '*gyre*' is to go round and round like a gyroscope. To '*gimble*' is to make holes like a gimlet."

"And '*the wabe*' is the grass-plot round a sun-dial, I suppose?" said Alice, surprised at her own ingenuity.

"Of course it is. It's called '*wabe*' you know, because it goes a long way before it, and a long way behind it—"

"And a long way beyond it on each side," Alice added.

"Exactly so. Well then, '*mimsy*' is 'flimsy and miserable' (there's another portmanteau for you). And a '*borogove*' is a thin shabby-looking bird with its feathers sticking out all round—something like a live mop."

"And then '*mome raths*'?" said Alice. "I'm afraid I'm giving you a great deal of trouble."

"Well, a '*rath*' is a sort of green pig: but '*mome*' I'm not certain about. I think it's short for 'from home'—meaning that they'd lost their way, you know."

"And what does '*outgrabe*' mean?"

"Well, '*outgribing*' is something between bellowing and whistling, with a kind of sneeze in the middle: however, you'll hear it done, maybe—down in the wood yonder—and, when you've once heard it, you'll be *quite* content. Who's been repeating all that hard stuff to you?"

"I read it in a book," said Alice. "But I *had* some poetry repeated to me much easier than that, by—Tweedledee, I think it was."

"As to poetry, you know," said Humpty Dumpty, stretching out one of his great hands, "I can repeat poetry as well as other folk, if it comes to that—"

"Oh, it needn't come to that!" Alice hastily said, hoping to keep him from beginning.

"The piece I'm going to repeat," he went on without noticing her remark, "was written entirely for your amusement."

Alice felt that in that case she really *ought* to listen to it; so she sat down, and said "Thank you" rather sadly,

"In winter, when the fields are white,
I sing this song for your delight—

only I don't sing it," he added, as an explanation.

"I see you don't," said Alice.

"If you can *see* whether I'm singing or not, you've sharper eyes than most," Humpty Dumpty remarked severely. Alice was silent.

"In spring, when woods are getting green,
I'll try and tell you what I mean:"

"Thank you very much," said Alice.

"In summer, when the days are long,
Perhaps you'll understand the song:

In autumn, when the leaves are brown,
Take pen and ink, and write it down."

"I will, if I can remember it so long," said Alice.

"You needn't go on making remarks like that," Humpty Dumpty said: "they're not sensible, and they put me out."

"I sent a message to the fish:
I told them 'This is what I wish.'

The little fishes of the sea,
They sent an answer back to me.

The little fishes' answer was
'We cannot do it, Sir, because—' "

"I'm afraid I don't quite understand," said Alice.

"It gets easier further on," Humpty Dumpty replied.

"I sent to them again to say
'It will be better to obey.'

> *The fishes answered, with a grin,*
> *'Why, what a temper you are in!'*
>
> *I told them once, I told them twice:*
> *They would not listen to advice.*
>
> *I took a kettle large and new,*
> *Fit for the deed I had to do.*
>
> *My heart went hop, my heart went thump:*
> *I filled the kettle at the pump.*
>
> *Then some one came to me and said*
> *'The little fishes are in bed.'*
>
> *I said to him, I said it plain,*
> *'Then you must wake them up again.'*
>
> *I said it very loud and clear:*
> *I went and shouted in his ear."*

Humpty Dumpty raised his voice almost to a scream as he repeated this verse, and Alice thought, with a shudder, "I wouldn't have been the messenger for *anything*!"

> *"But he was very stiff and proud:*
> *He said, 'You needn't shout so loud!'*
>
> *And he was very proud and stiff:*
> *He said 'I'd go and wake them, if—'*
>
> *I took a corkscrew from the shelf:*
> *I went to wake them up myself.*
>
> *And when I found the door was locked,*
> *I pulled and pushed and kicked and knocked.*
>
> *And when I found the door was shut,*
> *I tried to turn the handle, but—"*

There was a long pause.

"Is that all?" Alice timidly asked.

"That's all," said Humpty Dumpty. "Good-bye."

This was rather sudden, Alice thought: but, after such a *very* strong hint that she ought to be going, she felt that it would hardly be civil to stay. So she got up, and held out her hand. "Good-bye, till we meet again!" she said as cheerfully as she could.

"I shouldn't know you again if we *did* meet," Humpty Dumpty replied in a discontented tone, giving her one of his fingers to shake: "you're so exactly like other people."

"The face is what one goes by, generally," Alice remarked in a thoughtful tone.

"That's just what I complain of," said Humpty Dumpty. "Your face is the same as everybody has—the two eyes, so—" (marking their places in the air with his thumb) "nose in the middle, mouth under. It's always the same. Now if you had the two eyes on the same side of the nose, for instance—or the mouth at the top—that would be *some* help."

"It wouldn't look nice," Alice objected. But Humpty Dumpty only shut his eyes, and said "Wait till you've tried."

Alice waited a minute to see if he would speak again, but, as he never opened his eyes or took any further notice of her, she said "Good-bye!" once more, and, getting no answer to this, she quietly walked away: but she couldn't help saying to herself, as she went, "of all the unsatisfactory—" (she repeated this aloud, as it was a great comfort to have such a long word to say) "of all the unsatisfactory people I *ever* met—" She never finished the sentence, for at this moment a heavy crash shook the forest from end to end.

Content

1. Using specific examples from the essay, chracterize what you understand to be Humpty Dumpty's attitude toward language.
2. Given the piece as a whole, how would you characterize Lewis Carroll's attitude toward language? How does it differ from Humpty Dumpty's for instance?
3. To what extent does Alice seem to share Humpty Dumpty's view of poetry? What evidence would you cite to support your point of view?

Technique

1. Comparing and contrasting this piece of fiction with an essay of your choice from this chapter, analyze the different ways a fiction writer and an essayist make their points.
2. When Alice first meets Humpty Dumpty she says to herself that he had his name written all over his face; later the two of them have a

discussion about what names mean, their own included. Are there other paired episodes like this in the narration? How do such pairings contribute to the point of the narration?

3. Humpty Dumpty accuses Alice at one point of being "proud." To what extent would this label apply more appropriately to Humpty Dumpty himself?

Language

1. There is considerable word play in this narration, including, for example, Humpty Dumpty's remark to Alice about what names mean. What other examples can you find in the piece?
2. At one point Humpty Dumpty mentions "portmanteau words," words that have two meanings "packed" into them. Can you think of examples of portmanteau words in everyday use? Consider, for instance, puns and jokes.

Vocabulary

cravat   portmanteau
memorandum   gimlet

Writing Suggestions

1. In a brief essay, analyze the ways in which Alice, who is only seven years old, manages to take good care of herself in this episode. For a longer paper on the same subject, read the entire work, *Through the Looking Glass*; then write a paper in which you classify the various themes, besides language, you find in the book.
2. Humpty Dumpty says that words mean whatever we want them to mean. Write a paper in which you argue Humpty Dumpty's point of view. For example, what confusion would result if every time we used a word the listener interpreted it as meaning everything that the dictionary definition includes?

Notes on Punctuation
Lewis Thomas

Lewis Thomas (b. 1913) has had a distinguished career as a physician, administrator, researcher, teacher, and writer. He attended Princeton and the Harvard Medical School before moving on to the University of Min-

nesota Medical School, the New York University–Bellevue Medical Center, and the Yale University Medical School. He is currently president of the Memorial Sloan–Kettering Cancer Center. A series of essays he wrote for The New England Journal of Medicine *have been collected in two widely read books:* The Lives of a Cell *(1974) and* The Medusa and the Snail *(1979). "Notes on Punctuation" is taken from* The Medusa and the Snail. *In it, Thomas discusses the practical value of punctuation marks, but he goes on to describe and celebrate the shades of meaning and qualities of personality that such simple marks can add to prose.*

There are no precise rules about punctuation (Fowler lays out some general advice (as best he can under the complex circumstances of English prose (he points out, for example, that we possess only four stops (the comma, the semicolon, the colon and the period (the question mark and exclamation point are not, strictly speaking, stops; they are indicators of tone (oddly enough, the Greeks employed the semicolon for their question mark (it produces a strange sensation to read a Greek sentence which is a straightforward question: Why weepest thou; (instead of Why weepest thou? (and, of course, there are parentheses (which are surely a kind of punctuation making this whole much more complicated by having to count up the left-handed parentheses in order to be sure of closing with the right number (but if the parentheses were left out, with nothing to work with but the stops, we would have considerably more flexibility in the deploying of layers of meaning than if we tried to separate all the clauses by physical barriers (and in the latter case, while we might have more precision and exactitude for our meaning, we would lose the essential flavor of language, which is its wonderful ambiguity)))))))))))).

The commas are the most useful and usable of all the stops. It is highly important to put them in place as you go along. If you try to come back after doing a paragraph and stick them in the various spots that tempt you you will discover that they tend to swarm like minnows into all sorts of crevices whose existence you hadn't realized and before you know it the whole long sentence becomes immobilized and lashed up squirming in commas. Better to use them sparingly, and with affection, precisely when the need for each one arises, nicely, by itself.

I have grown fond of semicolons in recent years. The semicolon tells you that there is still some question about the preceding full sentence; something needs to be added; it reminds you sometimes of the Greek usage. It is almost always a greater pleasure to come across a semicolon than a period. The period tells you that that is that; if you didn't get all the meaning you wanted or expected, anyway you got all the writer intended to parcel out and now you have to move along. But with a semicolon there you get a pleasant little feeling of expectancy; there is more to come; read on; it will get clearer.

Colons are a lot less attractive, for several reasons: firstly, they give you the feeling of being rather ordered around, or at least having your nose pointed in a direction you might not be inclined to take if left to yourself, and, secondly, you suspect you're in for one of those sentences that will be labeling the points to be made: firstly, secondly and so forth, with the implication that you haven't sense enough to keep track of a sequence of notions without having them numbered. Also, many writers use this system loosely and incompletely, starting out with number one and number two as though counting off on their fingers but then going on and on without the succession of labels you've been led to expect, leaving you floundering about searching for the ninethly or seventeenthly that ought to be there but isn't.

Exclamation points are the most irritating of all. Look! they say, look at what I just said! How amazing is my thought! It is like being forced to watch someone else's small child jumping up and down crazily in the center of the living room shouting to attract attention. If a sentence really has something of importance to say, something quite remarkable, it doesn't need a mark to point it out. And if it is really, after all, a banal sentence needing more zing, the exclamation point simply emphasizes its banality!

Quotation marks should be used honestly and sparingly, when there is a genuine quotation at hand, and it is necessary to be very rigorous about the words enclosed by the marks. If something is to be quoted, the *exact* words must be used. If part of it must be left out because of space limitations, it is good manners to insert three dots to indicate the omission, but it is unethical to do this if it means connecting two thoughts which the original author did not intend to have tied together. Above all, quotation marks should not be used for ideas that you'd like to disown, things in the air so to speak. Nor should they be put in place around clichés; if you want to use a cliché you must take full responsibility for it yourself and not try to fob it off on anon., or on society. The most objectionable misuse of quotation marks, but one which illustrates the dangers of misuse in ordinary prose, is seen in advertising, especially in advertisements for small restaurants, for example "just around the corner," or "a good place to eat." No single, identifiable, citable person ever really said, for the record, "just around the corner," much less "a good place to eat," least likely of all for restaurants of the type that use this type of prose.

The dash is a handy device, informal and essentially playful, telling you that you're about to take off on a different tack but still in some way connected with the present course—only you have to remember that the dash is there, and either put a second dash at the end of the notion to let the reader know that he's back on course, or else end the sentence, as here, with a period.

The greatest danger in punctuation is for poetry. Here it is necessary to be as economical and parsimonious with commas and periods as with the words themselves, and any marks that seem to carry their own subtle meanings, like dashes and little rows of periods, even semicolons and question marks, should be left out altogether rather than inserted to clog up the thing with ambiguity. A single exclamation point in a poem, no matter what else the poem has to say, is enough to destroy the whole work.

The things I like best in T. S. Eliot's poetry, especially in the *Four Quartets*, are the semicolons. You cannot hear them, but they are there, laying out the connections between the images and the ideas. Sometimes you get a glimpse of a semicolon coming, a few lines farther on, and it is like climbing a steep path through woods and seeing a wooden bench just at a bend in the road ahead, a place where you can expect to sit for a moment, catching your breath.

Commas can't do this sort of thing; they can only tell you how the different parts of a complicated thought are to be fitted together, but you can't sit, not even take a breath, just because of a comma,

Content

1. Thomas speaks of four "stops" among the various marks of punctuation. What do you understand him to mean by this term? What other kinds of punctuation are there?
2. What fascinates Thomas as a reader about the semicolon as opposed to the period?

3. Why does Thomas say the colon is a "less attractive" mark of punctuation? Do you agree with him?
4. According to Thomas, punctuation is "dangerous" to poetry because it can "clog it up with ambiguity." What does this assertion mean? Can you find examples in poetry (or prose) of punctuation "clogging" the meaning?

Technique

1. We have described the tone of this essay as "playful." What specific examples substantiate this judgment. Do you agree?
2. Although nothing in the first seven paragraphs of this essay suggests that Thomas will necessarily end the essay by discussing poetry, in retrospect it seems like a natural, if not logical, conclusion. What, if anything, prepares us for Thomas' final concern with poetry?
3. Thomas uses four commas in a short sentence in which he warns us to use them sparingly, but none in the preceding long sentence in which he discusses the need for commas. What is Thomas' strategy here?
4. What seems to govern the order in which Thomas discusses each of the punctuation marks? In your opinion, would the essay be as interesting if he had used a different order? Explain.

Language

1. As we observed in the introduction to Part 1, Thomas' subject here, punctuation, applies only to written (not oral) forms of language. What, if anything, takes the place of punctuation in oral communication? To answer this question, listen to several different people talking over the next several days and note how each seems to "punctuate" his or her sentences. How, for that matter, do we recognize a "sentence" in nonwritten speech?
2. Most readers would expect to hear a list of rules in an essay about punctuation, yet Thomas does not offer any, at least as we traditionally conceive of rules. Instead, what particular forms of advice to writers are implicit in his essay? What advice would you be tempted to put into practice? Why?

Vocabulary

deploying	succession	fob
clauses	banal	parsimonious
exactitude	unethical	ambiguity

Writing Suggestions

1. Thomas calls attention to the specific punctuation mark that concerns him by making extensive use of it to illustrate his point. Using a similar technique, write a paragraph about the use of capital letters, circular "dots" over the letter "i," or another topic of your choice.

2. In a brief essay, write about your own attitudes toward punctuation. You might discuss why you particularly like one mark of punctuation or why the correct use of semicolons, commas, or quotation marks is so difficult to learn. Whatever your topic, try to parallel some of the same playfulness that occurs in Thomas' essay.

Language and the Community

2

Communication and community share the root word "commune," which as a verb conveys the sense of sharing, of making things common. The functions of languages and communities are interdependent as well: Whenever we use a language, we imply the presence of a community, whether we're talking or writing to many or to ourselves, writing grocery lists, or recording our own voices on a machine. There is, in other words, always at least the community of speaker and listener, writer and reader. Similarly, whenever we wish actually to create a community—whether it is a neighborhood club or an international corporation—a common language is our single indispensable tool.

The essays in this section, then, are particularly concerned with the connection between our notions of language and our notions of community. They allow us to explore and evaluate the ways in which we all use language to define our communities, large and small, and ways in which these same communities in turn use language to identify, rank, inform, and even deceive us. Because written religious and social laws may represent the clearest examples of the formal relationship between language and the values of our communities, some of the writers included here elaborate on this connection. Informal or even non-verbal languages can help establish communities, too; consequently, the essays in this section discuss language in topics as wide-ranging as secret clubs, lying, and marriage.

Some of the essayists address the topic of language and the community by focusing on relationships that have long been basic to human society. Diane Johnson, for example, examines the relationship between doctor and patient and the language of their communication. Doctors have a special power in this dialogue and in the community as a whole, Johnson suggests, because they are charged with healing us and because they often choose to speak the special language of medicine. Modern science has, of course, transformed the role of the doctor from tribal magician to trained professional, yet the language of modern medicine maintains for most of us a residue of that ancient magical power; Johnson investigates the conditions under which a doctor chooses to speak technically or familiarly with us.

Burton Bernstein, Joan Didion, and Maxine Hong Kingston illuminate the function and failure of language in other fundamental relationships. Bernstein describes the remarkable powers of a childhood language that binds together a small, secret society, which in turn provides its members with an identiy that they cling to even in adulthood. As Bernstein's memoir shows, the main purpose of such a secret language is to exclude others, to shut out the world. It does so most obviously by creating an unbreakable code consisting of names and words that no one else can understand. In a subtler way, moreover, it excludes the outside world by absorbing it, by ridiculing the words and names belonging to that world. "Anybody who 'talked funny,' " Bernstein writes, "was fair game when it came to the evolution of the [secret] language."

Joan Didion's "On Going Home" also concerns the way language can exclude others, sometimes unintentionally. She demonstrates how the special way her family communicates ultimately breaks down communication: They miss one another's points, mistake cousins for daughters, leave questions unfinished, and abandon answers. Just as the secret language of Bernstein's "family within a family" provides the members with identities separate from their identities in the outside world, the way Didion's family talks and socializes gives her an identity that has little to do with her life outside her family.

The implied thesis of Maxine Hong Kingston's essay combines Bernstein's and Didion's points of view. Kingston returns to an ethnic and filial past—represented by her aunt who lives in San Francisco's Chinatown—in which, like Didion, she initially feels resentment and apprehension. Ultimately, however, she is able to bring her understanding of the Chinese and American communities (and their languages) to bear on the situation. The result is a successful communication and a satisfying union of the two cultures; her aunt delights in the strange sounds and sense of English words and Kingston does the same with Chinese. Words fail them occasionally, but a sense of humor and a profound respect for one another make Kingston's visit to her aunt as fruitful and memorable as Bernstein's membership in the secret club.

In various ways, then, Johnson, Bernstein, Didion, and Kingston address the function of language in such fundamental relationships as those between brothers and sisters, doctors and patients, aunts and nieces. Alleen Pace Nilsen also focuses on a relationship fundamental to our culture—marriage. Whereas the other essayists emphasize the way language can create identity *within* the larger community, Nilsen shows how marriage reflects and transmits the national, ethnic, and religious values of that larger society. She specifically examines how the vocabulary we use to speak of marriage reveals these values, most of which she argues have been defined, like the idea of marriage itself, by males.

Daniel Yankelovich addresses the more general topic of lying in the community. Using examples from advertising, journalism, and business, he shows how public lying has become a way to " 'stick it' to authority, to strike back through the use of deceit." Because we lack confidence in political and social authority, Yankelovich argues, and because we often feel that those in power deceive us, we have come to accept public lying as a legitimate way to get along in the community. The effect, however, is ultimately destructive, for we lose "the sense of belonging to a larger community and sharing responsibility for it." Thus, when we can trust a common language, a community springs into being; but when lying becomes the common ground, the community is doomed.

In different ways, these essays all discuss the extent to which language allows communities to assimilate individuals and the ways it enables individuals to form relationships and thereby belong to families, groups, cities, nations, and other kinds of communities. In "Letter From Birmingham Jail," however, Martin Luther King, Jr., takes such analysis a step further by justifying the act of protest, in which the individual challenges the community. King's essay encompasses many of the themes contained in the other essays: the use of language to assert power; the use of lies and half-truths to manipulate others; the use of language to discover identity, conquer fear and hatred, and change the existing community. King's painstaking analysis and argumentation, his elaborate style, and his sense of history reflect a traditional attitude toward language and the community; but his sense of outrage and morality—and the occasion of his essay, which was written on scraps of paper while King was jailed following a civil rights protest—introduce personal, social, and political urgency to the subject of language and the community.

The essays in this section acknowledge the great power of language both to unify and to alienate people, and they all demonstrate how we can be both victims and agents of that power. When we begin new jobs, enter new schools, move to new cities, or travel to other countries, we feel immediately the capacity of language to exclude us—to "dry up," using Kingston's term, our ability to make ourselves understood. And yet we have all felt the satisfaction of getting our ideas and feelings across and thereby being accepted by new families, professions, communities, and nations. The essayists represented in this section try to further our understanding of the crucial connection between an awareness of language and the ability to function and prosper in a community. The community may be as small as Joan Didion's family or as large as the American society that Martin Luther King envisioned—and the language may be as simple and exclusive as Bernstein's "Rybernian" or as complex and inclusive as traditional English—but the connection each of us has to any type of *community* nonetheless depends on some form of *communication*.

Doctor Talk

Diane Johnson

> *Diane Johnson (b. 1934) received a B.A. from the University of Utah in 1957 and a Ph.D. from the University of California, Los Angeles, in 1968. She is the author of several novels and regularly writes reviews for* The New York Review of Books *and other magazines. A nominee for the National Book Award in 1973 and 1979 and a recipient of a Woodrow Wilson grant in 1968, Johnson is presently a Professor of English at the University of California, Davis. "Doctor Talk" analyzes the way doctors and patients communicate and what such dialogues reveal about our attitudes toward medicine. Of particular interest is the contrast between the scientific and the lay terms for explaining a medical condition.*

The Living Language

In Africa or the Amazon, the witch doctor on your case has a magic language to say his spells in. You listen, trembling, full of hope and dread and mystification; and presently you feel better or die, depending on how things come out. In England and America too, until recent times, doctors talked a magic language, usually Latin, and its mystery was part of your cure. But modern doctors are rather in the situation of modern priests; having lost their magic languages, they run the risk of losing their magic powers too.

For us, this means that the doctor may lose his ability to heal us by our faith; and doctors, sensing powerlessness, have been casting about for new languages in which to conceal the nature of our afflictions and the ingredients of cures. They have devised two main dialects, but neither seems quite to serve for every purpose—this is a time of transition and trial for them, marked by various strategies, of which the well-known illegible handwriting on your prescription is but one. For doctors themselves seem to have lost faith too, in themselves and in the old mysteries and arts. They have been taught to think of themselves as scientists, and so it is first of all to the language of science that they turn, to control and confuse us.

Most of the time scientific language can do this perfectly. We are terrified, of course, to learn that we have "prolapse of the mitral valve"—we promise to take our medicine and stay on our diet, even though these words describe a usually innocuous finding in the investigation of an innocent heart murmur. Or we can be lulled into a false sense of security when the doctor avoids a scientific term: "you have a little spot on your lung"—even when what he puts on the chart is "probable bronchogenic carcinoma."

With patients, doctors can use either scientific or vernacular speech but with each other they speak Science, a strange argot of Latin terms, new words, and acronyms, that yearly becomes farther removed from everyday speech and is sometimes comprised almost entirely of numbers and letters: "His pO_2 is 45; pCO_2, 40; and pH 7.4." Sometimes it is made up of peculiar verbs originating from the apparatus with which they treat people: "Well, we've bronched him, tubed him, bagged him, cathed him, and PEEPed him," the intern tells the attending physician. ("We've explored his airways with a bronchoscope, inserted an endotrachial tube, provided assisted ventilation with a resuscitation bag, positioned a catheter in his bladder to monitor his urinary output, and used positive end-expiratory pressure to improve oxygenation.") Even when discussing things that can be expressed in ordinary words, doctors will prefer to say "he had a pneumonectomy" to saying "he had a lung removed."

One physician remembers being systematically instructed, during the 1950s, in scientific-sounding euphemisms to be used in the presence of patients. If a party of interns were examining an alcoholic patient, the wondering victim might hear them say that he was "suffering from hyperingestation of ethynol." In front of a cancer victim they would discuss his "mitosis." But in recent years such discussions are not conducted in front of the patient at all, because, since Sputnik, laymen's understanding of scientific language has itself increased so greatly that widespread ignorance cannot be assumed.

Space exploration has had its influence, especially on the *sound* of medical language. A CAT-scanner (computerized automated tomography), *de rigueur* in an up-to-date diagnostic unit, might be something to look at the surface of Mars with. The resonance of physical, rather than biological, science has doubtless been fostered by doctors themselves, who, mindful of the extent to which their science is really like an art, would like to sound astronomically precise, calculable and exact, even if they cannot be so.

Acronyms and abbreviations play the same part in medical language that they do in other walks of modern life: We might be irritated to read on our chart that "this SOB patient complained of DOE five days PTA." (It means "this Short of Breath patient complained of Dyspnea On Exertion five days Prior To Admission.") To translate certain syllables, the doctor must have yet more esoteric knowledge. Doctor A, reading Dr. B's note that a patient has TTP, must know whether Doctor B is a hematologist or a chest specialist in order to know whether the patient has thrombotic thrombocytopoenic puerpura, or traumatic tension pneumothorax. That pert little word *ID* means identification to us, but Intradermal to the dermatologist, Inside Diameter to the physiologist, Infective Dose to the bacteriologist; it can stand for our inner self, it can mean *idem* (the same), or it can signify a kind of rash.

But sometimes doctors must speak vernacular English, and this is apparently difficult for them. People are always being told to discuss their problems with their doctors, which, considering the general inability of doctors to reply except in a given number of reliable phrases, must be some of the worst advice ever given. Most people, trying to talk to the doctor—trying to pry or to wrest meaning from his evasive remarks ("I'd say you're coming along just fine")—have been maddened by the vague and slightly inconsequential nature of statements which, meaning everything to you, ought in themselves to have meaning but do not, are noncommittal, or unengaged, have a slightly rote or rehearsed quality, sometimes a slight inappropriateness in the context ("it's nothing to worry about really"). This is the doctor's alternative dialect, phrases so general and bland as to communicate virtually nothing.

This dialect originates from the emotional situation of the doctor. In the way passers-by avert their eyes from the drunk in the gutter or the village idiot, so the doctor must avoid the personality, the individuality, any involvement with the destiny, of his patients. He must not let himself think and feel with them. This shows in the habit doctors have of calling patients by the names of their diseases: "put the pancreatitis in the other ward and bring the chronic lunger in here." In order to retain objective professional judgment, the doctor has long since learned to withdraw his emotions from the plight of the patient and has replaced his own ability to imagine them and empathize with them, with a formula language—the social lie and the understatement—usually delivered with the odd jocularity common to all gloomy professions.

"Well, Mrs. Jones, Henry is pretty sick. We're going to run a couple of tests, have a look at that pump of his." ("Henry is in shock. We're taking him to the Radiology Department to put a catheter in his aorta and inject contrast material. If he has what I think he has, he has a forty-two percent chance of surviving.") We might note an apparent difference of style in English and American doctors, with the English inclined to drollery in such situations. One woman I know reported that her London gynecologist said to her, of her hysterectomy, "We're taking out the cradle, but we're leaving in the playpen!" Americans on the other hand often affect tough talk: "Henry is sick as hell."

The doctor's *we*, by the way, is of especial interest. Medical pronouns are used in special ways that ensure that the doctor is never out alone on any limb. The referents are cleverly vague. The statement "we see a lot of that" designates him as a member of a knowledgeable elite, "we doctors"; while "how are we today" means you, or him and you, if he is trying to pass himself off as a sympathetic alter ego. Rarely does he stand up as an *I*. Rarely does he even permit his name to stand alone as Smith, but affixes syllables before and after—the powerful abbreviation *Dr.* itself, which can even be found on his golf bags or skis; or the letters *M.D.* after, or sometimes the two buttressing his name from both sides, like bookends: "Dr. Smart Smith, M.D."; in England a little train of other letters may trail behind: *F.R.C.P.* In America another fashionable suffix has been observed recently: *Inc.* Dr. Smart Smith, M.D., Inc. This stands for Incorporated, and indicates that the doctor has made himself into a corporation, to minimize his income taxes. A matrix of economic terms already evident in the vocabulary of some doctors is expected to become more pervasive as time goes on.

We may complain even of how the doctor talks to us; doctors will say, on the other hand, that it is we who do not listen. Very likely this is true. Our ears thunder with hope and dread. We cannot hear the doctor. He says "bone marrow test," we think he says "bow and arrow test." We have been struck with disbelief, listening to an account by a friend or family member of his trip to the doctor; the doctor cannot possibly have said it was okay to go on smoking, that she doesn't need to lose weight, that he must never eat carrots. This is the case. According to doctors, patients hear themselves. The patient says, "I can't even look at a carrot," and then imagines the doctor has interdicted them. Doctors' sense of our inability to understand things may increase their tendency to talk in simple terms to us, or not to speak at all. Nonetheless, we all hear them talking, saying things they say they never say.

Content

1. According to Johnson's argument, why do doctors speak to us in "dialects" different from everyday speech? Be prepared to define briefly these two "dialects" in your own words. Is her argument convincing? Does it correspond to your own experience?
2. In paragraph 2, Johnson says that doctors have turned to scientific language "to control and confuse us." Do you agree that this is a purpose of doctor talk? Can you think of any other reasons doctors might use language that is beyond the understanding of laymen?
3. At the conclusion of her essay, Johnson presents the other side of the argument that doctor talk excludes the patient: Doctors, she says, are probably right in saying that "patients hear themselves" rather than the doctor. Explain the meaning of this statement and discuss possible reasons for the patient's inability to hear the doctor.

Technique

1. Johnson supports her argument with specific examples of "doctor talk." How does she present these examples to make them interesting? Does she succeed?
2. Johnson's tone suggests that she is not particularly sympathetic to the way doctors use language. In the second paragraph, she states her feelings explicitly, saying that doctors turn to the language of science "to control and confuse us." Find two or three other places in the essay where Johnson's attitude is implied or explicitly stated; discuss the impact of her attitude on the essay as a whole.

Language

1. In paragraph 8, Johnson says that doctors must sometimes speak "vernacular" English. What is vernacular English and how does it differ from "doctor talk"? Why do you think Johnson believes that speaking vernacular English is difficult for doctors?
2. What does Johnson mean when she says in paragraph 9 that doctors often speak with the "odd jocularity common to all gloomy professions"? Look up "jocularity" in your dictionary.

Vocabulary

dialect	matrix	drollery
euphemism	interdict	esoteric
acronym	rote	vernacular

Writing Suggestions

1. Write a paragraph in which you describe a real or imaginary discussion with a doctor in which you use vernacular English, but the doctor insists on one of the many forms of doctor talk that Johnson describes.
2. There are other professions in which a special language is used. Write an essay about one of these professions and its language; offer an opinion about why the special language is used and about its affects on outsiders, supporting your opinion with specific examples.
3. We are all likely to speak at least two different "languages"—for example, one with our friends and one with our parents and their friends. Write an essay in which you analyze your own use of two languages or dialects. How would you characterize the differences between the two? In your analysis, be sure to use specific examples of both languages.

Rybernian

Burton Bernstein

> Burton Bernstein (b. 1932) has been a staff writer for The New Yorker magazine since 1957. His books include The Grove, The Lost Art, and Personal History, from which the following essay is taken. The essay combines narration and analysis to give a vivid portrait of his childhood family and the secret language that he invented with his brother (the composer and conductor Leonard Bernstein) and his sister Shirley.

The generational breach between my father, Samuel Joseph Bernstein, and his parents had insidiously duplicated itself with Sam and his own children—"the kids," as we were collectively referred to by Sam and Jennie, my mother, no matter what our ages. It was another case of those proverbial chickens coming home to roost. The latest Bernstein parent-child breach began as a normal one, but it widened with alarming speed. By 1941, it was a small canyon, which caused Sam to feel all the more isolated from his family—to see himself as the object of some sort of cabal. In his darkest, most depressed moments, he was given to saying, "I'm worth more dead to all of you."

The year 1941 was a critical period for Sam. Besides the guilt-producing burden of Dinah, his mother, whom he had brought to America from Russia, and who was only recently widowed, there was the war, which also had an adverse effect on his beauty-supplies-and-hair-goods business. Certain chemicals used in the manufacture of cosmetics were in short supply, and Sam feared that his business would be ruined. In 1927, he had received the New England franchise for the revolutionary Frederics Permanent Wave Machine, but the simpler cold-wave permanent, introduced around 1940, had just about finished off his once-lucrative Frederics franchise, and there was not the same exclusivity available for the several cold-wave products. And, because of an old dispute with Charles Revson, the founder of the Revlon Corporation, he still wasn't able to acquire the prized Revlon line of beauty products. His older son, Lenny, having graduated from Harvard, was in his second year at the Curtis Insititute of Music, in Philadelphia. His daughter, Shirley, was in her first year at Mount Holyoke. What with business and tuition worries and little confidence in the future, Sam panicked. He put his dream castle—the house in Newton, Massachusetts—up for sale, and enlarged and winterized the summer house we owned, in Sharon. Education for his children was more important to him than any house.

When we moved to Sharon in the summer of 1941, we moved for good. As we drove out of the driveway of the Newton house for the last time, I saw that my father was crying. I had never seen him cry before. He had probably lost his firstborn son to the cryptic, foreign world of music; his daughter was thriving in the also alien, if essential, world of academe; his business—another child, so to speak—was faltering; and now his magnificent Newton house, the symbol of his success in America, was gone. Of his progeny, I alone was left around the house to comfort him in his middle age, and I was suddenly a resentful and withdrawn nine-year-old, furious at having been snatched from my Newton home and friends.

In spite of his children's growing remoteness, Sam shouldn't have doubted our love. It was there, just as surely as his basic love for his own parents had been. But he did doubt, and a nagging riddle possessed him: If I have given my kids every advantage, sacrificing for their education, why don't they "pull with me," why don't they see things my way, why don't I have *nachas* from them? It was that ancient Jewish principle of *nachas*—the inner gratification that a parent feels from, say, a well-tutored older son's taking over the family business and settling down, or a bright daughter's marrying a nice boy, or a younger son's avidly following in the faith of his father—that spawned the riddle. The more devotedly one educated one's children, in order to have more *nachas* from them, the greater the gap that would ultimately deprive one of that *nachas*. It was a paradox peculiar to twentieth-century America, and there was no apparent resolution.

The key figure in the generational split was Lenny—the firstborn, the scion who led the way for the others. From the beginning, he was special. Asthmatic, sensitive, intelligent, he left a deep impression on everyone, whether because of his chronic wheezing or because of his unmistakable precocity. Jennie knew that she had an unusual child. "When he was a sickly little boy and he'd turn blue from his asthma, Sam and I were scared to death," she has said. "Every time he had an attack, we thought he was going to die. I would be up all night with steam kettles and hot towels, helping him to breathe. If Lenny so much as sneezed, we would turn pale with worry. The first thing Sam did when he came home from the office, he'd say, 'How's Lenny?' But, sickly or not, Lenny was such a brilliant boy—always the leader of his gang, always the best in school."

And, she might have added, always the most inventive. For instance, when he was ten years old and the family was living on Schuyler Street, in Roxbury (one of the Bernstein's many addresses in their climb up the economic ladder), he created an entire nation, with its own culture and language. Prehaps that in itself is not so remarkable, but how many such childhood creations have endured, even flourished, right up to the present day? Lenny and his best friend, Eddie Ryack, had been studying ancient history at the William Lloyd Garrison School, and, having been rather taken with the administration of the Roman republic, they decided to become consuls of a country called Rybernia—an acronym of their last names. Of equal stature as the nation's leaders, they set up stringent rules for citizenship, mainly testing one's courage to undergo hazing techniques. The elite who passed muster and were admitted into this secret national society were Daniel Salamoff (a neighborhood boy), Sid Ramin (another neighborhood boy, who is now an estimable composer-arranger), Harold Zarling (the son of Bessie Zarling, a weepy friend of my mother's), and Shirley (a five-year-old mascot). The culture and, especially, the language of Rybernia were rooted in prepubescent cruelty. Two children of a family in the neighborhood were nicknamed Sonny: the younger Sonny—called Baby Sonny—suffered from a speech defect and occasional fits of petit mal, during which he would become rigid for a few moments. With the distinctive heartlessness of youth, the Rybernians would stop Baby Sonny on the street and ask him his name, which came out of the poor child's mouth as "Babü Chonnü." If they questioned him long enough, he would go into a slight spasm and stand frozen and contorted. The giggling Rybernians would then imitate both his speech and his posture, and thus a deformed, ridiculing patois was born, to go with the already established nation. Almost everything could be translated into some variation of Babü Channü talk; for example, the Rybernian named Salamoff became "Schlaudümopsch," and Shirley, the mascot, was "Mascodü." The Rybernian national anthem was sung more or less to the words and music of "When the Moon Comes Over the Mountain," and it came out like this: "Ven da moonyagen come obyagen da montanü . . . " At the utterance of certain syllables, the anthem singers were compelled to freeze, like Babü Chonnü, into whatever positions they held at the moment.

The great era in the early development of Rybernian culture arrived a couple of years later, with the family's move to more spacious quarters, on Pleasanton Street, also in Roxbury. There a large attic served as a clubhouse and "labjtobj" (laboratory) for the growing membership. Because Lenny had by then matriculated at the illustrious Boston Latin School, the national direction of Rybernia had veered toward modern science, and the labjtobj was used for such projects as distilling pure alcohol from rubbing alcohol. "We set up some filched equipment, like a Bunsen burner and glass tubing, and proceeded to distill filched rubbing alcohol," Lenny has said. "When it came out pure alcohol—it never occurred to us to drink it—well, it was such a triumph, a miracle, that we were convinced a great scientific discovery had been achieved. We would then stand and sing the national anthem with reverence." (An earlier experiment was not quite as successful. Lenny and Shirley once wrapped two eggs in flannel and put them behind a hot radiator, in the belief that they would hatch. When no immediate results were manifested, they forgot about the whole matter. A week or so later, a mysterious stench filled the house. Just when Sam was threatening to move out, Jennie solved the offensive puzzle by discovering the wretched mess behind the radiator.) On Pleasanton Street, too, a new Rybernian song was created, about the latest object of mockery—Agnes, the amorous maid. Its first line went something like this: "Agitated Aggü, the red-hot momyagen . . . "

The keen-eyed linguist will detect a certain foreign influence in the language, particulary in the umlaut-"u" sound and the "agen" ending. Clearly, the accent of my father and many of his friends contributed to the development of Rybernian. In fact, anybody whose manner of speaking could be held up to ridicule—or, as Lenny sometimes put it, "anybody who talked funny"—was fair game when it came to the evolution of the language. Long after Roxbury, Eddie Ryack, and Baby Sonny were out of sight and mind, Rybernian continued to expand with locutions inspired by people who talked funny. Uncle Harry Levy, in Hartford, for instance, always said "I'll migh' " for "I might," and so "I'll migh' " became standard Rybernian. Annie Miller, the Polish-born wife of my father's cousin Abe, had a peculiar quality of speech that never failed to send the intolerant Bernstein kids into poorly stifled fits of laughter. In her plangent

Polish tones, she might say, "I'm decoratink mitt new drepps, and I got to hank dem mitt rots and rinks and festooents." All streets were "straats" to Annie (Roxbury's Harold Street, near where the Millers lived, was therefore "Harralt Straat"), and—most deliciously of all—she referred to her husband, Abe, as "Ape." The word "ape," as proper or common or adjectival noun, became an important Rybernianism.

Another Polish influence was Alice, a later maid, who when asked the time would reply, for instance, "It smose snapas seven;" consequently, Rybernian Standard Time was always "smose snapas" something. A retarded boy in Sharon tended to mumble, against all physical laws, through his nose, and that anomaly opened a whole new speech pattern in Rybernian—the hangdog, embarrassed, barely decipherable declaration, usually of affection. Perhaps the strangest influence on the language evolved from Serge Koussevitzky, the conductor of the Boston Symphony Orchestra, who became not only Lenny's mentor but also his spiritual father. Koussevitzky was well known in musical circles for his charming butchery of English. An example that particularly amused his protégé—Lenyushka—was his use of a verb's past tense for the imperative; most memorably, he once shouted in despair at an erratic student conductor, "Took it a tempo *und* kept it!" So the misuse of the past tense took its place in our private lexicon. "How ya gonna did it?" is a common Rybernian question, often weighted with grave significance.

Rybernian remains a living language. It is still developing, in the manner of any good living language. While the changes and additions are not as cruel and derisive as they used to be, Lenny, Shirley, and I—the three of us well into middle age—continue to call one another by our Rybernian names and to perform certain Rybernian rituals (when nobody is looking, usually).

I came on the Rybernian scene in the late nineteen-thirties, at a tender, impressionable age. I was then "Baudümü," and I still am. Lenny was "Laudü," but that gradually changed to "Lennuhtt" (a late Annie Miller influence). Shirley, after her "Mascodü" stage, was called "Suyaumü," which through the years became "Hilee," for complex reasons. We three were—and, in a sense, still are—a closed society, with our own language, culture, and humor. Above all, our own humor. Others have tried—have even been encouraged—to break into this society, but somehow they have never quite made it. Of course, most people who have encountered our extremely restricted world have found the esoteric jokes and allusions boring (and with good reason), but some have made brave attempts to storm the walls of Fortress Rybernia. Lenny's late wife, Felicia, came the closest, and his children and mine sometimes lapse into imitative Rybernian. But they have never felt truly comfortable in that curious land. Jennie and Sam were privy to the language from its birth, and they occasionally sought to ingratiate themselves by using, with frightening inaccuracy, a word here and there. However, I suspect that if they had picked up the spirit and text of the thing Rybernia would have immediately evaporated. The essential point of the private world of the kids was that it had to be a private world of the kids, sequestered from the parents. What we three had in fact achieved was the creation of an imaginary counter-family within the real family. Our Rybernian family had a father (Lenny), a mother (Shirley), and a child (me).

Content

1. In Leonard Bernstein's creation of "an entire nation," undoubtedly the most complex aspect of his invention was the Rybernian language. To what extent do you think the language was a necessary ingredient in the success of the nation? Support your answer with specific detail.
2. The objects of Rybernian cruelty, such as Baby Sonny, became unwilling contributors to the habits of the Rybernian nationals. What else served to bond this group into its own community? To what extent are these reminiscent of events that bonded one of your childhood (or adult) groups?
3. Bernstein points out that Rybernian is still a living language, still evolving (though less cruelly) in its (and its members') middle-age. Why do you think it has survived? Compare what you believe its current function might be to Bernstein's description of its adolescent function.

Technique

1. Bernstein introduces his discussion of the secret nation with an extended description of his family relationships, and at the end of the selection he comes back to a discussion of family, saying, "What we three had in fact achieved was the creation of an imaginary counter-family within the real family." In what ways does this description contribute to his central description of the children's secret society and language?

2. Bernstein includes in his essay detailed examples, providing, for instance, the names and biographical data of the elite members of the Rybernian nation. Find other examples of Bernstein's use of detail. In what ways do the details strengthen or weaken the essay?

Language

1. Early in the essay, Bernstein speaks of his father's frustrated yearning for "nachas" from his children. In your own words, describe the meaning of "nachas." From your experience, can you add to Bernstein's examples of "nachas"?
2. Bernstein frequently uses plain language to describe the evolution of Rybernian (much of it was inspired, for instance, by people who "talked funny"), but he also uses such words as "locutions," "patois," and "lexicon," often closely juxtaposed to the simpler descriptive words. What is the effect of Bernstein's mixed vocabulary on the description as a whole?

Vocabulary

insidious	prepubescent	locutions
progeny	derisive	patois
paradox	privy	lexicon
acronym	precocity	

Writing Suggestions

1. Write a paragraph in which you explain a word or phrase which you use or have used in a "private world" like that of the Bernstein children.
2. Bernstein says his brother's nation, and particularly its language, was "rooted in prepubescent cruelty," and the examples he offers tend to confirm this. Drawing from your own experience, write an essay analyzing the ways you think children use secret societies and language to inflict cruelty on others.

On Going Home
Joan Didion

Joan Didion (b. 1934) received a B.A. in English from the University of California, Berkeley, in 1956, after which she became an editor for Vogue *and contributed essays to* The National Review, *the* Saturday Evening

Post, New West, *and* Harper's. *Her books of essays include* Slouching Towards Bethlehem *(1968) and* The White Album *(1979). She has also written two novels,* A Book of Common Prayer *(1977) and* Play It As It Lays *(1970), and collaborated on three screenplays. In the narrative essay, "On Going Home," Didion combines vivid concrete details with intense analysis to show us how a visit home can be a complex, often alienating experience.*

I am home for my daughter's first birthday. By "home" I do not mean the house in Los Angeles where my husband and I and the baby live, but the place where my family is, in the Central Valley of California. It is a vital although troublesome distinction. My husband likes my family but is uneasy in their house, because once there I fall into their ways, which are difficult, oblique, deliberately inarticulate, not my husband's ways. We live in dusty houses ("D-U-S-T," he once wrote with his finger on surfaces all over the house, but no one noticed it) filled with mementos quite without value to him (what could the Canton dessert plates mean to him? how could he have known about the assay scales, why should he care if he did know?), and we appear to talk exclusively about people we know who have been committed to mental hospitals, about people we know who have been booked on drunk-driving charges, and about property, particularly about property, land, price per acre and C-2 zoning and assessments and freeway access. My brother does not understand my husband's inability to perceive the advantage in the rather common real-estate transaction known as "sale-leaseback," and my husband in turn does not understand why so many of the people he hears about in my father's house have recently been committed to mental hospitals or booked on drunk-driving charges. Nor does he understand that when we talk about sale-leasebacks and right-of-way condemnations we are talking in code about the things we like best, the yellow fields and the cottonwoods and the rivers rising and falling and the mountain roads closing when the heavy snow comes in. We miss each other's points, have another drink and regard the fire. My brother refers to my husband, in his presence, as "Joan's husband." Marriage is the classic betrayal.

Or perhaps it is not any more. Sometimes I think that those of us who are now in our thirties were born into the last generation to carry the burden of "home," to find in family life the source of all tension and drama. I had by all objective accounts a "normal" and a "happy" family situation, and yet I was almost thirty years old before I could talk to my family on the telephone without crying after I had hung up. We did not fight. Nothing was wrong. And yet some nameless anxiety colored the emotional charges between me and the place that I came from. The question of whether or not you could go home again was a very real part of the sentimental and largely literary baggage with which we left home in the fifties; I suspect that it is irrelevant to the children born of the fragmentation after World War II. A few weeks ago in a San Francisco bar I saw a pretty young girl on crystal take off her clothes and dance for the cash prize in an "amateur-topless" contest. There was no particular sense of moment about this, none of the effect of romantic degradation, of "dark journey," for which my generation strived so assiduously. What sense could that girl possibly make of, say, *Long Day's Journey into Night*? Who is beside the point?

That I am trapped in this particular irrelevancy is never more apparent to me than when I am home. Paralyzed by the neurotic lassitude engendered by meeting one's past at every turn, around every corner, inside every cupboard, I go aimlessly from room to room. I decide to meet it head-on and clean out a drawer, and I spread the contents on the bed. A bathing suit I wore the summer I was seventeen. A letter of rejection from *The Nation*, an aerial photograph of the site for a shopping center my father did not build in 1954. Three teacups hand-painted with cabbage roses and signed "E.M.," my grandmother's initials. There is no final solution for letters of rejection from *The Nation* and teacups hand-painted in 1900. Nor is there any answer to snapshots of one's grandfather as a young man on skis, surveying around Donner Pass in the year 1910. I smooth out the snapshot and look into his face, and do and do not see my own. I close the drawer, and have another cup of coffe with my mother. We get along very well, veterans of a guerilla war we never understood.

Days pass. I see no one. I come to dread my husband's evening call, not only because he is full of news of what by now seems to me our remote life in Los Angeles, people he has seen, letters which require attention, but because he asks what I have been doing, suggests uneasily that I get out, drive to San Francisco or Berkeley. Instead I drive across the river to a family graveyard. It has been vandalized since my last visit and the monuments are broken, overturned in the dry grass. Because I once saw a rattlesnake in the grass

The Living Language

I stay in the car and listen to a country-and-Western station. Later I drive with my father to a ranch he has in the foothills. The man who runs his cattle on it asks us to the roundup, a week from Sunday, and although I know that I will be in Los Angeles I say, in the oblique way my family talks, that I will come. Once home I mention the broken monuments in the graveyard. My mother shrugs.

I go to visit my great-aunts. A few of them think now that I am my cousin, or their daughter who died young. We recall an anecdote about a relative last seen in 1948, and they ask if I still like living in New York City. I have lived in Los Angeles for three years, but I say that I do. The baby is offered a horehound drop, and I am slipped a dollar bill "to buy a treat." Questions trail off, answers are abandoned, the baby plays with the dust motes in a shaft of afternoon sun.

It is time for the baby's birthday party: a white cake, strawberry-marshmallow ice cream, a bottle of champagne saved from another party. In the evening, after she has gone to sleep, I kneel beside the crib and touch her face, where it is pressed against the slats, with mine. She is an open and trusting child, unprepared for and unaccustomed to the ambushes of family life, and perhaps it is just as well that I can offer her little of that life. I would like to give her more. I would like to promise her that she will grow up with a sense of her cousins and of rivers and of her great-grandmother's teacups, would like to pledge her a picnic on a river with fried chicken and her hair uncombed, would like to give her *home* for her birthday, but we live differently now and I can promise her nothing like that. I give her a xylophone and a sundress from Madeira, and promise to tell her a funny story.

Content

1. Didion's trip home fills her with mixed, often conflicting, emotions. Summarize what you believe to be Didion's attitude toward going home, capturing as much of the conflicting attitudes as possible.
2. In your view, why doesn't Didion correct her great-aunts when she discovers (paragraph 5) that they think she still lives in New York City? In what way is this episode important to the point of the essay?
3. In the conclusion, Didion says that she would like to give her daughter *home*, but that "we live differently now and I can promise her nothing like that." Based on what you have learned in the rest of the essay, explain what Didion means by this statement.

Technique

1. In the first paragraph, Didion describes her husband's inability to understand her family. What do we find out about her family in this first paragraph, and how does this information fit in with the other ideas developed later in the essay?
2. Didion illustrates her feelings about going home with vivid details: her husband's writing the word "dust" in the dust of the living room, the contents of a drawer, the broken monuments of a graveyard. What attitudes do these details convey?
3. Didion's details help her evoke an image of her attitude toward home as well as an image of home itself. If you were to write an essay about going home to your own family, what details would you select?

Language

1. In the first paragraph, Didion uses the words "home" and "house." Discuss the connotations of these two words and the different meaning each carries for Didion.
2. In talking of her childhood (paragraph 2), why do you suppose Didion put the words "normal" and "happy" in quotation marks? Look up these commonplace words in your dictionary. Consider in what way they do or do not describe Didion's childhood.
3. Near the end of paragraph 1, Didion points out that her husband does not understand that her family frequently talks in "code" about the things they like best. Looking at the examples she gives in this passage, and considering the meaning of the word "code," what do you think Didion means by her statement?

Vocabulary

memento	lassitude	horehound
assay	guerilla	anecdote
assiduous		

Writing Suggestions

1. In a paragraph, describe some object, spot, or tradition at your family house that evokes in you a strong image of your response to home. Choose your details as carefully as Didion chooses hers for maximum effect.
2. In paragraph 2, Didion states that her generation might be the last to carry the burden of "home." Write an essay in which you analyze your

own generation's or your own individual relationship to home, considering especially whether or not you believe that your generation carries the burden of home.

3. Write a narrative of a visit you have made home since you've moved away. As Didion does, make the narrative vivid by using specific details and by choosing the details to convey a sense of what "going home" means to you.

A Visit to My Aunt
Maxine Hong Kingston

Maxine Hong Kingston (b. 1940) grew up in Stockton, California, the daughter of Chinese immigrants. She has been both a high school teacher and a Visiting Professor of English, and her stories and articles have appeared in such publications as Ms., New West, *and the* New York Times. *Her first book,* The Woman Warrior: Memoirs of a Girlhood Among Ghosts *(1976), won the National Book Critics Circle Award for general nonfiction. Her second book,* China Men, *appeared in 1980. In the following piece, Kingston describes a visit to her aunt's house in San Francisco's Chinatown. She reveals how she and her aunt managed to communicate with one another very well, despite differences in language, culture, and age.*

With no map sense, I took a trip by myself to San Francisco Chinatown and got lost in the Big City. Wandering in a place very different from Stockton's brown and gray Chinatown, I suddenly heard my own real aunt call my name. We screamed at each other the way our villagers do, hugged, held hands. "Have you had your rice yet?" we shouted. "I have. I have had my rice." "Me too, I've eaten too," letting the whole strange street know we had eaten, and me becoming part of the street, abruptly not a tourist, the street mine to shout in, not to worry if my accent be different. She introduced me to the group of women she'd been talking to. "This is my own actual niece," she said in a way that they would understand that I was not just somebody she called a niece out of politeness but a blood niece. "Hello, Aunt. Hello, Aunt," I said, but mumbling mumbling because there are different kinds of aunts depending on whether they're older or younger than one's mother, and both addresses familiar. And they'd tease also for being too distant, for calling them Lady or Mademoiselle, affectations. Some people feel insulted at young, low-rank titles, but there are also Americanized women who don't like being older, and me not good at ages anyway, and some not wanting to be roped into your family, and some not liking to be excluded. "Who is this?" the women asked, one of them pointing at me with her chin, the way Chinese people point, the other with her rolled up newspaper. This talking about me in the third person, this pointing at me—I shoved the resentment down my throat; they do not mean disdain—or they *do* mean disdain—but it's their proper way of treating young people—mustn't dislike them for it. "This is my real niece come to visit me," my aunt said, as if I had planned to run into her all along. "Come see my new apartment," she said to me, turned around and entered the doorway near which we were standing.

We went up the stairs, flight after flight. I followed her along a hallway like a tunnel. But her apartment need not be dismal, I told myself; these doors could open into surprisingly large, bright, airy apartments with shag carpets. "Our apartment is very small," she warned, her voice leading the way. "Not like a regular house. Not like your mother's big house." So she noticed space; I thought perhaps people from Hong Kong didn't need room, that Chinese people preferred small spaces.

When she opened the door, it just missed the sofa and didn't open up all the way because of a table. Stuff was stored along the walls on shelves above the furniture, which had things on top and underneath. I fitted myself in among the storage. "Cake?" asked my aunt. "Pie? Chuck-who-lick? Lemun?" She went into the one-person kitchen. There wasn't room in the space between the sink and the stove for me to help. I sat on the sofa, which could open into a bed.

"Small, isn't it?" she said. "Please have some cake."

"I just ate," I said, which was true.

She got herself some chocolate cake and lemon pie and sat next to me. "I saw those hoppies they tell about in the newspaper," she said. "Some of them talked to me. 'Spare change?' That's what they say. 'Spare change?' I memorized it." She held out her hand to show their ways. " 'Spare change?' What does 'spare change' mean?" "They're asking if you have extra money." "Oh-h, I see," she said laughing. " 'Spare change?' How witty." She was silly compared to my mother; she giggled and talked about inconsequentials. "Condo?" she asked. "Cottage cheese? Football? Foosball?"

"Are you working?" I asked because it was odd that she was home in the middle of a weekday. "Is it your day off?"

"No. I'm not working anymore."

"What happened to your hotel job? Didn't you have a hotel job? As a maid?" I said "maid" in English, not knowing the Chinese word except for "slave." If she didn't know the word, she wouldn't hear it anyway. Languages are like that.

"I've been fired," she said.

"Oh, no. But why?"

"I've been very sick. High blood pressure," she said. "And I got dizzy working. I had to clean sixteen rooms in eight hours. I was too sick to work that fast." Something I liked about this aunt was her use of exact numbers. "Ten thousand rooms per second," my mother would have said; "Uncountable. Infinite." I did some math while she tallked: half an hour per unit, including bathrooms. "People leave the rooms very messy," she said, "and I kept coughing from the ashes in the ashtrays. I was efficient until I fell sick. Once I was out for six weeks, but when I came back, the head housekeeper said I was doing a good job, and he kept me on." She said the name of the hotel; it was one of the famous ones. I had thought from the dirty work and low pay it was some flop house in Chinatown. She'd given us miniature soaps whenever she came to visit. "The head housekeeper said I was an excellent worker." My mother was the same way, caring tremendously how her employer praised her, never in so much trouble as when a boss reprimanded her, never so proud as when a forelady said she was picking cleanly or fast. ("Folaydee"; "chup-bo"—trouble; "bossu"; "day offu"—more Chinese American words.) "He said I speak English very well." She was proud of that compliment; I thought it was an insult, but it was too much trouble to try to explain to her why. When white demons said, "You speak English very well," I muttered, "It's my language too." The Japanese kids, who were always ahead of us socially, said the way to answer is, "Thank you. So do you."

"What do you do all day long now that you aren't cleaning hotel rooms?"

"The days go by very slowly. You know, in these difficult times in the Big City mothers can't leave their children alone. The kidnappers are getting two thousand dollars per child. And whoever reports a missing child to the FBI gets turned over to Immigration. So I posted ads, and one in the newspaper too, that I wanted to mind children, but I haven't gotten any customers. When the mothers see the apartment, they say No." Of course. No place to run, no yard, no trees. "I could mind four or five children," she said. "I'd make as much money as cleaning the hotel. They don't want me to watch their children because I can't speak English. My own son doesn't talk to me," she said. "What's nutrition?"

"It has to do with food and what people ought to eat to keep healthy."

"You mean like cooking? He's going to college to learn how to cook?"

"Well, no. It's planning menus for big companies, like schools and hospitals and the army. They study food to see how it works. It's the science of food," but I did not feel that I was giving an adequate explanation, the only word for "science" I knew was a synonym or derivative of "magic," something like "alchemy."

"You speak Chinese very well," she said. But I could talk to her. Some people dry up each other's language.

Content

1. In the first paragraph, Kingston suggests careful distinctions in the greetings used in the Chinese community: There are different greetings for nieces and "real" nieces, for instance, and for older and younger aunts. The essay suggests other significant differences in customs and manners between the Chinese and American cultures. Find as many of these as you can, and discuss the role that language frequently plays in these differences.

2. When her aunt offers her cake, Kingston declines by saying, "I just ate." For the reader's information, she adds, "which was true." Why do you think Kingston feels it necessary to provide this aside for the reader?

3. The aunt proudly says of her boss, "He said I speak English very well." Kingston views this remark as an insult, but, she says, "it was too much trouble to explain to her why." Considering the attitudes Kingston reveals in the rest of the essay, explain why you think she would view the statement as insulting.

Technique

1. At the beginning of the essay, Kingston says that she and her aunt screamed to one another in the street, "the way our villagers do . . . letting the whole strange street know we had eaten." Throughout the

essay, Kingston demonstrates her awareness of the differences between Chinese and American cultures, both of which she is a part. Find other examples of these distinctions, and discuss the role that Kingston's portrayal of them plays in the essay.

2. Most of Kingston's essay is devoted to dialogue between herself and her aunt, and she does not explicitly state a thesis, but rather implies one. Write what you think would be one or two possibilities for a thesis statement for the essay.

Language

1. In paragraph 1, Kingston tries to accept the disdain she senses as the Chinese ladies talk of her in the third person. "They do not mean disdain," she writes, "or they *do* mean disdain, but it's their proper way of treating young people." Look up the words "disdain" and "proper" and, based on their meaning, discuss Kingston's interpretation of the incident.
2. In paragraph 9, Kingston says of her aunt, "If she didn't know the word, she wouldn't hear it anyway. Languages are like that." In your view, what does Kingston mean by this statement.?

Vocabulary

disdain   alchemy   inconsequential
affectation   derivative

Writing Suggestions

1. Write a paragraph in which you analyze the difference between "I shoved resentment down my throat," and the more commonly heard, "I swallowed my resentment."
2. Though Kingston is Chinese, she is more clearly Chinese–American than her aunt who clings more closely to the old ways and language. As a result of the difference between them, Kingston's visit to her aunt is tinged by inadequate communication and different expectations and interpretations. Even without the barrier of language and culture that Kingston experiences, we all make visits to family members or acquaintances whose social, cultural, or generational attitudes differ considerably from our own. Write a narrative describing such a visit, evoking as Kingston does the rewards and frustrations of such a relationship.

Sexism in the Language of Marriage
Alleen Pace Nilsen

Alleen Pace Nilsen (b. 1936) has taught at various colleges and universities and is now a Professor of Education at Arizona State University. She has written a number of articles on linguistics and education and on sexism in language; she is the co-author of Language Play: An Introduction to Linguistics. *In the essay that follows, Nilsen provides several persuasive examples of the sexist attitudes that are imbedded in the ways we write and talk about the institution of marriage.*

One of the few songs I remember from the halcyon era of the fifties starts out with the bold claim "Love and marriage go together like a horse and carriage!" I was a teenager then and I thought it was a wonderful song. But today in my more cynical adulthood, I might be tempted instead to think of a threesome consisting of love, marriage, and sexism. They are as intertwined as any social institutions that we have.

I must hasten to add that I am speaking of society in general, not necessarily of the one marriage and the one husband I know best. Because instead of quarreling in the public press with my husband, Don, I should be paying tribute to him. We were married while we were still undergraduates. It was before the days of the pill and we started our family right away. But even with the responsibilities of three children he unselfishly shared, and shared alike, while we worked and went to school to earn both our master's and our Ph.D. degrees.

This attitude didn't come easily. What the conscious mind intellectually recognizes as fair is not the same as what the subconscious mind emotionally accepts as appropriate. "Growing pains" accompany any significant social change, and when a couple sets up a true partnership marriage, they are probably going against the example set by their own parents, as well as the expectations of their friends and society at large. For example, when I at last received a regular faculty appointment at Arizona State University, where my husband had been teaching for two years, my father came to a celebration dinner with a package under his arm and a twinkle in his eyes. He had brought a present. It was a pair of pants for Don. They were handed over with the good humored explanation that since we were now equal, he just wanted to remind everyone who was "to wear the pants in the family."

This old cliche about *the pants in the family* is just one of hundreds of ways that the language reminds us of the different expectations we have for the man and for the woman in a marriage. Some of these attitudes are revealed through our everyday language, in the ways we divide various aspects of marriage into male and female domains.

Parenthood and family relations in general are in the domain of the woman. For example, *wife and mother* is a phrase more commonly heard than *father and husband*. And we have many family related metaphors based on feminine, but not masculine, words, e.g., *gold star mother; alma mater; granny knot; mother lode; mother superior; mother tongue; mother, daughter and sister languages; mother wit; piamater; mother of pearl; mother earth; mother of vinegar; mother nature;* and *maternal* or *motherly instincts..*

Word Pairings and Male Precedence

"Ladies first" goes the old saying, but except in the phrase *ladies and gentlemen* we seldom follow this advice. Instead we have such pairings as:

Mr. and Mrs.
he/she
his and hers
Sonny and Cher
Jack and Jill
Fibber McGee and Molly
boys and girls
George and Martha Washington
men and women
sons and daughters
husbands and wives
kings and queens
brothers and sisters
guys and dolls
actors and actresses
host and hostess

This kind of male-female pairing is so set in our minds that it becomes automatic. I recently read that someone chided the National Organization of Women because their charter started out with "We, men and women . . . " instead of "We, women and men . . . ," which would have more accurately reflected their membership as well as their philosophy.

It is the general pattern in English for male words to come first. We make an exception only when something is so closely related to what we think of as the feminine domain that, without even realizing it, we switch over and break the pattern, putting the female first as in the following pairs, which all have to do with family relations and marriage.

> bride and groom
> mother and father
> mother and child
> aunt and uncle

Even these terms are sometimes interchanged so that the male comes first, and the phrase doesn't sound deviant except for *groom and bride*. We definitely think of a wedding as the bride's show, as evidenced by several language customs. It is the bride's parents who send out the announcements, and only recently have some people begun to name also the parents of the groom on the wedding announcement. The newspaper picture usually shows only the bride, and unless it's a celebrity couple the picture and accompanying story will appear on what is still called the *women's page* in many newspapers.

We went to a large wedding reception in a hotel the other night and the directory of events posted in the lobby read, "Cynthia Jenson Reception: Fiesta Room." I'm sure it was partly for the sake of efficiency that the sign maker didn't use the more complete "Cynthia Jenson and Robert Marshall Reception: Fiesta Room." During the couple's married life there will be hundreds of times when efficiency in listing their names is called for, but this announcement of the reception will probably be the last time Cynthia's name will be chosen over Robert's.

In nearly all semantic areas of English, nouns are considered basically masculine; if we need to specify that the referent is female, an extra word or an affix of some kind is attached. For example we have actor/actress, major/majorette, aviator/aviatrix, prince/princess, god/goddess, lawyer/woman lawyer, truck driver/lady truck driver. But when it comes to certain words related to marriage and sexual relations, the process is reversed. *Prostitute* is a female term, with *male prostitute* being the *unusual*. *Virgin* is another feminine term which must have a special context when it refers to a man. On the death of a spouse, the woman becomes a *widow*, the man, a *widower*.

Women are more often given the title *divorcé*, while a man is simply described as "being divorced." At the beginning of a marriage the woman is the *bride* and the man is the *bridegroom*. As we have already seen, *bride* is a more important word than *groom*. This is further shown by the fact that it appears in several compounds (bridal attendant, bridal wreath, etc.) while *groom* in the sense of *bridegroom* is seldom used. Even the males' prenuptial party is called a *bachelor party* as compared to the female *bridal shower*. And a woman considers herself a bride for a whole year after the wedding, while a man considers himself a groom only on the day of the wedding.

"Married" as a Goal for Women Only

Men are married just as much as women, but marriage isn't the center of their lives. We never give little boys dress-up clothes in which to play groom, but we give little girls old lace curtains and white dresses so they can play bride. And we train little girls, but not little boys, to respond to the question, "What are you going to do when you grow up?" with some form of "I'm going to get married."

At prenuptial celebrations, men look backward while women look forward. It is as if each sex wants to emphasize and honor the state it considers ideal, hence men stress the single state and women stress the married. At a bridal shower, the entertainment consists of looking to the future through gifts which will enhance the comfort and the glamour of the new home. Games are played which revolve around daydreams predicting a romanticized future for the couple. At the bachelor party, the entertainment consists of looking to the past. It's one last fling with *the boys*, a nostalgic celebration in honor of *single blessedness* and freedom from the sex-related constraints usually thought to go along with marriage. The comments and the jokes made at both the bridal party and the bachelor party reflect our underlying attitude that marriage signifies success for a woman but defeat for a man. Perhaps this is one of the reasons society seems to ignore the marital status of men. Our consciousness of whether or not a woman is married is shown by our use of two titles, *Miss* and *Mrs.*, as contrasted to the all-purpose *Mr.*

In English a man's wife is jokingly referred to as his *ball and chain*. A similar metaphor exists in Spanish. The word for wife is *esposa*; the plural *esposas*, means handcuffs.

Compare the positive connotations of *bachelor* with the negative connotations of *spinster* or *old maid*. *Old maid* is the name of a children's card game in which the loser is ridiculed by being given this uncomplimentary title. It is also used metaphorically to mean the left-over kernels of corn that failed to pop. These are all negative concepts. *Bachelor* has such positive connotations that unmarried girls have tried to borrow them by labelling themselves *bachelor girls* or *bachelorettes*. We hear *bachelor* in such phrases as *bachelor pad* and *most eligible bachelor*. The connotations of the word are such that in Arizona the local sex newspaper is called *Bachelor Beat*. Judging from the advertisements, it isn't read by bachelors at all. Nevertheless the title conveys the idea of sexual freedom. We would never hear the term *most eligible spinster*, because beauty and youth are considered prime qualifications of a female's eligibility, and supposedly both are gone by the time a female is old enough to be called an *old maid* or a *spinster*; hence the words are mutually exclusive.

Playboy might be a synonym for *eligible bachelor*, though the qualities of playboy are certainly not the same as those popularly ascribed to a "good" husband. Perhaps the reason a playboy is considered a *good catch* is that he supposedly has money and sophistication. It is as if we envy unmarried men because of the fullness of the life they lead with their extra freedom and extra money, while we pity unmarried women because we think they live only half a life. In an interesting bit of folk etymology, I heard of an *old maid* who specified in her will that she didn't want *Miss* written on her gravestone, because she hadn't missed as much as people thought she had.

It appears that society has certain expectations and that as long as behavior is fairly consistent with the expected, it goes unnoticed. For example, it is expected that every woman loves and serves her family, but such behavior is unusual in a man. We mark the unusual behavior with a word *family man*, but there's no such things as a *family woman*. The same type of reasoning probably explains why we have the term *career woman* but not *career man*.

Wife as Property

It is ironic that although we consider marriage to be a desirable thing for a woman, we also look on it as making her the property of her husband. This is probably a leftover from the days when women could not get jobs, and so getting married was a cause for celebration, just as we celebrate when children who cannot take care of themselves are adopted by responsible adults. Because proprietary attitudes toward women go back into the dim reaches of history, it is not surprising that the language reflects this idea of ownership.

The most obvious example is the traditional wedding ceremony, in which the clergyman asks, "Who gives the bride away?" The father of the bride answers, "I do." If the father is not available, a male substitute is found, usually an older relative or friend of the family. After the father both literally and figuratively hands the bride over to the groom, the clergyman says, "I now pronounce you man and wife."

This part of the ceremony has irritated many women, because the two words *man* and *wife* do not seem parallel; *wife* is a relational term, but *man* isn't. Actually, in Middle English these were matching terms, because *wife* meant *woman*. And because a woman's role in life was then primarily in relationship to her husband, the word gradually took on its current meaning. We see it in its original sense of female or woman in the terms *midwife* and *housewife*. *Mid* is cognate with the Germanic *mit*, meaning *with*. The literal meaning of *midwife* is someone who is "with women." If the panelists on the television show "What's My Line" had understood this, they wouldn't have been so easily fooled the night a male midwife was a guest. A *housewife* is not—or at least isn't supposed to be—someone married to a house. Instead the word means something like "the woman of the house." Chaucer's *Wife of Bath* is about a woman of Bath, and the word *alewife* simply means a woman who sold ale, as a *fishwife* is a woman who sold fish. *Old wives' tales* are nothing more than the stories of old women.

The reason the wedding ceremony uses the phrase *man and wife* is that religion is a traditional and conservative force and its language appropriately lags behind the volatile, common language of the land; witness the use of Latin in the Catholic Church several hundred years after it became a "dead" language, and think how long Jewish religious leaders kept Hebrew alive. Even in "modern" churches the archaic *thee* and *thou* are common in prayers and the King James Version of the Bible is far more popular than the modern Standard Revised Version. But since *wife* now has a different meaning and most people feel there is no religious or sacred reason for maintaining the exact wording of the marriage ceremony, many clergymen have changed the wording to the more parallel *husband and wife*.

In all close relationships, we use what appears to be possessive structures when we say *my husband, my wife, my secretary, my boss, my boyfriend*, etc. But these terms are not really possessive so much as they are relational. They are probably deleted forms for such thoughts as "The man who is my husband," "The woman who is my secretary," etc. However we do find inconsistent usage among young people when a female talks about her *boyfriend*, but a male talks about his *girl* or his *woman*. It is interesting that, he, but rarely she, can delete *friend*. This deletion of *friend* takes away the relational meaning and makes it possessive. If a female talks about *my boy*, a listener is apt to think of a child, i.e., the female's offspring.

The term *wife-swapping* is another example of the attitude that the male owns the female. Feminists would prefer the term *swinging*, but as a disillusioned friend confided, "It doesn't matter what you call it, it's still the woman who gets screwed!" Practically everything we say about sex revolves around the attitude that it is the domain of the man. He *possesses* the woman. He makes a *sexual conquest* when he *deflowers* her by *taking away her virginity*, a set phrase that doesn't even allow her the dignity of giving it away.

Surname Customs and Women's Identity

One of the most far-reaching and troublesome effects of the male-ownership idea is evident in surnames. A woman's taking her husband's name relates to the idea that she is his property. I looked through a standard desk-size dictionary for ways we treat men and women differently and was surprised to find what appears to be an attitude on the part of editors that it is almost indecent to let a respectable woman's name march unaccompanied across the pages of a dictionary. A woman's name must somehow be escorted by a male's name, regardless of whether the male contributed to the woman's reason for being in the dictionary, or whether he, in his own right, was as famous as the woman. For example, Charlotte Brontë was identified as Mrs. Arthur B. Nicholls, Amelia Earhart was identified as Mrs. George Palmer Putnam, Helen Hayes was identified as Mrs. Charles MacArthur, Zona Gale was identified as Mrs. William Llywelyn Breese, and Jenny Lind was identified as

Mme. Otto Goldschmidt. There were a few women such as temperance leader Carry Nation and slave Harriet Tubman who were listed without the benefit of a masculine escort, but most of the women were identified as someone's wife. Of all the men, and there were probably ten times as many men as women, only one was identified as the "husband of . . . " And even this one example was the rather unusual case of "Frederic Joliot-Curie (born Frederic Joliot), 1900-1958; husband of Irene; French chemist; shared Nobel prize . . . " Apparently when Irene and Frederic married they took the hyphenated name in honor of Irene's family.

This confusion indicates not so much the sexist attitude of the dictionary editors, as the complexity of making "two into one." Which *one* are they going to be? What name will the children have? Surely the Joliot-Curie compromise couldn't work for more than a generation. And what is an editor supposed to do with maiden names, professional names, married names, etc.? The complexity of the whole naming business may be a contributing factor to the general absence of women in the historical record keeping of the world.

Newspaper editors have a greater problem than dictionary editors, because most of the people they write about are very much alive and ready to object if they don't like the way their name was written. Also when a new person pops into the news there probably is no set pattern to be followed with regard to what version of her name this particular woman prefers.

In 1971, I clipped out the Associated Press listing of the "best dressed" because it illustrates the differences in the way we list names. The men were listed as:

> Frederic Byers III of Pittsburgh and New York; Yul Brynner, actor of Tartar stock now living in Switzerland; Hernando Courtwright, Mexican-born hotelier of Los Angeles; John Galliher, American socialite of New York and London; Angus Ogilvy, British businessman married to Princess Alexandra of Kent; Armando Orsini, New York restaurant owner; Giorgio Payone, Roman public relations executive; Baron Alexis de Rede, Austrian-born Paris financier; Thomas Shevlin, Palm Beach socialite; Bobby Short, nightclub star born in Rockford, Ill.; Lord Snowdon, photographer, husband of Princess Margaret; and Sargent Shriver, Washington.

Notice that of these twelve men, the only two identified in relationship to their wives are Angus Ogilvy and Lord Snowdon, who in true story-book fashion married real princesses. The list of women on the best dressed list started with Mrs. Harilaos Theodoracopulos, "American wife of the Greek ship owner," and then went on as follows:

> The Begum Aga Khan, British wife of the Moslem spiritual leader; Mme. Ahmed Benhima, wife of the Moroccan Ambassador to the United Nations; Diahann Carroll, American singer; Catherine Deneuve, French actress; Sophia Loren, Italian film star; Mrs. Denise Minnelli, Yugoslav residing in San Francisco; Mme. Georges Pompidou; Mrs. Richard Pistell, New York, former Marquesa Caroll de Portago; Mrs. Ronald Reagan, wife of the governor of California; Mrs. Samuel P. Reed, American socialite, daughter of Mrs. Charles Engelhard; and Mrs. Charles Revson, wife of the cosmetic magnate.

The five women given permanent status and elected to the Hall of Fame were:

> Mrs. William McCormick Blair, Jr., Chicago-born wife of the former U.S. ambassador who now heads the Kennedy Center for the Performing Arts in Washington; Mrs. Alfred Bloomingdale of Los Angeles, wife of the founder of the Diner's Club; Mrs. Wyatt (Gloria Vanderbilt) Cooper of New York; Mrs. Kirk Douglas, Hollywood, born in Paris; and Mrs. Patrick Guinness, Lausanne, Switzerland and Paris.

Notice that only three of the seventeen women are identified in a way separate from their relationship to a man. These three are all in show business, but Gloria Vanderbilt's name was given in parentheses in the middle of her husband's name, and it appears that Mrs. Denise Minnelli is using her married title along with her given name. Language purists object to this usage. Their feeling is that since *Mrs.* is an abbreviation for *Mistress* it must always be used with a man's name because someone cannot be the mistress of herself. But people who disagree point out that *Miss* is also a diminutive derived from *mistress.* If a woman must always use her husband's name with the title *Mrs.*, then when she marries she in effect loses not only her maiden name but also her given name.

Existing custom allows a woman no way to pass down either her family name or her given name. She cannot name her daughter

Jennifer, Jr. or Stacy Ann II, nor can she handicap a child with her own last name. This idea is so far removed from the realm of possibility that people talk about illegitimate children as "children without names." Some pregnant girls marry for no other reason than to "provide a name for the baby." The feeling is very strong that before a person is really part of our society, he or she must demonstrate an affiliation with a father, by means of a surname.

Probably the most forceful way our present custom of naming affects the average woman is by making it doubly difficult for her to "make a name for herself." Obviously it is a distinct disadvantage to have to stop midway in life and begin all over. Few women are able to bring their name to the public's attention so that it will be recognized in all its alternate forms as is Jacqueline Bouvier, Jackie Kennedy, Mrs. John F. Kennedy, Jacqueline Onassis, and Mrs. Aristotle Onassis.

Women are beginning to defy the anonymity and the self-effacement imposed by cultural attitudes and the accompanying naming customs of marriage. Witness the tendency of many to resume their maiden names after divorce and the daring of a few in carrying their maiden names beyond the altar. How far these innovations may spread is hard to guess, but the fact that they are occurring reflects an awareness of a woman's identity as being continuous throughout life and belonging to her rather than to "the men in her life."

Content

1. In paragraph 3, Nilsen says that her husband's share and share alike attitude toward marriage did not come easily. She notes that "what the conscious mind intellectually recognizes as fair is not the same as what the subconscious mind emotionally accepts as appropriate." In your own words, discuss the meaning of this statement and its importance to the essay as a whole.
2. In paragraph 4, Nilsen states her thesis, that "the different expectations we have for the man and for the woman in a marriage . . . are revealed through our everyday language. . . ." Cite several of the examples that Nilsen offers to support her argument. Do you, like Nilsen, find these examples revealing indicators of our cultural assumptions? Explain.
3. In her closing discussion of taking the male name in marriage, Nilsen notes (paragraph 28) that "some pregnant girls marry for no other

reason than to 'provide a name for the baby.' The feeling is very strong that before a person is really part of our society, he or she must demonstrate an affiliation with a father, by means of a surname." Do you agree that this feeling is strong in our society? Why or why not?

Technique

1. One problem frequently encountered in essays developed by example is that development and analysis can give way to listing. In what ways does Nilsen develop her essay and argue her point beyond more listing? Cite specific passages to support your answer.
2. Nilsen includes many examples to support her thesis that marriage is still a matter of possession of the female by the male, at least as reflected by our language. Which examples did you find most convincing, which the least convincing? Why?
3. Nilsen begins her essay with a pleasant early memory of a traditional song. How does she use this memory to introduce the thesis of her essay?

Language

1. What significant differences are there, in your own mind, between such terms as "bridal shower" and "bachelor party," "divorcée" (for a woman) and "being divorced" (for a man), or "bachelor" and "spinster"? You might want to conduct an informal poll in which you ask friends to tell you what each term means to them, and then report the results to your class. To what extent do the answers substantiate Nilsen's point about such terms?
2. We've had *Playboy* for years; now we have *Playgirl* as well. To what extent does the addition of *Playgirl* magazine and "playgirl" as part of our vocabulary reflect new social trends that contradict the "bachelor-spinster" syndrome Nilsen describes? Explain.
3. In her opening paragraph, Nilsen refers to the "halcyon era of the fifties." Look up the word "halcyon" in your dictionary. Why do you believe Nilsen refers to the era of the fifties as "halcyon"?

Vocabulary

halcyon	metaphor	entymology
cynical	connotation	domain
cliché	synonym	

Writing Suggestions

1. Write a paragraph in which you analyze the implications of such terms as "woman lawyer" and "male prostitute." Are they, as Nilsen suggests, sexist designations?

2. In paragraph 14, Nilsen asks you to compare the "positive connotations of 'bachelor' with the negative connotations of 'spinster' or 'old maid,'" then goes on to make that comparison from her own point of view. Write a paragraph in which you make the comparison based on your own interpretation of these terms.

3. Nilsen's last paragraph implies that the language of marriage, with its historical male bias, robs women of their identity. Write an essay discussing to what extent you feel our identity is bound up in the language used to describe us. Consider other language categories, such as name-calling, racial epithets, profesisonal titles, and the like.

4. It is widely argued that the English language is rich in male-dominant words. Nilsen gives several examples, and there are others: "chairman," "workman," "manpower," and others. As women increasingly take their place in the work world and become equal partners with men at home and at work, such male-dominated language troubles many people. Write an essay in which you analyze your own response to the dilemma. Should we continue, for instance, to use "he" as a generic pronoun, or do we need to revise the language to better reflect modern realities?

Lying Well is the Best Revenge

Daniel Yankelovich

Daniel Yankelovich (b. 1924), who graduated from Harvard University in 1946, is presently a Visiting Professor of Psychology at the New School for Social Research in New York City. His books include Ego and Instinct *(1969),* The New Morality: A Profile of American Youth in the Seventies *(1979), and* New Rules: Searching for Self-Fulfillment in a World Turned Upside Down *(1981). In "Lying Well is the Best Revenge," Yankelovich defines several kinds of lying and argues that when lying becomes acceptable, the community inevitably suffers.*

It is midwinter. A television commercial promoting vacations in Miami shows an elated middle-aged couple—he is stout, she is a bit matronly—sitting outdoors at a beautifully laid table. The plates in front of them are filled with what appears to be Alaskan king crab. The man is talking to his boss on the telephone. The wife snaps a crab leg. The man, suppressing a giggle, tells his boss, "You won't believe this, but my wife just broke a leg." The announcer punches home the message: "So pack your bags and plan your excuses. 'Cause you can't get enough of Miami."

This vignette is the last in a series that all conclude with the husband, his beaming wife beside him, giving his boss a false reason for extending his vacation.

We are accustomed to ads that make extravagant claims, but ads that make a joke of lying, conveying the message that it's okay to bend the truth to get what you want, are something new. Advertising has always been a good mirror of changing norms in our society, and this commercial, with its sympathetic portrait of husband and wife lying to get themselves another day of vacation, is a clue that social norms about lying are growing weaker. The commercial tells us that there are occasions on which lying is no longer to be regarded with social disapproval.

Of course, the deceptions of everyday private life have always been present. But now, new forms of public lying are beginning to surface. They take place in that common space where we do the business of society, and they represent a threat to the standards of truth that regulate our mutual behavior.

Consider the recent studies showing that 40 percent of the rising number of personal and business bankruptcies occur among people who have sufficient assets and could have avoided seeking the shelter of bankruptcy court. Many of these people report that they had been counseled by their lawyers to go on "spending sprees" before declaring themselves bankrupt, partly to reduce their resources and partly as a way of getting something for nothing. People are in effect receiving legal counsel to violate what until recently was a powerful social taboo that drenched in shame those who broke it. I remember from my childhood many stories of the moral anguish suffered by the friends of my parents who were forced into bankruptcy in the Depression, and the superhuman efforts that they made to cleanse their reputations.

Today, substantial numbers of people accept the deceit of self-induced bankruptcy as a reasonable strategy in a world in which, they believe, the economic cards are often marked. Interviews reveal that most people feel that because the "system" is unfair they have the right to take matters into their own hands.

Similar reasoning is offered as a defense in the by now familiar example of tax cheating (see "The Tax-Evasion Virus," *Psychology Today*, March 1982), and also for the "underground economy" of off-the-books employment and trading. Recent estimates indicate that these forms of deceit cost the Treasury between 80 billion and 100 billion dollars a year—nearly enough to balance the federal budget. As we grow more cynical about the fairness of our tax system, we become more adept at trimming our own share of the burden.

In at least one situation, public lying has become imbued with positive morality. In a recent television discussion about investigative journalism, both broadcast and print journalists openly and proudly described strategies of lying that extended from posing as gullible customers to forming friendships under false pretenses. The "crimes against society" that they were tracking, they maintained, were evil enough to justify whatever lies might be necessary.

Such journalistic uses of deception have grown to be common fare on nightly television news programs, and have even reached the classroom. In Marin County, California, high-school students working on a story for their school newspaper were given permission by their adviser and their parents to buy liquor illegally for the purpose of exposing stores that sell liquor to minors.

As a final example, consider the ABSCAM cases. Once again, lying was used to bring down elected officials who used their positions to peddle their influence. Here, though, the source of the justifiable lie—the FBI—generated a degree of social nervousness, for this powerful law-enforcement agency has sometimes seemed beyond public control.

All these examples of public lying have a common theme: the effort to "stick it" to authority, to strike back through the use of deceit. We see this theme in its mildest form in the vacation commercials. The husband is no angry militant agitating for longer vacations. He is an agreeable fellow who simply wants another day of fun in the sun and, with his wife's connivance, is delighted to trick the boss in order to get it. The tax cheating and the deliberate bankruptcy of those with assets are examples of people who have found ways to "get some of their own back." As for investigative reporting, its practitioners on the television forum defended it as a way of aiding the powerless against the powerful. Listen to ABC's Geraldo Rivera: "It goes back to the whole concept of civil disobedience . . . I was an instrument for positive social change. I'm proud of it." Rivera sees himself as a public avenger—a surrogate for the helpless and exploited. The drama of ABSCAM has the same strain, except that the public avenger in this instance is also an authority, which is what makes us uncomfortable.

12   Americans have always been nervous about authority, and quick to limit it and strike at it when they believe that it has abused its prerogatives. Watergate, for example, mystified European observers. They could not understand what the fuss was about, because, unlike Americans, they expect authorities to lie and deceive, and do not rush to overthrow governments that do.

13   From the victory of Andrew Jackson against those who put on airs, to the universal use of first names in the hierarchies of American corporate life, the theme of "leveling," at least in symbolic terms, is omnipresent in the United States. When we call the boss "Jim" or "Reg," we are saying, "Though you may be the boss, we are also equals."

14   Some years ago I interviewed a group of Greek workers who had made a tour of United States factories. I asked them what had impressed them most about the American workers whom they had met. I expected them to talk about the high standard of living of their American counterparts: their homes, cars, and television sets. The Greeks did not even mention these items. Instead, they spoke glowingly of the independence of American workers—their freedom to tell the boss to "shove it," even if saying it meant the loss of a job.

15   Yet those of us who monitor the public mind professionally have been aware of a steady erosion of social authority quite beyond the democratizing impulse to prevent anyone from getting "too big for his britches." Authority itself has become suspect. This attitude shows up in public-opinion surveys in the form of lower confidence scores for all institutions—government, business, the professions, the courts, the colleges, the press. It shows up in various new forms of consumer behavior—a new suspicion of brand names, prices, and middlemen. It shows up in the form of increasing crime and violence, and growing disrespect for our system of criminal justice. And

now it is starting to show up in tolerance for guile and subterfuge as modes of outwitting burdensome authority or flushing corrupt authority out into the open.

The decline of respect for authority has several major causes. One is the perception that no one in power is capable of dealing with society's problems. Nothing so undermines social authority as the public's doubt that those in charge, whether at the national or local level, know what they are doing. A second cause of declining respect is the suspicion that those in positions of authority often act in bad faith: protecting special interests, promoting unfairness, and putting personal gain and ambition ahead of the public weal.

Faltering confidence in the ability and good faith of authority plays havoc with social norms. People begin to feel that it no longer makes sense to observe the rules. In a 1981 survey conducted by my social-research firm, more than four out of five Americans (83 percent) agreed that "those who flout the rules are rewarded" while those who observe the rules typically end up empty-handed. This conviction breeds an "everyone for himself" state of mind—a self-fulfilling prophecy and a rationalization for one's own immoral behavior: "Since we live in an era when people are forced to scramble for themselves, I must, too."

The result is a distinct loss of civility and *civitas*—that sense of belonging to a larger community and sharing responsibility for it. Instead, one's vision narrows and one's responsibility shrinks to the tight world of self, family, and "one's own kind." And once this attitude takes hold, strategies of deception and lying that seem inappropriate and immoral against one's own kind are readily justified against everyone else. It is in this state of mind that our opposition to authority grows duplicitous. In the richly hedonistic life of the 1960s and 1970s, many Americans in effect took for their motto the slogan: "Living well is the best revenge." Now it appears that the slogan has been revised to read: "Lying well is the best revenge."

Content

1. In the opening paragraphs of his essay, Yankelovich points out that recent advertising makes a joke of lying and implies that it is acceptable to lie to get what you want. This concerns Yankelovich because, he says, "advertising has always been a good mirror of changing norms

in our society." What, in your own words, is the relationship that Yankelovich draws between advertising and society? Do you agree that the relationship is significant?

2. In paragraph 11, Yankelovich quotes ABC's Geraldo Rivera, who compares deceptive investigative reporting techniques to a form of civil disobedience. Based on the examples of such investigations that Yankelovich provides and on other examples you may think of (posing, for instance, as a bereaved relative in order to discover and expose corruption in the funeral industry), explain Rivera's statement. Rivera clearly believes that this is one acceptable, even admirable, form of "public lying." Do you agree?

3. In paragraph 17, Yankelovich says that "faltering confidence in the ability and good faith of authority plays havoc with social norms." What, in your own words, does Yankelovich mean by that statement, and what, according to the essay, is the relationship between this faltering confidence and public lying?

Technique

1. Yankelovich's essay is a serious analysis of the causes, effects, and varieties of public lying. He begins, however, with a descriptive narrative before moving on to his thesis statement and analysis. Is this an effective way to open the essay? Why or why not?

2. Yankelovich's thesis—that social norms about lying are growing weaker—is explicitly stated in the third paragraph. His point of view, whether or not he is alarmed by or accepting of this phenomenon, is never explicitly stated. Do you believe that his viewpoint is nevertheless clear? If so, how is it revealed in the essay?

3. Yankelovich's essay is carefully organized into three parts: He begins with a series of examples, then analyzes the phenomenon of public lying, then explores its causes. He then ends the essay with a statement about our times, a conclusion he has reached as a result of what comes earlier in the essay. Locate the points at which Yankelovich moves from one segment of the essay to the next, and be prepared to discuss the success of his organizational pattern.

4. Yankelovich cites several public opinion polls, surveys, and interviews that reveal public response to lying, authority, and other phenomena in American society. Find several instances where he cites such polls, and be prepared to discuss the effectiveness of this technique as a means of supporting his analysis and argument.

Language

1. In this essay, Yankelovich is exploring "public lying." What do you understand him to mean by this term? What, for instance, is the distinction between public and private lying?
2. In paragraph 13, Yankelovich says that "the theme of 'leveling,' at least in symbolic terms, is omnipresent in the United States," and he implies that this tendency to level is one cause of public lying. Look up the words "leveling" and "omnipresent" in your dictionary; then discuss ways in which leveling might be a cause of public lying.

Vocabulary

guile	connivance	leveling
subterfuge	prerogative	democratizing
imbued	omnipresent	duplicitous
deceit	symbolic	civility

Writing Suggestions

1. Write a paragraph in which you provide your own definition of public lying, using one example to clarify your definition.
2. Using Yankelovich's opening as a model, write an introductory paragraph for an essay similar to Yankelovich's, choosing as he does a narrative that dramatically demonstrates the casualness with which we accept public lying.
3. In paragraph 3, Yankelovich says that our "social norms about lying are growing weaker." He mentions many forms of public lying that he believes we have come to accept—tax evasion, contrived bankruptcy, journalistic posing to uncover corruption. Write an essay in which you analyze the causes or the effects of public lying. Use one form of public lying (any of those that Yankelovich discusses or another that you choose) as an extended example to support your analysis.
4. Is public lying ever justifiable? Write an essay defending one form of public lying or arguing that public lying, no matter how worthy the cause for which it is committed, is not an acceptable form of social behavior. In either case, support your argument with specific details and examples.

Letter from Birmingham Jail
Martin Luther King, Jr.

Martin Luther King, Jr., (1929–1968) was a gifted clergyman and a courageous leader of the American civil rights movement in the 1950s and 1960s. He won the Nobel Peace Prize in 1964; four years later he was assassinated. His books include Why We Can't Wait *(1964), which contains "Letter From Birmingham Jail." King wrote the letter/essay after being jailed during a civil rights protest in Alabama. The specific political occasion and the immediate audience (his fellow clergymen), therefore, give the otherwise formal essay an extraordinary sense of urgency. The essay is a painstaking analysis of racism and its effect on communities and nations. King draws upon a number of rhetorical methods—definition, analogy, comparison, example, and narration—to justify his commitment to civil rights and nonviolent protest.*

MARTIN LUTHER KING, JR.
Birmingham City Jail
April 16, 1963

Bishop C. C. J. CARPENTER
Bishop JOSEPH A. DURICK
Rabbi MILTON L. GRAFMAN
Bishop PAUL HARDIN
Bishop NOLAN B. HARMON
The Rev. GEORGE M. MURRAY
The Rev. EDWARD V. RAMAGE
The Rev. EARL STALLINGS

My dear Fellow Clergymen,

 While confined here in the Birmingham City Jail, I came across your recent statement calling our present activities "unwise and untimely." Seldom, if ever, do I pause to answer criticism of my work and ideas. If I sought to answer all of the criticisms that cross my desk, my secretaries would be engaged in little else in the course of the day and I would have no time for constructive work. But since I feel that you are men of genuine good will and your criticisms are sincerely set forth, I would like to answer your statement in what I hope will be patient and reasonable terms.

 I think I should give the reason for my being in Birmingham, since you have been influenced by the argument of "outsiders coming in." I have the honor of serving as president of the Southern Christian Leadership Conference, an organization operating in every Southern state with headquarters in Atlanta, Georgia. We have some eighty-five affiliate organizations all across the South—one being the Alabama Christian Movement for Human Rights. Whenever necessary and possible we share staff, educational, and financial resources with our affiliates. Several months ago our local affiliate here in Birmingham invited us to be on call to engage in a nonviolent direct action program if such were deemed necessary. We readily consented and when the hour came we lived up to our promises. So I am here, along with several members of my staff, because we were invited here. I am here because I have basic organizational ties here. Beyond this, I am in Birmingham because injustice is here. Just as the eighth century prophets left their little villages and carried their "thus saith the Lord" far beyond the boundaries of their home town, and just as the Apostle Paul left his little village of Tarsus and carried the gospel of Jesus Christ to practically every hamlet and city of the Graeco-Roman world, I too am compelled to carry the gospel of freedom beyond my particular home town. Like Paul, I must constantly respond to the Macedonian call for aid.

Moreover, I am cognizant of the interrelatedness of all communities and states. I cannot sit idly by in Atlanta and not be concerned about what happens in Birmingham. Injustice anywhere is a threat to justice everywhere. We are caught in an inescapable network of mutuality tied in a single garment of destiny. Whatever affects one directly affects all indirectly. Never again can we afford to live with the narrow, provincial "outside agitator" idea. Anyone who lives inside the United States can never be considered an outsider anywhere in this country.

You deplore the demonstrations that are presently taking place in Birmingham. But I am sorry that your statement did not express a similar concern for the conditions that brought the demonstrations into being. I am sure that each of you would want to go beyond the superficial social analyst who looks merely at effects, and does not grapple with underlying causes. I would not hesitate to say that it is unfortunate that so-called demonstrations are taking place in Birmingham at this time, but I would say in more emphatic terms that it is even more unfortunate that the white power structure of this city left the Negro community with no other alternative.

In any nonviolent campaign there are four basic steps: (1) collection of the facts to determine whether injustices are alive; (2) negotiation; (3) self-purification; and (4) direct action. We have gone through all of these steps in Birmingham. There can be no gainsaying of the fact that racial injustice engulfs this community. Birmingham is probably the most thoroughly segregated city in the United States. Its ugly record of police brutality is known in every section of this country. Its unjust treatment of Negroes in the courts is a notorious reality. There have been more unsolved bombings of Negro homes and churches in Birmingham than any city in this nation. These are the hard, brutal, and unbelievable facts. On the basis of these conditions Negro leaders sought to negotiate with the city fathers. But the political leaders consistently refused to engage in good faith negotiation.

Then came the opportunity last September to talk with some of the leaders of the economic community. In these negotiating sessions certain promises were made by the merchants—such as the promise to remove the humiliating racial signs from the stores. On the basis of these promises Rev. Shuttlesworth and the leaders of the Alabama Christian Movement for Human Rights agreed to call a moratorium on any type of demonstrations. As the weeks and months unfolded we realized that we were the victims of a broken promise. The signs remained. As in so many experiences of the past we were confronted with blasted hopes, and the dark shadow of a deep disappointment settled upon us. So we had no alternative except that of preparing for direct action, whereby we would present our very bodies as a means of laying our case before the conscience of the local and national community. We were not unmindful of the difficulties involved. So we decided to go through a process of self-purification. We started having workshops on nonviolence and repeatedly asked ourselves the questions, "Are you able to accept blows without retaliating?" "Are you able to endure the ordeals of jail?"

We decided to set our direct action program around the Easter season, realizing that with the exception of Christmas, this was the largest shopping period of the year. Knowing that a strong economic withdrawal program would be the by-product of direct action, we felt that this was the best time to bring pressure on the merchants for the needed changes. Then it occurred to us that the March election was ahead, and so we speedily decided to postpone action until after election day. When we discovered that Mr. Connor was in the run-off, we decided again to postpone so that the demonstrations could not be used to cloud the issues. At this time we agreed to begin our nonviolent witness the day after the run-off.

This reveals that we did not move irresponsibly into direct action. We too wanted to see Mr. Connor defeated; so we went through postponement after postponement to aid in this community need. After this we felt that direct action could be delayed no longer.

You may well ask, "Why direct action? Why sit-ins, marches, etc.? Isn't negotiation a better path?" You are exactly right in your call for negotiation. Indeed, this is the purpose of direct action. Nonviolent direct action seeks to create such a crisis and establish such creative tension that a community that has constantly refused to negotiate is forced to confront the issue. It seeks so to dramatize the issue that it can no longer be ignored. I just referred to the creation of tension as a part of the work of the nonviolent resister. This may sound rather shocking. But I must confess that I am not afraid of the word tension. I have earnestly worked and preached against violent tension, but there is a type of constructive nonviolent tension that is necessary for growth. Just as Socrates felt that it was necessary to create a tension in the mind so that individuals could rise from the bondage of myths and half-truths to the unfettered realm of creative analysis and objective appraisal, we must see the need of having nonviolent gadflies to create the kind of tension in society that will help men rise from the dark depths of prejudice and racism to the majestic heights of understanding and brotherhood. So the purpose of the direct action is to create a situation so crisis-packed that it will inevitably open the door to negotiation. We, therefore, concur with you in your call for negotiation. Too long has our beloved Southland been bogged down in the tragic attempt to live in monologue rather than dialogue.

One of the basic points in your statement is that our acts are untimely. Some have asked, "Why didn't you give the new administration time to act?" The only answer that I can give to this inquiry is that the new administration must be prodded about as much as the outgoing one before it acts. We will be sadly mistaken if we feel that the election of Mr. Boutwell will bring the millennium to Birmingham. While Mr. Boutwell is much more articulate and gentle than Mr. Connor, they are both segregationists dedicated to the task of maintaining the status quo. The hope I see in Mr. Boutwell is that he will be reasonable enough to see the futility of massive resistance to desegregation. But he will not see this without pressure from the devotees of civil rights. My friends, I must say to you that we have not made a single gain in civil rights without determined legal and nonviolent pressure. History is the long and tragic story of the fact that privileged groups seldom give up their privileges voluntarily. Individuals may see the moral light and voluntarily give up their unjust posture; but as Reinhold Niebuhr has reminded us, groups are more immoral than individuals.

We know through painful experience that freedom is never voluntarily given by the oppressor; it must be demanded by the oppressed. Frankly I have never yet engaged in a direct action movement that was "well timed," according to the timetable of those who have not suffered unduly from the disease of segregation. For years now I have heard the word "Wait!" It rings in the ear of every Negro with a piercing familiarity. This "wait" has almost always meant "never." It has been a tranquilizing thalidomide, relieving the emotional stress for a moment, only to give birth to an ill-formed infant of frustration. We must come to see with the distinguished jurist of yesterday that "justice too long delayed is justice denied." We have waited for more than three hundred and forty years for our constitutional and God-given rights. The nations of Asia and Africa are moving with jet-like speed toward the goal of political independence, and we still creep at horse and buggy pace toward the gaining of a cup of coffee at a lunch counter.

I guess it is easy for those who have never felt the stinging darts of segregation to say wait. But when you have seen vicious mobs lynch your mothers and fathers at will and drown your sisters and brothers at whim; when you have seen hate filled policemen curse, kick, brutalize, and even kill your black brothers and sisters with impunity; when you see the vast majority of your twenty million Negro brothers smothering in an air-tight cage of poverty in the midst of an affluent society; when you suddenly find your tongue twisted and your speech stammering as you seek to explain to your six-year-old daughter why she can't go to the public amusement park that has just been advertised on television, and see tears welling up in her little eyes when she is told that Funtown is closed to colored children, and see the depressing clouds of inferiority begin to form in her little mental sky, and see her begin to distort her little personality by unconsciously developing a bitterness toward white people; when you have to concoct an answer for a five-year-old son asking in agonizing pathos: "Daddy, why do white people treat colored people so mean?"; when you take a cross country drive and find it necessary to sleep night after night in the uncomfortable corners of your automobile because no motel will accept you; when you are humiliated day in and day out by nagging signs reading "white" men and "colored"; when your first name becomes "nigger" and your middle name becomes "boy" (however old you are) and your last name becomes "John," and when your wife and mother are never given the respected title "Mrs."; when you are harried by day and haunted by night by the fact that you are a Negro, living constantly at tip-toe stance never quite knowing what to expect next, and plagued with inner fears and outer resentments; when you are forever fighting a degenerating sense of "nobodiness";—then you will understand why we find it difficult to wait. There comes a time when the cup of endurance runs over, and men are no longer willing to be plunged into an abyss of injustice where they experience the bleakness of corroding despair. I hope, sirs, you can understand our legitimate and unavoidable impatience.

You express a great deal of anxiety over our willingness to break laws. This is certainly a legitimate concern. Since we so diligently urge people to obey the Supreme Court's decision of 1954 outlawing segregation in the public schools, it is rather strange and paradoxical to find us consciously breaking laws. One may well ask, "How can you advocate breaking some laws and obeying others?" The answer is found in the fact that there are two types of laws. There are *just* laws and there are *unjust* laws. I would be the first to advocate obeying just laws. One has not only a legal but moral responsibility to obey just laws. Conversely, one has a moral responsibility to disobey unjust laws. I would agree with Saint Augustine that "An unjust law is no law at all."

Now what is the difference between the two? How does one determine when a law is just or unjust? A just law is a man-made code that squares with the moral law or the law of God. An unjust law is a code that is out of harmony with the moral law. To put it in the terms of Saint Thomas Aquinas, an unjust law is a human law that is not rooted in eternal and natural law. Any law that uplifts human personality is just. Any law that degrades human personality is unjust. All segregation statutes are unjust because segregation distorts the soul and damages the personality. It gives the segregator a false sense of superiority and the segregated a false sense of inferiority. To use the words of Martin Buber, the great Jewish philosopher, segregation substitutes an "I-it" relationship for the "I-thou" relationship, and ends up relegating persons to the status of things. So segregation is not only politically, economically, and sociologically unsound, but it is morally wrong and sinful. Paul Tillich has said that sin is separation. Isn't segregation an existential expression of man's tragic separation, an expression of his awful estrangement, his terrible sinfulness? So I can urge men to obey the 1954 decision of the Supreme Court because it is morally right, and I can urge them to disobey segregation ordinances because they are morally wrong.

Let us turn to a more concrete example of just and unjust laws. An unjust law is a code that a majority inflicts on a minority that is not binding on itself. This is *difference* made legal. On the other hand a just law is a code that a majority compels a minority to follow that it is willing to follow itself. This is *sameness* made legal.

Let me give another explanation. An unjust law is a code inflicted upon a minority which that minority had no part in enacting or creating because they did not have the unhampered right to vote. Who can say the legislature of Alabama which set up the segregation laws was democratically elected? Throughout the state of Alabama all types of conniving methods are used to prevent Negroes from becoming registered voters and there are some counties without a single Negro registered to vote despite the fact that the Negro constitutes a majority of the population. Can any law set up in such a state be considered democratically structured?

These are just a few examples of unjust and just laws. There are some instances when a law is just on its face but unjust in its application. For instance, I was arrested Friday on a charge of parading without a permit. Now there is nothing wrong with an ordinance which requires a permit for a parade, but when the ordinance is used to preserve segregation and to deny citizens the First Amendment privilege of peaceful assembly and peaceful protest, then it becomes unjust.

I hope you can see the distinction I am trying to point out. In no sense do I advocate evading or defying the law as the rabid segregationist would do. This would lead to anarchy. One who breaks an unjust law must do it *openly*, *lovingly* (not hatefully as the white mothers did in New Orleans when they were seen on television screaming "nigger, nigger, nigger") and with a willingness to accept the penalty. I submit that an individual who breaks a law that conscience tells him is unjust, and willingly accepts the penalty by staying in jail to arouse the conscience of the community over its injustice, is in reality expressing the very highest respect for law.

Of course there is nothing new about this kind of civil disobedience. It was seen sublimely in the refusal of Shadrach, Meshach, and Abednego to obey the laws of Nebuchadnezzar because a higher moral law was involved. It was practiced superbly by the early Christians who were willing to face hungry lions and the excruciating pain of chopping blocks, before submitting to certain unjust laws of the Roman Empire. To a degree academic freedom is a reality today because Socrates practiced civil disobedience.

We can never forget that everything Hitler did in Germany was "legal" and everything the Hungarian freedom fighters did in Hungary was "illegal." It was "illegal" to aid and comfort a Jew in Hitler's Germany. But I am sure that, if I had lived in Germany during that time, I would have aided and comforted my Jewish brothers even though it was illegal. If I lived in a communist country today where certain principles dear to the Christian faith are suppressed, I believe I would openly advocate disobeying those antireligious laws.

I must make two honest confessions to you, my Christian and Jewish brothers. First I must confess that over the last few years I have been gravely disappointed with the white moderate. I have almost reached the regrettable conclusion that the Negroes' great stumbling block in the stride toward freedom is not the White Citizens' "Counciler" or the Ku Klux Klanner, but the white moderate who is more devoted to "order" than to justice; who prefers a negative peace which is the absence of tension to a positive peace which is the presence of justice; who constantly says "I agree with you in the goal you seek, but I can't agree with your methods of direct action"; who paternalistically feels that he can set the timetable for another man's freedom; who lives by the myth of time and who constantly advises the Negro to wait until a "more convenient season." Shallow understanding from people of good will is more frustrating than absolute misunderstanding from people of ill will. Lukewarm acceptance is much more bewildering than outright rejection.

I had hoped that the white moderate would understand that law and order exist for the purpose of establishing justice, and that when they fail to do this they become the dangerously structured dams that block the flow of social progress. I had hoped that the white moderate would understand that the present tension in the South is merely a necessary phase of the transition from an obnoxious negative peace, where the Negro passively accepted his unjust plight, to a substance-filled positive peace, where all men will respect the dignity and worth of human personality. Actually, we who engage in nonviolent direct action are not the creators of tension. We merely bring to the surface the hidden tension that is already alive. We bring it out in the open where it can be seen and dealt with. Like a boil that can never be cured as long as it is covered up but must be opened with all its pus-flowing ugliness to the natural medicines of air and light, injustice must likewise be exposed, with all of the tension its exposing creates, to the light of human conscience and the air of national opinion before it can be cured.

In your statement you asserted that our actions, even though peaceful, must be condemned because they precipitate violence. But can this assertion be logically made? Isn't this like condemning the robbed man because his possession of money precipitated the evil act of robbery? Isn't this like condemning Socrates because his unswerving commitment to truth and his philosophical delvings precipitated the misguided popular mind to make him drink the hemlock? Isn't this like condemning Jesus because His unique God consciousness and never-ceasing devotion to His will precipitated the evil act of crucifixion? We must come to see, as federal courts have consistently affirmed, that it is immoral to urge an individual to withdraw his efforts to gain his basic constitutional rights because the quest precipitates violence. Society must protect the robbed and punish the robber.

I had also hoped that the white moderate would reject the myth of time. I received a letter this morning from a white brother in Texas which said: "All Christians know that the colored people will receive equal rights eventually, but is it possible that you are in too great of a religious hurry? It has taken Christianity almost 2000 years to accomplish what it has. The teachings of Christ take time to come to earth." All that is said here grows out of a tragic misconception of time. It is the strangely irrational notion that there is something in the very flow of time that will inevitably cure all ills. Actually time is neutral. It can be used either destructively or constructively. I am coming to feel that the people of ill will have used time much more effectively than the people of good will. We will have to repent in this generation not merely for the vitriolic words and actions of the bad people, but for the appalling silence of the good people. We must come to see that human progress never rolls in on wheels of inevitability. It comes through the tireless efforts and persistent work of men willing to be co-workers with God, and without this hard work time itself becomes an ally of the forces of social stagnation.

We must use time creatively, and forever realize that the time is always ripe to do right. Now is the time to make real the promise of democracy, and transform our pending national elegy into a creative psalm of brotherhood. Now is the time to lift our national policy from the quicksand of racial injustice to the solid rock of human dignity.

You spoke of our activity in Birmingham as extreme. At first I was rather disappointed that fellow clergymen would see my nonviolent efforts as those of the extremist. I started thinking about the fact that I stand in the middle of two opposing forces in the Negro community. One is a force of complacency made up of Negroes who, as a result of long years of oppression, have been so completely drained of self-respect and a sense of "somebodiness" that they have adjusted to segregation, and of a few Negroes in the middle class who, because of a degree of academic and economic security, and because at points they profit by segregation, have unconsciously become insensitive to the problems of the masses. The other force is one of bitterness and hatred and comes perilously close to advocating violence. It is expressed in the various black nationalist groups that are springing up over the nation, the largest and best known being Elijah Muhammad's Muslim movement. This movement is nourished by the contemporary frustration over the continued existence of racial discrimination. It is made up of people who have lost faith in America, who have absolutely repudiated Christianity, and who have concluded that the white man is an incurable "devil." I have tried to stand between these two forces saying that we need not follow the "do-nothingness" of the complacent or the hatred and despair of the black nationalist. There is the more excellent way of love and nonviolent protest. I'm grateful to God that, through the Negro church, the dimension of nonviolence entered our struggle. If this philosophy had not emerged I am convinced that by now many streets of the South would be flowing with floods of blood.

And I am further convinced that if our white brothers dismiss us as "rabble rousers" and "outside agitators"—those of us who are working through the channels of nonviolent direct action—and refuse to support our nonviolent efforts, millions of Negroes, out of frustration and despair, will seek solace and security in black nationalist ideologies, a development that will lead inevitably to a frightening racial nightmare.

27 Oppressed people cannot remain oppressed forever. The urge for freedom will eventually come. This is what has happened to the American Negro. Something within has reminded him of his birthright of freedom; something without has reminded him that he can gain it. Consciously and unconsciously, he has been swept in by what the Germans call the *Zeitgeist*, and with his black brothers of Africa, and his brown and yellow brothers of Asia, South America, and the Caribbean, he is moving with a sense of cosmic urgency toward the promised land of racial justice. Recognizing this vital urge that has engulfed the Negro community, one should readily understand public demonstrations. The Negro has many pent-up resentments and latent frustrations. He has to get them out. So let him march sometime; let him have his prayer pilgrimages to the city hall; understand why he must have sit-ins and freedom rides. If his repressed emotions do not come out in these nonviolent ways, they will come out in ominous expressions of violence. This is not a threat; it is a fact of history. So I have not said to my people, "Get rid of your discontent." But I have tried to say that this normal and healthy discontent can be channeled through the creative outlet of nonviolent direct action. Now this approach is being dismissed as extremist. I must admit that I was initially disappointed in being so categorized.

28 But as I continued to think about the matter I gradually gained a bit of satisfaction from being considered an extremist. Was not Jesus an extremist in love? "Love your enemies, bless them that curse you, pray for them that despitefully use you." Was not Amos an extremist for justice—"Let justice roll down like waters and righteousness like a mighty stream." Was not Paul an extremist for the gospel of Jesus Christ—"I bear in my body the marks of the Lord Jesus." Was not Martin Luther an extremist—"Here I stand; I can do none other so help me God." Was not John Bunyan an extremist —"I will stay in jail to the end of my days before I make a butchery

of my conscience." Was not Abraham Lincoln an extremist—"This nation cannot survive half slave and half free." Was not Thomas Jefferson an extremist—"We hold these truths to be self evident that all men are created equal." So the question is not whether we will be extremist but what kind of extremist will we be. Will we be extremists for hate or will we be extremists for love? Will we be extremists for the preservation of injustice—or will we be extremists for the cause of justice? In that dramatic scene on Calvary's hill three men were crucified. We must never forget that all three were crucified for the same crime—the crime of extremism. Two were extremists for the preservation of injustice—or will we be extremists for the cause of justice? In that dramatic scene on Calvary's hill ness, and thereby rose above His environment. So, after all, maybe the South, the nation, and the world are in dire need of creative extremists.

I had hoped that the white moderate would see this. Maybe I was too optimistic. Maybe I expected too much. I guess I should have realized that few members of a race that has oppressed another race can understand or appreciate the deep groans and passionate yearnings of those that have been oppressed, and still fewer have the vision to see that injustice must be rooted out by strong, persistent, and determined action. I am thankful, however, that some of our white brothers have grasped the meaning of this social revolution and committed themselves to it. They are still all too small in quantity, but they are big in quality. Some like Ralph McGill, Lillian Smith, Harry Golden, and James Dabbs have written about our struggle in eloquent, prophetic, and understanding terms. Others have marched with us down nameless streets of the South. They have languished in filthy, roach-infested jails, suffering the abuse and brutality of angry policemen who see them as "dirty nigger lovers." They, unlike so many of their moderate brothers and sisters, have recognized the urgency of the moment and sensed the need for powerful "action" antidotes to combat the disease of segregation.

Let me rush on to mention my other disappointment. I have been so greatly disappointed with the white Church and its leadership. Of course there are some notable exceptions. I am not unmindful of the fact that each of you has taken some significant stands on this issue. I commend you, Rev. Stallings, for your Christian stand on this past Sunday, in welcoming Negroes to your worship service on a nonsegregated basis. I commend the Catholic leaders of this state for integrating Springhill College several years ago.

But despite these notable exceptions I must honestly reiterate that I have been disappointed with the Church. I do not say that as one of those negative critics who can always find something wrong with the Church. I say it as a minister of the gospel, who loves the church; who was nurtured in its bosom; who has been sustained by its spiritual blessings and who will remain true to it as long as the cord of life shall lengthen.

I had the strange feeling when I was suddenly catapulted into the leadership of the bus protest in Montgomery several years ago that we would have the support of the white Church. I felt that the white ministers, priests, and rabbis of the South would be some of our strongest allies. Instead, some have been outright opponents, refusing to understand the freedom movement and misrepresenting its leaders; all too many others have been more cautious than courageous and have remained silent behind the anesthetizing security of stained glass windows.

In spite of my shattered dreams of the past, I came to Birmingham with the hope that the white religious leadership of the community would see the justice of our cause and, with deep moral concern, serve as the channel through which our just grievances could get to the power structure. I had hoped that each of you would understand. But again I have been disappointed.

I have heard numerous religious leaders of the South call upon their worshippers to comply with a desegregation decision because it is the law, but I have longed to hear white ministers say follow this decree because integration is morally right and the Negro is your brother. In the midst of blatant injustices inflicted upon the Negro, I have watched white churches stand on the sideline and merely mouth pious irrelevancies and sanctimonious trivialities. In the midst of a mighty struggle to rid our nation of racial and economic injustice, I have heard so many ministers say, "Those are social issues with which the Gospel has no real concern," and I have watched so many churches commit themselves to a completely otherwordly religion which made a strange distinction between body and soul, the sacred and the secular.

So here we are moving toward the exit of the twentieth century with a religious community largely adjusted to the status quo, standing as a tail light behind other community agencies rather than a headlight leading men to higher levels of justice.

I have travelled the length and breadth of Alabama, Mississippi, and all the other Southern states. On sweltering summer days and crisp autumn mornings I have looked at her beautiful churches with their spires pointing heavenward. I have beheld the impressive outlay of her massive religious education buildings. Over and over again I have found myself asking: "Who worships here? Who is their God? Where were their voices when the lips of Governor Barnett dripped with words of interposition and nullification? Where were they when Governor Wallace gave the clarion call for defiance and hatred? Where were their voices of support when tired, bruised, and weary Negro men and women decided to rise from the dark dungeons of complacency to the bright hills of creative protest?"

Yes, these questions are still in my mind. In deep disappointment, I have wept over the laxity of the Church. But be assured that my tears have been tears of love. There can be no deep disappointment where there is not deep love. Yes, I love the Church; I love her sacred walls. How could I do otherwise? I am in the rather unique position of being the son, the grandson, and the great grandson of preachers. Yes, I see the Church as the body of Christ. But, oh! How we have blemished and scarred that body through social neglect and fear of being nonconformists.

There was a time when the Church was very powerful. It was during that period when the early Christians rejoiced when they were deemed worthy to suffer for what they believed. In those days the Church was not merely a thermometer that recorded the ideas and principles of popular opinion; it was a thermostat that transformed the mores of society. Wherever the early Christians entered a town the power structure got disturbed and immediately sought to convict them for being "disturbers of the peace" and "outside agitators." But they went on with the conviction that they were a "colony of heaven" and had to obey God rather than man. They were small in number but big in commitment. They were too Godintoxicated to be "astronomically intimidated." They brought an end to such ancient evils as infanticide and gladiatorial contest.

Things are different now. The contemporary Church is so often a weak, ineffectual voice with an uncertain sound. It is so often the archsupporter of the status quo. Far from being disturbed by the presence of the Church, the power structure of the average community is consoled by the Church's silent and often vocal sanction of things as they are.

But the judgment of God is upon the Church as never before. If the Church of today does not recapture the sacrificial spirit of the early church, it will lose its authentic ring, forfeit the loyalty of millions, and be dismissed as an irrelevant social club with no meaning for the twentieth century. I am meeting young people every day whose disappointment with the Church has risen to outright disgust.

Maybe again I have been too optimistic. Is organized religion too inextricably bound to the status quo to save our nation and the world? Maybe I must turn my faith to the inner spiritual Church, the church within the Church, as the true *ecclesia* and the hope of the world. But again I am thankful to God that some noble souls from the ranks of organized religion have broken loose from the paralyzing chains of conformity and joined us as active partners in the struggle for freedom. They have left their secure congregations and walked the streets of Albany, Georgia, with us. They have gone through the highways of the South on torturous rides for freedom. Yes, they have gone to jail with us. Some have been kicked out of their churches and lost the support of their bishops and fellow ministers. But they have gone with the faith that right defeated is stronger than evil triumphant. These men have been the leaven in the lump of the race. Their witness has been the spiritual salt that has preserved the true meaning of the Gospel in these troubled times. They have carved a tunnel of hope through the dark mountain of disappointment.

I hope the Church as a whole will meet the challenge of this decisive hour. But even if the Church does not come to the aid of justice, I have no despair about the future. I have no fear about the outcome of our struggle in Birmingham, even if our motives are presently misunderstood. We will reach the goal of freedom in Birmingham and all over the nation, because the goal of America is freedom. Abused and scorned though we may be, our destiny is tied up with the destiny of America. Before the pilgrims landed at Plymouth, we were here. Before the pen of Jefferson etched across the pages of history the majestic words of the Declaration of Independence, we were here. For more than two centuries our foreparents labored in this country without wages; they made cotton "king"; and they built the homes of their masters in the midst of brutal injustice and shameful humiliation—and yet out of a bottomless vitality they continued to thrive and develop. If the inexpressible cruelties of slavery could not stop us, the opposition we now face will surely fail. We will win our freedom because the sacred heritage of our nation and the eternal will of God are embodied in our echoing demands.

I must close now. But before closing I am impelled to mention one other point in your statement that troubled me profoundly. You warmly commended the Birmingham police force for keeping "order" and "preventing violence." I don't believe you would have so warmly commended the police force if you had seen its angry violent dogs literally biting six unarmed, nonviolent Negroes. I don't believe you would so quickly commend the policemen if you would observe their ugly and inhuman treatment of Negroes here in the city jail; if you would watch them push and curse old Negro women and young Negro girls; if you would see them slap and kick old Negro men and young Negro boys; if you will observe them, as they did on two occasions, refuse to give us food because we wanted to sing our grace together. I'm sorry I can't join you in your praise for the police department.

It is true that they have been rather disciplined in their public handling of the demonstrators. In this sense they have been rather publicly "nonviolent." But for what purpose? To preserve the evil system of segregation. Over the last few years I have consistently preached that nonviolence demands that the means we use must be as pure as the ends we seek. So I have tried to make it clear that it is wrong to use immoral means to attain moral ends. But now I must affirm that it is just as wrong, or even more so, to use moral means to preserve immoral ends. Maybe Mr. Connor and his policemen have been rather publicly nonviolent, as Chief Prichett was in Albany, Georgia, but they have used the moral means of nonviolence to maintain the immoral end of flagrant racial injustice. T. S. Eliot has said that there is no greater treason than to do the right deed for the wrong reason.

I wish you had commended the Negro sit-inners and demonstrators of Birmingham for their sublime courage, their willingness to suffer, and their amazing discipline in the midst of the most inhuman provocation. One day the South will recognize its real heroes. They will be the James Merediths, courageously and with a majestic sense of purpose, facing jeering and hostile mobs and the agonizing loneliness that characterizes the life of the pioneer. They will be old, oppressed, battered Negro women, symbolized in a seventy-two year old woman of Montgomery, Alabama, who rose up with a sense of dignity and with her people decided not to ride the segregated buses, and responded to one who inquired about her tiredness with ungrammatical profundity: "My feets is tired, but my soul is rested." They will be young high school and college students, young ministers of the gospel and a host of the elders, courageously and nonviolently sitting in at lunch counters and willingly going to jail for conscience sake. One day the South will know that when these disinherited children of God sat down at lunch counters they were in reality standing up for the best in the American dream and the most sacred values in our Judeo-Christian heritage, and thus carrying our whole nation back to great wells of democracy which were dug deep by the founding fathers in the formulation of the Constitution and the Declaration of Independence.

Never before have I written a letter this long (or should I say a book?). I'm afraid that it is much too long to take your precious time. I can assure you that it would have been much shorter if I had been writing from a comfortable desk, but what else is there to do when you are alone for days in the dull monotony of a narrow jail cell other than write long letters, think strange thoughts, and pray long prayers?

If I have said anything in this letter that is an overstatement of the truth and is indicative of an unreasonable impatience, I beg you to forgive me. If I have said anything in this letter that is an understatement of the truth and is indicative of my having a patience that makes me patient with anything less than brotherhood, I beg God to forgive me.

I hope this letter finds you strong in the faith. I also hope that circumstances will soon make it possible for me to meet each of you, not as an integrationist or a civil rights leader, but as a fellow clergyman and a Christian brother. Let us all hope that the dark clouds of racial prejudice will soon pass away and the deep fog of misunderstanding will be lifted from our fear-drenched communities and in some not too distant tomorrow the radiant stars of love and brotherhood will shine over our great nation with all their scintillating beauty.

Yours for the cause of
Peace and Brotherhood
MARTIN LUTHER KING, JR.

Content

1. King's critics, eight Alabama clergymen, had said that his activities were "unwise and untimely." Do you believe King's letter to them should have alleviated their concerns? Explain, using specific detail from the letter to support your response.
2. In paragraph 9, King defends "non-violent direct action," saying that its purpose is to make negotiation possible. In your own words, explain how you believe King thinks protest in the form of such nonviolent activities as sit-ins can lead to negotiation.
3. In paragraph 5, King lists what he considers to be the four basic steps in nonviolent protest: "collection of facts to determine whether injustices exist; negotiation; self-purification; and direct action." Based on your reading of King's letter, describe your understanding of these four steps. Be specific.
4. Does King's apology (paragraph 46) for writing such a long letter seem to you to be genuine? If it does not seem genuine, what other purpose might it serve?

Technique

1. King's topics, freedom and civil rights, are universal. The immediate audience for his essay was restricted, though, to eight of his fellow clergymen. How does his restricted audience affect the form and the tone of his essay?
2. King uses many techniques of argumentation in his letter. He analyzes the logic of his opponents, he draws analogies, and he relies on the authority of religious texts, history, and even emotion. Find examples of each of these methods in the essay and evaluate their effectiveness, identifying the passages that particularly convinced you or failed to convince you.
3. Two notable uses of definition in King's essay occur when he explains "nonviolent direction action" and just versus unjust laws. Paraphrase these definitions in your own words.

Language

1. Occasionally King uses metaphors to get his point across. For example, he writes, "I had hoped that the white moderate would understand that law and order exist for the purpose of establishing justice and that when they fail in this purpose they become dangerously structured dams that block the flow of social progress." Find two other examples

of metaphors in the essay; explain how each seems appropriate or inappropriate from your perspective as a reader.
2. In paragraph 12, King mentions some of the words that the white community uses (or will not use) to speak or write about blacks. These words, King suggests, allow the community to create a definition of blacks against which blacks must constantly struggle. What are some of these words that create what King calls a sense of "nobodiness"?
3. King objects to being called an "extremist." Why? Based on your reading of "Letter from Birmingham Jail," would you call King an extremist? Look up the word in your dictionary and consider your own idea of the meaning of the word.

Vocabulary

provincial	paradox	scintillating
deplore	anarchy	estrangement
gadfly	precipitate	unfettered
millennium	incorrigible	gainsay

Writing Suggestions

1. Throughout his letter, King uses vivid imagery to make his point: creeping at a "horse-and-buggy pace toward gaining a cup of coffee at a lunch counter," "the stinging darts of segregation," "the shadow of deep disappointment," and "the paralyzing chains of conformity," to name a few. Choose any one of King's images and write a paragraph in which you explain the success of the image in creating a vivid picture that strengthens or clarifies King's point.
2. Write a paragraph in which you explain your understanding of the term "nonviolent direct action."
3. A children's rhyme says that "names can never hurt you." In his list of grievances (paragraph 12), however, King implies that names really do hurt ("boy," "nigger"). Write an essay in which you analyze the impact of name-calling. You need not limit your analysis to racial epithets; consider as well other cases of abusive name-calling.
4. Civil disobedience takes many forms—draft resistance, illegal picketing, refusing to pay a portion of one's taxes, refusing to send one's child to school. Write a letter defending, to your critics, one such act of "nonviolent direct action." Support your stand with a well-reasoned, well-documented argument.

Language and the Media
3

In the past two decades, television has become our most potent form of public communication, shaping social, moral, and political attitudes. Television newscaster Walter Cronkite has been called the most trusted man in America; a generation grew up with the Vietnam war at its dinner table; we have watched a man walk on the moon and listened as he shared his reactions with us; and millions around the country spent a summer wondering who shot J.R., the villainous central character of the popular television serial, *Dallas*. Television is but one form of mass communication—or media—that provides us with shared knowledge and experience; books, newspapers, records, films, and radio all exert powerful influences in our everyday lives.

Because of their seeming omnipresence and omnipotence in our lives, the media have in recent years become the object both of careful scrutiny and controversy. With the advent of electronic media, mass communication is increasingly a one-way dialogue with no need for response from the recipients. For this reason, sociologists fear we are becoming passive "consumers" incapable of response. As magazine and book sales decline, critics fear that electronic media will replace reading in our lives. Many educators, fearing that the result will be illiteracy, have blamed declining college entrance exam scores on television mania. Increasing violence in our society is frequently attributed to media violence without moral or legal consequence, and women and ethnic minorities fight media stereotypes they feel perpetuate outdated images.

The essays in this section examine the role of the media in society and the ways in which we communicate with one another through them. The writers of these seven essays are aware of the power of the media in our lives; they recognize them as creations of man that, like Frankenstein, threaten to turn on the creator and control (or even destroy) him. At the same time, as writers, publishers, columnists, advertisers, and communication specialists themselves, they recognize the media's tremendous potential as positive instruments of social communication. They write, therefore, out of a belief in the future of the media, as well as out of a recognition of society's responsibility to shape what it has created.

In "The Second God," Tony Schwartz compares electronic media to our notion of a supreme being that is all-present and all-knowing. The media come into our homes and keep us company throughout the day, entering and affecting our lives even when we are not consciously aware of their presence. Schwartz points out that the media contain the knowledge man strives for and that in their dissemination of that knowledge they provide common values and shape social attitudes. Like the presence and the power of God, media are mysterious, "angel-like" in Marshall McLuhan's words, coming to man disembodied, communicating in ways not fully understood. Schwartz recognizes the irony and the implied danger of a god made by imperfect human beings, but he closes by suggesting that we can shape and control the unruly god we have created.

Television is the medium that is perhaps most like Schwartz's second god, all-powerful and ever-present, and it is the medium that elicits the greatest response from critics concerned with the possibility of the creature ruling the creator. In "Where Have the Children Gone?" Joshua Meyrowitz explores one result of television's pervasiveness; it has erased the traditional roles of adult and child. "Childhood as it once was," he says, "no longer exists." The change has occurred because television has given children access to "social knowledge" that was traditionally withheld from them until adolescence or adulthood. Before the advent of television, children had to read simple books before they could read the books that would give them access to the adult world; with television, all levels of knowledge are equally available to children from the beginning. Meyrowitz does not judge the change; it's too soon, he seems to believe, to know whether the loss of childhood innocence is a positive or negative phenomenon. It is to him, however, a significant instance of the media's power to work cultural change.

In addition to shaping new trends, the media frequently mirror cultural concerns, needs, and habits. Tom Wolfe, in "Porno-violence," examines the relationship between the media's portrayal of violence and society's violent inclinations. Wolfe calls this new media violence "porno-violence" because, like pornography, it is portrayed not from the point of view of the victim but through the eyes of the perpetrator. Through the media, we share vicariously in the violent act. Most disturbing to Wolfe is what he perceives as a new emphasis on porno-violence in the "pillars of the American press" and on television which seem to be responding in kind to our worst inclinations. When the thrill is gone from readily available porno-violence in the media, when that becomes "old hat," what, Wolfe wonders, will we do next to satisfy our lust for violence?

Tom Wolfe's criticism of the capitulation of "Establishment" magazines to porno-violence lends credence to Norman Cousins' sense that good taste is being preempted by sleaziness in the publishing industry. Cousins, former editor of *Saturday Review*, laments that magazine's demise, for it was, he says, a publication whose aim had been "to strengthen the cultural marketplace of good taste in America." Today, the national culture is less attracted to good taste than to bad, according to Cousins, and our magazines are responding to that cultural trend. The change is not only in subject matter, but also in the debasement of language—a shift from clear communication of high ideals to sensationally offensive language expressing gutter sentiments. Cousins believes that the decline of media language represents and even fosters a retreat from civility. Like Schwartz, Cousins warns us that the media we create can either elevate cultural standards and attitudes or debase them, and he reminds us that the choice is ours.

M. F. K. Fisher's subject, too, is the debasement of language in the media. Fisher, however, takes a more light-hearted look at one specialized form of media language, the culinary language in advertisements, cookbooks, and cooking columns. According to Fisher, the need to sell food (an odd need, she suggests, since the hunger drive should be enough to cause us to buy food) has made slaves of culinary writers and advertisers; consequently, their "culinary lingo" is in turn designed not to communicate but to dictate our tastes and behavior. To prove that language to describe food in the media lacks subtlety or accuracy and is frequently disgusting and insulting, Fisher takes a humorous romp through the world of hyphenated hyperbole ("freezer-fresh"); recipes that, we are promised, will make us "drool" (a dubious achievement, says Fisher); and the "lingo of gastronomical seduction" designed to make us link food with sexual success.

"It's Natural! It's Organic! Or Is It?" demonstrates, too, that advertising language is designed to make us buy specific products. Unlike Fisher, however, the Consumer's Union concentrates on the cleverness and duplicity of advertisers and food companies, not on their aesthetic abuse of the language. The Consumer's Union essay is particularly interesting insofar as it shows how even single words can trigger powerful—and profitable—responses in American consumers. The essay provides dozens of examples in which the words "natural" and "organic" are wrenched into new meanings or simply used recklessly. It also shows how the concept of "naturalness" seems to tap a longing in the American public to retreat from industrial society—the same society that has, ironically, created clever advertisers who manipulate language so as to exploit such emotional "soft spots."

Stanley Kauffmann's essay, "Why I'm Not Bored," brings together several of the concerns of the other essayists in this section, particularly the ways in which the media both mirror society's interests and shape communal attitudes. Kauffmann's medium is film, and his view of it is persuasively optimistic. Happily admitting he would be a regular moviegoer even if it were not required by his work, movie critic Kauffmann argues that film provides the community a sense of being part of a shared dream that draws viewers together in a way television, for instance, cannot. Communication between the individual and the movie maker is heightened, according to Kauffmann, by all that we bring with us to the theater; our hopes, dreams, and secret fantasies originated in part in the movie houses of our youth, and at the movies we continue to keep in touch with those fantasies. For Kauffmann, film is a hopeful medium, "pulsating with prospects," "life-crammed," and always possessing the potential to change the viewer's life.

Each of the writers in this section examines the ways in which we communicate, or fail to communicate, through the media. They speak about different media—television, film, books, magazines, and advertising—but each recognizes the power of mass communication to shape opinions, values, and behavior. The media undoubtedly reflect current cultural trends and create new ones. The writers represented in this section remind us that because the media have the power and potential for positive or negative influence on the community, the society that has created the media must be responsible for their direction.

The Second God

Tony Schwartz

Tony Schwartz is presently a professor of telecommunications at New York University. For more than thirty years, his weekly radio program, Around New York, was broadcast on station WNYC. As a specialist in political media, he has produced television and radio commercials for two presidents, as well as for candidates in various other levels of government. He has also designed sound for Broadway shows and produced dozens of records. In the following essay, taken from his book Media: The Second God *(1981), Schwartz develops an extended analysis of television's omnipotence as a god-like force in the lives of modern Americans.*

Ask someone raised in the religious traditions of the Western world to describe God, and this, with idiosyncratic variations, might be the answer:

"God is all-knowing and all-powerful. He is a spirit, not a body, and He exists both outside us and within us. God is always with us because He is everywhere. We can never fully understand Him because He works in mysterious ways."

In broad terms this describes the God of our fathers, but it also describes electronic media, the second god, which man has created.

Radio and television are everywhere and they are always with us. Millions listen to the same networks, hum the same commercial jingles, share with soap-opera characters the testing of souls, the mystery of love and death, the agony of the sinful and the triumph of the righteous. Stations transmit the same programs world-wide. In cramped apartments in Tokyo people watch *Charlie's Angels*. Lieutenant Columbo tracks down killers in Oslo, Rome, Madrid, and Bucharest. The whole world wanted to know who shot *Dallas's* J.R. And here in the United States we tune in the BBC's Masterpiece Theatre or watch Japanese and other foreign films on cable. Two billion people saw a man walk on the moon.

The similarities in people's feelings about God and their attitude about media are evident in the excerpts below. The following statements are taken from interviews I did dealing with religious habits conducted in the early 1960s for the television program *Lamp Unto My Feet*:

> *Woman*
> "I never feel alone because God is with me."
> *Child*
> "God is everywhere and I don't know how He could do it."

The following statements are from interviews I conducted in 1967 in the course of researching media habits:

> *Woman*
> "I never feel alone because I have my radio and television."
> *Child*
> "The same programs are in a lot of places."

The media are all-knowing. They supply a community of knowledge and feelings, and a common morality. Many people in the United States, literate and illiterate alike, simply do not read. They receive information from television whether or not they seek that information. It often comes to them in the form of entertainment.

Information is inherent in electronic entertainment, news, and commercials. Media are both a door to the mind and a window on the world. They provide insight and "outsight"—the introduction to hitherto unperceived realities. In one week a single television program, Alex Haley's *Roots*, influenced the way millions of people felt about the life, culture, and experience of American blacks. *Roots* provided the "outsight" about black history, tribal customs, patterns of ritual, all highly exotic to the white viewer who formerly had no knowledge of such things. But *Roots* also provided insight, the sudden understanding that all people share elemental emotions such as love, fear, hope, and despair—the common bonds of humanity that can unite otherwise disparate cultures.

Millions of Americans depend on radio and television rather than on newspapers for the news. Their indifference to the print medium has bankrupted newspapers in every major city in the country. In New York City alone we have seen the passing of the *Daily Mirror*, the *World-Telegram*, and the *Herald-Tribune*; only recently the venerable Chicago *Daily News* went under.

The media profoundly affect community attitudes, political structures, and the psychological state of entire countries. Godlike, the media can change the course of a war, bring down a president or a king, elevate the lowly and humiliate the proud, by directing the attention of millions on the same event and in the same manner. Media coverage of the Army-McCarthy hearings, which brought the proceedings into millions of homes at the same moment, ended the senator's career almost instantaneously. Because television coverage of the Vietnam war was so extensive, and because it brought the realities of armed conflict right into America's living rooms, it reduced concepts of heroism, gallantry, and self-sacrifice to the tawdry realities of battle, the suffering, the terror, the desperation and the agonizing pain, and created a national revulsion against that war. When the American hostages returned home from Iran, the joyful welcome they received was a reflection of how familiar they had become to us through the media, especially television. Television had brought those people into our homes. We had witnessed their suffering. When we welcomed them back, we felt that we were welcoming friends.

The side effects of media demonstrate the mysterious ways in which they work. These side effects are often more powerful than the intended message. For example, in advertising, whether commercial or political, we typically use media to achieve a straightforward result: to improve the sales of a product or to win votes for a candidate. We can measure these intended results. But the side effects of media campaigns are often exclusive because the people who see and hear these messages do not see and hear them in the same context as the people who devised them. The audience responds to the message in the context of their own lives and problems.

A newspaper whose employees were on strike sponsored a radio message which disclosed the salaries of all the workers, from pressmen to secretaries to office boys. The newspaper's management obviously considered these salaries generous, and the purpose of the message was to evoke certain feelings in listeners: "Well, they're making a pretty good living right now. Why should I miss my paper?"

To a large extent the message accomplished this primary purpose. But there was a secondary effect that no one could have foreseen. Upon learning the salary levels of these newspaper workers, people flooded the paper's employment office with job applications.

The proprietor of a furniture store advertised over radio for sales personnel who held decorator's certificates. The commercial achieved predictable results and the proprietor found qualified help. Curiously, the help-wanted commercial also increased sales. Potential customers realized that if they patronized the store, trained decorators rather than mere salespeople would assist them.

Sometimes the secondary results of a media campaign can take an amusing turn, as in the by now legendary case of a schoolchild who was participating in a spelling bee. When the teacher asked her to spell the word "relief," she spelled "r-o-l-a-i-d-s," taking her cue from the well-known Rolaids commercial.

The media are everywhere and nowhere. They are a spirit, a disembodied entity occupying no space and all space at the same time. The electronic voices we hear have no body. In fact, the entire output of electronic media is invisible. The late Marshall McLuhan called it "angel-like." On television and radio we experience other people, see them and hear them, but they have no corporeal form. The words we hear, the pictures we see on the television screen, exist only in our minds. We make the television picture ourselves as we assemble the scanning dots and from them construct a Walter Cronkite or a Mike Wallace. McLuhan observed, "at the speed of light nobody has a body."

The electronic waves of the media suffuse the atmosphere we live in. McLuhan equated the media environment with the traditional definition of God, whose "center is everywhere and whose margins are nowhere." This relates to the phenomenon of sound. Sound envelopes you because it is spatial, totally environmental. It functions by moving the air. Walk to any part of a room and the sound you hear is substantially the same. To ask, "Where is the center of sound?" is like asking, "Where is the center of the air in this room?" The center is everywhere. Where are the margins of sound? Nowhere. That is what we mean by such expressions as "The room was filled with music." Wherever we sit in a music-filled room the music is with us. Wherever we are, we are in the center of sound.

The media are within every one of us. The evangelist cries, "Open your hearts and receive God!" We open our eyes and ears and receive electronic media. What we receive exists only in our minds. Just as the idea of God is within us, we retain the memory of the voices and images of the media within us.

We don't need a special house, topped with a steeple, to commune with the second god. He comes into our homes every day and takes his place beside the family.

The second god is accessible to the humble and the mighty, the lettered and the ignorant, the child and the adult. This country has more radios than people, more television sets than bathtubs. The media audience cuts across all class and racial lines. The illiterate share a culture with the literate. The child of the sharecropper and the child of the banker absorb the same information through media.

We can talk to virtually anyone anywhere by telephone, and to anyone and everyone everywhere if we have access to radio and television. Any man, woman, or child on earth can hear you as though you were in the same room with them. We have even heard the man on the moon talk to us in our homes. The second god makes it possible for us to take for granted what was once an exercise of faith: the miracle of speaking and the listening to a disembodied voice.

The Judeo-Christian God observes mankind, finds it faulty in many respects, and tries to impose on it a sense of morality, but the relationship between mankind and the second god is different. We, mankind, find the second god faulty in many aspects as we try to impose society's ethics and morality upon the god we made. Many argue that this god is too fond of violence or too engrossed in trivia. At times we may ask this god to change his habits. The second god does not often oblige: although he was created by us, he *appears* to have the power to operate independently.

The analogy between electronic media and God obviously has its limits, and I don't want to carry it too far. However, let me suggest quite seriously that media have influenced our lives and shaped our beliefs as profoundly as any religion.

We have more control over the media god than we might think possible, yet we haven't begun to exercise this control and to use the second god as a social instrument in the hands of society.

Content

1. Schwartz compares the media to a godlike presence. What are some of the specific examples he gives of the media's power, and to what extent do these powers seem godlike?

2. "The side effects of media campaigns," Schwartz writes, "are often elusive because the people who see and hear these messages do not see and hear them in the same context as the people who devised them." What do you understand this statement to mean? How does it reinforce the idea that media work in "mysterious ways"?
3. According to Schwartz, the electronic media appear "to have the power to operate independently." To what extent do you believe a similar argument could be made for a non-electronic medium such as a newspaper? Explain.

Technique

1. Schwartz develops his essay in part through definition and analogy; he provides a general description of God and then shows how the same description applies to electronic media, admitting that "the analogy between electronic media and God obviously has its limits." Evaluate the effectiveness of Schwartz's analogy: Does he take it as far as it can go? Too far?
2. "The Second God" contains a number of examples of the media's power. In paragraph 10, Schwartz provides several examples of the ways television influences our view of national politics. How appropriate are these examples? What principle seems to govern the order in which Schwartz presents his examples?
3. Although Schwartz stresses the similarities between God and the media, toward the end of his essay he points out a crucial difference between the two. What is this difference and why is it important?

Language

1. Schwartz suggests that the media provide information in at least two ways—"insight" and "outsight." Explain what you understand him to mean by these terms.
2. "The words we hear, the pictures we see on the television screen, exist only in our minds," Schwartz writes. To what extent are you aware of this situation when you listen to or watch various types of electronic media? How might it change our response to what we hear if we were more conscious of this "electronic" component of the media?
3. Look up the words "medium" and "media" in the dictionary. How fully do the definitions apply to the specific types of electronic entertainment and communication that influence your life?

Vocabulary

righteous	disparate	patronize
idiosyncratic	elemental	sharecropper
inherent	tawdry	

Writing Suggestions

1. Write an essay about the most important electronic medium in your life; discuss whether or not its influence on you seems godlike. Describe the extent to which it controls you and *vice versa*.
2. Assume that you have been appointed to take charge of one electronic medium in America (television, electronic games, radio, for example). Write an essay about how you would alter the medium's control over our lives.

Where Have the Children Gone?
Joshua Meyrowitz

Joshua Meyrowitz (b. 1949) received a Ph.D. in communication from New York University in 1978. He has taught at Queens College and at the University of New Hampshire, where he is currently an Associate Professor of Communication. He has lectured and written widely on the nature and impact of modern media, particularly television. "Where Have the Children Gone?" is based on a portion of his forthcoming book, No Sense of Place, *which will be published by Oxford University. The essay analyzes the effects of television on childhood and growing up.*

About six years ago I was eating lunch in a diner in New York City when a woman and a young boy sat down in the next booth. I couldn't help overhearing parts of their conversation. At one point the woman asked: "So, how have you been?" And the boy—who could not have been more than seven or eight years old—replied, "Frankly, I've been feeling a little depressed lately."

This incident stuck in my mind because it confirmed my growing belief that children are changing. As far as I can remember, my friends and I didn't find out we were "depressed" until we were in high school.

The evidence of a change in children has increased steadily in recent years. Children don't seem childlike anymore. Children speak more like adults, dress more like adults and behave more like adults than they used to. The reverse is also true: adults have begun to speak, dress and act more like overgrown children.

It is not unusual to see children wearing three-piece suits or designer dresses, or adults in Mickey Mouse T shirts, jeans and sneakers. Adults now wear what were once considered play clothes to many work locations, including the White House.

Education, career choice and developmental stages were once discussed primarily in relation to children and adolescents. Now an increasing number of adults are enrolling in adult-education programs, changing careers in midlife and becoming concerned with their "life stages." Meanwhile, alcoholism, suicide, drug addiction and abortion have become children's issues. Children also commit adult crimes such as armed robbery and murder.

Cute: The merging of childhood and adulthood is reflected in the shifting image of children in entertainment. The Shirley Temple character of the past was a cute and outspoken child. Current child stars, such as Brooke Shields and Gary Coleman, seem to be adults imprisoned in children's bodies.

Whether this is good or bad is difficult to say, but it certainly is different. Childhood as it once was no longer exists. Why?

Human development is based not only on innate biological stages, but also on patterns of access to social knowledge. Movement from one social role to another usually involves learning the secrets of the new status. Children have always been taught adult secrets, but slowly and in stages: traditionally, we tell sixth graders things we keep hidden from fifth graders.

In the last 30 years, however, a secret revelation machine has been installed in 98 percent of American homes. It is called television.

Communication through print allows for a great deal of control over the social information to which children have access. Reading and writing involve a complex code of symbols that must be memorized and practiced. Children must read simple books before they can read adult books.

On TV, however, there is no complex code to exclude young viewers. There is no sharp distinction between the information available to the fifth grader, the high-school student and the adult. Even two-year-old children, unable to read or write their own names, find television accessible and absorbing. They watch over 27 hours a week.

While adults often demand more children's programming, children themselves prefer adult programs. In fact, everyone, regardless of age, tends to watch similar programs. In 1980, for example, "Dallas," "The Dukes of Hazzard," "Love Boat" and "The Muppets" were among the most popular programs in *all* age groups in the country, including ages 2 to 11.

The world of children's books can be insulated to present kids with an idealized view of adulthood. But television news and entertainment presents children with images of adults who lie, drink, cheat and murder.

Reading skill no longer determines the sequence in which social information is revealed to children. Through books, adults could communicate among themselves without being overheard by children. Advice books for parents, for example, can refer them to books that would be inappropriate for children. Similar attempts on television are relatively useless because they are as open to children as they are to adults. Advisory warnings on television often have a boomerang effect by *increasing* children's interest in what follows.

Even early conservative programs such as "Father Knows Best" and "Leave It to Beaver" reveal important social secrets to children. They portray adults behaving one way in front of children and another way when alone. "Father Knows Best," for example, reveals to the child viewer the ways in which a father hides his doubts and manipulates his behavior to make it appear to his children that he knows best.

Such programs teach children that adults play roles for their benefit and that the behavior adults exhibit to children is not necessarily their real or only behavior. Television not only exposes adult secrets, it also exposes the secret of *secrecy*. As a result, children become more suspicious of adults and adults may feel it no longer makes sense to try to keep some things hidden from children. Television undermines behavioral distinctions because it encompasses both children and adults in a single informational sphere or environment.

Rejection: Many formal reciprocal roles rely on lack of intimate knowledge of the other. If the mystery and mystification disappear, so do the formal behaviors. Stylized courtship behaviors, for example, must quickly fade in the day-to-day intimacy of marriage. Similarly, television's involvement of children in adult affairs undermines many traditional adult-child roles.

Given this analysis, it is not surprising that the first widespread rejection of both traditional child and traditional adult behavior occurred in the late 1960s among the first generation of Americans to have grown up with television. In the shared environment of television, children and adults know a great deal about each other's behavior and social knowledge—too much, in fact, for them to play out the traditional complementary roles of innocence versus omnipotence.

Content

1. According to Meyrowitz, children are becoming adults more quickly than in any previous generation. To what degree does this observation seem accurate to you? Do you think, for example, that you grew up more quickly than your older brothers and sisters or cousins? From your knowledge of today's children, do they seem to be growing up more quickly than members of your generation did?
2. Television, in Meyrowitz's opinion, has drastically affected the traditional roles of adult and child because children and adults can now find out so much about each other's "behavior and social knowledge." Assess the impact television had on your childhood and adolescence. Which television programs in particular seem to have influenced your perception of things? Were those perceptions accurate?
3. Speculate about what the consequences might be of children becoming adults more quickly. Do you have any friends, for instance, that seem to have grown up "too fast"?

Technique

1. Meyrowitz begins the essay by reporting a conversation that he overheard between a woman and a young boy. In your view, how effective was this paragraph as the opening of this essay?
2. The essay contrasts childhood today with childhood twenty or more years ago. List some of the more vivid examples Meyrowitz uses to support the contrast. Many of the examples come from television, of course, but pay attention to other types of examples, too. What could you add to his examples?
3. Choose one or two sentences in the essay that might serve as thesis statements and then assess how effectively Meyrowitz's analysis persuades you to agree with his thesis. Which observations of his seemed most convincing to you?

Language

1. Children nowadays speak more like adults and adults speak more like children, according to Meyrowitz. From your experience, is this observation generally accurate? As you answer this question, give some thought to your own definitions of "child" and "adult."
2. Meyrowitz calls television "a secret revelation machine" because through it children have access to what used to be thought of as "adult" information. First, explain whether you agree with this contention, and then think about whether television, as a form of communication, is more beneficial or harmful to children. Be prepared to justify your answer.
3. How has television affected your own use of language—your vocabulary, for instance, or your inclination to read, write, and converse? Has your attitude toward television changed since you entered college? If so, how?
4. Take time to watch 3 or 4 different popular television programs, taking note of the vocabulary used on the shows. What aged audience would you judge the show is intended for, based upon the vocabulary? How much of the language could children understand? Does your viewing support Meyrowitz's argument? Explain.

Vocabulary

idealized	reciprocal	complementary
encompass	stylized	(vs. complimentary)
omnipotence	mystification	

Writing Suggestions

1. One statistic Meyrowitz cites is that children in America watch over 27 hours of television per week. Given this statistic and Meyrowitz's other observations, write an essay explaining your attitude toward television viewing. Assume, for example, that you are the parent of a 10-year old child. Will you limit his or her viewing? How? Why?
2. Write an essay of your own about today's children. As Meyrowitz does, focus on one aspect of experience, such as television viewing, playing video games, listening to music, playing sports, reading, or any single activity that might vividly demonstrate how being a child has changed over the years.

3. Write a paragraph about a television program or a television "personality" (actor, newscaster, game-show host). Briefly describe the show or the person and then explain what children might learn from viewing such a show or such a person.

"Porno-violence"
Tom Wolfe

Tom Wolfe (b. 1931) graduated from Yale in 1957 and then became a correspondent and a reporter for the Washington Post, *the* New York Herald Tribune, *and the* New York World Journal Tribune; *many of his essays and sketches have appeared in* Esquire *and* New York Magazine. *His books include* The Electric Kool-Aid Acid Test *(1968),* The New Journalism *(1973) and* The Right Stuff *(1979). Wolfe's subjects range from the "hippies" and "beach bums" of the 1960s to modern architecture and astronauts. "Porno-violence" reflects his concern for the morality and meaning of a new phenomenon in popular culture; it also reflects the aggressive, unorthodox style of "New Journalism," as well as its technique of using large amounts of "raw material" (dialogue, headlines, etc.) as examples.*

Keeps His Mom-in-law in Chains, meet *Kills Son and Feeds Corpse to Pigs.* Pleased to meet you. *Teenager Twists Off Corpse's Head . . . To Get Gold Teeth,* meet *Strangles Girl Friend,* then *Chops Her to Pieces.* Likewise, I'm sure. *Nurse's Aide Sees Fingers Chopped Off in Meat Grinder,* meet. . . .

In ten years of journalism I have covered more conventions than I care to remember. Podiatrists, theosophists, Professional Budget Finance dentists, oyster farmers, mathematicians, truckers, dry cleaners, stamp collectors, Esperantists, nudists and newspaper editors—I have seen them all, together, in vast assemblies, sloughing through the wall-to-wall of a thousand hotel lobbies (the nudists excepted) in their shimmering grey-metal suits and Nicey Short Collar white shirts with white Plasti-Coat name cards on their chests, and I have sat through their speeches and seminars (the nudists included) and attentively endured ear baths such as you wouldn't believe. And yet some of the truly instructive conventions of our times I seem to have missed altogether. One, for example, I only heard about from one of the many anonymous men who have labored in . . . a curious field. This was a convention of the stringers for *The National Enquirer.*

The Enquirer is a weekly newspaper that is probably known by sight to millions more than know it by name. In fact, no one who ever came face-to-face with *The Enquirer* on a newsstand in its wildest days is likely to have forgotten the sight: a tabloid with great inky shocks of type all over the front page saying something on the order of *Gouges Out Wife's Eyes to Make Her Ugly, Dad Hurls Hot Grease in Daughter's Face, Wife Commits Suicide After 2 Years of Poisoning Fails to Kill Husband.* . . .

The stories themselves were supplied largely by stringers, i.e., correspondents, from all over the country, the world, for that matter, mostly copy editors and reporters on local newspapers. Every so often they would come upon a story, usually via the police beat, that was so grotesque the local sheet would discard it or run it in a highly glossed form rather than offend or perplex its readers. The stringers would preserve them for *The Enquirer*, which always rewarded them well and respectfully.

In fact, one year *The Enquirer* convened and feted them at a hotel in Manhattan. It was a success in every way. The only awkward moment was at the outset when the stringers all pulled in. None of them knew each other. Their hosts got around the problem by introducing them by the stories they had supplied. The introductions, I am told, went like this:

"Harry, I want you to meet Frank here. Frank did that story, you remember that story, *Midget Murderer Throws Girl Off Cliff After She Refuses To Dance With Him.*"

"Pleased to meet you. That was some story."

"And Harry did the one about *I Spent Three Days Trapped at Bottom of Forty-foot-deep Mine Shaft and Was Saved by a Swarm of Flies.*"

"Likewise, I'm sure."

And *Midget Murderer Throws Girl Off Cliff* shakes hands with *I Spent Three Days Trapped at Bottom of Forty-foot-deep Mine Shaft*, and *Buries Her Baby Alive* shakes hands with *Boy, Twelve, Strangles Two-year-old Girl*, and *Kills Son and Feeds Corpse to Pigs* shakes hands with *He Strangles Old Woman and Smears Corpse with Syrup, Ketchup and Oatmeal* . . . and. . . .

. . . There was a great deal of esprit about the whole thing. These men were, in fact, the avant-garde of a new genre that since then has become institutionalized throughout the nation without anyone knowing its proper name. I speak of the new pornography, the pornography of violence.

Pornography comes from the Greek word *porne*, meaning harlot, and pornography is literally the depiction of the acts of harlots. In the new pornography, the theme is not sex. The new pornography depicts practitioners acting out another, murkier drive: people staving teeth in, ripping guts open, blowing brains out and getting even with all those bastards. . . .

The success of *The Enquirer* prompted many imitators to enter the field, *Midnight, The Star Chronicle, The National Insider, Inside News, The National Close-up, The National Tattler, The National Examiner*. A truly competitive free press evolved, and soon a reader could go to the newspaper of his choice for *Kill the Retarded! (Won't You Join My Movement?)* and *Unfaithful Wife? Burn Her Bed!, Harem Master's Mistress Chops Him with Machete, Babe Bites Off Boy's Tongue*, and *Cuts Buddy's Face to Pieces for Stealing His Business and Fianceé.*

And yet the last time I surveyed the Violence press, I noticed a curious thing. These pioneering journals seem to have pulled back. They seem to be regressing to what is by now the Redi-Mix staple of literate Americans, plain old lust-o-lech sex. *Ecstasy and Me (By Hedy Lamarr)*, says *The National Enquirer*. *I Run A Sex Art Gallery*, says *The National Insider*. What has happened, I think, is something that has happened to avant-gardes in many fields, from William Morris and the Craftsmen to the Bauhaus group. Namely, their discoveries have been preempted by the Establishment and so thoroughly dissolved into the mainstream they no longer look original.

Robert Harrison, the former publisher of *Confidential*, and later publisher of the aforementioned *Inside News*, was perhaps the first person to see it coming. I was interviewing Harrison early in January of 1964 for a story in *Esquire* about six weeks after the assassination of President Kennedy, and we were in a cab in the West Fifties in Manhattan, at a stoplight, by a newsstand, and Harrison suddenly pointed at the newsstand and said, "Look at that. They're doing the same thing *The Enquirer* does."

There on the stand was a row of slick-paper, magazine-size publications, known in the trade as one-shots, with titles like *Four Days That Shook the World, Death of a President, An American Tragedy* or just *John Fitzgerald Kennedy (1921-1963)*. "You want to know why people buy those things?" said Harrison. "People buy those things to see a man get his head blown off."

And, of course, he was right. Only now the publishers were in many cases the pillars of the American press. Invariably, these "special coverages" of the assassination bore introductions piously commemorating the fallen President, exhorting the American people to strength and unity in a time of crisis, urging greater vigilance and safeguards for the new President, and even raising the nice metaphysical question of collective guilt in "an age of violence."

In the three and a half years since then, of course, there has been an incessant replay, with every recoverable clinical detail, of those less than five seconds in which a man got his head blown off. And throughout this deluge of words, pictures and film frames, I have been intrigued with one thing. The point of view, the vantage point, is almost never that of the victim, riding in the Presidential Lincoln Continental. What you get is . . . the view from Oswald's rifle. You can step right up here and look point-blank right through the very hairline cross in Lee Harvey Oswald's Optics Ordinance four-power Japanese telescopic sight and watch, frame by frame by frame by frame by frame, as that man there's head comes apart. Just a little History before your very eyes.

The television networks have schooled us in the view from Oswald's rifle and made it seem a normal pastime. The TV viewpoint is nearly always that of the man who is going to strike. The last time I watched *Gunsmoke*, which was not known as a very violent Western in TV terms, the action went like this: The Wellington agents and the stagecoach driver pull guns on the badlands gang leader's daughter and Kitty, the heart-of-gold saloonkeeper, and kidnap them. Then the badlands gang shoots two Wellington agents. Then they tie up five more and talk about shooting them. Then they desist because they might not be able to get a hotel room in the next town if the word got around. Then one badlands gang gunslinger attempts to rape Kitty while the gang leader's younger daughter looks on. Then Kitty resists, so he slugs her one in the jaw. Then the gang leader slugs him. Then the gang leader slugs Kitty. Then Kitty throws hot stew in a gang member's face and hits him over the back of the head with a revolver. Then he knocks her down with a rock. Then the gang sticks up a bank. Here comes the sheriff, Matt Dillon. He shoots a gang member and breaks it up. Then the gang leader shoots the guy who was guarding his daughter and the woman. Then the sheriff shoots the gang leader. The final exploding bullets signals The End.

It is not the accumulated slayings and bone-crushings that make this porno-violence, however. What makes it porno-violence is that in almost every case the camera angle, therefore the viewer, is with the gun, the fist, the rock. The pornography of violence has no point of view in the old sense that novels do. You do not live the action through the hero's eyes. You live with the aggressor, whoever he may be. One moment you are the hero. The next, you are the villain. No matter whose side you may be on consciously, you are in fact with the muscle, and it is you who disintegrate all comers, villains, lawmen, women, anybody. On the rare occasions in which the gun is emptied into the camera—i.e., into your face—the effect is so startling that the pornography of violence all but loses its fantasy charm. There are not nearly so many masochists as sadists among those little devils whispering into your ears.

In fact, sex—"sadomasochism"—is only a part of the pornography of violence. Violence is much more wrapped up, simply, with status. Violence is the simple, ultimate solution for problems of status competition, just as gambling is the simple, ultimate solution for economic competition. The old pornography was the fantasy of easy sexual delights in a world where sex was kept unavailable. The new pornography is the fantasy of easy triumph in a world where status competition has become so complicated and frustrating.

Already the old pornography is losing its kick because of overexposure. In the late Thirties, Nathanael West published his last and best-regarded novel, *The Day of the Locust*, and it was a terrible flop commercially, and his publisher said if he ever published another book about Hollywood it would "have to be *My Thirty-nine Ways of Making Love by Hedy Lamarr.*" *Ecstasy and Me* is not quite that . . . but maybe it is. I stopped counting. I know her account begins: "The men in my life have ranged from a classic case history of impotence, to a whip-brandishing sadist who enjoyed sex only after he tied my arms behind me with the sash of his robe. There was another man who took his pleasure with a girl in my own bed, while he thought I was asleep in it."

Yawns all around. The sin itself is wearing out. Pornography cannot exist without certified taboo to violate. And today Lust, like the rest of the Seven Deadly Sins–Pride, Sloth, Envy, Greed, Anger and Gluttony—is becoming a rather minor vice. The Seven Deadly

Sins, after all, are only sins against the self. Theologically, the idea of Lust—well, the idea is that if you seduce some poor girl from Akron, it is not a sin because you are ruining her, but because you are wasting your time and your energies and damaging your own spirit. This goes back to the old work ethic, when the idea was to keep every able-bodied man's shoulder to the wheel. In an age of riches for all, the ethic becomes more nearly: Let him do anything he pleases, as long as he doesn't get in my way. And if he does get in my way, or even if he doesn't . . . well . . . we have *new* fantasies for that. *Put hair on the walls.*

Hair on the walls is the invisible subtitle of Truman Capote's book *In Cold Blood*. The book is neither a who-done-it nor a will-they-be-caught, since the answers to both questions are known from the outset. It does ask why-did-they-do-it, but the answer is soon as clear as it is going to be. Instead, the book's suspense is based largely on a totally new idea in detective stories: the promise of gory details, and the withholding of them until the end. Early in the game one of the two murderers, Dick, starts promising to put "plenty of hair on them-those walls" with a shotgun. So read on, gentle readers, and on and on; you are led up to the moment before the crime on page 60—yet the specifics, what happened, the gory details, are kept out of sight, in grisly dangle, until page 244.

But Dick and Perry, Capote's killers, are only a couple of lower-class bums. With James Bond the new pornography has already reached dead center, the bureaucratic middle class. The appeal of Bond has been explained as the appeal of the lone man who can solve enormously complicated, even world problems through his own bravery and initiative. But Bond is not a lone man at all, of course. He is not the Lone Ranger. He is much easier to identify than that. He is a salaried functionary in a bureaucracy. He is a sport, but a believable one; not a millionaire, but a bureaucrat on expense account. He is not even a high-level bureaucrat. He is an operative. This point is carefully and repeatedly made by having his superiors dress him down for violations of standard operating procedure. Bond, like the Lone Ranger, solves problems with guns and fists. When it is over, however, the Lone Ranger leaves a silver bullet. Bond, like the rest of us, fills out a report in triplicate.

Marshall McLuhan says we are in a period in which it will become harder and harder to stimulate lust through words and pictures—i.e., the old pornography. In an age of electronic circuitry, he says, people crave tactile, all-involving experiences. The same thing may very well happen to the new pornography of violence. Even such able craftsmen as Truman Capote, Ian Fleming, NBC and CBS may not suffice. Fortunately, there are historical models to rescue us from this frustration. In the latter days of the Roman Empire, the Emperor Commodus became jealous of the celebrity of the great gladiators. He took to the arena himself, with his sword, and began dispatching suitably screened cripples and hobbled fighters. Audience participation became so popular that soon various *illuminati* of the Commodus set, various boys and girls of the year, were out there, suited up, gaily cutting a sequence of dwarves and feebles down to short ribs. Ah, swinging generations, what new delights await?

Content

1. In your own words, briefly define what you think Wolfe means by "porno-violence." How does porno-violence differ from pornography? What, according to Wolfe, are the principle objections to porno-violence?

2. Wolfe suggests that the mainstream of American media has absorbed the techniques of "porno-violence" that once belonged only to sensational newspapers such as *The Naitonal Enquirer*. Judging from the television news programs you watch and the newspapers you read, to what extent do Wolfe's observations seem accurate to you? Explain.

3. One example of mainstream porno-violence that Wolfe uses is the coverage of the assassination of President Kennedy in 1963. You may be more familiar, however, with such examples as the murder of John Lennon and the attempted assassination of President Reagan. In your view, did the mainstream newspapers, news magazines, and television networks engage in porno-violence, as Wolfe defines it, in their coverage of these occurrences? As you answer this question, think of specific examples of the news coverage as you remember it.

Technique

1. Review the first two pages of Wolfe's essay, paying particular attention to the examples he provides and the way he presents them. In your view, is the tone of these paragraphs effective? Why or why not?

2. How does Wolfe make his readers aware of his attitude toward "porno-

violence"? Select two or three sentences in the essay that appear to communicate his view and assess their effectiveness in persuading you.

3. One task that Wolfe sets for himself is to show how the mainstream media has begun to use the techniques that once belonged solely to sensational newspapers and magazines. How effective is his transition from discussing *The National Enquirer* to discussing television, books, and movies? As you answer this question, pinpoint what you think are the transitional paragraphs between the two topics.

Language

1. Wolfe's examples of headlines from *The National Enquirer* and similar newspapers are obvious in their sensational appeal. From your experience, do television news shows and news magazines make similar, if less obvious, appeals? As Wolfe does, cite examples of the kind of language such shows and magazines use.

2. How would you characterize Wolfe's own use of language? Choose two or three adjectives that describe it accurately. Is the style and tone of his essay appropriate to his discussion of the portrayal of violence in the media? Why or why not?

Vocabulary

tabloid	feted
perplex	exhort
grisly	functionary

Writing Suggestions

1. Write an essay about a television program, a movie, or a magazine story that demonstrates "porno-violence." Be sure to define the term in your own words, and provide examples to support your evaluation. As Wolfe does, communicate your attitude toward the program, movie, or story that you have chosen.

2. Clip an article from a sensational newspaper like *The National Enquirer;* then rewrite the piece in an informative but unsensational way. Then write a separate "cover" paragraph that summarizes the sorts of changes in tone, style, and diction you found yourself making.

3. Assume that you are the editor-in-chief of a daily newspaper. A particularly gruesome crime has occurred in your city, and you must advise your staff about how to report the incident with stories and photo-

graphs. The rival newspapers will probably report the incident in a sensational fashion. In a couple of paragraphs, briefly explain what your instructions to the staff would be and why you would handle the story in that particular way.

An Epitaph for the *Saturday Review*— And Culture, Too

Norman Cousins

(For biographical information on Norman Cousins, see page 32.) In the following essay, Cousins uses the occasion of a magazine's demise to compare and contrast attitudes toward language and the role of the media in defining values. His view of such things as "hope" is particularly noteworthy because he sees them not as luxuries or trite concepts, but as practical necessities.

The *Saturday Review* is dead, and I can no more be detached from its passing than I would be at the loss of a child. I was its editor for nearly half of my adult life.

As I write this obituary for what seems to me to be a member of my own family, I look out from my study over the distant ridges of the Santa Monica Mountains. The sky is soft overhead, and the day lends itself to reflection. And so I also look back over 35 years of my life on the magazine. Though I'd had no editorial authority over the magazine for a half-dozen years, my emotional connections are nonetheless deep. And I ask myself whether, now that it is gone, anything of value is lost.

A magazine, like almost everything else in life, has an evolving personality. It tries to do different things at different times. The underlying aim of the *Saturday Review*, through all the years and all the changes, was to serve and strengthen the cultural marketplace of good taste in America. Whatever success the magazine may have had was directly connected to its respect for the place of ideas and the arts in the life of the mind.

This emphasis takes on special significance in the light of the sleaziness that has infected the national culture in recent years. There seems to be a fierce competition, especially in the worlds of entertainment and publishing, to find ever-lower rungs on the ladder of taste. At the core of this competition is the apparent notion that intimacy does not require privacy, that genuine love is an irrelevance, and that sex is a toy to be played with and discarded when interest turns elsewhere. It is made to seem that the First Amendment was designed for the express purpose of shielding writers and editors who want to diagram the sex act in print or on film. In both media, human beings are flung at one another anatomically as though there is nothing more to life or love than random and mechanical exchange. The poetry of feeling has given way to puerile limericks and the fumblings of fools.

The annihilation of taste has not spared language. There is the curious notion that freedom is somehow synonymous with gutter jargon. At one time, people who worked in the arts would boast to one another about their ability to communicate ideas that attacked social injustice and brutality. Now some of them seem to feel that they have struck a blow for humanity if only they can use enough four-letter words. The trouble with this kind of verbiage is not just that it is offensive but also that it is trite to the point of being threadbare.

The decline of language has been marked by a corresponding rise of incoherence. The words "you know" or "I mean" are strewn like loose gravel through everyday communication. I don't believe in raising taxes, but I would happily support a bill that would tax the bejeebers out of people each time they use "you know" or "I mean."

Words are an important part of the civilizing process. Inevitably, the debasement of language not only reflects but also produces a retreat from civility. The slightest disagreement has become an occasion for violent reactions. Television has educated an entire generation of Americans to believe that the normal way of reacting to a slight is by punching someone in the face or by bashing him on the head with a stool. On every hand, there is evidence that people are losing the art of reasonable discourse. My friends in Congress tell me that in recent years the tone of letters from constituents has drastically changed. At one time, most letters tried to state a position reasonably. Today, people seem to feel that denunciation is the standard form.

My hope, from my earliest days at the *Saturday Review*, was that the magazine would help develop a language that transcends force. That was why it was one of the first journals to call attention to the implications of nuclear weapons. We didn't think that we could keep the planet from blowing up in our faces unless the language of force gave way to ideas that could institutionalize peace. To suppose that a nation could detach itself from moral dictates and yet remain free of violence was as irrational as imagining that an individual could live in anarchy and yet be secure.

I am sad, but not altogether so. There are good signs. Some of the things for which the magazine campaigned over the years are showing progress. Around the entire world today, people are coming to realize that they need not acquiesce in their own destruction. They dare to believe that this world and everything in it belongs to them. They insist that the conditions be created that will make it unnecessary for them to kill or be killed. They do not believe that they need be doomed by computer forecasts of a barren world. And they are ready for the leadership that will summon them to the cause of a rational collective existence.

Humanity's greatest problem has never been the absence of answers to complex situations. Its greatest problem has been the absence of will to attack problems. I could think of no higher function for the *Saturday Review* than to liberate people from feelings of helplessness or hopelessness. Progress begins with the belief that what is necessary is possible. Hope is a practical reality because it supplies the energy for converting intangibles into tangibles.

The *Saturday Review* tried to live within this philosophical frame. The general shape of this frame is recognizable by all those who have a high regard for minds like John Milton, John Stuart Mill, Thomas Jefferson, William James, Oliver Wendell Holmes, Alfred North Whitehead, Learned Hand. All these giants combined their love of language with devotion to the conditions of a free and creative society. All were energized by the possibilities of a humane and reasonably safe world.

I am especially proud of the magazine's role in organizing the relief and rehabilitation program in Hiroshima after the atomic bombing. Few experiences in my life have been more rewarding or gratifying than the project that brought disfigured young women from Hiroshima to the United States for plastic and reconstructive surgery. I am equally proud of the magazine's role in carrying out a similar project for victims of Nazi medical experimentation, as well as the project that brought medical relief to thousands of children in war-torn Biafra.

I suppose that, in the sum total of things today, the death of another magazine is not to be regarded as a matter of great consequence. Perhaps it is important only to the extent that the conditions of creativity, no less than the works of creativity, are considered important. It is important only to the extent that antidotes to shabbiness and schlock are important. It is important only to the extent that brutality, blood baths and squalor have to be eradicated. It is important only to the extent that radiant musings are important.

Content

1. Cousins uses the demise of the *Saturday Review* as an occasion to speak out against a number of things he finds objectionable about present-day American life. List the topics that he covers in the essay, then determine how he unites them under a common theme. In a sentence, explain the main theme of the essay.

2. Cousins seems to believe that the greatest obstacle to solving problems is not the absence of answers but rather "feelings of helplessness and hopelessness." To what extent does this view apply to problems you have encountered? In your opinion, are Americans feeling more helpless and hopeless than before?

3. Go to the library and look at one or two issues of the *Saturday Review*, then compare your impression of the magazine to Cousins' epitaph for it. How effectively does he capture the "personality" of the magazine? You may want to look at an early issue and a later one to determine how the magazine changed over the years.

Technique

1. In the second paragraph, Cousins describes the distant hills he sees as he is writing his essay. How did this description affect you? Why might a writer want to include such detail?

2. Cousins devotes the first half of his essay to a strong, perhaps even bitter, critique of declining taste and corrupt language. The latter half of the essay expresses more optimistic views. What are the advantages and disadvantages of organizing an essay in such a way?

3. Does the essay give a strong indication of what audience Cousins intended it for? Describe its audience, pointing to specific characteristics in the essay—the tone, the vocabulary, proper names, for example—that contributed to your conception of the audience.

Language

1. "The words 'you know' or 'I mean,' " Cousins complains, "are strewn like loose gravel through everyday communication." The next time you converse with friends, try to determine the extent to which they use these or similar words. Is Cousins justified in objecting strongly to the habitual use of such phrases? Explain your answer.
2. Judging from your experience, is Cousins correct in suggesting that Americans are becoming much less capable of solving disagreements verbally and more likely to solve even minor problems through violence? Explain.

Vocabulary

irrelevance   puerile
verbiage   antidote
intangible   denunciation
tangible

Writing Suggestions

1. Cousins writes, "My friends in Congress tell me that in recent years the tone of letters from constituents has drastically changed. At one time, most letters from constituents tried to state a position reasonably. Today, people seem to feel that denunciation is the standard form." Choose a political issue that particularly interests you and write two drafts of a letter to your Congressman. In the first draft, adopt an angry tone; in the second, state your position reasonably. Then try to assess which letter would be more effective from the Congressman's point of view and why.
2. Over a week's time, listen to conversations among your friends and acquaintances and observe the kind of words and tag-phrases they repeatedly use, such as "you know" or "I mean." At week's end try to classify the list and then write a brief essay in which you explain the types of words that are used and speculate about why people use them. Incorporate specific words and phrases in your essay for illustration.

As the Lingo Languishes
M. F. K. Fisher

> M. F. K. Fisher (b. 1908) has written on cooking and eating since 1937, when her first book, Serve It Forth, appeared. Since then she has written over a dozen books on gastronomical subjects as diverse as California wine, French provincial cooking, and the physiology of taste. Like most of her writing, "As the Lingo Languishes" is witty, opinionated and informative. The essay first defines "hunger," and then analyzes the language of food advertisers in the context of that definition. Her essential question seems to be "Why do we have to be told what to eat and how to eat it?"

Hunger is, to describe it most simply, an urgent need for food. It is a craving, a desire. It is, I would guess, much older than man as we now think of him, and probably synonymous with the beginnings of sex. It is strange that we feel that anything as intrinsic as this must continually be wooed and excited, as if it were an unwilling and capricious part of us. If someone is not hungry, it indicates that his body does not, for a time and a reason, want to be fed. The logical thing, then, is to let him rest. He will either die, which he may have been meant to do, or he will once more feel the craving, the desire, the urgency to *eat*. He will have to do that before he can satisfy most of his other needs. Then he will revive again, which apparently he was meant to do.

It is hard to understand why this instinct to eat must be importuned, since it is so strong in all relatively healthy bodies. But in our present Western world, we face a literal bombardment of cajolery from all the media, to eat this or that. It is as if we had been born without appetite, and must be led gently into an introduction to oral satisfaction and its increasingly dubious results, the way nubile maidens in past centuries were prepared for marriage proposals and then their legitimate defloration.

The language that is developing, in this game of making us *want* to eat, is far from subtle. To begin with, we must be made to feel that we really find the whole atavistic process difficult, or embarrassing or boring. We must be coaxed and cajoled to crave one advertised product rather than another, one taste, one presentation of something that we might have chosen anyway, if let alone.

The truth is that we are born hungry and in our own ways will die so. But modern food advertising assumes that we are by nature bewildered and listless. As a matter of fact, we come into the world howling for Mother's Milk. We leave it, given a reasonable length of time, satisfied with much the same bland if lusty precursor of "pap and pabulum," tempered perhaps with a brush of wine on our lips to ease the parting of body and spirit. And in between, today, now, we are assaulted with the most insulting distortion of our sensory linguistics that I can imagine. We are treated like innocents and idiots by the advertisers, here in America and in Western Europe. (These are the only two regions I know, even slightly, but I feel sure that this same attack on our innate common sense is going on in the Orient, in India, in Brazil . . .)

We are told, on radio and television and in widely distributed publications, not only how but what to eat, and when, and where. The pictures are colorful. The prose, often written by famous people, is deliberately persuasive, if often supercilious in a way that makes us out as clumsy louts, gastronomical oafs badly in need of guidance toward the satisfaction of appetites we are unaware of. And by now, with this constant attack on innate desires, an attack that can be either overt or subliminal, we apparently feel fogged-out, bombed, bewildered about whether we really crave some peanut butter on crackers as a post-amour snack, or want to sleep forever. And first, before varied forms of physical dalliance, should we share with our partner a French aperitif that keeps telling us to, or should we lead up to our accomplishments by sipping a tiny glass of Sicilian love potion?

The language for this liquid aphro-cut is familiar to most of us, thanks to lush ads in all the media. It becomes even stronger as we go into solid foods. Sexually the ads are aimed at two main groups: the Doers and the Dones. Either reader/viewer/listener is out to woo a lover or has married and acquired at least two children and needs help to keep the machismo-level high. Either way, one person is supposed to feed another so as to get the partner into bed and then, if possible, to pay domestic maintenance—that is, foot the bills.

One full-page color ad, for instance, shows six shots of repellently mingled vegetables, and claims boldly that these combinations "will do almost anything to get a husband's attentions." They will "catch his passing fancy . . . on the first vegetables he might even notice." In short, the ad goes on with skilled persuasion, "they're vegetables your husband can't ignore." This almost promises that he may not ignore the cook either, a heartening if vaguely lewd thought if the pictures in the ad are any intimation of his tastes.

It is plain that if a man must be kept satisfied at table, so must his progeny, and advertisers know how to woo mothers as well as plain sexual companions. Most of their nutritional bids imply somewhat unruly family life, that only food can ease: "No more fights over who gets what," one ad proposes, as it suggests buying not one but three different types of frozen but "crisp hot fried chicken at a price that take-out can't beat": thighs and drumsticks, breast portions, and wings, all coated with the same oven-crunchy-golden skin, and fresh from freezer to stove in minutes. In the last quarter of this family ad there is a garishly bright new proposal, the "no-fire, sure-fire, barbecue-sauced" chicken. Personal experience frowns on this daring departure from the national "finger-lickin' " syndrome: with children who fight over who gets what, it would be very messy . . .

It is easy to continue such ever-loving family-style meals, as suggested by current advertising, all in deceptively alluring color in almost any home-oriented magazine one finds. How about enjoying a "good family western," whatever that may be, by serving a mixture of "redy-rice" and leftover chicken topped with a blenderized sauce of ripe avocado? This is called "love food from California," and it will make us "taste how the West was won." The avocado, the ad goes on, will "open new frontiers of wholesome family enjoyment." And of course the pre-spiced-already-seasoned "instant" rice, combined with cooked chicken, will look yummy packed into the hollowed fruit shells and covered with nutlike green stuff. All this will help greatly to keep the kids from hitting each other about who gets what.

The way to a man's heart is through his stomach, we have been assured for a couple of centuries, and for much longer than that, good wives as well as noted courtesans have given their time and thought to keeping the male belly full (and the male liver equally if innocently enlarged). By now this precarious mixture of sex and gastronomy has come out of the pantry, so to speak, and ordinary cookbook shelves show *Cuisine d'amour* and *Venus in the Kitchen* alongside Mrs. Rombauer and Julia Child.

In order to become a classic, which I consider the last two to be, any creation, from a potato soufflé to a marble bust or a skyscraper, must be honest, and that is why most cooks, as well as their methods, are never known. It is also why dishonesty in the kitchen is driving us so fast and successfully to the world of convenience foods and franchised eateries.

If we look at a few of the so-called cookbooks now providing a kind of armchair gastronomy (to read while we wait for the wife and kids to get ready to pile in the car for supper at the nearest drive-in), we understand without either amazement or active nausea some such "homemade" treat as I was brought lately by a generous neighbor. The recipe she proudly passes along to me, as if it were her great-grandmother's secret way to many a heart, was from a best-selling new cookbook, and it included a large package of sweet chocolate bits, a box of "Butter Fudge" chocolate cake mix, a package of instant vanilla pudding, and a cup of imitation mayonnaise. It was to be served with synthetic whipped cream sprayed from an aerosol can. It was called *Old-Fashion Fudge Torte*.

This distortion of values, this insidious numbing of what we once knew without question as either True or False, can be blamed, in part anyway, on the language we hear and read every day and night, about the satisfying of such a basic need as hunger. Advertising, especially in magazines and books devoted to such animal satisfaction, twists us deftly into acceptance of the new lingo of gastronomical seduction.

A good example: an impossibly juicy-looking pork chop lies like a Matisse odalisque in an open microwave oven, cooked until "fall-from-the-bone-tender." This is a new word. It still says that the meat is so overcooked that it will fall off its bone (a dubious virtue!), but it is supposed to beguile the reader into thinking that he or she (1) speaks a special streamlined language and (2) deserves to buy an oven to match, and (3) appreciates all such finer things in life. It takes *know-how*, the ad assures us subliminally, to understand all that "fall-from-the-bone-tender" really means!

This strange need to turn plain descriptive English into hyphenated hyperbole can be found even in the best gastronomical reviews and articles, as well as magazine copy. How about "fresh-from-the-oven apple cobbler," as described by one of the more reputable food writers of today? What would be wrong, especially for someone who actually knows syntax and grammar, in saying "apple cobbler, fresh from the oven"? A contemporary answer is that the multiple adjective is more . . . uh . . . contemporary. This implies that it should reach the conditioned brain cells of today's reader in a more understandable, coherent way—or does it?

The vocabulary of our kitchen comes from every part of the planet, sooner or later, because as we live, so we speak. After the Norman Conquest in 1066, England learned countless French nouns and verbs that are now part of both British and American cooking language: *appetite, dinner, salmon, sausage, lemon, fig, almond*, and on and on. We all say *roast, fry, boil*, and we make *sauces* and put them in *bowls* or on *plates*. And the German kitchen, the Aztecan: they too gave us words like *cookie* and *chocolate*. We say *borscht* easily (Russian before it was Yiddish). From slave-time Africa there is the word *gumbo*, for okra, and in *benne* biscuits there is the black man's sesame. Some people say that *alcohol* came from the nonalcoholic Arabs.

But what about the new culinary language of the media, the kind we now hear and view and read? What can "freezer-fresh" mean? *Fresh* used to imply new, pure, lively. Now it means, at best, that when a food was packaged, it would qualify as ready to be eaten: "oven-fresh" cookies a year on the shelf, "farm-fresh" eggs laid last spring, "corn-on-the-cob fresh" dehydrated vegetable soup-mix. . .

Personal feelings and opinions and prejudices (sometimes called skunners) have a lot to do with our reactions to gastronomical words, and other kinds. I know a man who finally divorced his wife because, even by indirection, he could not cure her of "calling up." She called up people, and to her it meant that she used the telephone—that is, she was not calling across a garden or over a fence, but was calling up when she could not *see* her friends. Calling and calling up are entirely different, she and a lot of interested amateur semanticists told her husband. He refused to admit this. "Why not simply *telephone* them? To telephone you don't say telephone *up*," he would say. Her phrase continued to set his inner teeth, the ones rooted directly in his spiritual jaw, on such an edge that he finally fled. She called up to tell me.

This domestic calamity made me aware, over many years but never with such anguish, how *up* can dangle in our language. And experience has shown me that if a word starts dangling, it is an easy mark for the careless users and the overt rapists of syntax and meaning who write copy for mass-media outlets connected, for instance, with hunger and its current quasi-satisfactions. Sometimes the grammatical approach is fairly conventional and old-fashioned, and the *up* is tacked onto a verb in a fairly comprehensible way. "Perk up your dinner," one magazine headline begs us, with vaguely disgusting suggestions about how to do it. "Brighten up a burger," a full-page lesson in salad making with an instant powder tells us. (This ad sneaks in another call on home unity with its "unusually delicious . . . bright . . . tasty" offering: "Sit back and listen to the cheers," it says. "Your family will give them to this tasty-zesty easy-to-make salad!")

Of course *up* gets into the adjectives as well as the verbs: *souped up chicken* and *souped up dip* are modish in advertising for canned pudding-like concoctions that fall in their original shapes from tin to saucepan or mixing bowl, to be blended with liquids to make fairly edible "soups," or to serve in prefab sauces as handy vehicles for clams or peanuts or whatever is added to the can-shaped glob to tantalize drinkers to want one more Bloody Mary. They dip up the mixture on specially stiffened packaged "chips" made of imitation tortillas or even imitation reconditioned potatoes, guaranteed not to crumble, shatter, or otherwise mess up the landscape . . .

Verbs are more fun than adjectives, in this game of upmanship. And one of the best/worst of them is creeping into our vocabularies in a thoroughly unsubtle way. It is *to gourmet up*. By now the word *gourmet* has been so distorted, and so overloaded, that to people who know its real meaning it is meaningless. They have never misused it and they refuse to now. To them a gourmet is a person, and perforce the word is a noun. Probably it turned irrevocably into an adjective with descriptive terms like *gourmet-style* and *gourmet-type*. I am not sure. But it has come to mean fancy rather than fastidious. It means expensive, or exotic, or pseudo-elegant and classy and pricey. It rarely describes a person, the gourmet who knows how to eat with discreet enjoyment. It describes a style, at best, and at worst a cheap imitation of once-stylish and always costly affectation.

There is gourmet food. There are gourmet restaurants, or gourmet-style eating places. There are package frozen cubes of comestibles called gourmet that cost three times as much as plain fast foods because, the cunningly succulent mouth-watering ads propose, their sauces are made by world-famous chefs, whose magical blends of spices and herbs have been touched off by a personalized fillip of rare old Madeira. In other words, at triple the price, they are worth it because they have been gourmeted up. Not long ago I heard a young woman in a supermarket say to a friend who looked almost as gaunt and harried as she, "Oh god . . . why am I here? You ask! Harry calls to say his sales manager is coming to dinner, and I've got to gourmet up the pot roast!"

I slow my trundle down the pushcart aisle.

"I could slice some olives into it, maybe? Pitted. Or maybe dump in a can of mushrooms. Sliced. It's got to be more expensive."

The friend says, "A cup of wine? Red. Or sour cream . . . a kind of Stroganoff . . . ?"

I worm my way past them, feeling vaguely worried. I long to tell them something—perhaps not to worry.

There are, of course, even more personal language shocks than the one that drove a man to leave his dear girl because she had to call people up. Each of us has his own, actively or dimly connected with hunger (which only an adamant Freudian could call his!). It becomes a real embarrassment, for example, when a friend or a responsible critic of cookbooks or restaurants uses words like *yummy*, or *scrumptious*. There is no dignity in such infantile evasions of plain words like *good*—or even *delicious* or *excellent*.

My own word aversion is longstanding, and several decades from the first time I heard it I still pull back, like the flanges of a freshly opened oyster. It is the verb *to drool*, when applied to written prose, and especially to anything I myself have written. Very nice people have told me, for a long time now, that some things they have read of mine, in books or magazines, have made them drool. I know they mean to compliment me. They are saying that my use of words makes them oversalivate, like hapless dogs waiting for a bell to say "Meat!" to them. It has made them more alive than they were, more active. They are grateful to me, perhaps, for being reminded that they are still functioning, still aware of some of their hungers.

I too should be grateful, and even humble, that I have reminded people of what fun it is, vicariously or not, to eat/live. Instead I am revolted. I see a slavering slobbering maw. It dribbles helplessly, in a Pavlovian response. It *drools*. And drooling, not over a meaty bone or a warm bowl of slops, is what some people have done over my printed words. This has long worried me. I feel grateful but repelled. They are nice people, and I like them and I like dogs, but dogs *must* drool when they are excited by the prospect of the satisfaction of alerted tastebuds, and two-legged people do not need to, and in general I know that my reaction to the fact that some people slobber like conditioned animals is a personal skunner, and that I should accept it as such instead of meeting it like a stiff-upper-lipped Anglo-Saxon (and conditioned!) nanny.

I continue, however, to be regretfully disgusted by the word *drool* in connection with all writing about food, as well as my own. And a few fans loyal enough to resist being hurt by this statement may possibly call me up!

It is too easy to be malicious, but certainly the self-styled food experts of our current media sometimes seem overtly silly enough to be fair game. For anyone with half an ear for the English-American language we write and speak, it is almost impossible not to chuckle over the unending flow of insults to our syntax and grammar, not to mention our several levels of intelligence.

How are we supposed to react to descriptive phrases like "crisply crunchy, to snap in your mouth"? We know this was written, and for pay, by one or another of the country's best gastronomical hacks. We should not titter. He is a good fellow. Why then does he permit himself to say that some corn on the cob is so tender that "it dribbles milk down your chin"? He seems, whether or not he means well, to lose a little of the innate dignity that we want from our gourmet-judges. He is like a comedian who with one extra grimace becomes coarse instead of funny, or like an otherwise sensitive reader who says that certain writing makes him drool.

Not all our food critics, of course, are as aware of language as the well-known culinary experts who sign magazine articles and syndicated columns. And for one of them, there are a hundred struggling copywriters who care less about mouth-watering prose than about filling ad space with folksy propaganda for "kwik" puddings and suchlike. They say shamelessly, to keep their jobs, that Mom has just told them how to make instant homemade gravy taste "like I could never make before! *Believe* me," they beg, "those other gravies just aren't the same! This has a real homemade flavor and a rich brown color. Just add it to your pan drippings." And so on.

Often these unsung kitchen psalmists turn, with probably desperation, to puns and other word games. They write, for instance, that frozen batter-fried fish are so delicious that "one crunch and you're hooked!" Oh, hohoho ha ha. And these same miserable slaves produce millions of words, if they are fortunate enough to find and keep their jobs, about things like synthetic dough that is "pre-formed" into "old-fashioned shapes that taste cooky-fresh and crunchy" in just fifteen minutes from freezer to oven to the kiddies' eager paws and maws.

When the hacks have proved that they can sling such culinary lingo, they are promoted to a special division that deals even more directly with oral satisfaction. They write full-page ads in juicy color, about cocktail nibbles with "a fried-chicken taste that's lip-lickin' good." This, not too indirectly, is aimed to appeal to hungry readers familiar with a franchised fried chicken that is of course known worldwide as finger-lickin good, and even packaged Kitty Krums that are whisker-lickin good. (It is interesting and reassuring, although we must drop a few g's to understand it, that modern gastronomy still encourages us to indulge in public tongueplay.)

Prose by the copywriters usually stays coy, but is somewhat more serious about pet foods than humanoid provender. Perhaps it is assumed that most people who buy kibbles do not bother to read the printed information on all four sides of their sacks, but simply pour the formula into bowls on the floor and hope for the best. Or perhaps animal-food companies recognize that some of their slaves are incurably dedicated to correct word usage. Often the script on a bag of dry pet food is better written than most paperback novels. Possibly some renegade English instructor has been allowed to explain "Why Your Cat Will Enjoy This." He is permitted tiny professorial jokes, now and then: "As Nutritious As It Is Delicious," one caption says, and another section is called "Some Reading on Feeding," and then the prose goes all out, almost euphorically, with "Some Raving on Saving." The lost academician does have to toss in a few words like *munchy* to keep his job, but in general there is an enjoyably relaxed air about the unread prose on pet-food packages, as opposed to the stressful cuteness of most fashionable critics of our dining habits.

Of course the important thing is to stay abreast of the lingo, it seems. Stylish restaurants go through their phases, with beef Wellington and chocolate mousse high in favor one year and strictly for Oskaloossa, Missouri, the next. We need private dining-out guides as well as smart monthly magazines to tell us what we are eating tonight, as well as what we are paying for it.

A lot of our most modish edibles are dictated by their scarcity, as always in the long history of gastronomy. In 1979, for instance, it became *de rigueur* in California to serve caviar in some guise, usually with baked or boiled potatoes, because shipments from Iran grew almost as limited as they had long been from Russia. (Chilled caviar, regal fare, was paired with the quaintly plebeian potato many years ago, in Switzerland I think, but by 1979 its extravagant whimsy had reached Hollywood and the upper West Coast by way of New York, so that desperate hostesses were buying and even trying to "homemake" caviar from the Sacramento River sturgeons. Results: usually lamentable, but well meant.)

All this shifting of gustatory snobbism should probably have more influence on our language than it does. Writers for both elegant magazines and "in" guides use much the same word-appeal as do the copywriters for popular brands of convenience foods. They may not say "lip-smackin" or "de-lish," but they manage to imply what their words will make readers do. They use their own posh patter, which like the humbler variety seldom bears any kind of scrutiny, whether for original meaning or plain syntax.

How about "unbelievably succulent luscious scallops which boast a nectar-of-the-sea freshness"? Or "a *buerre blanc*, that ethereally light, grandmotherly sauce"? Or "an onion soup, baked *naturellement*, melting its knee-deep crust of cheese and croutons"? Dressings are "teasingly-tart," not teasing or tart or even teasingly tart. They have "breathtakingly visual appeal," instead of looking yummy, and some of them, perhaps fortunately, are "almost too beautiful to describe," "framed in a picture-perfect garnish of utter perfection and exquisiteness," "a pinnacle of gastronimical delight." (Any of these experiences can be found, credit card on the ready, in the bistrots-of-the-moment.)

It is somewhat hard to keep one's balance, caught between the three stools of folksy lure, stylish gushing, and a dictionary of word usage. How does one *parse*, as my grandfather would say, a complete sentence like, "The very pinkness it was, of mini-slices"? Or "A richly eggy and spiritous Zabaglione, edged in its serving dish with tiny dots of grenadine"? These are not sentences, at least to my grandfather and to me, and I think *spirituous* is a better word in this setting, and I wonder whether the dots of grenadine were wee drops of the sweet syrup made from pomegranates or the glowing seeds of the fruit itself, and how and why anyone would preserve them for a chic restaurant. And were those pink mini-slices from a lamb, a calf? Then there are always verbs to ponder on, in such seductive reports on what and where to dine. One soup "packs chunks" of something or other, to prove its masculine heartiness in a stylish lunchtime brasserie. "Don't forget to special-order!" Is this a verb, a split infinitive, an attempt of the reporter to sound down-to-earth?

Plainly it is as easy to carp, criticize, even dismiss such unworthy verbiage as it is to quibble and shudder about what the other media dictate, that we may subsist. And we continue to carp, criticize, dismiss—and to *eat*, not always as we are told to, and not always well, either! But we were born *hungry* . . .

Content

1. Fisher seems to have several reasons for objecting to the language of food advertising. List as many of these reasons as you can, stating them as complete sentences.
2. Two important words that Fisher takes some pains to define are "hunger" and "gourmet." In your own words, briefly summarize her definitions, and be prepared to speculate why Fisher gave these two words so much attention in the essay.
3. Fisher finds much to poke fun at in the language of ads for food and in the writings of food experts. What assumptions about food seem to underlie her objections?

Technique

1. Examine the structure of Fisher's essay and assess its effectiveness. For example, what purpose was served by dividing the essay into three parts? Does each section develop a single major point? Explain.
2. In paragraph 18, Fisher relates an anecdote about a man who divorced his wife. In your opinion, what is the point of this paragraph and what might have been Fisher's reason for including it?
3. One of Fisher's points is that food advertising is unnecessary because we are naturally hungry; consequently, it is difficult to take the language of such advertising seriously. On the other hand, she is genuinely disturbed by how copywriters use language. Does the tone of the essay reveal this mix of seriousness and humor? As you answer this question, cite examples in the essay that support your points and explain how they do so.
4. In paragraph 6, Fisher divides the audience of food advertisements into two groups, the Doers and the Dones. How helpful is this classification, and how does she distinguish between these two groups?

Language

1. Review and summarize Fisher's objections to the advertising phrases, "fall-from-the-bone-tender" (paragraph 14) and "freezer-fresh" (paragraph 17).
2. Fisher criticizes advertisers and restaurant critics for evading plain words like "good," "delicious," and "excellent." Speculate about why such writers would avoid using these plain words. Based on your own conversational habits, would you say that people are generally tempted to replace plain adjectives with more exotic ones?
3. Clip an article on cooking or on dining out from a newspaper; analyze its tone and diction, paying particular attention to the kinds of words and phrases to which Fisher objects in her essay. Do you find any new words or phrases you find particularly amusing or offensive? Explain.
4. Many readers will find Fisher's vocabulary in this essay difficult. Based on your own response to the diction of the essay, what audience do you suppose Fisher had in mind when she wrote the essay? Would these be the same people you would expect to "drool" over Fisher's writing, as she claims? Explain.

Vocabulary

capricious	nubile	affectation
defloration	supercilious	discreet
listless	overt	adamant
subliminal	progeny	culinary
importune	gastronomy	hyperbole

Writing Suggestions

1. Clip a full-page food advertisement from a magazine, then write an essay that analyzes the visual appeal and the use of language in the advertisement. You may want to speculate about the audience to which the advertisement was aimed and about how successful the presentation is in selling the product, from your point of view.
2. Over a two- or three-day period, make a list of the memorable words, phrases, and jingles in food advertising (for restaurants, food products, and so on) from radio, television, and magazines. Then write an essay in which you classify the various types of language that you listed.
3. Assume that you are an advertising copy-writer for a food product of your choice. Write a one-page radio commercial for the product, along

with a one-paragraph explanation of the rationale behind your choice of words, phrases, and overall advertising strategy. Do you suppose Fisher would approve of your ad?

It's Natural! It's Organic! Or Is It?
Consumer's Union

Consumer's Union is a nonprofit organization that informs consumers about the quality of various goods and services. In the following essay, the Union investigates Americans' susceptibility to "all-but-deceptive" advertising. The discussion is centered on the words "natural" and "organic," which are, as the numerous examples show, defined loosely and used less than truthfully by advertisers and producers of foods. The essay goes on to classify several methods of deception in the use of these words, and finally argues for consumer awareness and governmental regulation.

"No artificial flavors or colors!" reads the Nabisco advertisement in *Progressive Grocer*, a grocery trade magazine. "And research shows that's exactly what consumers are eager to buy." 1

The ad, promoting Nabisco's *Sesame Wheats* as "a natural whole wheat cracker," might raise a few eyebrows among thoughtful consumers of Nabisco's *Wheat Thins* and *Cheese Nips*, which contain artificial colors, or of its *Ginger Snaps* and *Oreo Cookies*, which have artificial flavors. But Nabisco has not suddenly become a champion of "natural" foods. Like other giants of the food industry, the company is merely keeping its eye on what will produce a profit. 2

Nabisco's trade ad, which was headlined "A Natural for Profits," is simply a routine effort by a food processor to capitalize on the concerns that consumers have about the safety of the food they buy. 3

Supermarket shelves are being flooded with "natural" products, some of them containing a long list of chemical additives. And some products that never did contain additives have suddenly sprouted "natural" or "no preservative" labels. Along with the new formulations and labels have come higher prices, since the food industry has realized that consumers are willing to pay more for products they think are especially healthful. 4

The mass merchandising of "natural" foods is a spillover onto supermarket shelves of a phenomenon once confined to health-food stores, as major food manufacturers enter what was once the exclu- 5

It's Natural! It's Organic! Or Is It?

sive territory of small entrepreneurs. Health-food stores were the first to foster and capitalize on the growing consumer interest in nutrition and are still thriving. Along with honey-sweetened snacks, "natural" vitamins, and other "natural" food products, the health-food stores frequently feature "organic" foods.

Like the new merchandise in supermarkets, the products sold at healthfood stores carry the implication that they're somehow better for you—safer or more nutritious. In this report, we'll examine that premise, looking at both "natural" foods, which are widely sold, and "organic" foods, which are sold primarily at health-food stores. While the terms "natural" and "organic" are often used loosely, "organic" generally refers to the way food is grown (without pesticides or chemical fertilizers) and "natural" to the character of the ingredients (no preservatives or artificial additives) and to the fact that the food product has undergone minimal processing.

Langendorf Natural Lemon Flavored Creme Pie contains no cream. It does contain sodium propionate, certified food colors, sodium benzoate, and vegetable gum.

That's natural?

Yes indeed, says L.A. Cushman Jr., chairman of American Bakeries Co., the Chicago firm that owns Langendorf. The word "natural," he explains, modifies "lemon flavored," and the pie contains oil from lemon rinds. "The lemon flavor," Cushman states "comes from the natural lemon flavor as opposed to artificial lemon flavor, assuming there is such a thing as artificial lemon flavor."

Welcome to the world of natural foods.

You can eat your "natural" way from one end of the supermarket to the other. Make yourself a sandwich of *Kraft Cracker Barrel Natural Cheddar Cheese* on *Better Way Natural Whole Grain Wheat Nugget Bread* spread with *Autumn Natural Margarine*. Wash it down with *Anheuser-Busch Natural Light Beer* or *Rich-Life Natural Orange NutriPop*. Snack on any number of brands of "natural" potato chips and "natural" candy bars. And don't exclude your pet: Feed your dog *Gravy Train Dog Food With Natural Beef Flavor* or, if it's a puppy, try *Blue Mountain Natural Style Puppy Food*.

The "natural" bandwagon doesn't end at the kitchen. You can bathe in *Batherapy Natural Mineral Bath* (sodium sesquicarbonate, isopropyl myristate, fragrance, D & C Green No. 5, D & C Yellow No. 10 among its ingredients), using *Queen Helen "All-Natural" Amino Peptide Shampoo* (propylene glycol, hydroxyethyl cellulose, methylparaben, D & C Red No. 3, D & C Brown No. 1) and *Organic Aid Natural Clear Soaps*. Then, if you're so inclined, you can apply *Naturade Conditioning Mascara with National Protein* (stearic acid, PVP, butylene glycol, sorbitan sesquioleate, triethanolamine, imidazolidinyl urea, methylparaben, propylparaben).

At its ridiculous extreme, the "natural" ploy extends to furniture, cigarettes, denture adhesives, and shoes.

The word "natural" does not have to be synonymous with "ripoff." Over the years, the safety of many food additives has been questioned. And a consumer who reads labels carefully can in fact find some foods in supermarkets that have been processed without additives.

But the word "natural" does not guarantee that. All too often, as the above examples indicate, the word is used more as a key to higher profits. Often, it implies a health benefit that does not really exist

Co-op News, the publication of the Berkeley Co-op, the nation's largest consumer-cooperative store chain, reported on "two 15-ounce cans of tomato sauce, available side-by-side" at one of its stores. One sauce, called *Health Valley*, claimed on its label to have "no citric acid, no sugars, no preservatives, no artificial colors or flavors." There were none of those ingredients in the Co-op's house brand, either, but their absence was hardly worth noting on the label, since canned tomato sauce almost never contains artificial colors or flavors and doesn't need preservatives after being heated in the canning process. The visible difference between the two products was price, not ingredients. The *Health Valley* tomato sauce was selling for 85 cents; the Co-op house brand, for only 29 cents.

One supermarket industry consultant estimates that 7 percent of all processed food products now sold are touted as "natural." And that could be just the beginning. A Federal Trade Commission report noted that 63 percent of people polled in a survey agreed with the statement, "Natural foods are more nutritious than other foods." Thirty-nine percent said they regularly buy food because it is "natural," and 47 percent said they are willing to pay 10 percent more for a food that is "natural."

According to those who have studied the trend, the consumer's desire for "natural" foods goes beyond the fear of specific chemicals. "There is a mistrust of technology," says Howard Moskowitz, a taste researcher and consultant to the food industry. "There is a movement afoot to return to simplicity in all aspects of life." A spokeswoman for Lever Bros., one of the nation's major food merchandisers, adds: "'Natural' is a psychological thing of everyone wanting to get out of the industrial world."

Because consumers are acting out of such vague, undefined feelings, they aren't sure what they should be getting when they buy a product labeled "natural." William Wittenberg, president of Grandma's Food Inc., comments: "Manufacturers and marketers are making an attempt to appeal to a consumer who feels he should be eating something natural, but doesn't know why. I think the marketers of the country in effect mirror back to the people what they want to hear. People have to look to themselves for their own protection." Grandma's makes a *Whole Grain Date Filled Fruit 'n Oatmeal Bar* labeled "naturally Good Flavor." The ingredients include "artificial flavor."

"Natural" foods are not necessarily preferable nor, as we have seen, necessarily natural.

Consider "natural" potato chips. They are often cut thick from unpeeled potatoes, packaged without preservatives in heavy foil bags with fancy lettering, and sold at a premium price. Sometimes, such chips include "sea salt," a product whose advantage over conventional "land" salt has not been demonstrated. The packaging is intended to give the impression that "natural" potato chips are less of a junk food than regular chips. But nutritionally there is no difference. Both are made from the same food, the potato, and both have been processed so that they are high in salt and in calories.

Sometimes the "natural" products may have ingredients you'd prefer to avoid. *Quaker 100% Natural* cereal, for example, contains 24 percent sugars, a high percentage, considering it's not promoted as a sugared cereal. (*Kellogg's Corn Flakes* has 7.8 percent sugar.) Many similar "natural" granola-type cereals have oil added, giving them a much higher fat content than conventional cereals.

Taste researcher Moskowitz notes that food processors are "trying to signal to the consumer a sensory impact that can be called natural." Two of the most popular signals, says Moskowitz, are honey and coconut. But honey is just another sugar, with no significant nutrients other than calories, and coconut is especially high in saturated fats.

While many processed foods are less nutritious than their fresh counterparts, processing can sometimes help foods: Freezing preserves nutrients that could be lost if fresh foods are not consumed quickly; pasteurization kills potentially dangerous bacteria in milk. Some additives are also both safe and useful. Sorbic acid, for instance, prevents the growth of potentially harmful molds in cheese and other products, and sodium benzoate has been used for more than 70 years to prevent the growth of microorganisms in acidic foods.

"Preservative" has become a dirty word, to judge from the number of "no preservative" labels on food products. Calcium propionate might sound terrible on a bread label, but this mildrew-retarding substance occurs naturally in both raisins and Swiss cheese. "Bread without preservatives could well cost you more than bread with them," says Vernal S. Packard Jr., a University of Minnesota nutrition professor. "Without preservatives, the bread gets stale faster; it may go moldy with the production of hazardous aflatoxin. And already we in the United States return [to producers] 100 million pounds of bread each year—this in a world nagged by hunger and malnutrition."

Nor are all "natural" substances safe. Sassafras tea was banned by the U.S. Food and Drug Administration several years ago because it contains safrole, which has produced liver cancer in laboratory animals. Kelp, a seaweed that is becoming increasingly fashionable as a dietary supplement, can have a high arsenic content. Aflatoxin, produced by a mold that can grow on improperly stored peanuts, corn, and grains, is a known carcinogen.

To complicate matters, our palates have become attuned to many unnatural tastes. "We don't have receptors on our tongues that signal "natural," says taste researcher Moskowitz. He points out, for instance, that a panel of consumers would almost certainly reject a natural lemonade "in favor of a lemonade scientifically designed to taste natural. If you put real lemon, sugar, and water together, people would reject it as harsh. They are used to flavors developed by flavor houses." Similarly, Moskowitz points out, many consumers say that for health reasons they prefer less salty food—but the results of various taste tests have contradicted this, too.

In the midst of all this confusion, it's not surprising that the food industry is having a promotional field day. Companies are using various tactics to convince the consumer that a food product is "natural"—and hence preferable. Here are some of the most common:

The indeterminate modifier. Use a string of adjectives and claim that "natural" modifies only the next adjective in line, not the product itself. Take *Pillsbury Natural Chocolate Flavored Chocolate Chip Cookies*. Many a buyer might be surprised to learn from the fine print that these cookies contain artificial flavor, as well as the chemical antioxidant BHA. But Pillsbury doesn't bat an eyelash at this. "We're not trying to mislead anybody," says a company representative, explaining that the word "natural" modifies only "chocolate flavored," while the artificial flavoring is vanilla. Then why not call the product "Chocolate Chip Cookies with Natural Chocolate Flavoring"? "From a labeling point of view, we're trying to use a limited amount of space" was the answer.

Innocence by association. Put nature on your side. *Life Cinnamon Flavor High Protein Cereal*, a Quaker Oats Co. product, contains BHA and artificial color, among other things. How could the company imply the cereal was "natural" and still be truthful? One series of *Life* boxes solves the problem neatly. The back panel has an instructional lesson for children entitled "Nature." The box uses the word "Nature" four times and "natural" once—but never actually to describe the cereal inside. Other products surround themselves with a "natural" aura by picturing outdoor or farm scenes on their packages.

The "printer's error." From time to time, readers send us food wrappers making a "natural" claim directly contradicted by the ingredients list. We have, for example, received a batch of individually wrapped *Devonsheer* crackers with a big red label saying: "A Natural Product, no preservatives." The ingredients list includes "calcium propionate (to retard spoilage)."

How could a manufacturer defend that? "At a given printing, the printer was instructed to remove 'no preservatives, natural product' when we changed ingredients, but he didn't do it," says Curtis Marshall, vice president for operations at Devonsheer Melba Corp.

The best defense. Don't defend yourself; attack the competition. Sometimes the use of the word "natural" is, well, just plain unnatural. Take the battle that has been brewing between the nation's two largest beer makers, Miller Brewing Co. and Anheuser-Busch. The latter's product, *Anheuser-Busch Natural Light Beer*, has been the object of considerable derision by Miller.

Miller wants the word "natural" dropped from Anheuser-Busch's advertisements because beers are "highly processed, complex products, made with chemical additives and other components not in their natural form."

Anheuser-Busch has responded only with some digs at Miller, charging Miller with using artificial foam stabilizer and adding an industrial enzyme instead of natural malt to reduce the caloric content of its *Miller Lite* beer.

No victor has yet emerged from the great beer war, but the industry is obviously getting edgy.

"Other brewers say it's time for the two companies to shut up," the Wall Street Journal reported. "One thing they [the other brewers] are worried about, says William T. Elliot, president of C. Schmidt & Sons, a Philadelphia brewery, is all the fuss over ingredients. Publicity about that issue is disclosing to beer drinkers that their suds include sulfuric acid, calcium sulfate, alginic acid, or amyloglucosidase."

The negative pitch. Point out in big letters on the label that the product doesn't contain something it wouldn't contain anyway. The "no artificial preservatives" label stuck on a jar of jam or jelly is true and always has been—since sugar is all the preservative jams and jellies need. Canned goods, likewise, are preserved in their manufacture—by the heat of the canning process. Then there is the "no cholesterol" claim of vegetable oils, margarines, and even (in a radio commercial) canned pineapple. Those are also true, but beside the point, since cholesterol is found only in animal products.

What can be done about such all-but-deceptive practices? One might suggest that the word "natural" is so vague as to be inherently deceptive, and therefore should not be available for promotional use. Indeed, the FTC staff suggested precisely that a few years ago but later backed away from the idea. The California legislature last year passed a weak bill defining the word "organic," but decided that political realities argued against tackling the word "natural."

"If we had included the word 'natural' in the bill, it most likely would not have gotten out of the legislature," says one legislative staff member. "When you've got large economic interests in certain areas, the tendency is to guard those interests very carefully."

Under the revised FTC staff proposal, which had not been acted on by the full commission as we went to press, the word "natural" can be used if the product has undergone only minimal processing and doesn't have artificial ingredients. That would eliminate the outright frauds, as well as the labeling of such products as Lever Bros.' *Autumn Natural Margarine*, which obviously has been highly processed from its original vegetable-oil state. But the FTC proposal might run into difficulty in defining exactly what "minimal processing" means. And it would also allow some deceptive implications. For instance, a product containing honey might be called "natural," while a food with refined sugar might not, thus implying that honey is superior to other sugars, which it is not.

A law incorporating similar regulations went into effect in Maine at the beginning of this year. If a product is to be labeled "natural" and sold in Maine, it must have undergone only minimal processing and have no additives, preservatives, or refined additions such as white flour and sugar.

So far, according to John Michael, the state legislator who sponsored the bill, food companies have largely ignored the law, but he expects the state to start issuing warnings this summer.

Content

1. According to the essay, why are American consumers susceptible to advertising campaigns featuring the words "natural" and "organic"?
2. The Consumer's Union suggests some ways in which "all-but-deceptive" advertising should be regulated. Briefly summarize these. In your view, should such advertising be regulated? Why or why not?

Technique

1. How effectively does this essay provide examples of the kind of advertising it describes? Find paragraphs in which several examples are provided, and be able to explain how the essayist avoids merely listing the examples.
2. To some extent, this essay is argumentative. Assess how fairly the essayist presents the viewpoints of "the opposition"—the companies and advertisers, that is.
3. How is this essay organized? Identify and label the sections of the essay, and explain how they are developed.
4. In your view, how effective is the essayist's classification of "the tactics of deception" toward the end of the essay? Briefly explain the categories that are set up.

Language

1. According to the essayist, how do manufacturers and advertisers manipulate and distort the meaning of the word "natural"?

2. What connotations do the words "natural" and "organic" suggest to you when you see them on the labels of products?

Vocabulary

entrepreneur	minimal	organic
ploy	natural	

Writing Suggestions

1. Write an essay about one or two other words which you believe manufacturers use deceptively in their advertising campaigns.
2. Write a one-paragraph advertisement for a product in which you manipulate a key term.

Why I'm Not Bored
Stanley Kauffmann

Stanley Kauffmann (b. 1916), who has been reviewing films for national magazines since 1958, is now regarded as one of America's best and most informed reviewers. He has been on the staff of The New Republic *since the late 1950s, although his reviews have also appeared in such magazines as* American Film *and* Horizon. *Kauffmann's collections of reviews include* A Word on Film, Figures of Light, Living Images, *and* Before My Eyes *(1980), from which "Why I'm Not Bored" is taken. In this essay, Kauffmann details the reasons for his capacity to view an average of three films a week and not become bored. As with other of his reviews and essays, this one demonstrates both his concern with film as an art form and his familiarity with the practical, business-like side of film-making as an industry.*

The two most frequent questions are: "How many films do you see a week?" "Don't you get bored with going to films?" I've been writing about them in *The New Republic* since 1958, with one intermission of a year and a half, have heard each of these questions at least once a week in that time, and am always pleased by them. As for the first, the number has varied sharply from none to twelve—usually it's about three—but the point is that most weeks it wouldn't have been less even if I weren't a critic. (And, grown gray in the ranks, I still get a thrill out of getting in free.) Once in a great while there have been too many. On two separate occasions there were two successive days in which I had to see four films each day—no kind of record but sickening to me. After each of those pairs of days it was a week before I could see another picture. But most of the time when I'm asked the question, I can't really remember how many times I've gone in the previous week or two, it all seems so natural. And therefore pleasant.

As to the second and more interesting question, the answer is a firm no. A happy no. To salute the obvious, this doesn't mean that I never see boring films or that I am unborable. On the contrary, I'm somewhat more acutely borable—by reason, I tell myself, of professional acuteness—than most of my friends. But the *idea* of going to films is never boring. The former editor of *The New Republic* once generously suggested that I also write about television from time to time. The prospect of merely crossing the living room to switch on television dramas was numbing. But even when I have to leave the house to see the most unpromising of films (and I limit myself to those with at least some sort of promise), there is something beyond the specifics of the film that tingles and attracts.

To begin with, there is the elemental kinetic aspect. As with billions of people throughout the world since 1900, the mere physical act of filmgoing is part of the kinesis of my life—the getting up and going out and the feeling of coming home, which is a somewhat different homecoming feeling from anything else except the theater (and which is totally unavailable from television). When I am not going out, rather frequently, to films (as a New Yorker this is also true for me of the theater), it's because I'm ill or sore beset with work or isolated somewhere in the country. To have my life unpunctuated by the physical act of filmgoing is almost like walking with a limp, out of my natural rhythm.

Past that there is the community, also known to billions, of being in a group dream, a group reality. This is true of the theater as well, but with films there is a paradox: because of the greater darkness there is, even in the middle of a group, the sense of private ownership of the occasion. That ownership has attachments. No one goes to a film theater—or a press screening-room—without taking with him all of his filmgoing past, including his initial fear. (For years students have been writing papers for me on their recollections of their very first film experiences, and more often than not, that first experience had included a feeling of fear.) That fear is never quite lost, perhaps, though gradually it is understood, is used to underpin and nourish other responses. No one can go to a film theater without taking with him his parents and childhood friends and the first grapplings of romance in the balcony. And no one can sit in a film theater without acknowledging, however secretly, that this is where some part of his psyche originated. Messenger boy or mogul, peasant or Pope, there can hardly be anyone alive whose secret fantasies, controlled and uncontrolled, have not in some measure been made by film. This has never been so widely true of any other art. My guess is that it is not yet true of television, may never be true in quite the same way. The size of the film screen in itself plays a part in its sacerdotal function; it ministers down to us while the television screen paws upward, smaller than we are, vulnerable to dials and switches. (If films ever really become principally available through television cassettes, as has been prophesied sporadically for years, whole psychic orders will have to be redeployed.)

All this exercise and enjoyment before we even touch matters of art, discrimination, esthetics! Once we get to the question of specific films rather than generic experience, the specter of boredom raises its threat. Some films turn out to be just as boring as feared, though not so many as the fulfilled dreads in the theater and not many more than with new fiction. No one assumes that a literary critic gets bored, yet, having worked in both kinds of criticism, I know that the rewards of poor films are more savorable, more certain, than those of poor novels.

In Westerns, however feeble, there are horses, the creak of leather, the reach of landscape. In any film there are likely to be attractive women or, if you prefer, attractive men. For myself, heterosexually straitened though I am, I get a kick out of seeing O'Toole and Newman and Redford, just as I did with Cooper and Grant and March. Then there are syntactical rewards. Richard Lester's maritime thriller *Juggernaut* missed the boat, but its editing and photography were in themselves thrilling. Visconti's *Ludwig* was drear, but the costumes were sumptuous. The music in *Once Upon a Time in the West* was like a Puccini sauna. I don't suggest that anyone go to see those films for those reasons: I'm just answering the once-a-week question.

There are other, greater things. Direction, for instance. Joseph Sargent, out of television, has done a really crisp job with *The Taking of Pelham One Two Three*. I enjoyed the way he used the subway tunnels and the racing through the streets and the compact arena of the hijacked subway car in a picture that, as a whole, was fading before it finished. (I couldn't read the novel.)

And in some dismal pictures one can often find bright spots of acting. A thriller called *11 Harrowhouse* is laden with Charles Grodin and Candice Bergen and a finale that was apparently devised by a moron on LSD; but James Mason plays an aging diamond expert, dying of cancer, who revenges himself on his niggardly employers by collaborating with thieves, and he creates a whole man, quietly, in the middle of roaring nonsense. Jon Voight has the leading role in a more seriously inane thriller, *The Odessa File*, and presents the young German journalist he is supposed to be, even to a beautifully precise accent. (Obeying the hilarious convention under which Germans in Germany, speaking English to one another in English-language films, have German accents.)

It would be easy to put together a large bouquet, a garden, several hothouses of flowers culled from poor pictures. They don't quite compensate for those pictures, not even for the waste of themselves in those pictures, still they are rewards not easily accessible in poor examples of other arts. Theater performances, yes, when they stand out from a bad script and/or a bad company. As for other matters, although the theater's symbolic systems are just as "real" as film's, they are less intensely packed to the square millimeter, and when one is forced away from the foreground by tedium, the theater's supportive symbols are less varied, less continuingly interesting. Boris Aronson's beautiful setting for *Company* didn't *continue* to make up for a dullish evening as Tonino delli Colli's cinematography almost did for Pasolini's *Decameron*.

But that's enough of scrounging, of beggarly gratitude for edible scraps amidst the swill. The chief reason for never being bored with the idea of film is that boredom is incompatible with hope, and hope is more of a constant in film than in virtually any other art in America. Fiction and poetry and dance and theater performance (as against playwriting) are in good estate, with good prospects; but (say the experts I've met) this is not true of painting or sculpture or musical composition or architecture. And no art is more persistently, almost irritatingly, pulsing with prospects than the film.

Distribution of films is in difficulties, but it always was: only the type of trouble changes. The vulgar and the violent are more popular than the good; so what else is new? Nothing rotten that happens in film—and most of what does happen is rotten—can negate the fact that it is still an avenue of possibilities, an expanding nebula of esthetic mysteries, a treasury of aptness for our time.

In 1966 I published an essay called "The Film Generation" that is now sometimes knocked because the size of the audience has not much increased, has not returned to anything like the size of the mid-1940s, and, worse, because some of the best pictures that come along—works by Bresson and Bellocchio, for instance—have short first-run lives. But I wouldn't alter much in that essay today. (Except for one addition: I've learned since writing it, by a lot of travel around the country and through four years' service on the Theater Panel of the National Endowment for the Arts, that theater appetite among young people is lesser only in size, not in urgency, to film appetite.) The film audience is smaller than it used to be because, obviously, free movies are available at home, as well as free vaudeville; but the fact that the film audience has not completely disappeared in the face of that situation is itself proof of that audience's vitality. Far from disappearing, that audience is now increasing. And if the television-threat argument were valid, there ought now to be no film theaters at all.

Blacks flocking to cheap "blaxploitation" films, yes. Kung-fu kooks, yes. Hard and soft porno for hard and soft fans, yes. But if statistics prove that those types account for a lot, statistics prove other things as well. *Somebody* is taking those thousands of film courses in those 1000-plus universities and colleges that offer them; *somebody* is buying those films books and magazines that continue to flood out, attending those festivals that continue to spring up and those film societies and campus and community series. It's not quite a nation of Bazins and Agees as yet, but to argue that the smaller audience has not improved qualitatively is either a confusion of cynicism with taste or a fear of improvement, a nostalgia for Hedda Hopper's Hollywood. The fact that Ozu doesn't run very long in the nation's biggest city doesn't prove any more about the status of the art and its audience than the fact that *Boesman and Lena* didn't break the *Hello Dolly!* record or that Berryman's *Dream Songs* didn't outsell Rod McKuen.

Film is in money trouble these days because of inflation, but so is everything, including book publishing. Relatively, money doesn't control the making of films much more than it does the publication of poetry and fiction: if film investments are higher, so are possible profits. The money squeeze is not new: finance has always worked cruelly in the film world even when money seemed to be more free (true of publishing, too), distribution has always been tyrannical, you've always been just as successful as your last picture, the putrid ones have always seemed to be surging up to our nostrils, and still the good ones have been made here and abroad—where the difficulties are different only in nomenclature or proportion—and the lesser ones have had their compensations.

To me this combination of views is hard-headed, with no touch of Pollyanna—unless there is also a touch of Pollyanna in the human race's general insistence on survival. Concurrent with our lives runs this muddied, quasi-strangulated, prostituted art, so life-crammed and responsive and variegated and embracing, so indefinable no matter how far one strings out phrases like these, that to deny it seems to me to deny the worst and the best in ourselves, a chance to help clarify which is which, and which is in the ascendant on any particular day. No matter how much I know about a film's makers or its subject before I go, I never *really* know what it's going to do to me: depress me with its vileness, or just roll past, or change my life in some degree, or some combination of all three, or affect me in some new way that I cannot imagine. So I like being asked whether filmgoing gets boring: it makes me think of what I don't know about the next film I'm going to see.

Content

1. In the middle of his essay, Kauffmann provides at least four reasons why he is not bored by films. Identify these and explain them in your own words.
2. Kauffmann states that "for years students have been writing papers for me on their recollections of their very first film experiences, and more often than not, that first experience had included a feeling of fear." To what extent does this statement characterize your own film-going experience? As you answer this question, try to define what kind of fear you think Kauffmann is referring to.
3. Kauffmann's chief reason for not being bored, he suggests, is that "boredom is incompatible with hope, and hope is more of a constant in film than in virtually any other art in America." Do you agree or disagree with this assessment of American films? Cite specific movies to support your answer. To what extent does the statement "boredom

is incompatible with hope" apply not just to film-going but to life in general?

Technique

1. "Why I'm Not Bored" is an argumentative essay insofar as it justifies Kauffmann's capacity to see several films a week throughout the year. What details of movie-going does Kauffmann provide to support his point of view? How convincing are these details?
2. Kauffmann develops his argument in part by contrasting films with both literature and television. According to Kauffmann, in what ways do movies differ from novels and television programs? In your view, how accurate are these observations?
3. Kauffmann waits until the latter part of his essay to present his chief reason for never being bored with the idea of going to movies. In your view, is this an effective technique? What might be the advantages of presenting your strongest evidence last in an essay? The disadvantages?

Language

1. As a "reviewer," Kauffmann has the job of making the reader "see" the film in his words. To what extent does he provide a vivid sense of the movies he likes and dislikes? Find at least two descriptive sentences in the essay that contain concrete images and lively verbs.
2. When Kauffmann discusses the few good aspects of what he feels are particularly bad films, he writes, "It would be easy to put together a large bouquet, a garden, several hothouses of flowers culled from poor pictures." How appropriate is this metaphor for the subject Kauffmann is attempting to describe? Explain.

Vocabulary

kinetic	deploy	esthetic
sacerdotal	laden	nomenclature
minister (verb)	niggardly	variegated
prophecy	cul	ascendant

Writing Suggestions

1. As Kauffmann indicates, the movie industry is suffering in part because so many movies are available on television. Write an essay in which

you argue either for or against the value of seeing movies in a theater instead of at home on television.

2. Write a 2–3 page review of a movie you have seen recently. In justifying your evaluation of the movie, be sure to give your readers a sense of the plot, the characters, and the theme of the movie.

3. Choose a hobby or an activity that particularly interests you, one that other people might consider boring, and explain why it still holds your interest. Like Kauffmann, you may want to support your essay by providing specific details and by contrasting the hobby or activity with related ones.

Language and Politics
4

Because the following essays examine the relationship between language and politics, they are also inevitably concerned with language and power. When we consider politics even in its most neutral light, as a necessary system for transferring the will of citizens into governmental policy and action, we cannot help but recognize the tremendous influence it exerts over us. This power becomes all the more apparent when politicians misrepresent, ignore, or surpress our wishes, or when gaining and keeping power seems to become the primary motivation of a politician or a political group.

Whether we view political power as necessary or excessive, dangerous or benign, however, we should not underestimate the crucial role language plays in politics of every kind. Politics offers a way for individuals to determine the nature of public life. To become part of a city's or a nation's politics, however, the individual must join, or at least be identified with, a group of some kind. Even when we cast our single votes in America, after all, we do so as members of a party; even those who refuse to belong to a party join the group known as "independents." Political action—the attempts of various groups to forward their causes—is necessarily accompanied by persuasive language that takes such forms as debate, political advertising, protest, editorial opinion, endorsement, statement of policy, and, ultimately, law, which is the most significant linking of the word and the political will. As law, political language tells us what we may and may not do in society, whether the law in question is a recently passed ordinance governing bicycle traffic or a "thou shalt not. . ." etched on the tablets of Moses several thousand years ago.

As one of the most widely read essays in the language, George Orwell's "Politics and the English Language" attests to our culture's continuing interest in the connection between language and politics. Orwell's essay assesses the damage that political power can inflict on our language as a whole; in his view, the political power of a few can lead to a linguistic powerlessness among the many. Orwell's premise is that using language imprecisely makes one's thinking foolish, and that foolish thinking in turn corrupts language further—and so on in a cycle that may, Orwell fears, devastate language entirely and transform us all into babblers. Political language, according to him, deserves special blame for this destructive cycle when those in power believe that they have to lie to stay in power: "In our time," he argues, "political speech and writing are largely the defense of the indefensible." Wholesome language can resist falsehood and corrupt language, he suggests, but only if each of us tirelessly concentrates on saying and writing as clearly as possible what we mean and if each of us demands that others do the same.

In suggesting that language corrupted by political power ends in failed communication and the disruption of any true dialogue, Orwell's essay leads naturally to the thesis of Walter Lippmann's essay, "The Indispensable Opposition." Lippmann's chief point is that a political system, if it is to remain effective, must at all costs preserve the dialogue between opposing points of view and different voices of power. This "creative principle of freedom of speech" is not, Lippmann argues, simply a matter of courtesy and tolerance, but constitutes the only way political communication can reveal the truth. Just as a doctor may tell us unpleasant but ultimately life-saving news, Lippmann suggests, someone with an opposing view may actually correct or sharpen our thinking. The opposition often accomplishes what Orwell prescribes; it forces us to ask ourselves what we mean, to clarify our thinking, and to use language carefully. The political system that acknowledges this creative relationship between language and politics will enrich the culture it serves. A statesman, according to Lippmann, "ought to pray never to be left without opponents, for they keep him on the path of reason and good sense."

The First Amendment to the United States Constitution may contain our nation's most forceful statement supporting the right of "opposing voices" to express themselves in print or speech. In "Confusion Worse Confounded," Lewis H. Lapham questions the extent to which pornography should fall under the protection of the First Amendment. In general, Lapham tells us, he subscribes to the idea that we should not curb even the most offensive uses of language, chiefly to avoid setting a precedent of limited free speech that might later be exploited to restrict the rights of newspapers and other mainstream publications. When confronted with a specific example of an extreme type of pornography, however, Lapham comes to doubt the value of an unqualified right of free speech. He asks, "How is it possible to construe the degradation of human beings as a constitutional right? Why should I protect the man who seeks to destroy what I have worked to build?" Like many people, Lapham finds himself caught in a dilemma between a general belief in free speech and an intense dislike for a particularly offensive publication. Although he offers no complete answers to this predicament, he does suggest that we should not expect the press to be perfect and that the press, in turn, "should not defend its elevated principles" on the basis of court cases involving pornography.

The remaining essays in this section reflect the perspective of several members of the "indispensable opposition," defined not in terms of political parties, but instead in terms of sexual and racial politics. In "The Political Vocabulary of Homosexuality," Edmund White shows how the social and political liberation of homosexuals has altered not only words belonging to America's standard vocabulary but also words that were part of the "secret language" of homosexuals before liberation occurred. And from another perspective, he provides examples of Orwell's premise that language and thought constantly reshape each other. As "gay liberation" has progressed, homosexual language has shifted from effeminacy to masculinity, he suggests, and the need for a private language has diminished.

Like White's essay, Richard Rodriguez's "Aria" is also about the language of a private and a public world. In this case, however, the conflict is not between the secret language of a sexual minority and the standard public language; instead it is between two standard languages: the Spanish of an earlier homeland and the English of the new country. To a great extent, Rodriguez's essay tracks his own development, when, as a "listening child," he had to learn the language of the new community; it also assesses the impact of this development on his Spanish-speaking family, including episodes of failed communication, embarrassment, and anger. Despite the heavy emotional toll, he finally perceives the changed home environment to have been an inevitable result of acquiring a public language and a sense of a public self. Rodriguez, then, gives the essay a controversially political and argumentative edge; he does this by linking his own experience with the issue of bilingual education, which, he argues, would have deprived him of both a public identity and a public language.

A sense of reasonableness and fairplay applies to all of the essays in this section; this is especially remarkable when we consider that the political issues under consideration constantly tempt us all to become angry or otherwise impassioned and close off the dialogue that Lippmann suggests must always remain open. As your own experience with political discussions no doubt shows, words themselves can be like sparks that touch off blazing arguments. Select words in these essays are no exception: "gay liberation," "bilingual education," and "pornography," to name but a few.

By preserving the sense of a reasonable audience and a dialogue, these essayists leave themselves and their arguments open to criticism. This apparent vulnerability reveals, however, an important strength. For by not allowing their language to overpower the reader, they show finally that their interest in truth outweighs their desire to win an argument or otherwise assert power. In so doing, they leave open the "path of reason and good sense" to which Lippmann refers, and they preserve the effectiveness of language that politics and power often jeopardize.

Politics and the English Language

George Orwell

George Orwell (1903–1950) is the pen name of Eric Arthur Blair, who was born in Burma and educated at Eton. He joined the Imperial Police in Burma after leaving school, but became disenchanted and returned to England. His first book, Down and Out in Paris and London, *appeared in 1933. For most of his life he was a socialist, and his political opinions are reflected in many of his books, including* Homage to Catalonia *(1939),* 1984 *(1949), and* Shooting an Elephant and Other Essays *(1950). "Politics and the English Language," one of the most reprinted essays in the language, is particularly remarkable for its extensive examples as well as its painstaking—and animated—analysis and argumentation.*

Most people who bother with the matter at all would admit that the English language is in a bad way, but it is generally assumed that we cannot by conscious action do anything about it. Our civilisation is decadent, and our language—so the argument runs—must inevitably share in the general collapse. It follows that any struggle against the abuse of language is a sentimental archaism, like preferring candles to electric light or hansom cabs to aeroplanes. Underneath this lies the half-conscious belief that language is a natural growth and not an instrument which we shape for our own purposes.

Now, it is clear that the decline of a language must ultimately have political and economic causes: it is not due simply to the bad influence of this or that individual writer. But an effect can become a cause, reinforcing the original cause and producing the same effect in an intensified form, and so on indefinitely. A man may take to drink because he feels himself to be a failure, and then fail all the more completely because he drinks. It is rather the same thing that is happening to the English language. It becomes ugly and inaccurate because our thoughts are foolish, but the slovenliness of our language makes it easier for us to have foolish thoughts. The point is that the process is reversible. Modern English, especially written English, is full of bad habits which spread by imitation and which can be avoided if one is willing to take the necessary trouble. If one gets rid of these habits one can think more clearly, and to think clearly is a necessary first step towards political regeneration: so that the fight against bad English is not frivolous and is not the exclusive concern of professional writers. I will come back to this presently, and I hope that by that time the meaning of what I have said here will have become clearer. Meanwhile, here are five specimens of the English language as it is now habitually written.

These five passages have not been picked out because they are especially bad—I could have quoted far worse if I had chosen—but because they illustrate various of the mental vices from which we now suffer. They are a little below the average, but are fairly representative samples. I number them so that I can refer back to them when necessary:

> 1. I am not, indeed, sure whether it is not true to say that the Milton who once seemed not unlike a seventeeth-century Shelley had not become, out of an experience ever more bitter in each

year, more alien (sic) to the founder of that Jesuit sect which nothing could induce him to tolerate.

Professor Harold Laski (Essay in Freedom of Expression*).*

2. Above all, we cannot play ducks and drakes with a native battery of idioms which prescribes such egregious collocations of vocables as the Basic *put up with* for *tolerate* or *put at a loss* for *bewilder*.

Professor Lancelot Hogben (Interglossa).

3. On the one side we have the free personality: by definition it is not neurotic, for it has neither conflict nor dream. Its desires, such as they are, are transparent, for they are just what institutional approval keeps in the forefront of consciousness; another institutional pattern would alter their number and intensity; there is little in them that is natural, irreducible, or culturally dangerous. But *on the other side*, the social bond itself is nothing but the mutual reflection of these self-secure integrities. Recall the definition of love. Is not this the very picture of a small academic? Where is there a place in this hall of mirrors for either personality or fraternity?

Essay on psychology in Politics *(New York).*

4. All the "best people" from the gentlemen's clubs, and all the frantic Fascist captains, united in common hatred of Socialism and bestial horror of the rising tide of the mass revolutionary movement, have turned to acts of provocation, to foul incendiarism, to medieval legends of poisoned wells, to legalise their own destruction to proletarian organisations, and rouse the agitated petty-bourgeoisie to chauvinistic fervour on behalf of the fight against the revolutionary way out of the crisis.

Communist pamphlet.

5. If a new spirit *is* to be infused into this old country, there is one thorny and contentious reform which must be tackled, and that is the humanisation and galvanisation of the BBC. Timidity here will bespeak canker and atrophy of the soul. The heart of Britain may be sound and of strong beat, for instance, but the British lion's roar at present is like that of Bottom in Shakespeare's *Midsummer Night's Dream*—as gentle as any sucking dove. A virile new Britain cannot continue indefinitely to be traduced in the eyes, or rather ears, of the world by the effete languors of Langham

Place, brazenly masquerading as "standard English." When the Voice of Britain is heard at nine o'clock, better far and infinitely less ludicrous to hear aitches honestly dropped than the present priggish, inflated, inhibited, school-ma'amish arch braying of blameless bashful mewing maidens!

Letter in Tribune.

Each of these passages has fault of its own, but, quite apart from avoidable ugliness, two qualities are common to all of them. The first is staleness of imagery: the other is lack of precision. The writer either has a meaning and cannot express it, or he inadvertently says something else, or he is almost indifferent as to whether his words mean anything or not. This mixture of vagueness and sheer incompetence is the most marked characteristic of modern English prose, and especially of any kind of political writing. As soon as certain topics are raised, the concrete melts into the abstract and no one seems able to think of turns of speech that are not hackneyed: prose consists less and less of *words* chosen for the sake of their meaning, and more of *phrases* tacked together like the sections of a prefabricated hen-house. I list below, with notes and examples, various of the tricks by means of which the work of prose construction is habitually dodged:

Dying metaphors. A newly invented metaphor assists thought by evoking a visual image, while on the other hand a metaphor which is technically "dead" (e.g. *iron resolution*) has in effect reverted to being an ordinary word and can generally be used without loss of vividness. But in between these two classes there is a huge dump of worn-out metaphors which have lost all evocative power and are merely used because they save people the trouble of inventing phrases for themselves. Examples are: *Ring the changes on, take up the cudgels for, toe the line, ride roughshod over, stand shoulder to shoulder with, play into the hands of, no axe to grind, grist to the mill, fishing in troubled waters, rift within the lute, on the order of the day, Achilles' heel, swan song, hotbed.* Many of these are used without knowledge of their meaning (what is a "rift," for instance?), and incompatible metaphors are frequently mixed, a sure sign that the writer is not interested in what he is saying. Some metaphors now current have been twisted out of their original meaning without those who use them even being aware of the fact. For example, *toe the line* is sometimes written *tow the line.* Another example is *the hammer and the anvil,* now always used with the implication that the anvil gets the worst of it. In real life it is always the anvil that breaks the hammer, never the other way about: a writer who stopped to think what he was saying would be aware of this, and would avoid perverting the original phrase.

Operators, or *verbal false limbs*. These save the trouble of picking out appropriate verbs and nouns, and at the same time pad each sentence with extra syllables which give it an appearance of symmetry. Characteristic phrases are: *render inoperative, militate against, prove unacceptable, make contact with, be subjected to, give rise to, give grounds for, have the effect of, play a leading part (rôle) in, make itself felt, take effect, exhibit a tendency to, serve the purpose of,* etc etc. The keynote is the elimination of simple verbs. Instead of being a single word, such as *break, stop, spoil, mend, kill,* a verb becomes a *phrase,* made up of a noun or adjective tacked on to some general-purposes verb such as *prove, serve, form, play, render.* In addition, the passive voice is wherever possible used in preference to the active, and noun constructions are used instead of gerunds (*by examination of* instead of *by examining*). The range of verbs is further cut down by means of the *-ise* and *de-* formations, and banal statements are given an appearance of profundity by means of the *not un-* formation. Simple conjunctions and prepositions are replaced by such phrases as *with respect to, having regard to, the fact that, by dint of, in view of, in the interests of, on the hypothesis that*; and the ends of sentences are saved from anticlimax by such resounding commonplaces as *greatly to be desired, cannot be left out of account, a development to be expected in the near future, deserving of serious consideration, brought to a satisfactory conclusion,* and so on and so forth.

Pretentious diction. Words like *phenomenon, element, individual* (as noun), *objective, categorical, effective, virtual, basic, primary, promote, constitute, exhibit, exploit, utilise, eliminate, liquidate,* are used to dress up simple statements and give an air of scientific impartiality to biased judgements. Adjectives like *epoch-making, epic, historic, unforgettable, triumphant, age-old, inevitable, inexorable, veritable,* are used to dignify the sordid processes of international politics, while writing that aims at glorifying war usually takes on an archaic colour, its characteristic words being: *realm, throne, chariot, mailed fist, trident, sword, shield, buckler, banner, jackboot, clarion.* Foreign words and expressions such as *cul de sac, ancien régime, deus ex machina, mutatis mutandis, status quo, Gleichschaltung, Weltanschauung,* are used to give an air of culture and elegance. Except for the useful abbreviations *i.e.*, *e.g.*, and *etc.*, there is no real need for any of the hundreds of foreign phrases now current in English. Bad writers, and especially scientific, political and sociological writers, are nearly always haunted by the notion that Latin or Greek words are grander than Saxon ones, and unnecessay words like *expedite, ameliorate, predict, extraneous, deracinated, clandestine, sub-aqueous* and hundreds of others constantly gain ground from their Anglo-Saxon opposite numbers.[1] The jargon peculiar to Marxist writing (*hyena, hangman, cannibal, petty bourgeois, these gentry, lacquey, flunkey, mad dog, White Guard*, etc) consists largely of words and phrases translated from Russian, German or French; but the normal way of coining a new word is to use a Latin or Greek root with the appropriate affix and, where necessary, the *-ise* formation. It is often easier to make up words of this kind (*deregionalise, impermissible, extramarital, non-fragmentatory* and so forth) than to think up the English words that will cover one's meaning. The result, in general, is an increase in slovenliness and vagueness.

Meaningless words. In certain kinds of writing, particularly in art criticism and literary criticism, it is normal to come across long passages which are almost completely lacking in meaning.[2] Words like *romantic, plastic, values, human, dead, sentimental, natural, vitality,* as used in art criticism, are strictly meaningless, in the sense that they not only do not point to any discoverable object, but are hardly even expected to do so by the reader. When one critic writes, "The outstanding feature of Mr X's work is its living quality," while another writes, "The immediately striking thing about Mr X's work is its peculiar deadness," the reader accepts this as a simple difference of opinion. If words like *black* and *white* were involved, instead of the jargon words *dead* and *living*, he would see at once that language was being used in an improper way. Many political words are similarly abused. The word *Fascism* has now no meaning except in so

8

---

[1] An interesting illustration of this is the way in which the English flower names which were in use till very recently are being ousted by Greek ones, *snapdragon* becoming *antirrhinum, forget-me-not* becoming *myosotis*, etc. It is hard to see any practical reason for this change of fashion: it is probably due to an instinctive turning-away from the more homely word and a vague feeling that the Greek word is scientific.

[2] Example: "Comfort's catholicity of perception and image, strangely Whitmanesque in range, almost the exact opposite in aesthetic compulsion, continues to evoke that trembling atmospheric accumulative hinting at a cruel, an inexorably serene timelessness . . . Wrey Gardiner scores by aiming at simple bullseyes with precision. Only they are not so simple, and through this contented sadness runs more than the surface bitter-sweet of resignation." *Poetry Quarterly*.)

far as it signifies "something not desirable." The words *democracy, socialism, freedom, patriotic, realistic, justice,* have each of them several different meanings which cannot be reconciled with one another. In the case of a word like *democracy,* not only is there no agreed definition, but the attempt to make one is resisted from all sides. It is almost universally felt that when we call a country democratic we are praising it: consequently the defenders of every kind of régime claim that it is a democracy, and fear that they might have to stop using the word if it were tied down to any one meaning. Words of this kind are often used in a consciously dishonest way. That is, the person who uses them has his own private definition, but allows his hearer to think he means something quite different. Statements like *Marshal Pétain was a true patriot, The soviet press is the freest in the world, The Catholic Church is opposed to persecution,* are almost always made with intent to deceive. Other words used in variable meanings, in most cases more or less dishonestly, are: *class, totalitarian, science, progressive, reactionary, bourgeois, equality.*

Now that I have made this catalogue of swindles and perversions, let me give another example of the kind of writing that they lead to. This time it must of its nature be an imaginary one. I am going to translate a passage of good English into modern English of the worst sort. Here is a well-known verse from *Ecclesiastes:* 9

> I returned, and saw under the sun, that the race is not to the swift, nor the battle to the strong, neither yet bread to the wise, nor yet riches to men of understanding, nor yet favour to men of skill; but time and chance happeneth to them all.

Here it is in modern English: 10

> Objective consideration of contemporary phenomena compels the conclusion that success or failure in competitive activities exhibits no tendency to be commensurate with innate capacity, but that a considerable element of the unpredictable must invariably be taken into account.

This is a parody, but not a very gross one. Exhibit 3, above, for instance, contains several patches of the same kind of English. It will be seen that I have not made a full translation. The beginning and ending of the sentence follow the original meaning fairly closely, but in the middle the concrete illustrations—race, battle, bread— dissolve into the vague phrase "success or failure in competitive activities." This had to be so, because no modern writer of the kind 11

I am discussing—no one capable of using phrases like "objective consideration of contemporary phenomena"—would ever tabulate his thoughts in that precise and detailed way. The whole tendency of modern prose is away from concreteness. Now analyse these two sentences a little more closely. The first contains 49 words but only 60 syllables, and all its words are those of everyday life. The second contains 38 words of 90 syllables: 18 of its words are from Latin roots, and one from Greek. The first sentence contains six vivid images, and only one phrase ("time and chance") that could be called vague. The second contains not a single fresh, arresting phrase, and in spite of its 90 syllables it gives only a shortened version of the meaning contained in the first. Yet without a doubt it is the second kind of sentence that is gaining ground in modern English. I do not want to exaggerate. This kind of writing is not yet universal, and outcrops of simplicity will occur here and there in the worst-written page. Still, if you or I were told to write a few lines on the uncertainty of human fortunes, we should probably come much nearer to my imaginary sentence than to the one from *Ecclesiastes*.

As I have tried to show, modern writing at its worst does not consist in picking out words for the sake of their meaning and inventing images in order to make the meaning clearer. It consists in gumming together long strips of words which have already been set in order by someone else, and making the results presentable by sheer humbug. The attraction of this way of writing is that it is easy. It is easier—even quicker, once you have the habit—to say *In my opinion it is a not unjustifiable assumption that* than to say *I think*. If you use ready-made phrases, you not only don't have to hunt about for words; you also don't have to bother with the rhythms of your sentences, since these phrases are generally so arranged as to be more or less euphonious. When you are composing in a hurry—when you are dictating to a stenographer, for instance, or making a public speech—it is natural to fall into a pretentious, latinised style. Tags like *a consideration which we should do well to bear in mind* or *a conclusion to which all of us would readily assent* will save many a sentence from coming down with a bump. By using stale metaphors, similes and idioms, you save much mental effort, at the cost of leaving your meaning vague, not only for your reader but for youself. This is the significance of mixed metaphors. The sole aim of a metaphor is to call up a visual image. When these images clash—as in *The Fascist octopus has sung its swan song, the jackboot is thrown into the melting pot*—it can be taken as certain that the writer is not seeing a mental image of the objects he is naming; in other words he is not really thinking. Look again at the examples I gave at the beginning of this essay. Professor Laski (1) uses five negatives in 53 words. One of these is superfluous, making nonsense of the whole passage, and in addition there is the slip *alien* for akin, making further nonsense, and several avoidable pieces of clumsiness which increase the general vagueness. Professor Hogben (2) plays ducks and drakes with a battery which is able to write prescriptions, and while disapproving of the everyday phrase *put up with*, is unwilling to look *egregious* up in the dictionary and see what it means. (3) if one takes an uncharitable attitude towards it, is simply meaningless: probably one could work out its intended meaning by reading the whole of the article in which it occurs. In (4) the writer knows more or less what he wants to say, but an accumulation of stale phrases chokes him like tea-leaves blocking a sink. In (5) words and meaninig have almost parted company. People who write in this manner usually have a general emotional meaning—they dislike one thing and want to express solidarity with another—but they are not interested in the detail of what they are saying. A scrupulous writer, in every sentence that he writes, will ask himself at least four questions, thus: "What am I trying to say? What words will express it? What image or idiom will make it clearer? Is this image fresh enough to have an effect? And he will probably ask himself two more: Could I put it more shortly? Have I said anything that is avoidably ugly? But you are not obliged to go to all this trouble. You can shirk it by simply throwing your mind open and letting the ready-made phrases come crowding in. They will construct your sentences for you—even think your thoughts for you, to a certain extent—and at need they will perform the important service of partially concealing your meaning even from yourself. It is at this point that the special connection between politics and the debasement of language becomes clear.

In our time it is broadly true that political writing is bad writing. Where it is not ture, it will generally be found that the writer is some kind of rebel, expressing his private opinions, and not a "party line." Orthodoxy, of whatever colour, seems to demand a lifeless, imitative style. The political dialects to be found in pamphlets, leading articles, manifestos, White Papers and the speeches of Under-Secretaries do, of course, vary from party to party, but they are all alike in that one almost never finds in them a fresh, vivid, homemade turn of speech. When one watches some tired hack on the platform mechanically repeating the familiar phrases—*bestial atrocities, iron heel, bloodstained tyranny, free peoples of the world, stand shoulder to shoulder*—one often has a curious feeling that one is not watching a live human being but some kind of dummy: a feeling which suddenly becomes stronger at moments when the light catches the speaker's spectacles and turns them into blank discs which seem to have no eyes behind them. And this is not altogether fanciful. A speaker who uses that kind of phraseology has gone some distance towards turning himself into a machine. The appropriate noises are coming out of his larnyx, but his brain is not involved as it would be if he were choosing his words for himself. If the speech he is making is one that he is accustomed to make over and over again, he may be almost unconscious of what he is saying, as one is when one utters the responses in church. And this reduced state of consciousness, if not indispensable, is at any rate favourable to political conformity.

In our time, political speech and writing are largely the defence of the indefensible. Things like the continuance of British rule in India, the Russian purges and deportations, the dropping of the atom bombs on Japan, can indeed be defended, but only by arguments which are too brutal for most people to face, and which do not square with the professed aims of political parties. Thus political language has to consist largely of euphemism, question-begging and sheer cloudy vagueness. Defenceless villages are bombarded from the air, the inhabitants driven out into the countryside, the cattle machine-gunned, the huts set on fire with incendiary bullets: this is called *pacification*. Millions of peasants are robbed of their farms and sent trudging along the roads with no more than they can carry: this is called *transfer of population* or *rectification of frontiers*. People are imprisoned for years without trial, or shot in the back of the neck or sent to die of scurvy in Arctic lumber camps: this is called *elimination of unreliable elements*. Such phraseology is needed if one wants to name things without calling up mental pictures of them. Consider for instance some comfortable English professor defending Russian totalitarianism. He cannot say outright, "I believe in killing off your opponents when you can get good results by doing so." Probably, therefore, he will say something like this:

> While freely conceding that the Soviet régime exhibits certain features which the humanitarian may be inclined to deplore, we

must, I think, agree that a certain curtailment of the right to political opposition is an unavoidable concomitant of transitional periods, and that the rigours which the Russian people have been called upon to undergo have been amply justified in the sphere of concrete achievement.

The inflated style is itself a kind of euphemism. A mass of Latin words falls upon the facts like soft snow, blurring the outlines and covering up all the details. The great enemy of clear language is insincerity. When there is a gap between one's real and one's declared aims, one turns as it were instinctively to long words and exhausted idioms, like a cuttlefish squirting out ink. In our age there is no such things as "keeping out of politics." All issues are political issues, and politics itself is a mass of lies, evasions, folly, hatred and schizophrenia. When the general atmosphere is bad, language must suffer. I should expect to find—this is a guess which I have not sufficient knowledge to verify—that the German, Russian and Italian languages have all deteriorated in the last ten or fifteen years, as a result of dictatorship.

But if thought corrupts language, language can also corrupt thought. A bad usage can spread by tradition and imitation, even among people who should and do know better. The debased language that I have been discussing is in some ways very convenient. Phrases like *a not unjustifiable assumption, leaves much to be desired, would serve no good purpose, a consideration which we should do well to bear in mind,* are a continuous temptation, a packet of aspirins always at one's elbow. Look back through this essay, and for certain you will find that I have again and again committed the very faults I am protesting against. By this morning's post I have received a pamphlet dealing with conditions in Germany. The author tells me that he "felt impelled" to write it. I open it at random, and here is almost the first sentence that I see: "(The Allies) have an opportunity not only of achieving a radical transformation of Germany's social and political structure in such a way as to avoid a nationalistic reaction in Germany itself, but at the same time of laying the foundations of a co-operative and unified Europe." You see, he "feels impelled" to write—feels, presumably, that he has something new to say—and yet his words, like cavalry horses answering the bugle, group themselves automatically into the familiar dreary pattern. This invasion of one's mind by ready-made phrases (*lay the foundations, achieve a radical transformation*) can only be prevented if one is constantly on guard against them, and every such phrase anaesthetises a portion of one's brain.

I said earlier that the decadence of our language is probably curable. Those who deny this would argue, if they produced an argument at all, that language merely reflects existing social conditions, and that we cannot influence its development by any direct tinkering with words and constructions. So far as the general tone or spirit of a language goes, this may be true, but it is not true in detail. Silly words and expressions have often disappeared, not through any evolutionary process but owing to the conscious action of a minority. Two recent examples were *explore every avenue* and *leave no stone unturned*, which were killed by the jeers of a few journalists. There is a long list of fly-blown metaphors which could similarly be got rid of if enough people would interest themselves in the job; and it should also be possible to laugh the *not un-* formation out of existence,[3] to reduce the amount of Latin and Greek in the average sentence, to drive out foreign phrases and strayed scientific words, and, in general, to make pretentiousness unfashionable. But all these are minor points. The defence of the English language implies more than this, and perhaps it is best to start by saying what it does *not* imply.

To begin with, it has nothing to do with archaism, with the salvaging of obsolete words and turns of speech, or with the setting-up of a "standard English" which must never be departed from. On the contrary, it is especially concerned with the scrapping of every word or idiom which has outworn its usefulness. It has nothing to do with correct grammar and syntax, which are of no importance so long as one makes one's meaning clear, or with the avoidance of Americanisms, or with having what is called a "good prose style." On the other hand it is not concerned with fake simplicity and the attempt to make written English colloquial. Nor does it even imply in every case preferring the Saxon word to the Latin one, though it does imply using the fewest and shortest words that will cover one's meaning. What is above all needed is to let the meaning choose the word, and not the other way about. In prose, the worst thing one can do with words is to surrender to them. When you

---

[3]One can cure oneself of the *not un-* formation by memorising this sentence: A *not unblack dog was chasing a not unsmall rabbit across a not ungreen field.*

think of a concrete object, you think wordlessly, and then, if you want to describe the thing you have been visualising, you probably hunt about till you find the exact words that seem to fit it. When you think of something abstract you are more inclined to use words from the start, and unless you make a conscious effort to prevent it, the existing dialect will come rushing in and do the job for you, at the expense of blurring or even changing your meaning. Probably it is better to put off using words as long as possible and get one's meaning as clear as one can through pictures or sensations. Afterwards one can choose—not simply *accept*—the phrases that will best cover the meaning, and then switch round and decide what impression one's words are likely to make on another person. This last effort of the mind cuts out all stale or mixed images, all prefabricated phrases, needless repetitions, and humbug and vagueness generally. But one can often be in doubt about the effect of a word or a phrase, and one needs rules that one can rely on when instinct fails. I think the following rules will cover most cases:

i. Never use a metaphor, simile or other figure of speech which you are used to seeing in print.
ii. Never use a long word where a short one will do.
iii. If it is possible to cut a word out, always cut it out.
iv. Never use the passive where you can use the active.
v. Never use a foreign phrase, a scientific word or a jargon word if you can think of an everyday English equivalent.
vi. Break any of these rules sooner than say anything outright barbarous.

These rules sound elementary, and so they are, but they demand a deep change of attitude in anyone who has grown used to writing in the style now fashionable. One could keep all of them and still write bad English, but one could not write the kind of stuff that I quoted in those five specimens at the beginning of this article.

I have not here been considering the literary use of language, but merely language as an instrument for expressing and not for concealing or preventing thought. Stuart Chase and others have come near to claiming that all abstract words are meaningless, and have used this as a pretext for advocating a kind of political quietism. Since you don't know what Fascism is, how can you struggle against Fascism? One need not swallow such absurdities as this, but one ought to recognise that the present political chaos is connected with the decay of language, and that one can probably bring about some improvement by starting at the verbal end. If you simplify your English, you are freed from the worst follies of orthodoxy. You cannot speak any of the necessary dialects, and when you make a stupid remark its stupidity will be obvious, even to yourself. Political language—and with variations this is true of all political parties, from Conservatives to Anarchists—is designed to make lies sound truthful and murder respectable, and to give an appearance of solidity to pure wind. One cannot change this all in a moment, but one can at least change one's own habits, and from time to time one can even, if one jeers loudly enough, send some worn-out and useless phrase—some *jackboot, Achilles' heel, hotbed, melting pot, acid test, veritable inferno* or other lump of verbal refuse—into the dustbin where it belongs.

Content

1. Orwell laments that most people are unwilling to bother to reverse the decline of accurate, clear language. What arguments does he offer to convince you there is reason to "bother" with the matter at all?
2. Orwell distinguishes between "words chosen for the sake of their meaning" and "phrases tacked together." Find two or three examples of such tacked-together phrases in Orwell's five sample passages and explain their probable appeal to the writer and failure for the reader.
3. Orwell's essay was written in 1946, yet it continues to be widely read and discussed. Are Orwell's warnings about politics and language still timely? Explain.

Technique

1. Orwell begins his essay with a premise that he does not believe—that it is useless to struggle against the decay of language. What is the effect of this technique on Orwell's argument?
2. Orwell is trying to persuade the reader to share his alarm at what he considers the deterioration of the English language. To do so, he uses several extended examples of inflated, wordy, and unclear prose. How effective do you find this technique?
3. In paragraph 2, Orwell states his thesis explicitly and attempts to clarify it by drawing an analogy between language decline and a man caught in the ugly circle of drinking and failure. What is Orwell's

thesis, and how effective do you find his use of analogy in clarifying that thesis?

Language

1. Why do you suppose Orwell includes such words as "democracy," "freedom," "patriotic," and "socialism" in his discussion of "meaningless words"? Do you agree that they have become meaningless?
2. Orwell's essay might seem dated in some of his examples of dying metaphors (paragraph 5). We no longer hear, for instance, "ring the changes on." But we can substitute current clichés, revealing that we still rely on the easy phrase, rather than the fresh image. Complete the following overused phrases; then try to replace them with vivid, new images:

    I was cool, calm, and _____ .
    I arose bright-eyed and _____ .
    The man was rotten to the _____ .
    I fought him tooth and _____ .
    To make a long story_____ .

3. In his own writing, Orwell strives for the fresh metaphor. In paragraph 4, for instance, he says that prose consists more and more of phrases "tacked together like the sections of a prefabricated hen-house." Find two or three additional examples of Orwell's figurative language and discuss their effectiveness as clarifying, interesting, and fresh visual images.

Vocabulary

| hackneyed | metaphor | imagery |
| abstract | euphemism | concrete |

Writing Suggestions

1. Write a paragraph in which you analyze the failure of one of Orwell's five examples of weak prose.
2. In paragraph 4, Orwell says that the tendency of modern prose is away from concreteness, that "the concrete melts into the abstract." The result, according to Orwell, is language that is ugly, stale, imprecise, and unclear. Write an essay analyzing the possible causes or effects of this trend. Use specific examples to support your analysis.

The Indispensable Opposition
Walter Lippmann

> Walter Lippmann (1889–1974) was one of the most prolific and respected political writers in modern America. He made a mark in both the world of government and the world of political journalism, serving as a captain in Army Military Intelligence. His dozens of books on politics and government have influenced the thinking of congressmen and presidents as well as the public at large. Lippmann won numerous awards for his writing and public service, including the Pulitzer Prize and the Legion of Honor Medal from Belgium. His books include Public Opinion (1922), The Cold War (1947), and The Public Philosophy (1955). "The Indispensable Opposition" reflects Lippmann's lifelong commitment to democracy. The essay is particularly noteworthy for the care and clarity with which Lippmann develops his thesis, which is "that we must protect the right of our opponents to speak because we must hear what they have to say."

1   Were they pressed hard enough, most men would probably confess that political freedom—that is to say, the right to speak freely and to act in opposition—is a noble ideal rather than a practical necessity. As the case for freedom is generally put to-day, the argument lends itself to this feeling. It is made to appear that, whereas each man claims his freedom as a matter of right, the freedom he accords to other men is a matter of toleration. Thus, the defense of freedom of opinion tends to rest not on its substantial, beneficial, and indispensable consequences, but on a somewhat eccentric, a rather vaguely benevolent, attachment to an abstraction.

2   It is all very well to say with Voltaire, "I wholly disapprove of what you say, but will defend to the death your right to say it," but as a matter of fact most men will not defend to the death the rights of other men: if they disapprove sufficiently what other men say, they will somehow suppress those men if they can.

3   So, if this is the best that can be said for liberty of opinion, that a man must tolerate his opponents because everyone has a "right" to say what he pleases, then we shall find that liberty of opinion is a luxury, safe only in pleasant times when men can be tolerant because they are not deeply and vitally concerned.

4 Yet actually, as a matter of historic fact, there is a much stronger foundation for the great constitutional right of freedom of speech, and as a matter of practical human experience there is a much more compelling reason for cultivating the habits of free men. We take, it seems to me, a naïvely self-righteous view when we argue as if the right of our opponents to speak were something that we protect because we are magnanimous, noble, and unselfish. The compelling reason why, if liberty of opinion did not exist, we should have to invent it, why it will eventually have to be restored in all civilized countries where it is now suppressed, is that we must protect the right of our opponents to speak because we must hear what they have to say.

5 We miss the whole point when we imagine that we tolerate the freedom of our political opponents as we tolerate a howling baby next door, as we put up with the blasts from our neighbor's radio because we are too peaceable to heave a brick through the window. If this were all there is to freedom of opinion, that we are too good-natured or too timid to do anything about our opponents and our critics except to let them talk, it would be difficult to say whether we are tolerant because we are magnanimous or because we are lazy, because we have strong principles or because we lack serious convictions, whether we have the hospitality of an inquiring mind or the indifference of an empty mind. And so, if we truly wish to understand why freedom is necessary in a civilized society, we must begin by realizing that, because freedom of discussion improves our own opinions, the liberties of other men are our own vital necessity.

6 We are much closer to the essence of the matter, not when we quote Voltaire, but when we go to the doctor and pay him to ask us the most embarrassing questions and to prescribe the most disagreeable diet. When we pay the doctor to exercise complete freedom of speech about the cause and cure of our stomachache, we do not look upon ourselves as tolerant and magnanimous, and worthy to be admired by ourselves. We have enough common sense to know that if we threaten to put the doctor in jail because we do not like the diagnosis and the prescription it will be unpleasant for the doctor, to be sure, but equally unpleasant for our own stomachache. That is why even the most ferocious dictator would rather be treated by a doctor who was free to think and speak the truth than by his own Minister of Propaganda. For there is a point, the point at which

things really matter, where the freedom of others is no longer a question of their right but of our need.

The point at which we recognize this need is much higher in some men than in others. The totalitarian rulers think they do not need the freedom of an opposition: they exile, imprison, or shoot their opponents. We have concluded on the basis of practical experience, which goes back to Magna Carta and beyond, that we need the opposition. We pay the opposition salaries out of the public treasury.

In so far as the usual apology for freedom of speech ignores this experience, it becomes abstract and eccentric rather than concrete and human. The emphasis is generally put on the right to speak, as if all that mattered were that the doctor should be free to go out into the park and explain to the vacant air why I have a stomachache. Surely that is a miserable caricature of the great civic right which men have bled and died for. What really matters is that the doctor should tell *me* what ails me, that I should listen to him; that if I do not like what he says I should be free to call in another doctor; and that then the first doctor should have to listen to the second doctor; and that out of all the speaking and listening, the give-and-take of opinions, the truth should be arrived at.

This is the creative principle of freedom of speech, not that it is a system for the tolerating of error, but that it is a system for finding the truth. It may not produce the truth, or the whole truth all the time, or often, or in some cases ever. But if the truth can be found, there is no other system which will normally and habitually find so much truth. Until we have thoroughly understood this principle, we shall not know why we must value our liberty, or how we can protect and develop it.

Let us apply this principle to the system of public speech in a totalitarian state. We may, without any serious falsification, picture a condition of affairs in which the mass of the people are being addressed through one broadcasting system by one man and his chosen subordinates. The orators speak. The audience listens but cannot and dare not speak back. It is a system of one-way communication; the opinions of the rulers are broadcast outwardly to the mass of the people. But nothing comes back to the rulers from the people except the cheers; nothing returns in the way of knowledge of forgotten facts, hidden feelings, neglected truths, and practical suggestions.

But even a dictator cannot govern by his own one-way inspiration alone. In practice, therefore, the totalitarian rulers get back the reports of the secret police and of their party henchmen down among the crowd. If these reports are competent, the rulers may manage to remain in touch with public sentiment. Yet that is not enough to know what the audience feels. The rulers have also to make great decisions that have enormous consequences, and here their system provides virtually no help from the give-and-take opinion in the nation. So they must either rely on their own institution, which cannot be permanently and continually inspired, or, if they are intelligent despots, encourage their trusted advisers and their technicians to speak and debate freely in their presence.

On the walls of the houses of Italian peasants one may see inscribed in large letters the legend, "Mussolini is always right." But if that legend is taken seriously by Italian ambassadors, by the Italian General Staff, and by the Ministry of Finance, then all one can say is heaven help Mussolini, heaven help Italy, and the new Emperor of Ethiopia.

For at some point, even in a totalitarian state, it is indispensable that there should exist the freedom of opinion which causes opposing opinions to be debated. As time goes on, that is less and less easy under a despotism; critical discussion disappears as the internal opposition is liquidated in favor of men who think and feel alike. That is why the early successes of despots, of Napoleon I and of Napoleon III, have usually been followed by an irreparable mistake. For in listening only to his yes men—the others being in exile or in concentration camps, or terrified—the despot shuts himself off from the truth that no man can dispense with.

We know all this well enough when we contemplate the dictatorships. But when we try to picture our own system, by way of contrast, what picture do we have in our minds? It is, is it not, that anyone may stand up on his own soapbox and say anything he pleases, like the individuals in Kipling's poem who sit each in his separate star and draw the Thing as they see it for the God of Things as they are. Kipling, perhaps, could do this, since he was a poet. But the ordinary mortal isolated on his separate star will have an hallucination, and a citizenry declaiming from separate soapboxes will poison the air with hot and nonsensical confusion.

If the democratic alternative to the totalitarian one-way broadcasts is a row of separate soapboxes, then I submit that the alternative is unworkable, is unreasonable, and is humanly unattractive. It is above all a false alternative. It is not true that liberty has developed among civilized men when anyone is free to set up a soapbox, is free to hire a hall where he may expound his opinions to those who are willing to listen. On the contrary, freedom of speech is established to achieve its essential purpose only when different opinions are expounded in the same hall to the same audience.

For, while the right to talk may be the beginning of freedom, the necessity of listening is what makes the right important. Even in Russia and Germany a man may still stand in an open field and speak his mind. What matters is not the utterance of opinions. What matters is the confrontation of opinions in debate. No man can care profoundly that every fool should say what he likes. Nothing has been accomplished if the wisest man proclaims his wisdom in the middle of the Sahara Desert. This is the shadow. We have the substance of liberty when the fool is compelled to listen to the wise man and learn; when the wise man is compelled to take account of the fool, and to instruct him; when the wise man can increase his wisdom by hearing the judgment of his peers.

That is why civilized men must cherish liberty—as a means of promoting the discovery of truth. So we must not fix our whole attention on the right of anyone to hire his own hall, to rent his own broadcasting station, to distribute his own pamphlets. These rights are incidental; and though they must be preserved, they can be preserved only by regarding them as incidental, as auxiliary to the substance of liberty that must be cherished and cultivated.

Freedom of speech is best conceived, therefore, by having in mind the picture of a place like the American Congress, an assembly where opposing views are represented, where ideas are not merely uttered but debated, or the British Parliament, where men who are free to speak are also compelled to answer. We may picture the true condition of freedom as existing in a place like a court of law, where witnesses testify and are cross-examined, where the lawyer argues against the opposing lawyer before the same judge and in the presence of one jury. We may picture freedom as existing in a forum where the speaker must respond to questions; in a gathering of scientists where the data, the hypothesis, and the conclusion are submitted to men competent to judge them; in a reputable newspaper which not only will publish the opinions of those who disagree but will reexamine its own opinion in the light of what they say.

Thus the essence of freedom of opinion is not in mere toleration as such, but in the debate which toleration provides: it is not in the venting of opinion, but in the confrontation of opinion. That this is the practical substance can readily be understood when we remember how differently we feel and act about the censorship and regulation of opinion purveyed by different media of communication. We find then that, in so far as the medium makes difficult the confrontation of opinion in debate, we are driven towards censorship and regulation.

There is, for example, the whispering campaign, the circulation of anonymous rumors by men who cannot be compelled to prove what they say. They put the utmost strain on our tolerance, and there are few who do not rejoice when the anonymous slanderer is caught, exposed, and punished. At a higher level there is the moving picture, a most powerful medium for conveying ideas, but a medium which does not permit debate. A moving picture cannot be answered effectively by another moving picture; in all free countries there is some censorship of the movies, and there would be more if the producers did not recognize their limitations by avoiding political controversy. There is then the radio. Here debate is difficult; it is not easy to make sure that the speaker is being answered in the presence of the same audience. Inevitably, there is some regulation of the radio.

When we reach the newspaper press, the opportunity for debate is so considerable that discontent cannot grow to the point where under normal conditions there is any disposition to regulate the press. But when newspapers abuse their power by injuring people who have no means of replying, a disposition to regulate the press appears. When we arrive at Congress we find that, because the membership of the House is so large, full debate is impracticable. So there are restrictive rules. On the other hand, in the Senate, where the conditions of full debate exist, there is almost absolute freedom of speech.

This shows us that the preservation and development of freedom of opinion are not only a matter of adhering to abstract legal rights, but also, and very urgently, a matter of organizing and arranging sufficient debate. Once we have firm hold on the central principle, there are many practical conclusions to be drawn. We then realize that the defense of freedom of opinion consists primarily in perfecting the opportunity for an adequate give-and-take of opinion; it consists also in regulating the freedom of those revolutionists who cannot or will not permit or maintain debate when it does not suit their purposes.

We must insist that free oratory is only the beginning of free speech; it is not the end, but a means to an end. The end is to find the truth. The practical justification of civil liberty is not that self-expression is one of the rights of man. It is that the examination of opinion is one of the necessities of man. For experience tells us that it is only when freedom of opinion becomes the compulsion to debate that the seed which our fathers planted has produced its fruit. When that is understood, freedom will be cherished not because it is a vent for our opinions but because it is the surest method of correcting them.

The unexamined life, said Socrates, is unfit to be lived by man. This is the virtue of liberty, and the ground on which we may best justify our belief in it, that it tolerates error in order to serve the truth. When men are brought face to face with their opponents, forced to listen and learn and mend their ideas, they cease to be children and savages and begin to live like civilized men. Then only is freedom a reality, when men may voice their opinions because they must examine their opinions.

The only reason for dwelling on all this is that if we are to preserve democracy we must understand its principles. And the principle which disintinguishes it from all other forms of government is that in a democracy the opposition not only is tolerated as constitutional but must be maintained because it is in fact indispensable.

The democratic system cannot be operated without effective opposition. For, in making the great experiment of governing people by consent rather than by coercion, it is not sufficient that the party in power should have a majority. It is just as necessary that the party in power should never outrage the minority. That means that it must listen to the minority and be moved by the criticisms of the minority. That means that its measures must take account of the minority's objections, and that in administering measures it must remember that the minority may become the majority.

The opposition is indispensable. A good statesman, like any other sensible human being, always learns more from his opponents than from his fervent supporters. For his supporters will push him to disaster unless his opponents show him where the dangers are. So if he is wise he will often pray to be delivered from his friends, because they will ruin him. But, though it hurts, he ought also to pray never to be left without opponents; for they keep him on the path of reason and good sense.

The national unity of a free people depends upon a sufficiently even balance of political power to make it impracticable for the administration to be arbitrary and for the opposition to be revolutionary and irreconcilable. Where that balance no longer exists, democracy perishes. For unless all the citizens of a state are forced by circumstances to compromise, unless they feel that they can affect policy but that no one can wholly dominate it, unless by habit and necessity they have to give and take, freedom cannot be maintained.

Content

1. Lippmann believes that freedom of speech is much more than a political abstraction or national ideal. Explain in your own words what Lippmann sees as the principle function of freedom of speech.
2. Lippmann argues that it is essential to the survival of a democratic society that citizens confront divergent opinions. To what extent is hearing and confronting the opposition also important in our daily, more personal lives? Cite specific examples to support your point of view.
3. Lippmann quotes Socrates as saying that the unexamined life is not worth living. What do you understand Socrates' statement to mean? How does the statement relate to Lippmann's argument?

Technique

1. Frequently, Lippmann clarifies the difficult abstraction "freedom of speech" with a concrete analogy. Cite one of his analogies and evaluate its success.
2. In this argumentative essay, Lippmann uses techniques such as explanation, clarification, and contrast to persuade the reader that oppo-

sition is indispensable to the success of society. Choose one of these techniques and evaluate its effectiveness in the essay as a whole.
3. How does Lippmann's extended comparison between totalitarianism and American or British political systems further his argument?

Language

1. "Liberty," "freedom," "democratic," "dictator," and "totalitarian" are abstract words with strong connotations. Discuss their connotations and the effect they might have on our response to Lippmann's essay.
2. Look up the word "eccentric" in your dictionary. Discuss the use of the term in paragraph 8 and elsewhere.

Vocabulary

| indispensable | tolerate | confrontation |
| eccentric | totalitarian | arbitrary |

Writing Suggestions

1. Write a paragraph in which you clarify, in your own words, the significant distinction between allowing someone to speak his or her opinion and having that opinion heard.
2. Lippmann says that any sensible human being learns more from opponents than from supporters. Write an essay describing such a situation in your own life. What, for example, did you learn from your opponent that you would never have learned from your supporters?

Confusion Worse Confounded
Lewis H. Lapham

Lewis Lapham (b. 1935) has worked as a reporter for the San Francisco Examiner *and the* New York Herald Tribune, *and he has served as an editor for* Life *and* The Saturday Evening Post. *From 1975 to 1981 he was the editor of* Harper's. *A collection of his essays,* Fortune's Child, *appeared in 1980. In "Confusion Worse Confounded," Lapham addresses the controversial issue of pornography in the context of the First Amendment's guarantee of free speech, a topic that is particularly complex for an editor who is offended by pornography but committed to the ideal of free* speech. *The essay attempts to justify Lapham's withdrawal of support for the embattled publisher of* Hustler *magazine.*

On a Friday afternoon in February I received a telephone call from a gentleman who identified himself as an editor of *Hustler* magazine and who said that he was enlisting volunteers for a defense of the First Amendment. His publisher, Larry Flynt, had been sent to jail in Cincinnati on charges of pandering obscenity, and so the editor had drafted a statement that likened Mr. Flynt's sufferings to those of Alexander Solzhenitsyn. The statement was to appear as an advertisement in the *New York Times*, and the editor was looking for interested parties, most of them in the publishing business, to set their names to it. If Mr. Flynt could be persecuted for the courage of his convictions, then nothing was safe.

Ordinarily it wouldn't have occurred to me to sign any manifesto, no matter what the cause in question. I have an aversion to polemics, partly because I think of them as futile gestures taking place in an empty hall and partly because I am accustomed to seeing them in the hands of overly excited celebrities who have trouble remembering which social justice it is that they have been asked to sponsor on which television show.

But from what I could tell by reading the papers it appeared that Mr. Flynt had been badly used by the courts. Having been convicted of pandering obscenity, a misdemeanor, he had been sentenced to between seven and twenty-five years in prison on a charge of "engaging in organized crime." It wasn't clear what the court meant by this, or why the statute obtained only in Cincinnati. Nor was it clear why Mr. Flynt had been denied bail or why the jury had not seen fit merely to prevent the local sale of his magazine.

The summary judgment reminded me that an angry suspicion of the press had been making itself increasingly manifest during the past two or three years. In New York last spring a federal judge awarded $250,000 to a restaurant because its premises had been invaded by a camera crew from CBS News. During the Congressional hearings into the matter of Daniel Schorr, the more belligerent members of the subcommittee kept asking witnesses to define the press, to tell them of what it consisted and by what divine right, as they chose to put it, did the press set itself above the duly elected representatives of the people. Elsewhere in the country small-town judges had lapsed into the habit of sending reporters to jail.

Within my own sphere of interest I had noticed that I was being accosted, more frequently than in years past, by people who wanted to make fairly long speeches about the vanity, ignorance, and hypocrisy of the press. I found it impossible to disagree with them, but I found it equally impossible to make them understand that it was in the nature of the press to be vain, ignorant, and hypocritical. What in God's name did they expect? Did they imagine that it was possible to write *Faust* on an afternoon deadline? Had they not found proof of vanity, ignorance, and hypocrisy in themselves, or in any other institution about which they knew slightly more than what they read in the papers? Their unhappiness always proceeded from mistaken assumptions, as if they expected the press to conform to the idealizations given credence by the Watergate news. They objected to the lackluster but accurate definition of the press as that which gets printed, sold, bought, and read. Their disappointment suggested that they were looking for God revealed as a headwaiter, flatteringly subservient but sufficiently omniscient to answer all their questions and so excuse them from the tedious business of having to think for themselves.

All of which prompted me to take seriously the imprisonment of Mr. Flynt. Not having seen his magazine, I assumed I could make the conventional argument in support of the so-called free press. The argument relies on the paradox that the freest press is also, by definition, the most licentious press. If it is possible to assert, with Jefferson, that a free press constitutes the hope of man's enlightenment, so must it also be possible, with Balzac and Orwell, to define the press as a compendium of gossip and lies. As an abstract principle the argument has the advantage of symmetry. I think I may have said as much to Mr. Flynt's editor. That was on Friday afternoon.

On Saturday, I made the mistake of buying Mr. Flynt's magazine. This complicated the question. Mr. Flynt doesn't make it easy to quote passages from Milton's *Areopagitica*. The juxtaposition would be as ludicrous as the juxtaposition of Larry Flynt and Alexander Solzhenitsyn. Except as a matter of arbitrary impression I never have been able to distinguish between the categories of obscenity, pornography, and erotic art. The words mean different things to different people. One man's good time is another man's sermon. But what was I to say to Mr. Flynt? Looking through the pages of his magazine, I couldn't place him in any category but that of nihilist.

He presented me with an object, with a product that I conceivably could defend in an argument before the Federal Trade Commission, on more or less the same grounds that I might defend the sale and manufacture of cigarettes or automatic weapons. But what did this have to do with the First Amendment? The First Amendment states that Congress shall make no law abridging the freedom of speech, or of the press. But unless I made nonsense of the language, I couldn't see how Mr. Flynt's magazine qualified under the meaning of the word *speech*. The noun implies the adjective *human*. Mr. Flynt achieved his effects with the subliminal suggestions of cannibalism, homosexuality, sadism, narcissism, and homicide. I grant that each of these occupations has its pleasures, but what have they to do with speech? How is it possible to construe the degradation of human beings as a constitutional right? Probably I put the proposition in too subjective a form, but I do not know how else to phrase it. In Mr. Flynt's magazine I found myself confronted by the negation of the meaning embodied not only in the First Amendment but also in the idea of civilization. Why should I protect the man who seeks to destroy what I have worked to build? If I found somebody passing out leaflets that demanded my assassination, would I argue for his right to free expression?

I have no answers to these questions. Neither, apparently, do the courts. In 1973 the Supreme Court failed to define obscenity, choosing instead to assign the task to local jurisdictions. Each community sets its own standards and takes whatever course of action it deems necessary for the protection of the public morals. In theory I can agree with this approach to the difficulty, but what happens when the local jury extends its authority beyond the local newsstand? Obviously the law remains obscure, and I expect that it will be brought back to the Supreme Court for further clarification. But I can see no reason for the press to make loud protestations about the First Amendment. Given the shabbiness of its present circumstances, the press does itself a disservice by choosing to defend its elevated principles on such doubtful and muddy ground as that offered by Mr. Flynt in Cincinnati.

On Monday I called Mr. Flynt's editor and asked that my name be removed from his advertisement. I thought no more about the subject until later in the afternoon when a reporter from the *New York Post* called to ask if it was true that I had abandoned the faith of her forefathers. She went on to say that all the best people in

New York literary society (among them John Dean) had subscribed to the declaration. Her line of questioning suggested that the defense of Larry Flynt, eminent pornographer, had become as much of a *cause célèbre* as the Dreyfus affair.

No wonder the press has fallen so low in the public esteem. If the leading exponents of what passes for thoughtful opinion make such careless distinctions between their real and their illusory interests, then what can be the worth of the rest of their scribbling? What is the use of listening to people who chase after slogans as if they were butterflies, and by so doing allow themselves to be exploited in no less grotesque a manner than the men and women who pose for the photographs in Mr. Flynt's magazine? The people who plead the First Amendment in Mr. Flynt's behalf no doubt will say (as many of them already have said, although queasy with embarrassment) that if the constitutional guarantee can be breached in this one, admittedly distasteful, instance, then who knows what will happen next? What other trespasses will the state commit? Concede so much as a fraction of the principle, so runs the speech to the freshman class, and the enemies of freedom will descend like ravening crows.

But this is mostly let's pretend, the argument of rich children who can afford to play at being poor. In Czechoslovakia or Chile it would be seen as an absurd joke. In New York, among people who have not the opportunity to make the acquaintance of a totalitarian state, the argument costs less than a ticket to the movies. By pretending to descry fascism on the horizon, the people who would uphold the theory in defiance of the practice ignore the fascism implicit in the most vicious levels of pornography. Sooner or later the dehumanized vision of man leads to the raising of pornographic theaters at Dachau and Auschwitz.

Certainly I couldn't prove such an assertion in a court of law, and I doubt that I could even carry the point in a conversation with people who insisted on statistical tabulations. The best I could do would be to offer the historical record and to quote, exhaustively if necessary, from the works of wiser and more eloquent writers. Even this become difficult in an age when the meanings of words can be so easily shifted to balance the weight of money. Take for example the dictum, which happens to be Tocqueville's, that usually accompanies the loftier arguments about the paradoxes necessary to the freedom of the press.

"In this question, therefore, there is no medium between servitude and license; in order to enjoy the inestimable benefits that the liberty of the press ensures, it is necessary to submit to the inevitable evils that it creates."

But what does he mean by "license," and what constitutes an "inevitable evil"? He was writing in an age of political pamphlets, many of them seditious, and I suspect that he referred to the profligacy and ignorance characteristic of even the most well-intentioned newspaper. But if the press no longer accepts this somewhat unflattering view of things, choosing instead to imagine itself courageous, truthful, and omnipotent, then where must it look for its supposed weaknesses except in the images purveyed by Mr. Flynt? By refusing to acknowledge its own inevitable corruptions, the press has no choice but to wrap itself in the sorcerer's robe of inhuman villainy. This is a foolish and wasteful deception.

The raucous confusion of the press is not nihilism. If as many people as possible can publish whatever information they can find (much of it wrong), or as many opinions as possible (most of them misleading), then somebody with a purpose in mind might come across something useful in the rubble. In this respect the press resembles a gigantic midden heap from which, over varying periods of time, the innumerable but miscellaneous fragments of truth can be fitted together into the shape of invention or a new idea. Like the profligacy of biological combination, the profligacy of the press nourishes the gradual awakening of an infinite number of human possibilities. The process, which is also the process of life, reaches forward into the future. The nihilist impulse slouches backward in time toward barbarism, magic, and death.

In the latter years of the eighteenth century people like Jefferson associated the oppression of the human spirit with the coercions of priests and kings. It was against this tyranny that they raised up the idea of the freedom of the press. I find it ironic that their would-be successors have no better use of their liberty than to substitute for the old antagonists the coercions of Mr. Flynt.

Content

1. Lapham decided not to help defend the publisher of *Hustler* because he felt the magazine had nothing to do with "human speech." What reasons does he give for regarding the magazine as "an object" rather

than language? To what extent do you agree with his view of what constitutes pornography?
2. Lapham suggests that "fascism" is "implicit in the most vicious levels of pornography." He goes on to say, "Sooner or later the dehumanized vision of man leads to the raising of pornographic theaters at Dachau and Auschwitz." From Lapham's point of view, what is the potential relationship between pornography and fascism? Do you agree or disagree?
3. Granted that Lapham's vocabulary is often difficult and his references sometimes unfamiliar, paraphrase one paragraph in the final six in the essay. Be prepared to discuss in class what conclusion you draw about the nature of Lapham's original audience.

Technique

1. The first paragraph of Lapham's essay is a narrative setting the scene for the decision that he had to make to sign or not sign a statement supporting publisher Larry Flynt. What in that narration makes the reader understand Lapham's initial sympathy for the cause?
2. The essay is divided sharply at the point where Lapham says, "On Saturday I made the mistake of buying Mr. Flynt's magazine." What differences do you see in the points of view expressed before and after that statement? How effective is this short sentence in signaling a significant change of direction for the essay?
3. Lapham titles his essay "Confusion Worse Confounded." Analyze the significance of this title. What is the original confusion, and how and by what has that confusion been confounded?

Language

1. Lapham discusses the meaning of a "free press." Explain your own interpretation of this abstract word "free" as it applies to the press.
2. Commenting on the critics of the press, Lapham complains that their disappointment suggests that they wree "looking for God revealed as a headwaiter." What does this image suggest, and how does it help explain what Lapham believes we expect from the press?
3. The public expectation of the press as "God revealed as a headwaiter" is just one of many fresh, vivid images that Lapham uses in this essay. Find two or three others and discuss how effective they are in strengthening or clarifying Lapham's argument.

Vocabulary

manifesto	pornography	licentious
polemic	hypocrisy	nihilist
fascism	paradox	profligacy
pander	omniscient	midden
obscenity		

Writing Suggestions

1. Write a paragraph in which you define, from your own point of view, the term "freedom of the press." Be as specific as possible.

2. At the bottom of paragraph 5, Lapham complains that the public wants newspapers to "excuse them from the tedious business of having to think for themselves." Write an essay in which you analyze what you believe the role of the press should be. Lapham implies several possibilities for your consideration: that which thinks for us, that which is "subservient" to us, that which is "omniscient," or just "that which gets printed."

3. Write an essay in which you argue for or against extending freedom of the press so far as to include pornography, which (according to Lapham) degrades human beings. Consider, for example, whether to preserve freedom of the press we, as Tocqueville said, "have to submit to the inevitable evils it creates," or whether, as Lapham suspects, we have to stop short of protecting a press that "seeks to destroy what (we) have worked to build" in our personal lives, families, and society.

The Political Vocabulary of Homosexuality
Edmund White

Edmund White (b. 1940), who has taught creative writing at Yale and Johns Hopkins, is a novelist and essayist. His novels include Forgetting Elena *(1976),* Nocturnes for the King of Naples *(1978), and* A Boy's Own Story *(1982). He is co-author, with Charles Silverstein, of* The Joy of Gay Sex *(1978). In the following essay, White analyzes the extent to which the social and political liberation of homosexuals has affected both their language and America's standard vocabulary.*

Gay liberation is a new phenomenon, yet it has already transformed attitudes among homosexuals and modified the ways in which they speak. In June 1969 a group of lesbians and gay men resisted a routine police raid on the Stonewall, a popular dance bar in Greenwich Village. Opposition to police harrassment was unusual enough to signal a quickening sense of solidarity. Soon after the Stonewall Resistance gay organizations and publications were springing up across the country and, by now, gay liberation has become both a national and an international movement.

I was present at that original event and can recall how the participants cast about for political and linguistic models. Black power, feminism, resistance to the war in Vietnam and the New Left were all available, and each contributed to the emerging gay style and vocabulary. Discussing the beginning of the movement in this way, however, makes it sound too solemn and deliberate. Our recognition that we formed an oppressed minority struck us as *humorous* at first; only later did we come to take ourselves seriously.

I can remember that after the cops cleared out the bar we clustered in Christopher Street around the entrance to the Stonewall. The customers were not being arrested, but a paddy wagon had already hauled off several of the bartenders. Two or three policemen stayed behind, locked inside with the remaining members of the staff, waiting for the return of the paddy wagon. During that interval someone in the defiant crowd outside called out, "Gay Power," which caused us all to laugh. The notion that gays might become militant after the manner of blacks seemed amusing for two reasons—first because we gay men were used to thinking of ourselves as too effeminate to protest anything and secondly because most of us did not consider ourselves to be a legitimate minority.

At that time we perceived ourselves as separate individuals at odds with society because we were "sick" (the medical model), "sinful" (the religious model), "deviant" (the sociological model) or "criminal" (the legal model). Some of these words we might have said lightly, satirically, but no amount of wit could convince us that our grievances should be remedied or our status defended. We might ask for compassion but we could not demand justice. Many gays either were in therapy or felt they should be, and the words *gay liberation* would have seemed as preposterous to us as *neurotic liberation* (now, of course, Thomas S. Szasz in the United States, R.D. Laing in England and Felix Guattari on the Continent have, in their different ways, made even that phrase plausible enough.)

What I want to stress is that before 1969 only a small (though courageous and articulate) number of gays had much pride in their homosexuality or a conviction that their predilections were legitimate. The rest of us defined our homosexuality in negative terms, and those terms isolated us from one another. We might claim Plato and Michelangelo as homosexuals and revere them for their supposed affinities to us, but we could just as readily dismiss, even despise, a living thinker or artist for being gay. Rich gays may have derived pleasure from their wealth, educated gays from their knowledge, talented gays from their gifts, but few felt anything but regret about their homosexuality as such. To be sure, particular sexual encounters, and especially particular love relationships, were gratifying then as now, but they were explained as happy accidents rather than as expected results.

Moreover, the very idea that sexual identity might demarcate a political entity was still fairly novel. Minority status seemed to be vouchsafed by birth, to be involuntary. One was born into a race or religion or nationality or social class—that was the way to become a member of a *real* minority. One could also be born a woman, though the large claims advanced by feminists still struck many people then as preposterous. Women, after all, formed a majority and they scarcely seemed to have much in common. Did an upper-class WASP woman from Boston share a perspective with a poor Chicano Catholic woman from Waco? The same question could be asked about gays: what was our common bond? This "category confusion" assailed us and may have been one source of our laughter upon hearing the phrase *gay power*.

Then there was the problem about how people become gay. If they're born that way, they may represent, depending on the point of view, a genetic mistake or an evolutionary advance or a normal variation. If, on the other hand, they choose to be gay, then their rights seem less defensible; what has been chosen can be rejected. A third possibility is that the environment makes people gay against their will—but this etiology, because of conventional associations if not logical arguments, again smacks of pathology and suggests gays should seek to be "cured."

I raise these issues not because I propose answers (the whole discussion strikes me as politically retrograde, since at this point any etiology would disguise a program for prevention). I bring up the matter only because I want to demonstrate what a strange sort of "minority" homosexuals belong to and why we were reluctant to embrace the political vocabulary (and stance) that had been useful in securing the civil rights of other groups.

Nevertheless, because the black movement was highly vocal and visible at the time of Stonewall, slogans such as "black is beautiful" were easily translated into "gay is good" and "black power" became "gay power." Some of the resistants even dubbed themselves "pink panthers," but that name did not catch on. These derivations, I should hasten to point out, were not approved of by black militants who, like most young white leftists, regarded homosexuality as "decadent" and "bourgeois." In 1971, I believe, H. Rap Brown did propose a coalition between blacks and gays, but that suggestion was not very popular among his constituents.

A less obvious imitation of the black movement by gays was the elevation of the word *gay* itself. Just as *Negro* had been rejected as something contaminated because it had been used by (supposedly hypocritical) liberals and the seemingly more neutral *black* was brought into currency, in the same way *homosexual*, with its medical textbook ring, was dismissed in favor of the more informal and seemingly more innocuous *gay* (I say "seemingly" because these words, *black* and *gay*, do have complex etymologies).

No one I know has any real information about the origins of the word *gay*; the research all remains to be done. Those who dislike the word assume that it is synonymous with *happy* or *lighthearted* and that its use implies that homosexuals regard heterosexuals, by contrast, as "grim." But *gay* has had many meanings, including "loose" and "immoral," especially in reference to a prostitute (a whorehouse was once called a "gay house"). In the past one asked if a woman was "gay," much as today one might ask if she "swings." The identification of *gay* with "immoral" is further strengthened by the fact that *queen* (a male homosexual) is almost certainly derived from *quean* (the Elizabethan word for prostitute).

In American slang at the turn of the century, a "gay cat" was a younger, less experienced man who attached himself to an older, more seasoned vagrant or hobo; implicit in the relationship between gay cat and hobo was a sexual liaison. Yet another slang meaning of *gay* is "fresh," "impertinent," "saucy" (not so very distant from "immoral"). In French *gai* can mean "spicy" or "ribald." My hunch (and it's only a hunch) is that the word may turn out to be very old, to have originated in France, worked its way to England in the eighteenth century and thence to the colonies in America. It has died out in Europe and England and is now being reintroduced as a new word from the United States. But this is only speculation.

If the exact etymology is vague, no wonder; the word served for years as a shibboleth, and the function of a shibboleth is to exclude outsiders. Undoubtedly it has had until recently its greatest vogue among Americans. In England, the standard slang word has been *queer*. In Bloomsbury *bugger* was the preferred term, presumably because it was salty and vulgar enough to send those rarefied souls into convulsions of laughter. One pictures Virginia Woolf discussing "buggery" with Lytton Strachey; how they must have relished the word's public school, criminal and eighteenth-century connotations.

Today heterosexuals commonly object to *gay* on the grounds that it has ruined for them the ordinary festive sense of the word; one can no longer say, "How gay I feel!" It seems frivolous, however, to discuss this semantic loss beside the political gain the word represents for American homosexuals. An English novelist visiting the States, after boring everyone by saying she felt gay life was actually sad (an observation she presented as though it were original), proceeded to call gay men "queer," which I presume is less offensive in England than in America (a few older Americans use the word).

Many homosexuals object to *gay* on other grounds, arguing that it's too silly to designate a life-style, a minority or a political movement. But, as the critic Seymour Kleinberg has mentioned in his introduction to *The Other Persuasion: Short Fiction about Gay Men and Women*, "For all its limitations, 'gay' is the only unpompous, unpsychological term acceptable to most men and women, one already widely used and available to heterosexuals without suggesting something pejorative." *Gay* is, moreover, one of the few words that does not refer explicitly to sexual activity. One of the problems that has beleaguered gays is that their identity has always been linked to sexual activity rather than to affectional preference. The word *gay* (whatever its etymology) at least does not *sound* sexual.

In any event, *gay* is so workable a word that in the last ten years it has shifted from being just an adjective to being both an adjective and a noun. One now says, "Several gays were present," though such a construction sounds awkward to older American homosexuals.

Just as Fowler in *A Guide to Modern English Usage* objects to *human* as a noun and prefers *human being*, so many homosexuals still prefer *gay person* or *gay man*.

The connection between feminism and gay liberation has been strong for a decade, though now it has broken down. Because of this break, the word *gay* now generally refers to homosexual men alone. Homosexual women prefer to be called *lesbians*, pure and simple. Most lesbian radicals feel they have more in common with the feminist movement than with gay liberation. Since political lesbians tend to resent a male spokesman, I have confined most of my remarks in this essay to the gay male experience which, in any event, is more within my range of competence and understanding.

This fairly recent rupture, however, should not obscure the debt that gay liberation owes to feminism. The members of both movements, for instance, regard their inner experiences as political, and for both gays and feminists the function of consciousness-raising sessions has been to trace the exact contours of their oppression. Women and gay men, as the argument goes, have been socialized into adopting restricting roles that are viewed with contempt by heterosexual men (despite the fact that these very roles reinforce the values of a virilist society). Accordingly, at least one aspect of feminism and gay liberation has been to end the tyranny of stereotyped behavior. Much of this stereotyping, of course, is perpetuated by the victimized themselves. Many women have a low opinion of other women, and many gays are quick to ridicule other gays.

For example, political gays have fought the use of the feminine gender when employed by one homosexual man of another. In the past a regular feature of gay male speech was the production of such sentences as: "Oh, *her*! She'd do anything to catch a husband . . ." in which the "she" is Bob or Jim. This routine gender substitution is rapidly dying out, and many gay men under twenty-five fail to practice it or even to understand it. This linguistic game has been attacked for two reasons: first, because it supposedly perpetuates female role playing among some gay men; and second, because it is regarded in some quarters as hostile to women. Since one man generally calls another "she" in an (at least mildly) insulting context, the inference is that the underlying attitude must be sexist: to be a woman is to be inferior.

Following the same line, a large segment of the lesbian and gay male population frowns on drag queens, who are seen as mocking women, all the more so because they get themselves up in the most *retardataire* female guises (show girls, prostitutes, sex kittens, Hollywood starlets).

This rejection of transvestites has been harsh and perhaps not well thought out. As long ago as 1970 Kate Millett in *Sexual Politics* saw the drag queen in quite another light—as a useful subversive:

> . . . as she minces along a street in the Village, the storm of outrage an insouciant queen in drag may call down is due to the fact that she is both masculine and feminine at once—or male, but feminine. She has made gender identity more than frighteningly easy to lose, she has questioned its reality at a time when it has attained the status of a moral absolute and a social imperative. She has defied it and actually suggested its negation. She has dared obloquy, and in doing so has challenged more than the taboo on homosexuality, she has uncovered what the source of this contempt implies—the fact that sex role is sex rank.

Anyone familiar with drag knows that it is an *art* of impersonation, not an act of deception, still less of ridicule. The drag queen performing in a night club, for instance, is often careful to reveal his true masculinity (deep voice, flat chest, short hair) at some point in his performance; such a revelation underscores the achievements of artifice. Since, in addition, most gay transvestites are from the working class and many are either black or Puerto Rican, discrimination against them may be both snobbish and racist. The greatest irony is that the Stonewall Resistance itself and many other gay "street actions" were led by transvestites.

As for why drag queens have singled out prostitutes and show girls to imitate, the explanation may be at least partially historical. In Jonathan Katz's *Gay American History*, one discovers a clue. Testimony given to the New York police in 1899 has this to say of male prostitutes: "These men that conduct themselves there—well, they act effeminately; most of them are painted and powdered; they are called Princess this and Lady So and So and the Duchess of Marlboro, and get up and sing as women, and dance; ape the female character; call each other sisters and take people out for immoral purposes."

Obviously, then, many of the early drag queens actually were prostitutes. Others may have found that the world of the theater and prostitution was the only one where overt homosexuals were welcome. Or perhaps the assertive make-believe of such women, purveyors of sex and fantasy, seemed naturally related to the forbidden pleasures of gay men. Or perhaps the assault on convention staged by prostitutes and performers appealed to gay men because it was a gaudy if ambiguous expression of anger. In any event, this legacy can still be faintly heard in gay speech today, though less and less often ("Don't be such a cunt," "Look, bitch, don't cross me," "Go, girl, shake that money-maker" and in a vagueness about proper names and the substitution of the generic *darling* or *Mary*). Much more hardy is a small but essential vocabulary derived from prostitute's slang, including: *trick* (a casual sex partner as a noun, to have quickie sex as a verb); *box* (the crotch); *trade* (one-sided sex); *number* (a sex partner); *john* (a paying customer); *to hustle* (to sell sex); *to score or to make out* (to find sex) and so on. Few young gays, however, know the origins of these words, and certain locutions borrowed from prostitutes have been modified in order to obscure their mercenary connotations. For instance, few homosexuals still say, "I'd like to turn that trick." Instead, they say, "I'd like to trick with him." That homosexual slang should be patterned after the slang of prostitutes suggests that in the past the only homosexual men who dared talk about their sexual tastes and practices either were prostitutes themselves or lived in that milieu. Curiously, that vocabulary has flourished among gay men who have never dreamed of selling sex.

In the past, feminization, at least to a small and symbolic degree, seemed a necessary initiation into gay life; we all thought we had to be a bit *nelly* (effeminate) in order to be truly gay. Today almost the opposite seems to be true. In any crowd it is the homosexual men who are wearing beards, army fatigues, checked lumberjack shirts, work boots and T-shirts and whose bodies are conspicuously built up. Ironically, at a time when many young heterosexual men are exploring their androgeny by living with women in platonic amicability and by stripping away their masculine stoicism and toughness, young gays are busy arraying themselves in these castoffs and becoming cowboys, truckers, telephone linemen, football players (in appearance and sometimes also in reality).

This masculinization of gay life is now nearly universal. Flamboyance has been traded in for a sober, restrained manner. Voices are lower, jewelry is shed, cologne is banished and, in the decor of houses, velvet and chandeliers have been exchanged for functional carpet and industrial lights. The campy queen who screams in falsetto, *dishes* (playfully insults) her friends, swishes by in drag is an anachronism; in her place is an updated Paul Bunyan.

Personal advertisements for lovers or sex partners in gay publications call for men who are "macho," "butch," "masculine" or who have a "straight appearance." The advertisements insist that "no femmes need apply." So extreme is this masculinization that it has been termed "macho fascism" by its critics. They point out that the true social mission of liberated homosexuals should be to break down, not reinforce, role-playing stereotypes. Gay men should exemplify the dizzying rewards of living beyond gender. But they have betrayed this promise and ended up by aping the most banal images of conventionally "rugged" men—or so the anti-macho line would have it.

In the heady, early days of gay liberation, certainly, apologists foresaw the speedy arrival of a unisex paradise in which gay angels, dressed in flowing garments and glorying in shoulder-length, silken hair, would instruct heterosexual men in how to discard their cumbersome masculinity and ascend to the heights of androgyny. Paradoxically, today it is the young straights who wear their hair long and style it daily, who deck themselves out in luxurious fabrics and gold filaments, who cover their bodies with unguents, dive into a padded conversation pit and squirm about in "group gropes" (in which, mind you, lesbianism may be encouraged for its entertainment value to male spectators but never the swains shall meet). Simultaneously but elsewhere, crew-cut gays, garbed in denim and rawhide are manfully swilling beer at a country and western bar and, each alone in the crowd, tapping a scuffed boot to Johnny Cash's latest.

Another objection to the masculinization of gay life is that it has changed a motley crew of eccentrics into a highly conformist army of clones. Whereas gays in the past could be slobs or bohemians or Beau Brummels or aesthetes striking "stained glass attitudes" or tightly closeted businessmen in gray flannel suits, today this range of possibility has been narrowed to a uniform look and manner that is uninspiredly butch. The flamboyance and seediness and troubling variety of gay life (a variety that once embraced all the outcasts of society, including those who were not gay) have given way to a militant sameness.

This argument, I think, ignores our historical moment. In the past gay men embraced the bias of the oppressor that identified homosexuality with effeminacy, degeneracy, failure. To have discovered that this link is not necessary has released many homosexuals into a forceful assertion of their masculinity, normality, success—an inevitable and perhaps salutary response. Moreover, the conformism of gay life, I suspect, is more on the level of appearance than reality. The butch look is such a successful get-up for cruising that some sort of "natural selection" in mating has made it prevail over all other costumes. But this look does not preclude the expression of individuality, of tenderness and zaniness, in conversation and private behavior.

Yet another thought occurs to me. In the past many homosexuals despised each other and yearned for even the most fleeting and unsatisfactory sexual (or even social) contact with straight men. Some gays considered sex with other homosexuals pointless and pitiable, a poor second best, and thirsted for the font of all value and authenticity, a "real" (i.e., straight) man. Today, fortified by gay liberation, homosexuals have become those very men they once envied and admired from afar.

The apotheosis of the adult macho man has meant that the current heart-throb in gay pornography—and in actual gay cruising situations—is no longer the lithe youth of nineteen but rather the prepossessing stud of thirty-five. The ephebe with hyacinthine curls has given way to the bald marine drill sergeant, and Donatello's *David* demurs to Bernini's.

The change has affected the language of approbation. In the past one admired a "boy" who was "beautiful" or "pretty" or "cute." Now one admires a man who is "tough" or "virile" or "hot." Perhaps no other word so aptly signals the new gay attitudes as *hot*. Whereas *beautiful* in gay parlance characterizes the face first and the body only secondarily, *hot* describes the whole man, but especially his physique. One may have a lantern jaw or an assymmetrical nose or pockmarked skin and still be "hot," whereas the signs of the "beautiful" face are regular features, smooth skin, suave coloring—and youth. The "hot" man may even fail to have an attractive body; his appeal may lie instead in his wardrobe, his manner, his style. In this way "hotness" is roughly equivalent to "presence" with an accent on the sexy rather than the magisterial sense of that word. In addition, "hot" can, like the Italian *simpatico*, modify everything from people to discos, from cars to clothing. Gay chartered cruises promise a "hot" vacation and designers strive after a "hot" look. If an attractive man strolls by, someone will murmur, "That's hot." The "that" in place of "he" may be an acknowledgment that the person is as much a package as a human being, though more likely the impersonal pronoun is a last echo of the old practice (now virtually abandoned) of referring to a one-time-only sex partner as an "it" (as in, "The trick was fine in bed, but I had to throw it out this morning—couldn't get it to shut up").

Gay male culture, as though in flight from its effeminate past, is more and more gravitating towards the trappings of sado-masochism. The big-city gay man of today no longer clusters with friends around a piano at a bar to sing songs from musicals; now he goes to a leather and western bar to play pool and swill beer. Gay men belong to motorcycle clubs or engage in anonymous sex in backrooms, those dimly lit penetralia behind the normally sociable bar.

The popularity of sado-masochistic sex has introduced new words into the gay vocabulary—as well as their domesticated, more casual variants. The original terms, such as *slave* and *master*, must have seemed too absurd, too theatrical, not quite plausible, too . . . well, *embarrassing*. It is socially awkward to ask a stranger if he wants to be your "slave" for the night. The word invokes dungeons, chains, pornographic novels of the eighteenth century—a sort of period claptrap. As a result, nearly every word in the original vocabulary has found its more conversational, more up-to-date euphemism. "Sado-masochism" itself has thus become "S and M" or, more recently and innocuously, "rough stuff." Bondage and discipline is now "B and D." "Sadist" and "masochist" have become "top man" and "bottom man." The way to ask someone to be your slave, therefore, is "Are you into a bottom scene?" Similarly, sexual aggression kept on the level of fantasy is a "head trip," whereas to want physical abuse is to be "into pain." And the "dungeon" has become the "game room."

Interestingly, gay men, usually so fastidious about staying *au courant*, are willing to utter outmoded hippy words from the drug culture of the sixties such as *scene*, *trip* and *into* if those words enable periphrases that stand in for the still more ludicrous vocabulary of classical sadism.

I have tried to point out that gay male culture and language have registered a shift in taste away from effeminacy to masculinity and from youth to maturity. But now a larger question might be posed: has the status of—and the need for—a private language itself become less important to homosexuals?

I think it has. In the past homosexuality was regarded with such opprobrium and homosexuals remained so inconspicuous that we faced some difficulty in detecting one another. A familiar game was to introduce into an otherwise normal conversation a single word that might seem innocent enough except to the initiated ("I went to a very lively and gay party last night"). If that risk was greeted with words from the same vocabulary ("I'm afraid the party I went to was a real drag; everyone acted like royalty," i.e., "queens"), a contact was established. Two businessmen could thus identify themselves to one another in the midst of a heterosexual gathering.

But the value of a private language was not merely practical. It also allowed gays to name everything anew, to appropriate experience in terms that made sense only to the few. Sailors became "sea food," "chicken" (always singular) were teenage boys and so on—there is a whole book, *The Queen's Vernacular*, that lists these words. Equally amusing and subversive was the pleasure of referring to a revered public leader as "Miss Eisenhower," or to oneself (as Auden does at the end of an otherwise serious poem) as "Miss Me." When gay frustration had no outlet in action it could find expression only in language. But even in language the impulse had become sour and self-destructive through long suppression; its target was more often other gays than straights or in the fiction that respectable straights were actually outrageous queens. In self-satire lies the reflexive power of thwarted anger. Gay identity, now rehearsed nightly in thronged discos and in a myriad of gay bars, was once much more tenuous. It was an illegitimate existence that took refuge in language, the one system that could swiftly, magically, topple values and convert a golf-playing general into a co-conspirator in a gingham frock and turn a timid waiter into a queen for a night—or at least into the Duchess of Marlboro.

Now that homosexuals have no need for indirection, now that their suffering has been eased and their place in society adumbrated if not secured, the suggestion has been made that they will no longer produce great art. There will be no liberated Prousts, the argument goes, an idea demonstrated by pointing to the failure of *Maurice* in contrast to Forester's heterosexual novels. A review of my novel, *Nocturnes for the King of Naples*, claimed that it was not as strong as my earlier, "straight" *Forgetting Elena* precisely because I no longer need to resort to the pretense of heterosexuality.

This position strikes me as strange and unexamined. Proust, of course, *did* write at length about homosexual characters—in fact, one of the complaints against his novel is that so many characters implausibly turn out to be homosexual. *Maurice*, I suspect, is a failure not because it is homosexual but because it is a rather exalted, sentimentalized masturbation fantasy. When he wrote *Maurice*, Forester had even less knowledge of the homosexual than of the heterosexual world, and he was forced back on his day-dreams rather than on his observations from life. It is not for me to judge the merits of my own books, but what strikes me as most "homosexual" about *Nocturnes* is not the content so much as the technique, one that uses endless dissolves of time and geography, as though the same party were being reassembled over decades and on different continents, something like that "marvellous party" in the Noel Coward song. Anyone who has experienced the enduring and international links of gay life will recognize how the technique is a formal equivalent to the experience.

Unless one accepts the dreary (and unproved) Freudian notion that art is a product of sublimated neuroses, one would not predict that gay liberation would bring an end to the valuable art made by homosexuals. On the contrary, liberation should free gays from tediously repetitious works that end in madness or suicide, that dwell on the "etiology" of the characters' homosexuality (shadowy Dad, suffocating Mom, beloved, doomed, effeminate Cousin Bill) and that feature long, static scenes in which Roger gently weeps over Hank's mislaid hiking boot. Now a new range of subject matter has opened up to gays, much of it comic; Feydeau, after all, would have loved gay life, since every character can cheat with every other and the mathematical possibilities of who may be hiding under the bed (if not in the closet) have been raised geometrically. Still more importantly, gay liberation means that not so many talentless souls need to continue lingering about in the sacred precincts (i.e., the gay ghetto) of high culture. Finally they are free to pursue all those other occupations they once feared to enter—electrical engineering, riding the range, plumbing. The association between homosexuals and the arts, I suspect, suited some of us but not most; the great majority of gays are as reassuringly philistine as the bulk of straights.

Content

1. Summarize the reasons White offers for gay men's earlier reluctance "to embrace the political vocabulary (and stance) that had been useful in securing the civil rights of other groups" (paragraph 8).
2. What do you understand to be the relationship between the new language of gays and what White calls "the masculinization of gay life" (paragraph 7)? In your opinion, did the new language cause the masculinization or is the new language merely a reflection of the changes taking place?
3. White entitles this essay, "The Political Vocabulary of Homosexuality," and the first incident he describes involves what he calls "police harassment" and "a quickening sense of solidarity." What definition of "politics" does White imply in this essay?

Technique

1. Why do you suppose White includes so many examples of older gay terms in this essay? In what way does his careful analysis of gay language explain or even defend gay life?
2. Would you describe the tone of this essay as formal, conversational, angry, or defensive? Citing specific passages to support your answer, be prepared to discuss whether or not the tone he chooses seems effective. Why or why not?

Language

1. The words "colored" and "Negro," once acceptable, have been largely replaced by the word "black." Similarly, "homosexual" has now given way to "gay." Do you think these words reflect a new position in society for these groups they describe? Explain.
2. Why do you suppose White feels the semantic loss of the word "gay" is small "beside the political gain the word represents for American homosexuals" (paragraph 13)? Do you find his argument convincing?
3. The vocabulary of this essay could be described as mixed in that words such as "shibboleth" appear in the same paragraph (12) as "salty" and "vulgar." For what audience do you suppose this essay was originally intended? Explain.

Vocabulary

solidarity	shibboleth	semantic
political	stereotype	androgeny
etiology	pejorative	approbation

Writing Suggestions

1. Write a paragraph in which you analyze your own response to the term "gay."
2. People who are not members of minorities also develop a language unique to the group. Write an essay in which you classify the private language of some group other than a politically active minority group, one with which you are familiar. Explain, if possible, its origins and its purpose within the group.
3. The women's movement has been called "women's liberation," then "feminism," and now we begin to hear the term "womanism." Blacks have called themselves "colored," then "Negro," then "black." In this essay, White discusses the importance of the term "gay" to the movement for homosexual rights. Write an essay in which you analyze the significance of identifying terms to the self-image of minority and politically active groups.

Aria

Richard Rodriguez

Richard Rodriguez (b. 1944), a graduate of Stanford and Columbia universities, did graduate work at the University of California, Berkeley, and at the Warburg Institute in London. His essays have appeared in The American Scholar, College English, *and in* Change *magazine.* Hunger of Memory, *the autobiography which contained a controversial argument against bilingual education, appeared in 1982. "Aria" is taken from that book; it details the hardships and complexities of growing up in a world of two languages.*

1   I remember to start with that day in Sacramento—a California now nearly thirty years past—when I first entered a classroom, able to understand some fifty stray English words.

The third of four children, I had been preceded to a neighborhood Roman Catholic school by an older brother and sister. But neither of them had revealed very much about their classroom experiences. Each afternoon they returned, as they left in the morning, always together, speaking in Spanish as they climbed the five steps of the porch. And their mysterious books, wrapped in shopping-bag paper, remained on the table next to the door, closed firmly behind them.

An accident of geography sent me to a school where all my classmates were white, many the children of doctors and lawyers and business executives. All my classmates certainly must have been uneasy on that first day of school—as most children are uneasy—to find themselves apart from their families in the first institution of their lives. But I was astonished.

The nun said, in a friendly but oddly impersonal voice, "Boys and girls, this is Richard Rodriguez." (I heard her sound out: *Rich-heard Road-ree-guess.*) It was the first time I had heard anyone name me in English. "Richard," the nun repeated more slowly, writing my name down in her black leather book. Quickly I turned to see my mother's face dissolve in a watery blur behind the pebbled glass door.

Many years later there is something called bilingual education—a scheme proposed in the late 1960s by Hispanic-American social activists, later endorsed by congressional vote. It is a program that seeks to permit non-English-speaking children, many from lower-class homes, to use their family language as the language of school. (Such is the goal its supporters announce.) I hear them and am forced to say no: It is not possible for a child—any child—ever to use his family's language in school. Not to understand this is to misunderstand the public uses of schooling and to trivialize the nature of intimate life—a family's "language."

Memory teaches me what I know of these matters; the boy reminds the adult. I was a bilingual child, a certain kind—socially disadvantaged—the son of working-class parents, both Mexican immigrants.

In the early years of my boyhood, my parents coped very well in America. My father had steady work. My mother managed at home. They were nobody's victims. Optimism and ambition led them to a house (our home) many blocks from the Mexican south side of town. We lived among *gringos* and only a block from the biggest, whitest houses. It never occurred to my parents that they couldn't live wherever they chose. Nor was the Sacramento of the fifties bent on teaching them a contrary lesson. My mother and father were more annoyed than intimidated by those two or three neighbors who tried initially to make us unwelcome. ("Keep your brats away from my sidewalk!") But despite all they achieved, perhaps because they had so much to achieve, any deep feeling of ease, the confidence of "belonging" in public was withheld from them both. They regarded the people at work, the faces in crowds, as very distant from us. They were the others, *los gringos*. That term was interchangeable in their speech with another, even more telling, *los americanos*.

I grew up in a house where the only regular guests were my relations. For one day, enormous families of relatives would visit and there would be so many people that the noise and the bodies would spill out to the backyard and front porch. Then, for weeks, no one came by. (It was usually a salesman who rang the doorbell.) Our house stood apart. A gaudy yellow in a row of white bungalows. We were the people with the noisy dog. The people who raised pigeons and chickens. We were the foreigners on the block. A few neighbors smiled and waved. We waved back. But no one in the family knew the names of the old couple who lived next door; until I was seven years old, I did not know the names of the kids who lived across the street.

In public, my father and mother spoke a hesitant, accented, not always grammatical English. And they would have to strain—their bodies tense—to catch the sense of what was rapidly said by *los gringos*. At home they spoke Spanish. The language of their Mexican past sounded in counterpoint to the English of public society. The words would come quickly, with ease. Conveyed through those sounds was the pleasing, soothing, consoling reminder of being at home.

During those years when I was first conscious of hearing, my mother and father addressed me only in Spanish; in Spanish I learned to reply. By contrast, English (inglés), rarely heard in the house, was the language I came to associate with *gringos*. I learned my first words of English overhearing my parents speak to strangers. At five years of age, I knew just enough English for my mother to trust me on errands to stores one block away. No more.

I was a listening child, careful to hear the very different sounds of Spanish and English. Wide-eyed with hearing, I'd listen to sounds more than words. First, there were English (*gringo*) sounds. So many words were still unknown that when the butcher or the lady at the drugstore said something to me, exotic polysyllabic sounds would bloom in the midst of their sentences. Often, the speech of people in public seemed to me very loud, booming with confidence. The man behind the counter would literally ask, "What can I do for you?" But by being so firm and so clear, the sound of his voice said that he was a *gringo*; he belonged in public society.

I would also hear then the high nasal notes of middle-class American speech. The air stirred with sound. Sometimes, even now, when I have been traveling abroad for several weeks, I will hear what I heard as a boy. In hotel lobbies or airports, in Turkey or Brazil, some Americans will pass, and suddenly I will hear it again—the high sound of American voices. For a few seconds I will hear it with pleasure, for it is now the sound of *my* society—a reminder of home. But inevitably—already on the flight headed for home—the sound fades with repetition. I will be unable to hear it anymore.

When I was a boy, things were different. The accent of *los gringos* was never pleasing nor was it hard to hear. Crowds at Safeway or at bus stops would be noisy with sound. And I would be forced to edge away from the chirping chatter above me.

I was unable to hear my own sounds, but I knew very well that I spoke English poorly. My words could not stretch far enough to form complete thoughts. And the words I did speak I didn't know well enough to make into distinct sounds. (Listeners would usually lower their heads, better to hear what I was trying to say.) But it was one thing for *me* to speak English with difficulty. It was more troubling for me to hear my parents speak in public: their high-whining vowels and guttural consonants; their sentences that got stuck with "eh" and "ah" sounds; the confused syntax; the hesitant rhythm of sounds so different from the way *gringos* spoke. I'd notice, moreover, that my parents' voices were softer than those of *gringos* we'd meet.

I am tempted now to say that none of this mattered. In adulthood I am embarrassed by childhood fears. And, in a way, it didn't matter very much that my parents could not speak English with ease. Their linguistic difficulties had no serious consequences. My mother and father made themselves understood at the county hospital clinic and at government offices. And yet, in another way, it mattered very much—it was unsettling to hear my parents struggle with English. Hearing them, I'd grow nervous, my clutching trust in their protection and power weakened.

There were many times like the night at a brightly lit gasoline station (a blaring white memory) when I stood uneasily, hearing my father. He was talking to a teenaged attendant. I do not recall what they were saying, but I cannot forget the sounds my father made as he spoke. At one point his words slid together to form one word—sounds as confused as the threads of blue and green oil in the puddle next to my shoes. His voice rushed through what he had left to say. And, toward the end, reached falsetto notes, appealing to his listener's understanding. I looked away to the lights of passing automobiles. I tried not to hear anymore. But I heard only too well the calm, easy tones in the attendant's reply. Shortly afterward, walking toward home with my father, I shivered when he put his hand on my shoulder. The very first chance that I got, I evaded his grasp and ran on ahead into the dark, skipping with feigned boyish exhuberance.

But then there was Spanish. *Español*: my family's language. *Español*: the language that seemed to me a private language. I'd hear strangers on the radio and in the Mexican Catholic church across town speaking in Spanish, but I couldn't really believe that Spanish was a public language, like English. Spanish speakers, rather, seemed related to me, for I sensed that we shared—through our language—the experience of feeling apart from *los gringos*. It was thus a ghetto Spanish that I heard and I spoke. Like those whose lives are bound by a barrio, I was reminded by Spanish of my separateness from *los otros, los gringos* in power. But more intensely than for most barrio children—because I did not live in a barrio—Spanish seemed to me the language of home. (Most days it was only at home that I'd hear it.) It became the language of joyful return.

A family member would say something to me and I would feel myself specially recognized. My parents would say something to me and I would feel embraced by the sounds of their words. Those sounds said: *I am speaking with ease in Spanish. I am addressing you in words I never use with* los gringos. *I recognize you as someone special, close, like no one outside. You belong with us. In the family.*

(Ricardo.)

At the age of five, six, well past the time when most other children no longer easily notice the difference between sounds uttered at home and words spoken in public, I had a different experience.

I lived in a world magically compounded of sounds. I remained a child longer than most; I lingered too long, poised at the edge of language—often frightened by the sounds of *los gringos*, delighted by the sounds of Spanish at home. I shared with my family a language that was startlingly different from that used in the great city around us.

For me there were none of the gradations between public and private society so normal to a maturing child. Outside the house was public society; inside the house was private. Just opening or closing the screen door behind me was an important experience. I'd rarely leave home all alone or without reluctance. Walking down the sidewalk, under the canopy of tall trees, I'd warily notice the—suddenly—silent neighborhood kids who stood warily watching me. Nervously, I'd arrive at the grocery store to hear there the sounds of the *gringo*—foreign to me—reminding me that in this world so big, I was a foreigner. But then I'd return. Walking back toward our house, climbing the steps from the sidewalk, when the front door was open in summer, I'd hear voices beyond the screen door talking in Spanish. For a second or two, I'd stay, linger there, listening. Smiling, I'd hear my mother call out, saying in Spanish (words): "Is that you, Richard?" All the while her sounds would assure me: *You are home now; come closer; inside. With us.*

"Sí," I'd reply.

Once more inside the house I would resume (assume) my place in the family. The sounds would dim, grow harder to hear. Once more at home, I would grow less aware of that fact. It required, however, no more than the blurt of the doorbell to alert me to listen to sounds all over again. The house would turn instantly still while my mother went to the door. I'd hear her hard English sounds. I'd wait to hear her voice return to soft-sounding Spanish, which assured me, as surely as did the clicking tongue of the lock on the door, that the stranger was gone.

Plainly, it is not healthy to hear such sounds so often. It is not healthy to distinguish public words from private sounds so easily. I remained cloistered by sounds, timid and shy in public, too dependent on voices at home. And yet it needs to be emphasized: I was an extremely happy child at home. I remember many nights when my father would come back from work, and I'd hear him call out to my mother in Spanish, sounding relieved. In Spanish, he'd sound light and free notes he never could manage in English. Some nights

I'd jump up just at hearing his voice. With *mis hermanos* I would come running into the room where he was with my mother. Our laughing (so deep was the pleasure!) became screaming. Like others who know the pain of public alienation, we transformed the knowledge of our public separateness and made it consoling—the reminder of intimacy. Excited, we joined our voices in a celebration of sounds. *We are speaking now the way we never speak out in public. We are alone—together*, voices sounded, surrounded to tell me. Some nights, no one seemed willing to loosen the hold sounds had on us. At dinner, we invented new words. (Ours sounded Spanish, but made sense only to us.) We pieced together new words by taking, say, an English verb and giving it Spanish endings. My mother's instructions at bedtime would be lacquered with mock-urgent tones. Or a word like *sí* would become, in several notes, able to convey added measures of feeling. Tongues explored the edges of words, especially the fat vowels. And we happily sounded that military drum roll, the twirling roar of the Spanish *r*. Family language: my family's sounds. The voices of my parents and sisters and brother. Their voices insisting: *You belong here. We are family members. Related. Special to one another. Listen!* Voices singing and sighing, rising, straining, then surging, teeming with pleasure that burst syllables into fragments of laughter. At times it seemed there was steady quiet only when, from another room, the rustling whispers of my parents faded and I moved closer to sleep.

Supporters of bilingual education today imply that students like me miss a great deal by not being taught in their family's language. What they seem not to recognize is that, as a socially disadvantaged child, I considered Spanish to be a private language. What I needed to learn in school was that I had the right—and the obligation—to speak the public language of *los gringos*. The odd truth is that my first-grade classmates could have become bilingual, in the conventional sense of that word, more easily than I. Had they been taught (as upper-middle-class children are often taught early) a second language like Spanish or French, they could have regarded it simply as that: another public language. In my case such bilingualism could not have been so quickly achieved. What I did not believe was that I could speak a single public language.

Without question, it would have pleased me to hear my teachers address me in Spanish when I entered the classroom. I would have felt much less afraid. I would have trusted them and responded with ease. But I would have delayed—for how long postponed?—having to learn the language of public society. I would have evaded—and for how long could I have afforded to delay?—learning the great lesson of school, that I had a public identity.

Fortunately, my teachers were unsentimental about their responsibility. What they understood was that I needed to speak a public language. So their voices would search me out, asking me questions. Each time I'd hear them, I'd look up in surprise to see a nun's face frowning at me. I'd mumble, not really meaning to answer. The nun would persist, "Richard, stand up. Don't look at the floor. Speak up. Speak to the entire class, not just to me!" But I couldn't believe that the English language was mine to use. (In part, I did not want to believe it.) I continued to mumble. I resisted the teacher's demands. (Did I somehow expect that once I learned the public language my pleasing family life would be changed?) Silent, waiting for the bell to sound, I remained dazed, diffident, afraid.

Because I wrongly imagined that English was intrinsically a public language and Spanish an intrinsically private one, I easily noted the difference between classroom language and the language of home. At school, words were directed to a general audience of listeners. ("Boys and girls.") Words were meaningfully ordered. And the point was not self-expression alone but to make oneself understood by many others. The teacher quizzed: "Boys and girls, why do we use that word in this sentence? Could we think of a better word to use there? Would the sentence change its meaning if the words were differently arranged? And wasn't there a better way of saying much the same thing?" (I couldn't say. I wouldn't try to say.)

Three months. Five. Half a year passed. Unsmiling, ever watchful, my teachers noted my silence. They began to connect my behavior with the difficult progress my older sister and brother were making. Until one Saturday morning three nuns arrived at the house to talk to our parents. Stiffly, they sat on the blue living room sofa. From the doorway of another room, spying the visitors, I noted the incongruity—the clash of two worlds, the faces and voices of school intruding upon the familiar setting of home. I overheard one voice gently wondering, "Do your children speak only Spanish at home, Mrs. Rodriguez?" While another voice added, "That Richard especially seems so timid and shy."

That Rich-heard!

With great tact the visitors continued, "Is it possible for you and 31
your husband to encourage your children to practice their English
when they are at home?" Of course, my parents complied. What
would they not do for their children's well-being? And how could
they have questioned the Church's authority which those women
represented? In an instant, they agreed to give up the language (the
sounds) that had revealed and accentuated our family's closeness.
The moment after the visitors left, the change was observed. "*Ahora,
speak to us en inglés,*" my father and mother united to tell us.

At first, it seemed a kind of game. After dinner each night, the 32
family gathered to practice 'our' English. (It was still then *inglés*, a
language foreign to us, so we felt drawn as strangers to it.) Laughing,
we would try to define words we could not pronounce. We played
with strange English sounds, often over-anglicizing our pronuncia-
tions. And we filled the smiling gaps of our sentences with familiar
Spanish sounds. But that was cheating, somebody shouted. Everyone laughed. In school, meanwhile, like my brother and sister, I
was required to attend a daily tutoring session. I needed a full year
of special attention. I also needed my teachers to keep my attention
from straying in class by calling out, *Rich-heard*—their English
voices slowly prying loose my ties to my other name, its three notes,
Ri-car-do. Most of all I needed to hear my mother and father speak
to me in a moment of seriousness in broken—suddenly heartbreak-
ing—English. The scene was inevitable: One Saturday morning I
entered the kitchen where my parents were talking in Spanish. I
did not realize that they were talking in Spanish however until, at
the moment they saw me, I heard their voices change to speak
English. Those *gringo* sounds they uttered startled me. Pushed me
away. In that moment of trivial misunderstanding and profound
insight, I felt my throat twisted by unsounded grief. I turned quickly
and left the room. But I had no place to escape to with Spanish.
(The spell was broken.) My brother and sisters were speaking English
in another part of the house.

Again and again in the days following, increasingly angry, I was 33
obliged to hear my mother and father: "Speak to us *en inglés.*" (*Speak.*).
Only then did I determine to learn classroom English. Weeks after,
it happened: One day in school I raised my hand to volunteer an
answer. I spoke out in a loud voice. And I did not think it remarkable when the entire class understood. That day, I moved very far

from the disadvantaged child I had been only days earlier. The belief, the calming assurance that I belonged in public, had at last taken hold.

Shortly after, I stopped hearing the high and loud sounds of *los gringos*. A more and more confident speaker of English, I didn't trouble to listen to *how* strangers sounded, speaking to me. And there simply were too many English-speaking people in my day for me to hear American accents anymore. Conversations quickened. Listening to persons who sounded eccentrically pitched voices, I usually noted their sounds for an initial few seconds before I concentrated on *what* they were saying. Conversations became contentfull. Transparent. Hearing someone's *tone* of voice—angry or questioning or sarcastic or happy or sad—I didn't distinguish it from the words it expressed. Sound and word were thus tightly wedded. At the end of a day, I was often bemused, always relieved, to realize how "silent," though crowded with words, my day in public had been. (This public silence measured and quickened the change in my life.)

At last, seven years old, I came to believe what had been technically true since my birth: I was an American citizen.

But the special feeling of closeness at home was diminished by then. Gone was the desperate, urgent, intense feeling of being at home; rare was the experience of feeling myself individualized by family intimates. We remained a loving family, but one greatly changed. No longer so close; no longer bound tight by the pleasing and troubling knowledge of our public separateness. Neither my older brother nor sister rushed home after school anymore. Nor did I. When I arrived home there would often be neighborhood kids in the house. Or the house would be empty of sounds.

Following the dramatic Americanization of their children, even my parents grew more publicly confident. Especially my mother. She learned the names of all the people on our block. And she decided we needed to have a telephone installed in the house. My father continued to use the word *gringo*. But it was no longer charged with the old bitterness or distrust. (Stripped of any emotional content, the word simply became a name for those Americans not of Hispanic descent.) Hearing him, sometimes, I wasn't sure if he was pronouncing the Spanish word *gringo* or saying gringo in English.

Matching the silence I started hearing in public was a new quiet at home. The family's quiet was partly due to the fact that, as we children learned more and more English, we shared fewer and fewer words with our parents. Sentences needed to be spoken slowly when a child addressed his mother or father. (Often the parent wouldn't understand.) The child would need to repeat himself. (Still the parent misunderstood.) The young voice, frustrated, would end up saying "Never mind"—the subject was closed. Dinners would be noisy with the clinking of knives and forks against dishes. My mother would smile softly between her remarks; my father at the other end of the table would chew and chew at his food, while he stared over the heads of his children.

My mother! My father! After English became my primary language, I no longer knew what words to use in addressing my parents. The old Spanish words (those tender accents of sound) I had used earlier—*mamá* and *papá*—I couldn't use anymore. They would have been too painful reminders of how much had changed in my life. On the other hand, the words I heard neighborhood kids call *their* parents seemed equally unsatisfactory. *Mother* and *Father*; *Ma, Papa, Pa, Dad, Pop* (how I hated the all-American sound of that last word especially)—all these terms I felt were unsuitable, not really terms of address for *my* parents. As a result, I never used them at home. Whenever I'd speak to my parents, I would try to get their attention with eye contact alone. In public conversations, I'd refer to "my parents" or "my mother and father."

My mother and father, for their part, responded differently, as their children spoke to them less. She grew restless, seemed troubled and anxious at the scarcity of words exchanged in the house. It was she who would question me about my day when I came home from school. She smiled at small talk. She pried at the edges of my sentences to get me to say something more. (What?) She'd join conversations she overheard, but her intrusions often stopped her children's talking. By contrast, my father seemed reconciled to the new quiet. Though his English improved somewhat, he retired into silence. At dinner he spoke very little. One night his children and even his wife helplessly giggled at his garbled English pronunciation of the Catholic Grace before Meals. Thereafter he made his wife recite the prayer at the start of each meal, even on formal occasions, when there were guests in the house. Hers became the public voice of the family. On official business, it was she, not my father, one would usually hear on the phone or in stores, talking to strangers. His children grew so accustomed to his silence that, years later, they would speak routinely of his shyness. (My mother would often try to explain: Both his parents died when he was eight. He was raised by an uncle who treated him like little more than a menial servant. He was never encouraged to speak. He grew up alone. A man of few words.) But my father was not shy, I realized, when I'd watch him speaking Spanish with relatives. Using Spanish, he was quickly effusive. Especially when talking with other men, his voice would spark, flicker, flare alive with sounds. In Spanish, he expressed ideas and feelings he rarely revealed in English. With firm Spanish sounds, he conveyed confidence and authority English would never allow him.

The silence at home, however, was finally more than a literal silence. Fewer words passed between parent and child, but more profound was the silence that resulted from my inattention to sounds. At about the time I no longer bothered to listen with care to the sounds of English in public, I grew careless about listening to the sounds family members made when they spoke. Most of the time I heard someone speaking at home and didn't distinguish his sounds from the words people uttered in public. I didn't even pay much attention to my parents' accented and ungrammatical speech. At least not at home. Only when I was with them in public would I grow alert to their accents. Though, even then, their sounds caused me less and less concern. For I was increasingly confident of my own public identity.

I would have been happier about my public success had I not sometimes recalled what it had been like earlier, when my family conveyed its intimacy through a set of conveniently private sounds. Sometimes in public, hearing a stranger, I'd hark back to my past. A Mexican farmworker approached me downtown to ask directions to somewhere. "¿Hijito. . .?" he said. And his voice summoned deep longing. Another time, standing beside my mother in the visiting room of a Carmelite convent, before the dense screen which rendered the nuns shadowy figures, I heard several Spanish-speaking nuns—their busy, singsong overlapping voices—assure us that yes, yes, we were remembered, all our family was remembered in their prayers. (Their voices echoed faraway family sounds.) Another day, a dark-faced old woman—her hand light on my shoulder—steadied herself against me as she boarded a bus. She murmured something I couldn't quite comprehend. Her Spanish voice came near, like the face of a never-before-seen relative in the instant before I was kissed. Her voice, like so many of the Spanish voices I'd hear in public, recalled the golden age of my youth. Hearing Spanish then, I continued to be a careful, if sad, listener to sounds. Hearing a Spanish-speaking family walking behind me, I turned to look. I smiled for an instant, before my glance found the Hispanic-looking faces of strangers in the crowd going by.

Today I hear bilingual educators say that children lose a degree of "individuality" by becoming assimilated into public society. (Bilingual schooling was popularized in the seventies, that decade when middle-class ethnics began to resist the process of assimilation—the American melting pot.) But the bilingualists simplistically scorn the value and necessity of assimilation. They do not seem to realize that there are *two* ways a person is individualized. So they do not realize that while one suffers a diminished sense of *private* individuality by becoming assimilated into public society, such assimilation makes possible the achievement of *public* individuality.

The bilingualists insist that a student should be reminded of his difference from others in mass society, his heritage. But they equate mere separateness with individuality. The fact is that only in private—with intimates—is separateness from the crowd a prerequisite for individuality. (An intimate draws me apart, tells me that I am unique, unlike all others.) In public, by contrast, full individuality is achieved, paradoxically, by those who are able to consider themselves members of the crowd. Thus it happened for me: Only when I was able to think of myself as an American, no longer an alien in *gringo* society, could I seek the rights and opportunities necessary for full public individuality. The social and political advantages I enjoy as a man result from the day that I came to believe that my name, indeed, is *Rich-heard Road-ree-guess*. It is true that my public society today is often impersonal. (My public society is usually mass society.) Yet despite the anonymity of the crowd and despite the fact that the individuality I achieve in public is often tenuous—because it depends on my being one in a crowd—I celebrate the day I acquired my new name. Those middle-class ethnics who scorn assimilation seem to me filled with decadent self-pity, obsessed by the burden of public life. Dangerously, they romanticize public separateness and they trivialize the dilemma of the socially disadvantaged.

My awkward childhood does not prove the necessity of bilingual education. My story discloses instead an essential myth of childhood—inevitable pain. If I rehearse here the changes in my private life after my Americanization, it is finally to emphasize the public gain. The loss implies the gain: The house I returned to each afternoon was quiet. Intimate sounds no longer rushed to the door to greet me. There were other noises inside. The telephone rang. Neighborhood kids ran past the door of the bedroom where I was reading my schoolbooks—covered with shopping-bag paper. Once I learned public language, it would never again be easy for me to hear intimate family voices. More and more of my day was spent hearing words. But that may only be a way of saying that the day I raised my hand in class and spoke loudly to an entire roomful of faces, my childhood started to end.

I grew up victim to a disabling confusion. As I grew fluent in English, I no longer could speak Spanish with confidence. I continued to understand spoken Spanish. And in high school, I learned how to read and write Spanish. But for many years I could not pronounce it. A powerful guilt blocked my spoken words; an essential glue was missing whenever I'd try to connect words to form sentences. I would be unable to break a barrier of sound, to speak freely. I would speak, or try to speak, Spanish, and I would manage to utter halting, hiccuping sounds that betrayed my unease.

When relatives and Spanish-speaking friends of my parents came to the house, my brother and sisters seemed reticent to use Spanish, but at least they managed to say a few necessary words before being excused. I never managed so gracefully. I was cursed with guilt. Each time I'd hear myself addressed in Spanish, I would be unable to respond with any success. I'd know the words I wanted to say, but I couldn't manage to say them. I would try to speak, but everything I said seemed to me horribly anglicized. My mouth would not form the words right. My jaw would tremble. After a phrase or two, I'd cough up a warm, silvery sound. And stop.

It surprised my listeners to hear me. They'd lower their heads, better to grasp what I was trying to say. They would repeat their questions in gentle, affectionate voices. But by then I would answer in English. No, no, they would say, we want you to speak to us in Spanish. (". . . *en español.*") But I couldn't do it. *Pocho* then they called me. Sometimes playfully, teasingly, using the tender diminutive—*mi pochito.* Sometimes not so playfully, mockingly, *Pocho.* (A Spanish dictionary defines that word as an adjective meaning "colorless" or "bland." But I heard it as a noun, naming the Mexican-American who, in becoming an American, forgets his native society.) "¡*Pocho!*" the lady in the Mexican food store muttered, shaking her head. I looked up to the counter where red and green peppers were strung like Christmas tree lights and saw the frowning face of the stranger. My mother laughed somewhere behind me. (She said that her children didn't want to practice "our Spanish" after they started going to school.) My mother's smiling voice made me suspect that the lady who faced me was not really angry at me. But, searching her face, I couldn't find the hint of a smile.

Embarrassed, my parents would regularly need to explain their children's inability to speak flowing Spanish during those years. My mother met the wrath of her brother, her only brother, when he came up from Mexico one summer with his family. He saw his nieces and nephews for the very first time. After listening to me, he looked away and said what a disgrace it was that I couldn't speak Spanish, "*su proprio idioma.*" He made that remark to my mother; I noticed, however, that he stared at my father.

I clearly remember one other visitor from those years. A longtime friend of my father from San Francisco would come to stay with us for several days in late August. He took great interest in me after he realized that I couldn't answer his questions in Spanish. He would grab me as I started to leave the kitchen. He would ask me something. Usually he wouldn't bother to wait for my mumbled response. Knowingly, he'd murmur: "*¿Ay Pocho, Pocho, adónde vas?*" And he would press his thumbs into the upper parts of my arms, making me squirm with currents of pain. Dumbly, I'd stand there, waiting for his wife to notice us, for her to call him off with a benign smile. I'd giggle, hoping to deflate the tension between us, pretending that I hadn't seen the glittering scorn in his glance.

I remember that man now, but seek no revenge in this telling. I recount such incidents only because they suggest the fierce power Spanish had for many people I met at home; the way Spanish was associated with closeness. Most of those people who called me a *pocho* could have spoken English to me. But they would not. They seemed to think that Spanish was the only language we could use, that Spanish alone permitted our close association. (Such persons are vulnerable always to the ghetto merchant and the politician who have learned the value of speaking their clients' family language to gain immediate trust.) For my part, I felt that I had somehow committed a sin of betrayal by learning English. But betrayal against whom? Not against visitors to the house exactly. No, I felt that I had betrayed my immediate family. I *knew* that my parents had encouraged me to learn English. I *knew* that I had turned to English only with angry reluctance. But once I spoke English with ease, I came to *feel* guilty. (This guilt defied logic.) I felt that I had shattered the intimate bond that had once held the family close. This original sin against my family told whenever anyone addressed me in Spanish and I responded, confounded.

But even during those years of guilt, I was coming to sense certain consoling truths about language and intimacy. I remember playing with a friend in the backyard one day, when my grandmother appeared at the window. Her face was stern with suspicion when she saw the boy (the *gringo*) I was with. In Spanish she called out to me, sounding the whistle of her ancient breath. My companion looked up and watched her intently as she lowered the window and moved, still visible, behind the light curtain, watching us both. He wanted to know what she had said. I started to tell him, to say—to translate her Spanish words into English. The problem was, however, that though I knew how to translate exactly *what* she had told me, I realized that any translation would distort the deepest meaning of her message: It had been directed only to me. This message of intimacy could never be translated because it was not *in* the words she had used but passed *through* them. So any translation would have seemed wrong; her words would have been stripped of an essential meaning. Finally, I decided not to tell my friend anything. I told him that I didn't hear all she had said.

This insight unfolded in time. Making more and more friends outside my house, I began to distinguish intimate voices speaking through *English*. I'd listen at times to a close friend's confidential tone or secretive whisper. Even more remarkable were those instances when, for no special reason apparently, I'd become conscious of the fact that my companion was speaking only to me. I'd marvel just hearing his voice. It was a stunning event: to be able to break through his words, to be able to hear this voice of the other, to realize that it was directed only to me. After such moments of intimacy outside the house, I began to trust hearing intimacy conveyed through my family's English. Voices at home at last punctured sad confusion. I'd hear myself addressed as an intimate at home once again. Such moments were never as raucous with sound as past times had been when we had had "private" Spanish to use. (Our English-sounding house was never to be as noisy as our Spanish-speaking house had been.) Intimate moments were usually soft moments of sound. My mother was in the dining room while I did my homework nearby. And she looked over at me. Smiled. Said something—her words said nothing very important. But her voice sounded to tell me *(We are together)* I was her son.

(Richard!)

Intimacy thus continued at home; intimacy was not stilled by English. It is true that I would never forget the great change of my life, the diminished occasions of intimacy. But there would also be times when I sensed the deepest truth about language and intimacy: *Intimacy is not created by a particular language; it is created by intimates.* The great change in my life was not linguistic but social. If, after becoming a successful student, I no longer heard intimate voices as often as I had earlier, it was not because I spoke English rather than Spanish. It was because I used public language for most of the day. I moved easily at last, a citizen in a crowded city of words.

This boy became a man. In private now, alone, I brood over language and intimacy—the great themes of my past. In public I expect most of the faces I meet to be the faces of strangers. (How do you do?) If meetings are quick and impersonal, they have been efficiently managed. I rush past the sounds of voices attending only to the words addressed to me. Voices seem planned to an even surface of sound, soundless. A business associate speaks in a deep baritone, but I pass through the timbre to attend to his words. The crazy man who sells me a newspaper every night mumbles something crazy, but I have time only to pretend that I have heard him say hello. Accented versions of English make little impression on me. In the rush-hour crowd a Japanese tourist asks me a question, and I inch past his accent to concentrate on what he is saying. The Eastern European immigrant in a neighborhood delicatessen speaks to me through a marinade of sounds, but I respond to his words. I note for only a second the Texas accent of the telephone operator or the Mississippi accent of the man who lives in the apartment below me.

My city seems silent until some ghetto black teenagers board the bus I am on. Because I do not take their presence for granted, I listen to the sounds of their voices. Of all the accented versions of English I hear in a day, I hear theirs most intently. They are *the* sounds of the outsider. They annoy me for being loud—so self-sufficient and unconcerned by my presence. Yet for the same reason they seem to me glamorous. (A romantic gesture against public acceptance.) Listening to their shouted laughter, I realize my own quiet.

Their voices enclose my isolation. I feel envious, envious of their brazen intimacy.

I warn myself away from such envy, however. I remember the black political activists who have argued in favor of black English in schools. (Their argument varies only slightly from that made by foreign-language bilingualists.) I have heard "radical" linguists make the point that black English is a complex and intricate version of English. And I do not doubt it. But neither do I think that black English should be a language of public instruction. What makes black English inappropriate in classrooms is not something *in* the language. It is rather what lower-class speakers make of it. Just as Spanish would have been a dangerous language for me to have used at the start of my education, so black English would be a dangerous language to use in the schooling of teenagers for whom it reenforces feelings of public separateness.

This seems to me an obvious point. But one that needs to be made. In recent years there have been attempts to make the language of the alien public language. "Bilingual education, two ways to understand . . . ," television and radio commercials glibly announce. Proponents of bilingual education are careful to say that they want students to acquire good schooling. Their argument goes something like this: Children permitted to use their family language in school will not be so alienated and will be better able to match the progress of English-speaking children in the crucial first months of instruction. (Increasingly confident of their abilities, such children will be more inclined to apply themselves to their studies in the future.) But then the bilingualists claim another, very different goal. They say that children who use their family language in school will retain a sense of their individuality—their ethnic heritage and cultural ties. Supporters of bilingual education thus want it both ways. They propose bilingual schooling as a way of helping students acquire the skills of the classroom crucial for public success. But they likewise insist that bilingual instruction will give students a sense of their identity apart from the public.

Behind this screen there gleams an astonishing promise: One can become a public person while still remaining a private person. At the very same time one can be both! There need be no tension between the self in the crowd and the self apart from the crowd! Who would not want to believe such an idea? Who can be surprised that the scheme has won the support of many middle-class Americans? If the barrio or ghetto child can retain his separateness even while being publicly educated, then it is almost possible to believe that there is no private cost to be paid for public success. Such is the consolation offered by any of the current bilingual schemes. Consider, for example, the bilingual voters' ballot. In some American cities one can cast a ballot printed in several languages. Such a document implies that a person can exercise that most public of rights—the right to vote—while still keeping apart, unassimilated from public life.

It is not enough to say that these schemes are foolish and certainly doomed. Middle-class supporters of public bilingualism toy with the confusion of these Americans who cannot speak standard English as well as they can. Bilingual enthusiasts, moreover, sin against intimacy. An Hispanic-American writer tells me, "I will never give up my family language; I would as soon give up my soul." Thus he holds to his chest a skein of words, as though it were the source of his family ties. He credits to language what he should credit to family members. A convenient mistake. For as long as he holds on to words, he can ignore how much else has changed in his life.

It has happened before. In earlier decades, persons newly successful and ambitious for social mobility similarly seized upon certain "family words." Working-class men attempting political power took to calling one another "brother." By so doing they escaped oppressive public isolation and were able to unite with many others like themselves. But they paid a price for this union. It was a public union they forged. The word they coined to address one another could never be the sound (brother) exchanged by two in intimate greeting. In the union hall the word "brother" became a vague metaphor; with repetition a weak echo of the intimate sound. Context forced the change. Context could not be overruled. Context will always guard the realm of the intimate from public misuse.

Today nonwhite Americans call "brother" to strangers. And white feminists refer to their mass union of "sisters." And white middle-class teenagers continue to prove the importance of context as they try to ignore it. They seize upon the idioms of the black ghetto. But their attempt to appropriate such expressions invariably changes the words. As it becomes a public expression, the ghetto idiom loses its sound—its message of public separateness and strident intimacy. It becomes with public repetition a series of words, increasingly lifeless.

The mystery remains: intimate utterance. The communication of intimacy passes through the word to enliven its sound. But it cannot be held by the word. Cannot be clutched or ever quoted. It is too fluid. It depends not on word but on person.

My grandmother!

She stood among my other relations mocking me when I no longer spoke Spanish. "*Pocho*," she said. But then it made no difference. (She'd laugh.) Our relationship continued. Language was never its source. She was a woman in her eighties during the first decade of my life. A mysterious woman to me, my only living grandparent. A woman of Mexico. The woman in long black dresses that reached down to her shoes. My one relative who spoke no word of English. She had no interest in *gringo* society. She remained completely aloof from the public. Protected by her daughters. Protected even by me when we went to Safeway together and I acted as her translator. Eccentric woman. Soft. Hard.

When my family visited my aunt's house in San Francisco, my grandmother searched for me among my many cousins. She'd chase them away. Pinching her granddaughters, she'd warn them all away from me. Then she'd take me to her room, where she had prepared for my coming. There would be a chair next to the bed. A dusty jellied candy nearby. And a copy of *Life en Español* for me to examine. "There," she'd say. I'd sit there content. A boy of eight. *Pocho*. Her favorite. I'd sift through the pictures of earthquake-destroyed Latin American cities and blond-wigged Mexican movie stars. And all the while I'd listen to the sound of my grandmother's voice. She'd pace around the room, searching through closets and drawers, telling me stories of her life. Her past. They were stories so familiar to me that I couldn't remember the first time I'd heard them. I'd look up sometimes to listen. Other times she'd look over at me. But she never seemed to expect a response. Sometimes I'd smile or nod. (I understood exactly what she was saying.) But it never seemed to matter to her one way or another. It was enough I was there. The words she spoke were almost irrelevant to that fact—the sounds she made. Content.

The mystery remained: intimate utterance.

I learn little about language and intimacy listening to those social activists who propose using one's family language in public life. Listening to songs on the radio, or hearing a great voice at the opera, or overhearing the woman downstairs singing to herself at an open window, I learn much more. Singers celebrate the human voice. Their lyrics are words. But animated by voice those words are subsumed into sounds. I listen with excitement as the words yield their enormous power to sound—though the words are never totally obliterated. In most songs the drama or tension results from the fact that the singer moves between word (sense) and note (song). At one moment the song simply "says" something. At another moment the voice stretches out the words—the heart cannot contain!—and the voice moves toward pure sound. Words take flight.

Singing out words, the singer suggests an experience of sound most intensely mine at intimate moments. Literally, most songs are about love. (Lost love; celebrations of loving; pleas.) By simply being occasions when sound escapes word, however, songs put me in mind of the most intimate moments of my life.

Finally, among all types of song, it is the song created by lyric poets that I find most compelling. There is no other public occasion of sound so important for me. Written poems exist on a page, at first glance, as a mere collection of words. And yet, despite this, without musical accompaniment, the poet leads me to hear the sounds of the words that I read. As song, the poem passes between sound and sense, never belonging for long to one realm or the other. As public artifact, the poem can never duplicate intimate sound. But by imitating such sound, the poem helps me recall the intimate times of my life. I read in my room—alone—and grow conscious of being alone, sounding my voice, in search of another. The poem serves then as a memory device. It forces remembrance. And refreshes. It reminds me of the possibility of escaping public words, the possibility that awaits me in meeting the intimate.

The poems I read are not nonsense poems. But I read them for reasons which, I imagine, are similar to those that make children play with meaningless rhyme. I have watched them before: I have noticed the way children create private languages to keep away the adult; I have heard their chanting riddles that go nowhere in logic but harken back to some kingdom of sound; I have watched them listen to intricate nonsense rhymes, and I have noted their wonder. I was never such a child. Until I was six years old, I remained in a magical realm of sound. I didn't need to remember that realm because it was present to me. But then the screen door shut behind me as I left home for school. At last I began my movement toward words. On the other side of initial sadness would come the realization that intimacy cannot be held. With time would come the knowledge that intimacy must finally pass.

I would dishonor those I have loved and those I love now to claim anything else. I would dishonor our closeness by holding on to a particular language and calling it my family language. Intimacy is not trapped within words. It passes through words. It passes. The truth is that intimates leave the room. Doors close. Faces move away from the window. Time passes. Voices recede into the dark. Death finally quiets the voice. And there is no way to deny it. No way to stand in the crowd, uttering one's family language.

The last time I saw my grandmother I was nine years old. I can tell you some of the things she said to me as I stood by her bed. I cannot, however, quote the message of intimacy she conveyed with her voice. She laughed, holding my hand. Her voice illumined disjointed memories as it passed them again. She remembered her husband, his green eyes, the magic name of Narciso. His early death. She remembered the farm in Mexico. The eucalyptus nearby. (Its scent, she remembered, like incense.) She remembered the family cow, the bell round its neck heard miles away. A dog. She remembered working as a seamstress. How she'd leave her daughters and son for long hours to go into Guadalajara to work. And how my mother would come running toward her in the sun—her bright yellow dress—to see her return. "Mmmaaammmmáááá," the old lady mimicked her daughter (my mother) to her son. She laughed. There was the snap of a cough. An aunt came into the room and told me it was time I should leave. "You can see her tomorrow," she promised. And so I kissed my grandmother's cracked face. And the last thing I saw was her thin, oddly youthful thigh, as my aunt rearranged the sheet on the bed.

At the funeral parlor a few days after, I knelt with my relatives during the rosary. Among their voices but silent, I traced, then lost, the sounds of individual aunts in the surge of the common prayer. And I heard at that moment what I have since heard often again—the sounds the women in my family make when they are praying in sadness. When I went up to look at my grandmother, I saw her through the haze of a veil draped over the open lid of the casket. Her face appeared calm—but distant and unyielding to love. It was not the face I remembered seeing most often. It was the face she made in public when the clerk at the Safeway asked her some question and I would have to respond. It was her public face the mortician had designed with his dubious art.

Content

1. Throughout this essay, Rodriguez weaves together two themes, language and intimacy. Be prepared to discuss in your own words how these two themes are related in the essay.
2. In Rodriguez's narration of his youth, how does his home life change? What is the significance of that change in terms of his argument against bilingual education?
3. Rodriguez distinguishes between private and public identity and between private and public language. How did Rodriguez and his parents each respond to their growing awareness of the differences between private and public life?
4. In paragraph 43, Rodriguez says, "In public, by contrast, full individuality is achieved, paradoxically, by those who are able to consider themselves members of the crowd." In your own words, explain what you understand this statement to mean in general and in the context of Rodriguez's thesis.

Technique

1. Rodriguez develops his argument against bilingual education through an intensely personal, often painfully frank narration. What are the advantages of using this technique? The disadvantages?
2. Throughout the essay, Rodriguez interweaves his adult point of view with his perspective as a young child. Find a specific instance in the essay when he does so, and be prepared to discuss its significance.
3. Rodriguez's essay is, on the whole, organized chronologically. Why is that technique particularly appropriate to this essay?

Language

1. Rodriguez says he is now part of the American middle-class. Why, then, do you suppose he uses so many Spanish words in his essay?
2. Rodriguez distinguishes between *"gringo"* in Spanish and "gringo" in English, between "mama" and "mother," "papa" and "father," and between "Ricardo" and "Richard." What is the significance of these distinctions and what do the pairs of words have in common?

3. Look up "resume" and "assume" in your dictionary. What is revealed by Rodriguez's use of these words in paragraph 22: "Once more inside the house I would resume (assume) my place in the family"?

Vocabulary

gringo	aria	assimilation
bilingual	intrinsic	paradox
counterpoint	eccentric	

Writing Suggestions

1. Write a narrative about your own changing sense of home. As Rodriguez does, use vivid images and examples to communicate your experiences to your audience.
2. Write an essay in which you examine your own awareness of the importance of language. Such an essay might, for example, focus on the first time you had to speak in public, a time when language failed you, your first encounter with a foreign language, or an incident that taught you the importance of using the "right" word at the right time.

Language and Sports
5

Given the enormous amount of time and money we spend on sports, the American interest in them might legitimately be called an obsession. Sport pervades virtually every part of our society. Children can begin playing organized sports at very early ages and continue to participate in school, city, college, and adult leagues for the rest of their lives. The sports heroes we admire and sometimes worship earn millions of dollars by playing their sports and by trading on their exalted place in the public eye. We devote hours and days to following our favorite athletes and teams, and as a nation we spend millions of dollars annually for the accessories required for competing and staying fit ourselves. When athletes form labor unions, "the game" has clearly become an industry. When teams from unfriendly nations compete, games can seem like diplomacy—or war. And when our spirits sink or rise depending on an athlete's or a team's fortunes, the game has become a play that dramatizes our frustrations and aspirations.

Although the intensity of and motives for our commitment to sport may vary widely, the influence of games goes well beyond the boundaries of the field and the court; the essays in this section trace that influence, and most of them pay particular attention to the effect of sports terminology on language. Francine Hardaway, for instance, views the abundance of sports metaphors in everyday language as a harmful development that reveals a failure to distinguish between sports situations and problems in the larger world. Because sports reflect the values of society and because we often identify with sports figures, our use of the terminology of football, boxing, baseball, and other games is often excessive. Those who compete in other occupations, such as business and politics, are more susceptible to this tendency, Hardaway argues. They come to view their actions and decisions solely as those of an athlete.

Hardaway acknowledges that metaphors and other comparisons are useful insofar as they "explain unfamiliar or difficult concepts in terms of familiar images." She argues, however, that when we restrict the comparisons to a set of specialized terms and use the comparisons without thinking, we trick both our audience and ourselves. We can adequately describe some situations as "striking out" or "running with the ball," but other situations deserve fresh comparisons and a more sophisticated vocabulary than sports, or any single occupation, can provide.

Joseph Durso's "You Could Look It Up" and A. B. Giamatti's "Hyperbole's Child" show the importance of language to two sports world "insiders," Casey Stengel and Muhammad Ali—figures whose theatrics made their sports low comedy and high drama, foolish at one moment and poignant the next. As well as being natural actors, Stengel and Ali were masters of "sports English," using it to create roles for themselves, to defend themselves and their sports. Durso shows how Stengel's antics and his use of "Stengelese" masked his shrewd management of a baseball team and his own financial affairs. Similarly, Giamatti argues that Ali's theatrics sprang in part from a fear of being an average boxer, as well as from calculated self-promotion and a defense against racism.

A more obvious place to begin to study the meaning of sports and their influence on language is of course the "sports page." The fact that sports occupies its own substantial section of our daily news attests to its status in society, certainly. But the sports page can also show us the extent to which those who habitually describe games become addicts of sports jargon. This type of "sports English" is the subject of William Zinsser's essay, "Sports."

In Zinsser's view, sports writers become ineffective when they write "sports English" because they neglect their main responsibility, which is to describe the events of the sports world to the general reader. By cramming their prose with jargon and statistics, such writers create what amounts to an indecipherable code, thereby losing their audience. After quoting an example of such sports writing, Zinsser speaks for the general reader when he asks, "But can anybody read it? And does anybody care?"

Roger Angell's "Stories for A Rainy Afternoon" and Red Smith's "Unconquerable" do not address the issue of language and sports directly, but rather exemplify the kind of sports writing Zinsser praises in his essay: writing that demonstrates humor, originality, fresh imagery, and a sense of the humanity of sports. Good sports writers like Angell and Smith avoid using "sports English," Zinsser suggests, because they realize that the most interesting sports issues transcend the sport itself and appeal to the general reader and the fan alike.

Thus, Angell shows us that recalling unheroic, comic moments in sport is as important as describing championships or broken records, chiefly because such moments remind us that athletes are humans, not superhumans. Similarly, Smith's essay reminds us that we will remember Jackie Robinson more as a man than a sportsman. For while his courage "established the black man's right to play second base," it also went far beyond the game of baseball. "American sport has always been interwoven with social history," writes Zinsser, "and the best sports writers are those who will make the connection."

Foul Play: Sports Metaphors as Public Doublespeak

Francine Hardaway

Francine Hardaway (b. 1941) received a Ph.D. from Syracuse University in 1968. She worked as a copywriter for several publishing houses before becoming an assistant professor of English at Le Moyne College in 1967. She is presently the director of program development at Rio Salado College in Phoenix, Arizona. Her books include Writing Through Reading *(1976),* Doublespeak and Teaching *(1976), and* Thinking Into Writing *(1978). She contributes essays to numerous professional journals and was the recipient of a National Endowment for the Humanities Fellowship in 1974. In "Foul Play: Sports Metaphor as Public Doublespeak," Hardaway analyzes the frequently negative impact that sports metaphors have on communication that takes place outside the world of sports.*

Nobody would argue the place of sports in American life; they are big business. And they are big business because they fit philosophically with the widely accepted American dream of open competition in a free market economy. Americans believe in competition, foster it, and encourage it. They live by its rules. No wonder the language of athletic competition has found its way as metaphor into every aspect of American life. If we are at a disadvantage, we say we've "got two strikes against us," things have "taken a bad bounce," or we're "on the ropes." If we are being aggressive, we "take the ball and run with it," "take the bull by the horns," "come out swinging," or "make a sweep." If the fates still conspire against us, we "take it on the chin," "throw in the towel," or "roll with the punches" until we're "saved by the bell."

It's worth taking some time to think about how these sports metaphors, so ubiquitous and so ignored until Watergate brought them to our attention, describe the quality of life in America. 2

The purpose of such metaphors is to explain unfamiliar or difficult concepts in terms of familiar images. But recently there have been some changes in our national self-concept and these changes are duly reflected in sports metaphors. We seem to have changed drastically from a society in which "it isn't whether you win or lose, but how you play the game," to one in which, to use Vince Lombardi's words, "winnng isn't everything, it's the only thing." And our sports metaphors have changed with us. "The good fight" and "the old college try" have given way to the more sophisticated "game plans," "play-calling," and quarterbacking rhetoric of Vietnam and Watergate. Sports metaphors now often function as public doublespeak: language meant to manipulate its audience unconsciously. Analyzing sports doublespeak reveals some scary truths about how we Americans look at life. In John Mitchell's words, "when the going gets tough, the tough get going," and we turn out to be a society in which "nice guys finish last," and everybody wants to "be on the winning side." 3

The rhetoric of the playing field appears in advertising, business, and government. Let's take an obvious example first. President Ford, in publicizing his economic strategies when he first took office, devised the W.I.N. button. An offshoot of Ford's other unfortunate sports metaphor, the promise to "hold the line" on inflation, the W.I.N. button was meant to appeal by familiarity to the sports-minded American who will "get up for the game," and "tackle the job" if the coach just tells him what to do. Ford hoped that the "win" mentality was so strongly ingrained in America that the very word would alter attitudes and behavior. 4

With the W.I.N. button, Ford hoped to make use of a sports metaphor the way advertising does. He wanted to make the analogy from athletic success to success in other fields. We all expect to be manipulated by advertising, so it is no surprise to see professional athletes advertising hair tonic, shaving cream, even frozen pizza or panty hose. The doublespeak is implicit: use this product, and you will enjoy the same success as Frank Gifford, Arthur Ashe, Joe Namath. Associating the athlete with the product, however, makes another claim for the athlete: it extends his expertise beyond the playing field. Ad agencies hope we will take the advice of these "pros" about shaving cream, hair tonic, frozen pizza, or panty hose; after all, the pro wouldn't make a wrong choice about these products any more than he would throw the ball away at a crucial moment of the game. So the athlete is an expert, as well as a hero. His ability to "score" carries over into financial and the sexual arenas as well; there is even a product named "Score."

Since it has been established by advertising that the athlete is both hero and expert, sports metaphors are used more subtly to sell products. In the MGB ad that reads "MGB. Think of it as a well-coordinated athlete," we can see how much athletic ability is admired. No longer do we compare the good athlete or the good team to a well-oiled machine: now we're comparing the machine to the good athlete. Like a well-conditioned athlete, you'll "score" in your MGB.

But advertising is an easy target for doublespeak analysis. More complex by far is the way sports metaphors function in business, where their analysis leads to crucial revelations about American ethics. Business has always been fond of the football analogy, as William H. Whyte, Jr. points out:

> No figure of speech is a tenth as seductive to the businessman. Just why this should be—baseball curiously is much less used—is generally explained by its adaptability to all sorts of situations. Furthermore, the football analogy is *satisfying*. It is bounded by two goal lines and is thus finite. There is always a solution. And that is what makes it so often treacherous.[1]

---

[1] William H. Whyte, Jr., "The Language of Business," in *Technological and Professional Writing*, ed. Herman A. Estrin (New York: Harcourt, Brace & World, 1963), p. 83. In this part of the paper, I am indebted to an unpublished paper on "Sports Metaphors in Business" by John Driscoll.

Business uses the team philosophy, says Whyte, to hedge on moral issues. By making analogies to sports, business convinces the outside world that its decisions aren't truly consequential: they are "games" executed by good "team players." The fact that dollars and human lives may also be involved is not included when the sports metaphor is used, for the sports metaphor imposes automatic limits on the way business activity is seen.

> The goal of sports activity is always unambiguous and non-controversial: participants do not come together to discuss or debate the ends for which the activity has been established, but rather take this end for granted and apply themselves in a single-minded fashion to the task of developing the most efficient means to achieve the predetermined unchanging and non-controversial end: winning.[2]

So the sports metaphor precludes thought; it operates on unconscious and irrational levels, manipulating its users as well as its audiences. Perhaps its use in business, where the idea of competition in the free marketplace still carries moral force, has something to do with man's aggressive nature; what sports and business have in common that allows the sports metaphor to be drawn so often and so successfully by American businessmen is aggressiveness. Sports are an acceptable form of releasing aggressive impulses, if business uses the sports metaphor, isn't the aggressiveness of business automatically acceptable?

> . . . [the] same aggressive impulse which can lead to strife and violence also underlies man's urge to independence and achievement. Just as a child could not possibly grow up into an independent adult if it were not aggressive, so an adult must needs continue to express at least part of his aggressive potential if he is to maintain his own autonomy.[3]

No wonder the Duke of Wellington was able to observe that "the battle of Waterloo was won on the playing fields of Eton." The skills learned on the playing field by the child are translated into the battles of the adult.

But there is also a certain cynicism associated with the use of the sports metaphor by business:

---

[2]Ike Balbus, "Politics as Sports: The Political Ascendancy of the Sports Metaphor in America," *Monthly Review*, March 1975, p. 30.
[3]Anthony Stoor, *Human Aggression* (New York: Atheneum, 1970), p.59.

What happens to some guys is — well, I'll draw the analogy to sports again. Baseball has its hot players and the next year the hot players cool off, and what happens is that their salaries drop and they get optioned out to Toledo.[4]

In Jerry Della Femina's description of what happens to advertising men who don't produce, the sports metaphor obscures the human position of the advertising executive, the man who has a good year followed by a bad year and suddenly finds himself nursing an ulcer and out of a job. Like most sports metaphors, this one permits the reader to ignore the ethical implications of cut-throat competition among advertising agencies for top talent.

But business still isn't the "Big Game"—that's government. And, as we might now expect, the bigger the game, the more prevalent the sports metaphor as doublespeak. Watergate revealed the wholesale use of the sports lexicon by politicians, but Watergate was neither the beginning nor the end of the sports metaphor. As William Safire points out in his excellent book *The New Language of Politics*,[5] Shakespeare may have been the first to use the comparisons. King Henry V told his troops before Harfleur, "I see you stand like greyhounds in the slips, straining upon the start. The game's afoot; . . ." But Safire also notes that Shakespeare wasn't the last; the section on "Sports Metaphors" in *The New Language of Politics* is a wonderful compendium of quotations from past political greats beginning with Woodrow Wilson's "I have always in my own thought summed up individual liberty, and business liberty, and every other kind of liberty, in the phrase that is common in the sporting world, 'A free field and no favor,' " and stopping at JFK's "Politics is like football. If you see daylight, go through the hole."

Amusingly enough, politics doesn't content itself only with the football metaphor so favored by business. Instead, it inadvertently reveals its seamier side by the frequent use of the horse race analogy. There are front-runners and dark horses, long shots and shoo-ins. The winner takes the reins of government, while the loser is an also-ran who was "nosed out." Harry Truman said, "I am trying to do in politics what Citation has done in the horse races. I propose at the finish line on November 2 to come out ahead . . . ." It seems that in politics, more than in advertising or in business, the use of

---

[4]Jerry Della Femina, *From Those Wonderful Folks Who Brought You Pearl Harbor* (New York: Simon & Shuster, 1971), p. 124.
[5]New York: Random House, 1968, p. 421.

the sports metaphor reveals more than gamesmanship, competition, or vicarious aggression; it also reveals an affinity with gambling.

But Safire's compendium, while amusing and instructive, is pre-Watergate and he therefore views the sports metaphor as innocuous. He says,

> Sports metaphors relate closely to many people, which is why politicians spend the time to create them; at other times they are tossed off without thinking because they are already a part of the language. After a Kennedy aide appeared on Lawrence Spivak's television panel show *Meet the Press*, the President called to say "They never laid a glove on you." It is the classic remark of a trainer to a prize fighter who has been belted all over the ring. (pp. 421–22)

Since Watergate, we have become more attuned to the way sports metaphors are often used to make big decisions involving all our lives seem trivial and inconsequential.

> Nixon's "jocko' macho" talk (as Nicholas von Hoffman called it) was amply demonstrated; the limited supply of tough-guy metaphors, akin to verbal locker room swaggering of muscle-flexing *machismo* at the beach: . . . Years earlier, some critics had felt that Nixon's overt enthusiasm for spectator sports (shaking hands with athletes, telegrams and phone calls to coaches) was simply a calculated ploy ("a grandstand play") to win the favor of certain voters, to create the illusion that he was "just one of the guys." It was no illusion. Nixon was not the first politician to use the imagery of athletics . . . but the transcripts reveal that the traditional emphasis on "fair play," "following the rules," and "good sportsmanship" had been replaced by a "win at all costs" mentality.[6]

One need hardly comment further on what Watergate did to the language; its only good effect was to alert many Americans to the way language does both form and corrupt thinking. For that, we should probably be grateful.

Unfortunately, the effects of Watergate aren't longlasting. In the midst of the recent New York City financial crisis, the *Wall Street Journal* carried the following story:

> After a seven-month game of political brinkmanship, the Ford administration has browbeaten New York City into "fiscal respon-

---

[6]Hugh Rank, "Watergate and the Language," in *Language and Public Policy*, ed. Hugh Rank (Urbana, Ill.: NCTE, 1974), pp. 8–9.

sibility" and the city has pressured Washington into limited federal help.

But the path to that outcome proved to be far different than either side had expected, and the ultimate results happier than either would have predicted just a short time ago. There seems to be no clear winner in the long struggle—just losers of varying degrees. . . .

The reconstruction of these events leading up to the Wednesday statement discloses basic miscalculations by every player in the game. . . .

The city's fiscal crisis, surfacing last May, rapidly developed into a high-level game of political chess—played out in Washington and New York and Albany, full of bluff and bombast, maneuver and surprise.

Only the name of the game has changed; the article goes on to discuss how New York's crisis developed into a standoff between Ford and the city, in which participants in the negotiations between New York and Washington felt that "it was hardball both ways, and nothing was spared." The "hardball season" of negotiations ran from September through November, when Ford and New York City finally reached a compromise.

This story illustrates very well the dangers of relying too heavily on sports metaphors. Here a genuine crisis has been reduced for readers to a game in which participants are trying to out-bluff and out-maneuver each other while New York and perhaps the rest of the nation await the consequences. And the crisis is portrayed as a strategy problem, rather than a human problem or a problem in responsible government.

What is the lesson to be learned from looking at our culture's continuing use of sports metaphors to render important situations innocuous in advertising, in business, and in government? If it is true, as Walker Gibson said to the NCTE[8] Convention in 1973, that "learning to read is learning to infer dramatic character from linguistic evidence," then examining the metaphors used in popular culture provides good insight into our character as a nation. And if it is also true, as Orwell remarked in *Politics and the English Language*, that "language can corrupt thought," then sports metaphors become not merely ways of revealing our adolescent preoccupation with

[7]November 28, 1975.
[8]National Council of Teachers of English.

aggressiveness, with winning, with games, but also ways of perpetuating those concerns, of glorifying them, of passing them on unexamined to our children through our national culture. It is at least worth a few minutes of our time to wrestle (there it is again) with the decision of whether we really want to see ourselves forever as a nation of teamplayers and sports fans.

Content

1. Hardaway begins her essay by saying, "Nobody would argue the place of sports in American life; they are big business." What does her equation of the big business of sports and the place of sports in American life suggest about Hardaway's view of sports? Does her view of sports influence your reading of the essay? Explain.
2. Hardaway has no objection to metaphors themselves. Metaphors, she says, explain the unfamiliar in familiar terms. Why, then, does she not accept the sports metaphor as merely a way of clarifying the complicated arenas of business and politics? What does she find dangerous about this particular use of metaphor?
3. In paragraph 8, Hardaway notes that the sports metaphor manipulates "its users as well as its audiences." In other words, the politican who uses the sports metaphor as doublespeak is as much its victim as is the listener. Explain how the metaphor as doublespeak might victimize even its user.

Technique

1. Hardaway places the fullest statement of her thesis at the end of the essay, when she says that sports metaphors offer insight into our national character and that their use, in turn, glorifies the flaws we find there. What has Hardaway done throughout the essay to prepare the reader to accept her thesis?
2. To make her argument convincing, Hardaway chooses examples of sports metaphors drawn from several sports and used in three areas of our public life—advertising, business, and politics. Choose two or three of these examples and discuss how they strengthen or weaken her argument.

Language

1. The concept of "doublespeak" is central to Hardaway's concerns about the use of sports metaphors in advertising, business, and politics. In

your own words, explain doublespeak and the relationship that Hardaway sees between doublespeak and sports metaphors.
2. In paragraph 11, Hardaway says that the use of sports metaphors reveals, among other things, our "vicarious aggression." Look up the word "vicarious" in your dictionary and explain Hardaway's statement in your own words.

Vocabulary

ubiquitous	rhetoric	vicarious
metaphor	manipulate	innocuous
analogy	lexicon	

Writing Suggestions

1. In a single paragraph, use one sports metaphor (one of Hardaway's or one of your own) to compare the familiar to the unfamiliar, then discuss how the metaphor clarifies the issue or event in question.
2. In a paragraph, use one sports metaphor to demonstrate how doublespeak can purposely mislead or confuse the audience, then discuss how the confusion arises.
3. Hardaway believes that sports metaphors are dangerous because they oversimplify and mislead and because they perpetuate and glorify our "adolescent preoccupation with aggressiveness, with winning. . . ." William Safire, at least before Watergate, found them less dangerous, believing they are used because they "relate closely to many people" and because they are, simply, "a part of the language." Write an essay in which you argue for or against Hardaway's contention. Like Hardaway, use specific examples to support your viewpoint.
4. Sports metaphors are commonly used in social situations as well as in the busines snad political worlds. Over several days and evenings, make note of the sports metaphors you hear in different social settings: What metaphors get used, who uses them most frequently and who least frequently, and what situations seem to occasion the greatest use? Based on your observations, write an essay in which you compare and contrast the use of metaphors in two different social situations, showing how their use might tell us something about social assumptions or social distinctions.

You Could Look It Up

Joseph Durso

Joseph Durso is a Phi Beta Kappa graduate of New York University and received a masters degree from Columbia University. After serving as a fighter pilot in the Air Force, Durso joined the New York Times in 1950, subsequently working as an assistant city editor, a sports writer, and a columnist. He has covered such major sports events as the Olympics and the Kentucky Derby, and for the last twenty years he has written about the World Series. For the past fifteen years, he has also taught at the Columbia Graduate School of Journalism. "You Could Look It Up" is taken from one of Durso's ten books about sports, Casey: The Life and Times of Charles Dillon Stengel *(1967). The narrative essay is peppered with lively anecdotes about one of baseball's most famous, and most talkative, characters.*

1 His name was Charles Dillon Stengel, but because he had been born in Kansas City, Missouri, he was the man from K.C.—Casey. But he also was called "Dutch," because his family was German; "the Professor," because of his Socratic manner of presiding over baseball dugouts; "the Swami," because, under mild promotional prompting, he affected exotic headgear and stared wildly into crystal balls, and "Doctor," simply because he had an uncertain memory for names and called everybody else "Doctor."

2 Branch Rickey, the "deacon" of major league baseball, called him "the perfect link between the team and the public."

3 It was a link he had started to establish as a 19-year-old outfielder in a place called Kankakee, Illinois, in a league called the Northern Association in 1910. That was four years before World War I, a decade before Babe Ruth became a Yankee, half a century before the first big league game was played indoors. The league folded in July.

4 Stengel thereupon squirreled a couple of Kankakee uniforms into a suitcase and moved over to Shelbyville, Kentucky, in the Blue Grass League. The franchise collapsed.

5 He packed again and moved to Maysville, Kentucky, where a stream skirted the outfield grass, and one day he drifted back for a

fly ball, sloshed a few feet farther back and caught the ball while standing in the stream. The link was taking shape.

For the next 55 years, Casey Stengel grew old, rich and famous while the United States moved from William Howard Taft to John F. Kennedy and beyond, with talking pictures, the automobile and the Lunar Excursion Module revolutionizing life, and baseball expanding as a multimillion-dollar business into the West Coast, the Deep South, Central America and even Japan. He had been transported to his early baseball games in horse-drawn surreys and he wound up a regular traveler from Los Angeles to New York in Boeing 727 jetliners.

He owned oil wells in Texas, was vice president of a bank in California and controlled real estate that made him a millionaire. His face was heavily wrinkled, his ears were floppy, his voice was guttural, his endurance beyond belief. Like Mickey Mouse and Charles de Gaulle, he was a household figure of towering identification.

But for all his status, he was best known as a baseball man, earned his "source" money in baseball and for 55 years exerted his greatest influence on baseball players, fans and franchises.

He had been a player, coach or manager on 17 professional baseball teams. He had been traded four times as a left-handed outfielder in the major leagues. He had been dropped or relieved three times as a manager in the big leagues. He had even been paid twice for *not* managing.

He had retired at the age of 71, had returned at 72, and had been re-hired at 73 and 74. Then, as he turned 75, he fell and broke his left hip somewhere between Toots Shor's restaurant in Manhattan and a house in Whitestone, Queens, and had to watch on television from a room in Roosevelt Hospital while 39,288 persons in Shea Stadium sang "Happy Birthday, Dear Casey, Happy Birthday to You."

One year later, to the day, he limped into the Baseball Hall of Fame alongside Ted Williams, having completed the course from Kankakee to Cooperstown as a national figure, an average player, a controversial coach, a wheeler and dealer of minor league talent, a second-division manager of dismal teams, a first-division manager of the Olympian Yankees, a man criticized as an expert at *overmanaging* wherever he managed—a mixture of Santa Claus and Jimmy Durante as he duck-walked out to home plate with his lineup card, wearing flannel pinstripes and No. 37 on the back of his uniform.

Was he the greatest baseball manager who ever lived? Was he the luckiest manager who ever lived? Was he simply a manager whose fortunes oscillated with the talent available? Was he a meddler, a tyrant in the dugout, a slave to the "book," a wizard, a patriarch, a Merlin, a charming old man or an "angry old man" with great press notices?

Whatever he was, when he signed his final contract as manager of the New York Mets on September 29, 1964, he received the following telegram from Rickey, then seven years younger than Winston Churchill and eight years older than Stengel—who was 74 years and two months old:

"You are exactly the right age to manage a major league baseball team in my book."

Later, sitting in his box seat between home plate and third base in Busch Stadium, St. Louis, Rickey leaned forward on a gnarled cherrywood cane, chewed on a cigar and watched the St. Louis Cardinals bat their way into a tie for first place in the National League.

Rickey had been born on a farm in Ohio 82 years earlier, once had pedaled a bicycle 18 miles each way to teach school and later had become a lawyer with three degrees, the creator of baseball's first farm system and the dominant figure in the major leagues in three cities. But what excited him now was that Casey Stengel—in his 75th year—had just signed a $100,000 contract to manage a baseball team. And he reacted as though he suddenly had put his finger on something constant in the sweep of a busy life.

"Exactly the right age," he said. "You know, it's a great waste for universities to force brilliant men to retire at 65, when they're at the peak of their ability. And baseball needs men like that, too—like Casey Stengel—who are so able, so alive, so articulate, so aroused."

"People in New York have spent a lot of time and effort trying to ferret out the reason for the Mets' astounding attendance," he said, peering out beneath strong, bushy eyebrows, his hands folded across the knob of the cherrywood cane. "You need look no farther than Casey Stengel. He is the perfect link between the team and the public."

The perfect link between the team and the public, at that moment, was landing in Milwaukee aboard a jet airliner from New York. In 72 hours, his team would arrive in Deacon Rickey's St. Louis and cause panic in much of the Midwest by reaching up from the league cellar to defeat the Cardinals twice at the climax of one of the great finishes in baseball history. He had the knack, it seemed, of living at the eye of the hurricane.

The Mets required one full page in their handbook that season to record his three-quarters of a century, but somehow managed to compress his vital statistics into these four lines of spectacular understatement:

> STENGEL, Charles Dillon. 'Casey.' Manager. Born July 30, 1890, at Kansas City, Mo. Height: 5 ft., 10 in. Weight: 175 pounds. Batted and threw lefthanded. Married and lives in Glendale, Calif. Former outfielder.

Before he had become a "former outfielder," though, Stengel had played baseball from 1910 to 1931 for four minor league teams, five major league teams and two more minor league teams. Then, as a manager, he lived through 25 seasons of almost abject frustration in both the major and minor leagues, finishing no higher than fifth in an eight-team league during one entire decade, before suddenly graduating to the New York Yankees as the 15th manager in their 46-year history of dominating the sport. He won 10 pennants in 12 years and finally, at the age of 72, wound up with the Mets where he had started—at the bottom of the ladder.

During the next four years, the Mets fielded a team that won 194 games, lost 452 and ran dead last in the National League each time. But they fielded a team that was cast in the precise image of the waddling old man who directed it, a team whose sins were pardoned by an adoring public, whose life was surrounded by legend—and could be understood only in terms of legend—and a team whose bank credit grew as indisputably as the lore.

In 1965, Casey Stengel's last year in a baseball uniform, 1,768,389 persons paid up to $3.50 each to watch the Old Man and his celebrated Youth of America in their new ball park on Flushing Bay, and 1,075,431 paid to see them on the road.

Only the Los Angeles Dodgers, en route to the world championship, and the Houston Astros, en route to great wealth under baseball's first roof, did better business at home, and with a World's Fair enlivening the Meadow next to the stadium, Stengel completed the "perfect link" to the public that had so enthralled Branch Rickey.

But Stengel's rapport with the American public went far beyond the box office.

"He's not a clown," his wife Edna said after 40 years of marriage. "He's one of the smartest men in baseball, in business, in anything he'd try."

He was a turn-of-the-century athlete, country boy and Broadway character rolled into one and, it was widely believed, was the model for Carey in Ring Lardner's *Alibi Ike*. He drove a taxicab as a husky, rather oldish teen-ager in Kansas City; played football and basketball as well as baseball in high school; turned to semi-pro baseball in 1910 to earn money for dental school; consternated his laboratory instructors by attempting to practice dentistry left-handed; was paid 25 cents for pumping the organ in St. Mark's Episcopal Church in Kansas City, $1 a day for pitching with the Kansas City Red Sox, $135 a month for playing the outfield with Kankakee and, 55 years later, $100,000 a year for managing the New York Mets.

When he was poor, he was duly impressed by small wealth. "I found they'd pay me $135 a month for playing ball," he told the members of the Senate Antitrust and Monopoly Subcommittee on July 9, 1958, during hearings on baseball's business growth. "I thought it was amazing." But, he said later when private conversations got around to his personal fortune, "people are always talking about how much money I got; they never remember how much money I lost."

He earned all this to the loud accompaniment of theatrical antics both on and off the baseball field, until he was accused of carrying on in order to distract people from the less effectual performances of his teams. But even in his heyday as skipper of the lordly Yankees, he performed from a full repertoire of practical jokes, pantomine, and anecdotes.

"He can talk all day and all night," John Lardner said, "on any kind of track, wet or dry."

His talent for outlandish behavior outraged owners like Barney Dreyfuss of the Pittsburgh Pirates, officials like Judge Emil Fuchs of the Boston Braves, commissioners like Kenesaw Mountain Landis and umpires like Bill Klem.

"Every time two owners got together with a fountain pen," observed Quentin Reynolds, "Casey Stengel was being sold or bought."

"I never played with the Cubs, Cards or Reds," Stengel acknowledged. "I guess that was because the owners of those clubs didn't own no fountain pens."

When he was installed as a one-man triumvirate—president, manager and outfielder—for the Braves' farm club at Worcester, Massachusetts, in the Eastern League in 1925, he fretted through his first assignment as an executive for one season. He even played in 100 of the team's 125 games and the team finished third. But at the end of the season he executed a monumental front-office triple play to escape. As manager, he released Stengel the player. As president, he fired Stengel the manager. And as Stengel, he resigned as president.

He once slid into a potted plant in the Sheraton-Cadillac Hotel in Detroit to demonstrate Ty Cobb's famous fallaway slide. But when he was criticized in 1918 for not sliding home during a close game when he was, according to his own judgment, a grossly underpaid member of the Pittsburgh Pirates, he replied: "With the salary I get here, I'm so hollow and starving that I'm liable to explode like a light bulb if I hit the ground too hard."

Putting him into the outfield was likely to become an adventure for both sides. When he returned to Ebbets Field in Brooklyn for the first time as a member of the Pirates, he was welcomed back with a rousing round of catcalls from the same fans who had applauded his tricks for his first five years in the major leagues. In reply, he marched to home plate, bowed with courtliness to the grandstand, doffed his cap, and out flew a sparrow.

When he took over right field for Montgomery of the Southern Association in the spring of 1912, he achieved a complicated variation of the fly-ball-in-the-stream routine that had helped launch his histrionic career two years earlier. He found a drainage hole in the outfield and simply disappeared from sight. A short time later he rose like Triton from the sea, drainage cover under his arm, just in time to grab a fly ball. His manager, Kid Elberfeld, was not amused.

When umpires pulled rank to thwart his tricks, he sometimes counterattacked with passive resistance. He would swoon in a mock faint and just lie down on the ground while they raged. He did this effectively one day against Beans Reardon, one of the National League's senior umpires, but Reardon trumped Stengel's ace by lying down alongside him.

"When I peeked outa one eye and saw Reardon on the ground, too," he recalled later, "I knew I was licked."

When another umpire rejected his suggestion that it was growing too dark to continue playing, Stengel goaded him by signaling his pitcher with a flashlight. When yet another umpire appeared to give him the worst of a series of decisions, he stripped off his uniform shirt on the field, held it out and said impudently: "You try to play on our side for a change."

When John J. McGraw, his idol as a manager, attempted to stifle him, Stengel rebelled somewhat more gently. McGraw hired a private detective to shadow Stengel and Irish Meusel, the two most celebrated hell-raisers on the New York Giants. So the two players simply split up, forcing McGraw's man to track one quarry and neglect the other. Stengel, with pretended petulance, then went to McGraw and complained: "If you want me followed, you'll have to get me a detective of my own."

Later, when he became a manager himself, Stengel looked back on his wayward years and said: "Now that I'm a manager, I see the error of my youthful ways. If any player pulled that stuff on me now, I would probably fine his ears off."

Indeed, he was frequently accused of intolerance in the face of others' antics, though the degree of intolerance appeared to fluctuate with the degree of the culprit's success with ball, bat and glove.

When he was a new manager at Toledo in the American Association in the late nineteen-twenties, his players, like most other working adults in the country, became Wall Street buffs who played the soaring stock market and showed more frenzy over the stock averages than over their batting averages. The team dropped off from first place in 1927 to sixth in 1928 and plunged to eighth in 1929 just before the market plunged even deeper.

He called the team together one day at the height of the boom and said, with a tone of formality: "You fellows better start buying Pennsylvania Railroad and Baltimore & Ohio stock, because when we start shipping you out to the bushes next week those roads are going to get rich."

A quarter-century later, his New York Yankees eased into a game of Twenty Questions aboard a train en route from a catastrophic series against the meek Philadelphia Athletics. When he could stand the frivolity no longer, he poked his head around from the manager's front seat in the special car and growled: "I'll ask *you* a question. How many of you fellas think you're earning your salary?"

Still, he proved unregenerate himself no matter what rank he occupied. Arthur Daley wrote in *The New York Times:* "His humor is constant and ever-flowing, but most of it is strictly visual. You have to see him in action to appreciate him, an item which perpetually confounds those chroniclers who strive to capture his hilarious antics in print. He acts funny but he doesn't write funny because his violent pantomime and mimicry need a much broader stage than the confining limitations of type."

He displayed this bent on a sufficiently broad stage sometimes in situations that might have been perilous for a less-talented mimic. On a tour of the Pacific he once devoted an entire 20-minute "speech" at a rally to a violent pantomime of arm-waving, finger-pointing and head-shaking, clenching his fist and going through all the signs of an orator without actually saying anything, while the crowd roared.

He was not insensitive to the possibility of diplomatic or physical dangers, however, exhibiting a kind of Charlie Chaplin stoicism to the tightrope course he often plunged along.

In the spring of 1915, his third with Wilbert Robinson's Dodgers, a sports writer was driving across the trestle between Charles Ebbets's "beautiful Daytona" and the beach when his headlights caught the figure of a man leaning over the railing toward the water. He stopped, ran over and looked into the anguished face of Casey Stengel. "I'm sick," the young outfielder moaned, "and Uncle Robbie doesn't like me and I can't hit, and I'm deliberatin' whether to jump in."

When he became manager of the same Dodgers 20 years later, he slumped into a barber's chair after the team had fumbled away a doubleheader with flourishes, ordered a shave and cautioned the barber: "Don't cut my throat. I may want to do that later myself."

When he became manager of Oakland in the Pacific Coast League in 1946, he noted the geographical advantages of the area with appreciation. "Just like Brooklyn," he said, "wherever I go they throw in a bridge as part of the service. Every manager wants to jump off a bridge sooner or later, and it is very nice for an old man like me to know he don't have to walk 50 miles to find one."

He did not have to walk 50 miles to find an audience, either, for his nonstop, marathon, circuitous style of speaking that became known as "Stengelese."

It was a kind of rambling semi-doubletalk laced with ambiguous, assumed or unknown antecedents, a liberal use of "which" instead of "who" or "that," a roundabout narrative framed in great generalities and dangling modifiers, a lack of proper names for "that fella" or simply "the shortstop," plus flashes of incisiveness tacked onto the ends of sentences, like: "And, of course, they got Perranoski."

When a listener's interest appeared to wane, Stengel recaptured his attention by suddenly exclaiming, "Now, wait; let me ask you," etc. And he would then pose a question in the form of a lengthy monologue. Finally, when the central point was delivered, he would extend a finger, wink with exaggeration and ask: "Got it?" Strict followers of Stengelese always found a point at the end of his trail, though often an hour later; between the layers of dangling participles and fused phrases, a point lurked.

Sometimes the point was made rather quickly in a form of short, clipped, Stengelese, most frequently to summarize a baseball player's ability or idiosyncrasies or to define a situation starkly.

Of Jim Bunning, who had pitched successfully for both the Detroit Tigers of the American League and the Philadelphia Phillies of the National League, he said: "He must be good. He gets 'em out in both leagues."

Of Van Lingle Mungo, his impetuous pitcher with the Dodgers in the nineteen-thirties: "Mungo and I get along fine. I just tell him I won't stand for no nonsense—and then I duck."

Of Roger Maris, the aloof, arch power-hitter of the Yankees: "That Maris. You'd tell him something and he'd stare at you for a week before answering."

Of baseball itself and the nature of the game: "You got to get 27 outs to win."

Of the logic of the double play: "It gives you two twenty-sevenths of a ball game."

Of a pitcher who throws sinking balls that tend to be hit onto the ground into such double plays: "He throws grounders."

Of ball players and their occasional lack of hustle: "I ain't seen no one die on a ball field chasing flies. And the pitchers. I bet I lost six games fieldin' by a pitcher. He's got an eighteen-dollar glove, ain't he?"

Of Willie Mays, who played for the San Francisco Giants in windy Candlestick Park: "If a typhoon is blowing, he catches the ball."

Of a ball player with a problem: "That feller runs splendid but he needs help at the plate, which coming from the country chasing rabbits all winter give him strong legs, although he broke one falling out of a tree, which shows you can't tell, and when a curve ball comes he waves at it and if pitchers don't throw curves you have no pitching staff, so how is a manager going to know whether to tell boys to fall out of trees and break legs so he can run fast even if he can't hit a curve ball?"

Stengelese flowered, though, in even longer, fuller public utterances that reached Olympian heights in Congress, where a rambler of Stengel's range might be accused of carrying coal to Newcastle. When he testified in 1958 before the Senate's Antitrust and Monopoly Subcommittee, he took the members back in history and syntax as he reviewed the ramifications of Oliver Wendell Holmes's decision of 1922 that baseball was not a business subject to trust laws but was "a local exhibition."

"I had many years that I was so successful as a ball player, as it is a game of skill," Stengel said, appearing as the manager of Yankees and the patriarch of the national game. "And then I no doubt was discharged by baseball, in which I had to go back to the minor leagues as a manager and after being in the minor leagues as a manager I became a major league manager in several cities and was discharged, we call it 'discharged' because there is no question I had to leave."

But should there be a new law governing professional baseball's relations with its players?

"Well," the Professor replied into the microphone, "I would have to say at the present time that I think baseball has advanced in this respect for the player help. That is an amazing statement for me to make, because you can retire with an annuity at 50 and what organization in America allows you to retire at 50 and receive money?"

"I want to further state that I am not a ball player, that is, put into that pension fund committee. At my age, and I have been in baseball, well, I will say that I am possibly the oldest man in baseball. I would say that when they start an annuity for ball players to better their conditions, it should have been done and I think it has been done."

Estes Kefauver, the tall Tennesseean who became a Presidential contender after staring down Frank Costello and other powerful starers in other Senate hearings, received the loudest laugh of the day when he cleared his throat and said: "Mr. Stengel, I'm not sure I made my question clear."

The feeling persisted, after performances like these, that Stengelese was at least 50 per cent "put on" and 50 per cent "personality." As a vice president and director of the Valley National Bank of Glendale, which he and his wife's family controlled, Casey was considered as clownish as a barracuda despite straight-faced monologues like this one during an exposition on his bank's branch at Toluca Lake:

"We're a national bank and that is what you call a subsidiary. That's correct. Our main office is over in Glendale and this is a subsidiary—a branch. You can't ask me to go downstairs and run an I.B.M. machine without a college I.B.M. course. And I'm not supposed to talk about the banking business at all, because gold is leaving the country."

"Now this is a board room. See over there on the chart—capital assets and all that. Now you ask me: if this is the board room, where is the board, and I say this ain't the day the board meets. Okay?"

"Now, in there where it says 'escrows' is where they can take people in and talk about escrows so it won't be out in public."

Part of the anatomy of Stengelese consisted of certain understated adjectives, like "fairly" as in "fairly amazing," and certain rich or mid-Victorian words or usages that he dropped neatly among the "ain'ts" and "fellas," such as "commerce" and "numerous" and "splendid."

When 1,400 banners were paraded around the perimeter of Shea Stadium in New York during the Mets' Annual Banner Day contest, "numerous splendid" hand-made signs carried messages in short, pure Stengelese, including one that caught the essence of the Stengel philosophy toward his astonishingly forlorn ball club in the Professor's own metier: "Commence Bein' Amazin'."

Even the Stengel telephone had a touch of the legend. His home number in California for years carried the exchange "Citrus"; his office exchange, appropriately, "Popular." One day in January 1965, just before he began what turned into his final season as manager, the phone rang in the bank and the vice president, who had been alerted for a call from this writer on the East Coast, answered.

"I feel fairly good, yes, sir," he boomed, his flair for understatement in mid-season form. "We've been going to all them big football games at Southern Cal. And now we're going ahead with our new bank building here in Glendale, and then there's a branch in North Hollywood that we're goin' to dig ground for, and if I had Berra and Spahn and some of those pitchers here I'd see that they'd dig in and I'd show 'em who's the boss—around the bank, anyway."

"Spahn and Berra the opening-day battery?" he asked, barely pausing to field a question. "Well, I tell you. You know the amazing fans we have in Shea Stadium, which have stormed us with mail from all over, and now we have a girls' group and a women's group. There's nobody in the world I've seen will buy more tickets, and more fans are going to show up on opening day whether the Dodgers show up or not. So maybe we'll fill the park anyway and let those boys play 'em another day."

The point being delivered was that Stengel the Banker never let Stengel the Manager indulge in non sequiturs in money matters. The Los Angeles Dodgers, with Sandy Koufax, Don Drysdale, Maury Wills and many memories of the team's 67 years in Brooklyn, were scheduled to open the season three months later in New York. It was to be a one-day stand and a certain sellout, followed for two days by the Houston Astros, who were certain not to sell out the stadium. So behind the doubletalk lay the seeds of a plan to fill the Mets' coffers on those quieter days with Stengel's "money" combination of Yogi Berra and Warren Spahn, two of the game's ranking stars who had been signed by the Mets near the end of their careers.

"I think we have a number of spots on the ball club," Stengel went on, having, as usual, all of his time-outs left. "We have numerous jobs which our men can fill on the pitching staff, in the outfield and in the infield, too. You could look it up, but very few players last more than five years, or maybe ten, and you'll find that the annuities are made out that way."

Did he know that his second-baseman, Ron Hunt, had returned his contract unsigned?

"Is that so?" he asked with interest. "Well, Mr. Hunt has given 100 per cent, and he'll probably have to be a second-baseman again this year. I have a proposition with Hunt that he'd have to beat out several outstanding players, and he did win the job against competition without ever being in Triple-A baseball."

Translation: Hunt resented suggestions that he shift to third base to make way for unproved players at second base, and he probably was right.

Edna Stengel added a postscript to the conversation, displaying some Stengel understatement herself, by saying: "We're kind of an active family, you know."

Stengel's entourage of baseball players and writers had watched one-half of the active family that season in cities from San Francisco to Philadelphia, as they traveled the country with their 74-year-old manager, watching him in action before the public around the clock.

In Milwaukee, we watched him rush onto the field when the Mets and the Braves got into a ninth-inning rumble one night. Some players said later that they were so surprised to stumble over "the Old Man" in the dust that they broke up laughing. Hours after, the Old Man was enthralling friends and writers by reenacting great team fights of two generations earlier.

In Pittsburgh one day, a family named Stengel sent a birth certificate into the dugout with the name David Casey Stengel written on it—their son, who had been born nine years earlier after Casey's Yankees won their fifth straight championship. He bounced over to the dugout railing and held court with his namesake for 20 minutes.

In St. Louis, before a glittering mink-and-tails crowd on Robert Goulet's opening night in the ballroom of the Chase Hotel, Goulet eased into his first number, cruising around a raised dance floor murmuring a love song to the ringside tables. He turned left and ("Why not take all of me?") came face to face with the unmistakable features of Casey Stengel, who was sitting at the ringside, too. The singer did a double take, fell to one knee, stopped his show and, to deafening applause, introduced the manager of the Mets, who stood and croaked: "You know, I've got a way with the ladies myself." After that, Goulet sang and Stengel was besieged by dozens of stunningly gowned women, who thronged his table pleading for autographs, and it became the Robert Goulet and Casey Stengel show.

In Cincinnati, a radio interviewer asked about Washington's place in the national life and Casey said proudly that "people want to see three things there, don't they? the White House, the Washington Monument because Gabby Street once caught a ball dropped off it and the ball park—because in what other sport does the President throw out the first ball every year?"

In Houston, a man brought his skeptical son to the visiting team's dugout and said hesitantly: "I wonder if you remember me. I pitched against you when you broke in with Kankakee." The Mets had just traveled from the Coast, were sleepless and, as usual, somewhat hopeless, and they were showing signs of total collapse as a baseball team. But the old manager looked at the visitor and his son and said: "Sure, sure. The old fireball himself. Why, I was sure glad when you quit that league. Did you make me look bad. I never could hit you."

In San Francisco, a minister leaned over the visiting team's dugout, introduced himself and said he had pitched batting practice to Stengel in 1910 in Kankakee. The census listed Kankakee, Illinois, at 27,666, and that was half a century after Stengel and all of his visitors supposedly had crowded the little town, but he showed no flicker of disbelief this time, either. He turned in astonishment to a man standing near him in the dugout and, spanning the 54 turbulent years since Kankakee, said warmly: "You know, he helped me hit."

That was a depression, two world wars, three generations and a dozen leagues earlier. And now, Branch Rickey was saying on that mild September evening in 1964 just before Casey Stengel headed into his last season as the most splendidly flamboyant, influential and controversial figure in the game, "he is exactly the right age to manage a major league baseball team."

Content

1. Former baseball executive Branch Rickey called Stengel "the perfect link between the team and the public." In his article, Durso attempts to explain that link. Citing several examples from the essay, explain Stengel's great appeal to the fans.
2. In paragraph 22, Durso says that Stengel's life was surrounded by and could be "understood only in terms of legend." Based on this essay and on other things you might have heard about Stengel, what do you think Durso means by this statement?
3. Like Muhammad Ali (see "Hyperbole's Child"), Stengel enjoyed putting on a show. Some have even said that both men made the sports event anti-climatic to the show as a whole. Judging from your reading of the essays on Ali (pages 267–74) and Stengel, in what ways do you think their theatrics were similar? Dissimilar?

The Living Language

Technique

1. To what extent do the details of Durso's narrative make Stengel's life and times interesting to those who are baseball fans or those who were born after Stengel's time? Cite several examples to support your answer.
2. Durso incorporates many direct quotations in this essay. Find 2 or 3 specific quotations that you feel help the reader envision Stengel's theatrics and various poses; explain why you chose these passages in particular.
3. In paragraphs 1–24, Durso presents the legend of Casey Stengel. Beginning in paragraph 25, he goes further, analyzing the intelligence and technique behind the legend. Find one or two examples of the portrayal of the legend and one or two of the explanations of its magic. Has Durso succeeded in showing us more than just the image that Stengel projected to his public?

Language

1. Stengel entertained audiences for years with what has come to be known as "Stengelese," his unique brand of English. What characterizes "Stengelese," and why, according to Durso, did Stengel communicate this way?
2. In paragraph 47, Durso quotes Arthur Daley as saying that Stengel did not "write funny." What does he mean by this term?
3. Stengel was famous for his own vivid images. In paragraph 35, for instance, he describes his "poverty" by saying, "I'm so hollow and starving, I'm liable to explode like a light bulb if I hit the ground too hard." Find one other example of Stengel's colorful language and discuss the image it conveys.
4. Many of Stengel's antics consisted of body language. In paragraph 48, for instance, Durso describes a 20-minute speech consisting entirely of gesture. Find descriptions of two other examples of Stengel's pantomime and gesture, and discuss the way in which he communicated in body language. Do you think, in these cases, that words would have been as effective? Why or why not?

Vocabulary

antics	rapport	ambiguous
histrionics	repertoire	antecedents
unregenerate		

Writing Suggestions

1. Write a brief character sketch of someone you know who has developed a unique personal language, like Stengelese. Combine anecdotes with analysis, as Durso does.

2. On A. B. Giamatti's worker-athlete-actor spectrum (see "Hyperbole's Child", pages 267–74), both Stengel and Ali emphasize the theatrical. Write an essay in which you argue that such theatrics are either good or bad for sports, and in what ways. Use specific examples to support your argument.

Hyperbole's Child
A. B. Giamatti

A. Bartlett Giamatti (b. 1938), who received a Ph.D. in Comparative Literature from Yale University in 1964, has taught at Princeton, Yale, and New York University, and has been a Guggenheim Fellow and a Fellow of the American Academy of Arts and Sciences. Among his scholarly works are numerous articles and books on Renaissance literature, including Play of Double Senses: Spenser's Fairie Queen *(1975), and* Poems of John Milton *(1970). In "Hyperbole's Child," Giamatti turns from the world of the English Renaissance to the world of boxing. He provides a perceptive analysis of boxing, both as work and drama, then goes on to unearth the motives behind the outlandish antics of the three-time heavyweight champion, Muhammad Ali.*

It suddenly became clear to me, sitting in Madison Square Garden on September 29, watching the preliminary bouts to the Ali-Shavers fight, that the basis of sport is work. Running, jumping, lifting, pushing, bending, pulling, planting the legs and using the back—these exertions are essential to physical labor and to athletic competition. The closeness of a given game to the rituals and effort of work invests the game with dignity; without that proximity to labor, the game would be merely a release from work instead of a refinement of it. The radical difference between work and game, however, occurs when limits or rules are imposed on this labor, patterns which acknowledge that this new work, this sport, is not a matter of life and death. Whereas that work, the work of your back and arms, in field or mill, on ship or in forest, was crucial to your survival, and to the survival of those dependent on you, this work is different; it is delimited, separate, independent, a refinement of reality but distinct. This work is fully as serious and difficult as real work, but this unreal work is not coextensive with life. This work of sport, usually but not always at some predetermined point, will have an end. It will be over, not to begin again with the sun. This work, unlike that real work, does not sustain life in any immediate and practical way, such as providing food; but this unreal serious work does sustain life in the sense that it makes life bearable. It allows all of us to go back renewed to whatever real work we do, perhaps to go back for a moment redeemed. I have often thought that the world-wide appeal of soccer lies in part in its unabashed emphasis on penetrating the other's territory; partly in its wonderfully seamless and continuous quality, where no quarter is given, no pause taken, but like the tides men come and go; but mostly in its denial of the use of the hands. For the millions who work with their hands, there can be no greater relief than to escape the daily focus on those instruments of labor, and no greater confirmation of the centrality of hands to life than their denial in this sport.

These notions formed while I waited for the Ali-Shavers fight. I had been watching the undercard, and admiring the way Alfredo Evangelista of Uruguay would get his back into his punches, like a man digging a hole, and how the sheer expenditure of effort had forced Pedro Soto to fight Evangelista's fight until, in the eighth round, Soto was so badly punished by the patient, awkward digging of Evangelista that the referee stopped the bout. At this moment of victory, which is also a moment of reunion, as the men finish work and leave together, the crowd's attention was diverted from Soto and Evangelista by the presence of Ali, who suddenly appeared in the back of the garden and roared through the aisles shaking his finger, surrounded by about ten of his entourage. The crowd responded with delight—"A-li, A-li, A-li," they chanted; and when they turned from that spectacle, Evangelista and Soto were gone. If for most athletes and spectators sport is work conceived in some special way as play, for Muhammad Ali sport is work conceived as theater.

Ali has theatricalized his work in that, rather than continuing to serve his work as a worker, or slave, he has made what he does serve him as a setting. Ali has extended himself and boxing, the sport most like work, in the direction of theater by emphasizing the other being that lives beside the worker in every athlete, the actor.

In the athlete worker and actor meet, the expenditure of energy and the power to give shape come together. Of course, workers "perform" tasks and actors work hard; the spectrum worker-athlete-actor is not a broad one and the three points are distinguished by emphasis more than anything else. As the athlete resembles the worker in the way he exerts his body, and in the way he catches the deep rhythms in work, so the athlete resembles the actor in the way he uses the body to express what I can only call an inner vision. Both athlete and actor release energy in order to restrain it and in restraining it, to give shape to a new idea. Both are judged effective or ineffective (that is what "good" or "bad" means in these two professions) by how well they execute what is set them; and for both athlete and actor execution depends not on inspiration or luck or the weather, inner or outer, but on coordination, economy of gesture, timing, good coaching.

It is Ali who has brought to the surface the actor in every athlete more successfully and obsessively than anyone else. Ali is in many ways profoundly bored, and he knows only one craft. In order to remain interested in what he must do, Ali has allowed the performer to erupt unchecked, burying the worker in him, the skilled artisan with extraordinary hands and legs and specific, wordly ambitions, under the sulfurous, scaling lava of his improvisations. Improvisation is the only way he has found to order the endless days: the monologizing, poeticizing, and prophesying, all that grimacing and exhorting and praying, is the style of a man who is not sure even he knows when his acts are simply acting, but who does know he does not care.

And when a fight is in view, and training is required, a regimen guaranteed to exacerbate boredom with brutal fatigue, Ali goes deeper into his protean reserves and whole dramas emerge. There is often the heroic beast fable—Ali will slay a dragon in the form of a Bear, a Rabbit, a Gorilla, or lately, an Acorn. As time goes on, other subplots emerge. Howard Cosell once reguarly took a part; occasionally whole countries, like Zaire, are cast. In recent years the press has been less and less willing to be the megaphone to this sideshow, but the press has no choice but to be megaphone when the source of news insists on defining himself as a barker. So we are treated to sermons, doggerel, parables, myths, even creations from whole cloth: "JIMMY ELLIS, SPARRING PARTNER, KNOCKS DOWN CHAMP

The Living Language

TWICE TODAY." That particular story, out of Ali's Pennsylvania training camp some eight days before the bout, is a good example of the problems Ali poses and the problem he has.

Perhaps only a headline announcing the pope's intention to remarry would be as immediately unconvincing as the news that Ellis knocked Ali down twice in one round. The gloves used in sparring sessions weigh sixteen ounces apiece; Billy Carter would have trouble knocking over a schooner of Schlitz with one of those mitts. Then there is the fact that these two know each other well, having met more than twenty years ago in Louisville when they were both young teen-agers. Ali and Ellis cannot surprise each other and while Ellis would work for a man he could knock down, Ali would not hire a man who might even try it. Even once. But *twice!* Such an idea staggers the imagination.

Why put out the story then? In part because where the rest of us were born under a star, Ali was born under a rhetorical figure, hyperbole, defined by the great Quintilian as "an elegant straining of the truth." Surely Ali was also impelled by a realization that the advance sale for September 29 was slow; that the publicity, at the time of the Lance affair and a hot mayoral primary race in New York, had been soggy; and he was propelled by that instinct of his to hype the gate, to work his own crowd (as he would do as Soto and Evangelista finished work), to shill for himself, to be both the show and the man who hustled them into the tent. If there is one born every minute, Ali wants to be the midwife. But does that deep instinct justify putting out such a palpably transparent story as the one about being knocked down twice? No, that instinct does not justify straining the truth quite so inelegantly. An even deeper need justifies the story, the need to pump up once again the white man's hope to see the black champion beaten.

Here we engage Ali's deepest game, the only work he does with a will. While you are being encouraged to think he can be beaten, you are being allowed to understand that the form the encouragement takes is fraudulent. Your ability to see through the con undermines your belief in his vulnerability (he can't be beaten if he says he can) and reaffirms your faith in his theatrical mastery (knocked down twice, my foot! What a showman). You are now his. Ali has transformed all the potential spectators, the fight crowd, into something far different, an audience; he has enticed the naive, titillated the devoted, amused the jaded, outraged the mass; he has had it out with his opponent now in the press and on television for at least two weeks, his sense of pace inpeccable, the whole spectacle building to the grand final number, the climax just before the last curtain, the weigh-in; and, most important, he has managed to legitimize race as an issue in the fight by making it part of the show, or, for those so inclined, the whole show. One so inclined is Ali, and the last scene is played.

At the weigh-in, the state lends whatever moral and legal credibility it has to the ritual of assessing the fighters' weight and physical fitness. They are always found to be fit. (Examinations and X rays conducted on September 28 could find no injuries, indeed no trace of trauma, resulting from the two knockdowns suffered by the champion during training.) And after the tape and scales, Ali takes over, and tears a passion to tatters, splitting the ears of the groundlings in the press, o'erdoing Termagant and out-heroding Herod, now the player, now the Prince, doing all the parts and, at the weigh-in on September 28, ranting at length about the theatrical nature of his ranting, exposing the structure of his illusion, the old actor getting himself worked up for the part, doing what Elvis Presley could no longer do, getting into the circle, recapturing the energy and interest to go out on stage by pretending to have it—all of this working precisely to the extent that all the hangers-on and reporters and onlookers and cuties and commission people and cameramen and friends and spies and flunkies and acolytes, who have seen it dozens of times, get pulled in, and begin to laugh and nudge and shake their heads and stamp their feet as if it were the first time; and yet, if you listen rather than acquiesce, at the center of this whirlwind of words and gestures and postures and poses the chosen epithet of the chosen opponent is chanted and honed and, finally, hurled like a knife at the man it signifies. The real fight is now almost over, as Ali turns on his opponent all the power of the opponent, turning the man's physical characteristics, his background, his class, his worth as a man against him. Ali deflects the opponent's strength from Ali, and now the opponent is left, in the weeks or hours remaining (for this process does not start at the weigh-in), to fight himself, to fight his ugliness or his awkwardness or his lack of education or, in the most savage blow of all, to fight his race. If the man is white, he is not allowed to be the White Hope. Ali bestows this duty as if it were a dukedom, and then watches while the opponent tries to figure out whether to hoist this load, and, if he

9

will, how to gain a purchase on it, and, once it is up, where to take it. It is too easy.

With black fighters there is more sport, though the press here draws a line and the public does not, evidently, get the full force of Ali's treatment of black opponents. But the technique is clear. In calling Frazier a gorilla, or Shavers "shiftless," Ali simply unleashes the power of traditional racist epithets. He thus sets his black opponent to battling two chimeras, both now identified with himself. The opponent must confront his main sense of himself, his strength, his identity as a black man, as if it were a weakness; he must struggle with, rather than use, the source of his power, because this black champion has turned their race into a vicious insult. Lest the opponent miss the point to the burden that he alone now carries, Ali will during the fight clarify his status for him as he did for Shavers by calling him throughout the fight, according to reports, "nigger." It is a technique as simple, and decent, as rubbing your glove's laces on an opponent's swollen eye.

But while Ali has a black opponent fighting his blackness, he also has the other man fighting his whiteness. Everyone who fights Ali must be the white hope. The gate demands it, and hyperbole's child would have it no other way. Every opponent is the champion of that vast, hostile white mass that, since February 28, 1964, when Ali annnounced that he had a few months before joined the Nation of Islam, and especialy since his refusal in Houston on April 28, 1967, to be inducted into the army, has wanted to see him knocked out. So, at least, Ali believes; and so believed the elegantly dressed, affable black man who sat behind me at the Ali-Shavers bout, and who laughingly insisted for fifteen rounds that I had come to see Ali beaten by my fighter, Shavers. But I believe that the act at Houston and the announcement about the Nation of Islam were themselves not the causes of an attitude, but the results of an even older attitude of Ali's. For those acts of 1967 and 1964 were acts of separation, of secession from black and white America's traditional assumptions about how to behave, and were themselves responses to the conviction, held by the boy who by his account in *My Own Story* felt a "deep kinship" with Emmett Till, that they wanted him out, and that he would dance inside and sting them before they could put him down and put him out.

Ali's boredom with training and fighting only masks a fear, a fear of being peripheral, a terror of being out, and that fear accounts for his need to be at the center of something, a stage, a ring, a Nation, a cosmic racial drama. His fear of being marginal accounts for the savagery of his desire to get in, to land the first blow, and for the outlandish intensity of his acting center stage, before the bell has ever rung or the lights have dimmed. Ali's sense of racial antagonism forces him to scorn his black opponents for being black, while at the same time smearing Frazier, Norton, Shavers with whiteface, grotesquely deforming the other's face in every way while trumpeting the beauty of his own, that clean-shaven, smooth, unblemished face so unlike the scarred, roughened laborers' faces his mocks. His is an extraordinary series of performances, culminating in the weigh-in, each scene contributing, as do rounds, to that over-all accumulation of episode and pace and shaped energy we call a starring role. He has, particularly in the last year or so as preparation gets more and more difficult, set up the actual fight as an anticlimax to the weeks before it. And certainly the bout on the evening of September 29 was an anticlimax; for, regardless of what you saw on television, where closeups on intense faces covered a great deal of standing, leaning, peek-a-booing, clowning, missing, waiting, the Shavers-Ali fight was a good fight only once you had accepted how much less good a fighter Ali has become.

The real struggle goes on earlier, when Ali transforms the coming fight into a ghastly minstrel show, he never more black than when the other end man is daubed in white, the other never blacker than when Ali sneers at his color, the races locked together, at one and at odds, the whole a parody of race relations in every city street and union and school and firehouse and subway and unemployed black waking hour in America, the prizefight finally only a skirmish in the larger race war, this little battle masquerading as a show starring Muhammad Ali and a cast of everyone else.

Ali has known from the beginning what every good athlete learns: make him play your game, fight your fight, and you will beat him every time. but Ali has also learned a lesson kept from most athletes precisely by the pleasure of their work, a pleasure now beneath Ali, a pleasure in work insufficiently exhilarating to one who has the art born in him, the art of filling a scene: and that subtler lesson is that while you can beat him if he fights your fight, you can destroy him if he acts in your play. If, like Othello, he will accept the role you set for him, you will master him as you master all scenes. And if you can make him play nigger and white racist all at once, surely you are the greatest and he is yours. This is, after all, an old drama and an old style, learned from the white slavemasters; they were the ones who based their play on others' brutal work and who forced the others to enact roles simply to survive. Ali, with his incredible gifts of body and mind, has brought the central drama of his people's history in America to a bright, gaudy life, for everyone to see. He has brought the patterns of work, play, and acting that commingle in slaves and athletes to the surface, and he has refined his techniques for communicating, through the media, what those old patterns mean.

Sitting in Madison Square Garden on September 29, I did not think Ali beat Shavers; even giving Ali all the even rounds, I scored the fight for Shavers, 8–7. I do not think Ali beat Shavers this September any more than many think he beat Ken Norton in September of 1976, or beat Jimmy Young in the spring of 1976. I also do not believe that Ali, at this point, really cares what anyone thinks, or cares what really happened. The fights in the ring, vastly remunerative, full of effort and clowning, are only incidental to the real battle. I believe he will participate in the ring fights longer than he should because he cannot stop until he has fought down the need, compounded of fear and fury, to act out completely what, in his view, it is to be black in America, to be always living at the margin, on the edge, in a position where, despite the pain of your work and the beauty of your play, a man may announce with superb casualness at any given moment that you have been counted out.

Content

1. In Giamatti's opinion, Ali's outrageous behavior outside the ring is an act to conceal fear. In your own words, summarize what Giamatti feels that fear is.
2. William Zinsser admires the sports writer who successfully links the world of sport to the broader social scene. Discuss the way in which Giamatti links boxing and Ali to American social history.
3. Giamatti believes that Ali's playacting communicates to the public in at least three ways: it entertains, it advertises, and it makes a serious social statement. Using examples of each from the essay or your own memory of Ali's hyperbolic language, explain how Ali's communication to the public serves these functions.

Technique

1. To argue that Ali's bragging is more significant than it first appears, Giamatti employs the technique of analogy, explaining one thing by comparing it to another. His analogies liken Ali's hyperbole to Shakesperian theater, to the circus, to minstrel shows, and to Elvis Presley. What do these seemingly very different phenomena have in common that help Giamatti make a statement about Ali's language?
2. The structure of this essay is difficult. Giamatti begins his essay with a serious discussion of the relation between reality and sport; his discussion about Ali's language does not immediately appear to be related to this earlier discussion. How does the conclusion of the essay, with its mention of "race war" and "the cosmic racial drama" bring the two topics of the essay together? Consider the final analogy of the essay in forming your answer.

Language

1. "Hyperbole," Giamatti points out, has been defined as the "elegant straining of the truth." For an additional definition, look up the word in your dictionary. In what way would you say Ali is "hyperbole's child"?
2. Giamatti says that "Ali roared through the aisles." Discuss the way in which the word "roar" contributes to our image of Ali.
3. Ali demands attention, Giamatti says, by "dignifying himself as a barker." What is a barker, and how can we apply the word to Ali's show?

Vocabulary

delimited	hyperbole	barker
coextensive	improvisation	ritual
chimera	protean	spectrum

Writing Suggestions

1. Write a paragraph in which you describe Ali or some other flamboyant sports personality. As Giamatti does with the word "roar," choose words that catch the personality of the sports figure.

2. Giamatti says that with Ali the fight is anticlimatic to the performance. The same has been said of many sports, sports figures, and sportscasters. Write an essay in which you analyze the relationship between theater and sport, using a particular sport (wrestling or hockey, for instance) or sports figure.
3. Giamatti says that the "spectrum worker–athlete–actor is not a broad one and the three points are distinguished by emphasis more than anything." Write an essay in which you contrast two sports, one which seems closer to theater and one which seems closer to work.

Sports

William Zinsser

William Zinsser (b. 1922) has been a successful writer, editor, and teacher. He was a feature writer for the New York Herald-Tribune *from 1946 to 1949, also serving as drama editor, feature writer, editorial writer, and film critic for this newspaper. He has also been a columnist for the New York Times, Look, and Life. His books include* The City Dwellers *(1962),* The Lunacy Boom *(1970), and* On Writing Well *(1976). Currently, he is Executive Director of the Book-of-the-Month Club. In "Sports," Zinsser defines what he perceives to be a good style of sportswriting; as he does so, he provides examples of what constitutes bad sportswriting. He finds sports jargon and the excessive use of statistics particularly objectionable.*

1   I learned about the circuit clout before I learned about the electrical circuit. I also learned early—as a child addict of the sports pages—that a hurler (or twirler) who faces left when he toes the slab is a southpaw or a portsider. Southpaws were always lanky, portsiders always chunky, though I have never heard "chunky" applied to anything else except peanut butter (to distinguish it from "creamy") and I have no idea what a chunky person would look like. When hurlers fired the old horsehide, a batsman would try to solve their slants. If he succeeded he might rap a sharp bingle to the outfield, garnering a win for the home contingent, or at least knotting the count. If not, he might bounce into a twin killing, snuffing out a rally and dimming his team's hopes in the flag scramble.

2   I could go on, mining every sport for its lingo and extracting from the mother lode a variety of words found nowhere else in the mother tongue. Do we ever "garner" anything except a win? I could

write of hoopsters and pucksters, grapplers and matmen, strapping oarsmen and gridiron standouts. I could rhapsodize about the old pigskin—far more passionately than any pig farmer—or describe the frenzied bleacherites caught up in the excitement of the autumn classic. I could, in short, write in sports English instead of good English, as if they were two different languages. Of course they're not. As in the case of writing about science or any other special subject, there is no substitute for the best.

What, you might ask, is wrong with "southpaw"? Shouldn't we be grateful for the addition to our language of a word so picturesque? Why isn't it a relief to have twirlers and circuit clouts instead of the same old pitchers and home runs? The answer is that these words have become even cheaper currency than the coins they were meant to replace. They come flooding automatically out of the typewriter of every scribe (sportswriter) in every pressbox.

The man who first thought of "southpaw" had a right to be pleased. I like to think that he allowed himself the small smile that is the due of anyone who invents a good novelty. But how long ago was that? The color that "southpaw" added to the language has paled with decades of repetition, along with the hundreds of other idioms that now form the fabric of daily sportswriting. There is a weariness about them that leaves us numb. We read the articles to find out who won, and how, but we don't read them with any real enjoyment.

The best sportswriters know this. They avoid the exhausted synonyms and strive for freshness elsewhere in the construction of a sentence. You can search the columns of Red Smith and never find a batsman bouncing into a twin killing. Smith is not afraid to let a batter hit into a double play. But you will find hundreds of unusual words—good English words—chosen with precision and fitted into situations where no other sportswriter would put them. They gratify us because the writer obviously cares about using fresh imagery in a field where his competitors settle for the same old stuff. This is why Red Smith is still in business after more than fifty years of writing, and why his competitors have long since been sent—as they would be the first to say—to the showers.

Across the years I remember countless phrases in Red Smith's columns that took me by surprise with their humor and originality. It was a pleasure to read about a quarterback who was "scraped off the turf like apple butter." I remember countless times when Smith, a devout angler, baited his hook and came up with that slippery fish, a sports commissioner, gasping for air.

"In most professional sports, the bottom has just about dropped out of the czar business," he wrote in 1971, noting once again that the cupidity of team owners has a tendency to outrun the courage of the sport's monitors. "The first and toughest of the overlords was Kenesaw Mountain Landis, who came to power in 1920 and ruled with a heavy hand until his death in 1944. But if baseball started with Little Caesar, it wound up with Ethelred the Unready." Red Smith is the daily guardian of our perspective, a writer who keeps us honest. But this is largely because he is writing good English. His style is not only graceful but strong enough to carry strong convictions.

What keeps the average sportswriter from writing good English is, first, the misapprehension that he shouldn't be trying to. He has been reared on so much jargon, so many clichés, that he thinks they are the required tools of the trade.

He is also obsessed by synonyms. He has a dread of repeating the word that is easiest for the reader to visualize—batter, runner, golfer, boxer—if a synonym can be found. And usually, with exertion, it can. This excerpt from a college newspaper is typical:

> Bob Hornsby extended his skein yesterday by toppling Dartmouth's Jerry Smithers, 6-4, 6-2, to lead the netmen to victory over a surprisingly strong foe. The gangling junior put his big serve to good use in keeping the Green captain off balance. The Memphis native was in top form as he racked up the first four games, breaking the Indian's service twice in the first four games. The Exeter graduate faltered and the Hanover mainstay rallied to cop three games. But the racquet ace was not to be denied, and Smithers' attempt to knot the first stanza at 4-4 failed when he was passed by a cross-court volley on the sixth deuce point. The redhead was simply too determined, and . . . .

Whatever became of Bob Hornsby? Well might you ask. Hornsby has been metamorphosed within one paragraph into the gangling junior, the Memphis native, the Exeter graduate, the racquet ace and the redhead. The reader doesn't know him in these various disguises—or care. He only wants the clearest picture of what happened. Never be afraid to repeat the player's name and to keep the details of the game simple. A set or an inning doesn't have to be recycled into a stanza or a frame just to avoid redundancy. The cure is worse than the ailment.

Another obsession is with numbers. True, every sports addict lives with a head full of statistics, cross-filed for ready access, and many a baseball fan who once flunked simple arithmetic can perform prodigies of instant calculation in the ball park on a summer afternoon. Still, some statistics are more important than others. If a pitcher wins his twentieth game, if a golfer shoots a 61, if a runner runs the mile in 3:48, please mention it. But don't get carried away:

> AUBURN, Ala., Nov. 1 (UPI)—Pat Sullivan, Auburn's sophomore quarterback, scored two touchdowns and passed for two today to hand Florida a 38-12 defeat, the first of the season for the ninth-ranked Gators.
> John Reaves of Florida broke two southeastern Conference records and tied another. The tall sophomore from Tampa, Fla., gained 369 yards passing, pushing his six-game season total to 2,115. That broke the S.E.C. season record of 2,012 set by the 1966 Heisman trophy winner, in 10 games.
> Reaves attempted 66 passes—an S.E.C. record—and tied the record of 33 completions set this fall by Mississippi's Archie Manning.
> Fortunately for Auburn, nine of Reaves's passes were intercepted—breaking the S.E.C. record of eight interceptions suffered by Georgia's Zeke Bratkowski against Georgia Tech in 1951.
> Reaves's performance left him only a few yards short of the S.E.C. season total offense record of 2,187 set by Georgia's Frank Sinkwich in 11 games in 1942. And his two touchdown passes against Auburn left him only one touchdown pass short of the S.E.C. season record of 23 set in 1950 by Kentucky's Babe Parilli . . . .

Those are the first five paragraphs of a six-paragraph story that was prominently displayed in my New York newspaper, a long way from Auburn. It has a certain mounting hilarity—a figure freak amok at his typewriter. But can anybody read it? And does anybody care? Only Zeke Bratkowski—finally off the hook.

Sports is one of the richest fields now open to the nonfiction writer. Many authors better known for "serious" books have done some of their most solid work as observers of athletic combat. John McPhee's *Levels of the Game* and George Plimpton's *Paper Lion*—one a book about tennis, the other about professional football—take us deeply into the lives of the players. In mere detail they have enough information to keep any fan happy. But what makes them special is their humanity. Who is this strange bird—the winning athlete—and what mysterious engines keep him going?

One of the classics in the literature of baseball is John Updike's account of Ted Williams' final game, on September 28, 1960. The article builds to the almost mythical moment in the eighth inning when the forty-two-year-old "Kid," coming up for his last time at bat in Fenway Park, hits one over the wall. But before that Updike has compressed much of the career of "this brittle and temperamental player" in one paragraph that is as graceful as Williams' own swing:

> I remember watching one of his home runs from the bleachers of Shibe Park; it went over the first baseman's head and rose meticulously along a straight line and was still rising when it cleared the fence. The trajectory seemed qualitatively different from anything anyone else might hit. For me, Williams is the classic ballplayer of the game on a hot August weekday, before a small crowd, when the only thing at stake is the tissue-thin difference between a thing done well and a thing done ill. Baseball is a game of the long season, of relentless and gradual averaging-out. Irrelevance—since the reference point of most individual games is remote and statistical—always threatens its interest, which can be maintained not by the occasional heroics that sportswriters feed upon but by players who always care; who care, that is to say, about themselves and their art. Insofar as the clutch hitter is not a sportswriter's myth, he is a vulgarity, like a writer who writes only for money. It may be that, compared to managers' dreams, such as Joe DiMaggio and the always helpful Stan Musial, Williams is an icy star. But of all team sports, baseball, with its graceful intermittences of action, its immense and tranquil field sparsely settled with poised men in white, its dispassionate mathematics, seems to me best suited to accommodate, and be ornamented by, a loner. It is essentially a lonely game. No other player visible to my generation has concentrated within himself so much of the sport's poignance, has so assiduously refined his natural skills, has so constantly brought to the plate that intensity of competence that crowds the throat with joy.

From the "sparsely settled" diamond to the densely populated chessboard may seem an unlikely leap. But to a good writer there is always the central mystery of a game's fascination for the player, whatever the game. George Steiner's *Fields of Force*, an account of the Fischer-Spassky chess championship and of past title matches and champions, is a masterpiece of sports reporting, taking the reader into terrain more dizzying than any bobsled run:

> Whatever Fischer's idiosyncrasies, there are abundant impulses to paranoia and unreality in chess itself, in the violence and autistic passion of the game. Like the inner workings of mathematics and music, these qualities are next to impossible to communicate in words . . .
>
> [But] something of the full horror and harmony of the abysmal depths, of the lunatic magic of endless vertigo, can be expressed numerically. The first four moves can lead to 70,000 different positions. The number of possible ways of playing the first ten moves on each side is such that if every man, woman and child on earth played without respite it would require more than 217 billion years to go through them all. The most recent estimate of the number of different games that can be played is of the order of 25×10^{115}, a product fantastically larger than the generally assumed sum of atoms in the universe. This does not mean that identical *positions* will not turn up. Openings will often run the same course, and an end-game problem set by al-Adli in an Arab manuscript of the ninth century came up in actual play in 1945 (Jorgensen-Sorensen). But the odds against a duplication of a major portion of a game are far more than astronomical. In brief, as far as we can look ahead to a future for the species and this galaxy, the variety of play in chess remains inexhaustible.

Good sportswriting has crossed over into whole new realms, undreamed of by the hacks who still sit in the pressbox reporting the stellar exploits of chunky portsiders and Ruthian sluggers. It's one of the richest frontiers, incidentally, for women writers. Even Ruth has been ushered down from the sanitized slopes of Olympus and converted into a real person, with appetites as big as his girth, in Robert W. Creamer's fine biography, *Babe*. "The legend comes alive," says the book's subtitle, which is certainly what Ruth would have wanted, hard though some of the facts may be on those who would like him to stay legendary.

This is only one of many realities that have come crowding into what was until recently a simple fairyland world. Just to process the daily medical news, for instance, is no easy task for the modern fan—matters of fitness, injury and orthopedic disarray. Hardly a man is now alive who can't draw a transverse section of the human knee after surgery, or digress on bone chips and rotator disks in a pitcher's arm.

Another new element is high finance. In the few years since baseball's hired hands were legally sprung from bondage and allowed to peddle themselves to the highest bidder, I have often opened the sports section and thought that I had stumbled into the business pages by mistake. Million-dollar contracts of infinite complexity swim before my eyes, replete with deferred payments, bonuses and annuities, some extending beyond the year 2000.

Big money in turn has brought big emotional trouble. Envy is the new worm in the apple of sport. To read about the New York Yankees as they bickered through the summer of 1977, when Reggie Jackson had arrived toting his monetary bundle, was like reading Ann Landers. The game was secondary; first we had to learn whose feelings were hurt, whose pride was wounded. In once-sedate tennis, the pot of gold is now enormous and the players are strung as tightly as their racquets. In football and basketball the pay is sky-high and so is the umbrage.

"It wasn't my idea for basketball to become tax-shelter show biz," Bill Bradley writes in *Life on the Run*, a chronicle of his seasons with the New York Knicks. Bradley's book is one of the best examples of the new sportswriting because it ponders the darker forces that are altering the quality of American sport—the greed of entrepreneurs, the blind worship of stars, the inability to accept defeat:

> After Van's departure, I realized that no matter how kind, friendly and genuinely interested the owners may be, in the end most players are little more than depreciable assets to them.
>
> Self-definition comes from external sources, not from within. While their physical skill lasts, professional athletes are celebrities—fondled and excused, praised and believed. Only toward the end of their careers do the stars realize that their sense of identity is insufficient.
>
> The winning team, like the conquering army, claims everything in its path and seems to say that only winning is important. Yet victory has very narrow meanings and can become a destructive force. The taste of defeat has a richness of experience all its own.

Bradley's book is also an excellent travel journal, catching the fatigue and loneliness of the professional athlete's nomadic life—the countless night flights and bus rides, the dreary days and endless waits in motel rooms and terminals:

In the airports that have become our commuter stations we see so many dramatic personal moments that we are calloused. To some, we live romantic lives. To me, every day is a struggle to stay in touch with life's subtleties.

American sport has always been interwoven with social history, and the best sportswriters are those who will make the connection. A small but pleasant example of making the connection was a small but pleasant piece by Jean Shepherd about the Indianapolis 500. The article, which ran in the Sunday sports section of the *New York Times*, explains that the Indy has only one counterpart in American sport—the Kentucky Derby—and that both "can only be understood by the outsider in terms of folklore":

> Any horse that wins the Derby enters the pearly gates of history forever. Hundreds of horses have won "classics" over the years, but even non-horseplayers remember Derby winners. So it is with the 500. Who knows or cares what other races Wilbur Shaw might have won in his great career? The fact that he took the 500 three times makes him immortal.
>
> Why the Derby when there are other, richer races? A little history helps. Kentucky, with its great plantations, its soft rolling hills and lazy summers, was the true horse country of America, and 100 years ago when the Derby was born it pitted one aristocratic horse against the other. It was not just another race, but something that came out of the air and the land and the people who lived on it . . .
>
> Indiana in the early days was to the automobile as Kentucky was and is to the horse. Some of the truly great machines by any world standard were born and bred on the Indiana flatlands. The stylish and terrifying Dusenbergs created by the almost mythical Dusenberg brothers, Fred and August, were hammered out a few miles from the brick track. The Auburn, the Cord and the great racing Studebakers were all spawned in dusty Indiana hamlets and came together every spring in the dawn of automobiling to battle it out.
>
> The automobile also means much more to the common people of the great plains than it does to the city folk who huddle jammed together in the great urban East. It meant, and still means, freedom, mobility and, above all, a way out for lives that are often as monotonous as the landscape they are lived in.

These are the values to look for when you write about sport—people, places, the link between past and present, the tug of the future. Observe closely. Hang around the track and the paddock, the ball park and the rink. Interview in depth. Listen to old-timers. Ponder the changes. Write well.

Content

1. Explain Zinsser's thesis. Why, according to Zinsser, do we need fresh sports language?
2. Choose two or three of Zinsser's examples of sports language and two or three examples from your own sports experiences and be prepared to discuss why Zinsser does not or would not consider these "good English." Do you agree? Why or why not?
3. Despite Zinsser's dislike of sports jargon, it has a lasting appeal to players, announcers, and writers. Professional jargon develops in part to establish the unique identity of the "insiders"—to set them apart from the non-member, the uninitiated. To what extent do you think the appeal of sports lingo is that it, like professional jargon, identifies the user as an insider? Cite specific examples from a sport you know well.
4. In paragraph 13, Zinsser implies that the best sportswriter will acknowledge the "realities" and thus the "humanity" of sports. Certainly we frequently speak of sports heroes in legendary, superhuman terms. Consider specifically two or three modern "legends" from various sports. What effect do you believe taking these players "down from the sanitized slopes of Olympus" has on our image of the sports world?

Technique

1. Zinsser begins his argument for fresher sports language with a paragraph that depends largely on "sports lingo." How effective is this technique, given Zinsser's argument against using such overused terms as "southpaw" or "the old horsehide"?
2. Zinsser is not primarily a sportswriter; he is instead a craftsman in the writing of good English. But in the final paragraph he makes it clear that his intended audience is the potential sportswriter. His primary technique of instruction is example. Choose one of his examples of "good" sports English and be prepared to discuss how it supports Zinsser's argument in favor of fresh language.
3. Zinsser uses many images and figures of speech in his discussion of sports. The "sanitized slopes of Olympus" is one example; find two

other examples and describe their effect on you as a reader. Are they, for instance, fresh, vivid, and clear, as Zinsser believes all writing, including sports writing, should be?

Language

1. Do you agree or disagree with Zinsser that words like "twirler," "chunky," and "southpaw" grow stale too quickly to have a real place in sportswriting? Explain.
2. Zinsser uses the word "lingo" to describe sports talk. Look up "lingo" in your dictionary; explain the impression this carefully chosen word gives you as the reader.
3. John Updike, whom Zinsser quotes at length in paragraph 14, chooses his words carefully: "icy star," "tissue-thin difference," "the long season," "tranquil field." These and other phrases are chosen to evoke images in the reader. Find one or two other examples of effective, colorful wording in Updike's paragraph and discuss their effect.

Vocabulary

| hack | umbrage | rhapsodize |
| lingo | cupidity | |

Writing Suggestions

1. Zinsser gives one vivid example, from a college newspaper, of the kind of lingo-filled sportswriting he dislikes. Choose an example of your own from your college or local newspaper or from a sports magazine; rewrite one or two of its paragraphs in vivid, precise prose, developing new images to replace worn ones.
2. Write an essay in which you compare and contrast two sports articles or essays—one you consider effective, the other ineffective. Be specific in your analysis of what makes sportswriting successful, considering, perhaps, such factors as tone, image, language, or point of view.
3. Zinsser's aim is to instruct in the art of sports writing. He suggests, for instance, fresh images, clear language, a "sense of humanity," and the connection between sports and social history. He would have you avoid sports lingo, clichés, the "mounting hilarity" of excessive statistics, and the mythological "sanitized slopes of Olympus." Attend a sports event (or watch one on TV) and write a brief article about the event, attempting to incorporate some of Zinsser's suggestions into your own writing.

The Living Language

Stories for a Rainy Afternoon

Roger Angell

Roger Angell (b. 1920), a native of New York City and a graduate of Harvard University, has served as a contributing editor for the New Yorker since 1956. His writings include a book of short stories, The Stone Arbor *(1960); a collection of humorous essays,* A Day in the Life of Roger Angell *(1967); and three books about baseball. "Stories for a Rainy Afternoon" sheds light on the difference between the sports article, which reports an event, and the sports story, which is more likely to recall an accidental, outlandish, or legendary incident. The essay also shows how important narration and dialogue are to the sportswriter.*

The tarpaulin is down, and a midafternoon rain is falling steadily. Play has been halted. The lights are on, and the wet, pale green tarp throws off wiggly, reptilian gleams. The scoreboard is lit up, too, bringing us fair-weather scores from other cities, and showing us where this game stood a few minutes ago, when the home-plate umpire threw up his hands to call time and everybody on the field ran for cover. Now the players are back in their locker rooms, and both dugouts are empty. A few fans have stayed in their seats, huddling under big, brightly colored golf umbrellas, but almost everybody else has moved back under the shelter of the upper decks, standing there quietly, behind the seats, watching the rain. The press box is deserted except for a couple of writers knocking out sidebars or an early column; a teletype operator is sitting next to his machine and reading a newspaper. The huge park, the countless rows of shiny-blue wet seats, the long emerald outfield lawns, the rain-spattered tarps—all stand silent and waiting. By the look of it, this shower may hold things up for a good half-hour or more. Time for a few baseball stories.

One story concerns another rain delay, a deluge that interrupted a night game in Baltimore, way back in the nineteen fifties. This happened only a year after the Orioles came to town, in 1954, when the American League franchise in St. Louis was shifted east and the worn-out Browns suddenly became the brand-new Orioles. For a while, everybody in Baltimore was happy about the team, but it became clear within a few weeks that the new uniforms could not alter the abilities of the players who had done so horribly in their previous incarnation. The team finished seventh in its first eastern season, losing one hundred games. A new manager, Paul Richards, came aboard the next year, and he shifted the lineup around a little and tinkered with his pitchers, while the front office put out hopeful reports about better times ahead, but the team went right on losing, and by this time it had also begun to lose its following. On this particular damp midsummer night, the Orioles were behind again (the name of the other team has been forgotten), in a game that had been held up two or three times by brief showers. By the bottom of the ninth, only a few hundred silent, pessimistic fans were still in attendance at Memorial Stadium. A light rain had started again. Unexpectedly, the Orioles rallied. A couple of runs scored, and another base hit drove out the enemy pitcher; suddenly the Orioles had the bases loaded, with the tying run at third base and the winning run at second. The reporters paused over their typewriters, where they had begun their customary irritable or apologetic lead paragraphs for further bad-news stories; a few hoarse cries of hope came out of the stands. The next batter was Clint Courtney, probably the most reliable player on the club. Richards came out of the dugout and whispered into Courtney's ear and whacked him encouragingly on the rump. Clint stepped into the box and scowled at the pitcher through the deepening damp. The count went to two and two. Courtney fouled off a couple of pitches, then there was another ball. Three and two, and the bases loaded! There was some real yelling from the stands. Now, however, the rain suddenly became a downpour, almost hiding the outfielders from view. The umpire unwillingly called time, the players came in, and the tarps went back on the field.

It rained and rained. The perpetually gloomy Baltimore fans stared up at the sky and nodded their head disconsolately. The thing would be called, of course, and the score would revert to the bottom of their eighth—another game gone. Nobody went home, though; this one had to be waited out. Midnight struck, and still the rain went on. Then, wonder of wonders, it began to ease up. It lightened to a drizzle, then to a mist, and then stopped. The ground crew appeared and rolled back the tarp. The field had been flooded, and another fifteen or twenty minutes went by while the men worked with rakes and shovels, and scattered sawdust on the mound and in the batters' boxes. The umps came back on the field, and the pitcher returned to the mound and warmed up for a considerable time, as

The Living Language

was his privilege. The teams took the field at last, more than an hour after they had left it, and the few dozen surviving fans came down to the front rows and took up a hopeful caterwauling.

The home-plate umpire checked his indicator and looked out at the scorecard. Still three and two. He pointed to the pitcher. Play ball! Courtney stood in, chomped down on his wad of tobacco, waggled his bat, and glared out at the pitcher. The fans screamed. The pitcher got his sign. He went into his stretch, paused, rocked back, and threw. The three base runners were off with his motion, running like jackrabbits. The pitch crossed the heart of the plate. Courtney looked at it, motionless. The ump threw up his hand. Strike three. Everybody went home.

That may not be a story to please every palate. I am fond of it, but I can see that as drama it wants work. Baseball-haters will complain about it for their old, dumb reason: nothing *happens*. But never mind. The best baseball stories are probably appreciated only by true fans, who know the possibilities for unlikelihood, letdown, and wild mischance in their game, which can swing in an instant from morality play to variety show to farce.

Anything can happen in baseball, but it may almost be taken as a rule that the most appalling accidents happen to the worst teams. It was the Mets—the early Mets, of course—who were involved in a play one day at Wrigley Field in which an errant heave from one of their outfielders wound up in the Cubs' ball bag. And it was the Cubs themselves—a similarly gentle and innocuous club—who once were caught up in a calamity undreamed of even in the *Metsungsaga*. On an afternoon in 1959, the Cardinals were the visitors at Wrigley Field, and the batter was Stan Musial. Nobody on base. With the count at three and one, Musial almost offered at the next pitch but checked his swing, and the ball somehow skipped by the Chicago catcher, Sammy Taylor, and went all the way back to the screen. The umpire, Vic Delmore, called ball four, and Musial, unaware of the misplay, trotted toward first. Taylor whirled on Delmore and shouted that the ball had been foul-tipped, and Cub manager Bob Scheffing ran out to back him up. The ball, meantime, was picked up by a ball boy and handed to the Cubs' field announcer, who in those days sat in a chair near the home dugout. Two other Cubs—pitcher Bob Anderson and third baseman Alvin Dark—now made their entrances in the plot, each sprinting in to retrieve the ball. Musial, becoming aware at last of these disturbances, rounded first at full speed and set sail for second. The announcer, horrified to observe that he was somehow an active participant in the National League pennant race, hastily dropped the ball on the ground, where it was seized simultaneously by Anderson and Dark, with Alvin finally winning possession.

Meantime, in another part of the forest—back at home plate— Ump Delmore, frazzled by the importunings of Taylor and Scheffing, suddenly and inexplicably extracted a fresh ball—hereinafter to be known as Ball No. 2—and plopped it into Taylor's glove. Taylor, spotting Musial on the base path, threw the new pill down to second, a bare instant after Alvin Dark had made the same peg, from well behind him, with Ball No. 1. Musial, sliding into second, saw an unmistakable baseball (it was No. 2) sail untouched past his ear and on into center field. He scrambled up and turned happily toward third, only to be tagged after two or three steps by Ernie Banks, the shortstop, with Ball No. 1. Ball No. 2 was chased down in the outfield by the Cubs' Bobby Thomson, who now threw it wildly past *third* base. But here, at last, both baseballs may be allowed to make their exit, for at this juncture the chief umpire, Al Barlick, who had been working at second base, mercifully threw up his hands, calling time. The ensuing confabulations and plea-bargainings need not be explicated. Barlick's next ruling, which caused the game to be played under official protest by the Cardinals, was that Musial was out at second, because he, Barlick, had seen the tag made there with the ball—or with *a* ball. The game went back a step, then resumed, eventually being won by the Cards, and the sport, once again, survived.

For continuous baseball melodrama, there probably never was a better theater than the Phillies' shabby little park, Baker Bowl, which was finally abandoned in 1938. The field was better suited for a smaller, narrower game—croquet, perhaps—and its very short right-field wall, a bare 270 feet from home, was detested by every pitcher and outfielder in the league. One afternoon in 1934, the starting hurler for the visiting Brooklyn Dodgers was Walter (Boom-Boom) Beck—the nickname was onomatopoetic—and the dangerous starboard garden was being defended by Hack Wilson. Always a robust slugger, Wilson unfortunately got to spend far less time at the plate than he had to put in afield, where he was, to put the matter kindly, less than adequate. Hack was also known to spend an occasional evening at his local tavern, pondering this injustice.

On this day, he had experienced a particularly trying afternoon in pursuit of assorted line drives and scorching grounders rifled in his direction off Boom-Boom's deliveries—often getting extra practice as he spun around and tried to field the caroms and ricochets, off that extremely adjacent wall, of the same hits he had missed outward-bound.

The Dodger manager, Casey Stengel, even then accustomed to severe adversity, watched several innings of this before he called time and made his familiar journey to the mound, where he suggested to Beck that he take the rest of the afternoon off. Beck's performance had been perfectly within his genre, but for some reason he was enraged at this derricking, and instead of handing the ball over to Stengel he suddenly turned and heaved it away in a passion. Fate, of course, sent the ball arching out into right field, where Hack Wilson, with his head down and his hands on his knees, was quietly reflecting on last night's excesses and this day's indignities. Boom-Boom's throw struck the turf a few feet away from Wilson, who, although badly startled, whirled and chased manfully after the ball, fielded the carom off the wall, and got off a terrific, knee-high peg to second base—his best fielding play, Casey always said, of the entire summer.

A more recent epochal disorder came in a game played in the Florida Instructional League last year. This time, things began with an outfielder's peg to a rookie catcher (all the players in the Instructional League are rookies), who grabbed the ball and made a swipe at an inrushing, sliding base runner at the plate. As sometimes happens, the catcher missed the tag and the base runner missed the plate. The runner jumped up, dusted himself off, and trotted to his dugout, convinced that he had scored. The umpire made no call either way, which is the prescribed response, and after a moment or two the pitcher and the infielders, analyzing the situation, hurried in and implored the catcher to make the tag.

"What?" said the catcher. "Tag who?"

"The runner, the runner!" they cried, severally. "You missed him. He didn't score. Go tag him!"

"Ah," said the young receiver, the light bulb over his head at last clicking on. Still holding the ball, he ran eagerly toward the enemy dugout, with the umpire close behind. When the catcher got there, however, he gazed up and down the line of seated fresh-faced rookies without recognizing anyone who looked like a recent passerby. He frowned, then went to one end of the bench and tagged the first two or three men sitting in line. He looked around at the umpire, who was watching with folded arms. The umpire made no sign. The catcher tagged four more players. The ump shook his head almost imperceptibly: nothing doing. Now the erstwhile base runner, seeing the catcher inexorably working up the line toward him, suddenly leaped onto the field and made a dash for the plate. The pitcher, who had been standing bemused near home, screamed for the ball, and he and catcher executed a rundown, more or less in the style of stadium attendants collecting a loose dog on the field, and tagged the man out in the on-deck circle.

I have dismissed the Mets too quickly—the progenitors of so many legendary baseball disasters. Some of the legends were true. During the early stages of their terrible first summer, in 1962, their center fielder, Richie Ashburn, suffered a series of frightful surprises while going after short fly balls, because he was repeatedly run over by the shortstop, the enthusiastic but modestly talented Elio Chacon. After several of these encounters, Ashburn took Chacon aside and carefully explained that, by ancient custom, center fielders were allowed full freedom to catch all flies they could get to and signal for. The collisions and near-collisions and dropped fly balls continued exactly as before, and Ashburn eventually concluded that Chacon, who spoke very little English, simply didn't understand what it meant when he saw his center fielder waving his arms and yelling "Mine! Mine! I got it!" Richie thought this over and then went to Joe Christopher, a bilingual teammate on the Mets, and asked for help.

"All you have to do is say it in Spanish," Christopher said. "Yell out '*Yo la tengo!*' and Elio will pull up. I'll explain it to him, too—OK? You won't have any more trouble out there."

"*Yo la tengo?*" Ashburn said.

"That's it," Christopher said.

Before the next game, Ashburn saw Chacon in the clubhouse. "*Yo la tengo?*" Richie said tentatively.

"*Sí, sí! Yo la tengo! Yo la tengo!*" Chacon said, smiling and nodding his head.

"*Yo la tengo!*" Ashburn said. They shook hands.

In the second or third inning that night, an enemy batter lifted a short fly to center. Ashburn sprinted in for the ball. Chacon thundered out after it. "Yo la tengo! Yo la tengo!" Richie shouted.

Chacon jammed on the brakes and stopped, happily gesturing for Ashburn to help himself. Richie reached up to make the easy catch—and was knocked flat by Frank Thomas, the Mets' left fielder.

Interesting baseball happenings sometimes take place away from the field. Consider, for example, the memorable and uplifting public-relations outing made in the mid-sixties by Cy Tatum (this is not his real name). Cy was a remarkable hitter, and he had the good fortune to play for a big-league team in a city close to the town where he had grown up. Like some other players in the majors, he had run into trouble with the law when young, and he had served a few semesters at a state trade school for wayward boys. He mended his ways, went into baseball, and became a great local favorite. One summer when his team was in the process of winning a pennant, its first in many years, somebody in the front office realized what a dynamite PR event it would be if Cy were invited to come back to the trade school and address the boys there. The date was quickly arranged, and Tatum turned up at the appointed time and was introduced by the principal of the school to the full, enraptured student body. Cy spoke eloquently, praising the virtues of the straight-and-narrow path and a level swing at the ball, and sat down, to wild applause.

"Thank you, Cy!" said the principal, coming to the center of the stage. "That was splendid. Now, I know the boys want to ask you a lot of questions, and I wonder if you could give us a few more minutes out of your busy day?"

Cy nodded graciously.

"Fine, fine," said the principal. "Perhaps I could just start things off with a question of my own. I think the boys would be really interested to know what you took when you were at school here. Can you recall, Cy?"

Tatum looked faintly surprised, but he recovered himself quickly. "Mostly," he said, "it was overcoats."

Tom LaSorda's story also begins in boyhood. LaSorda, of course, is the long-term third-base coach for the Los Angeles Dodgers who recently was named the successor to Walter Alston as the Dodger manager, after Alston's twenty-third season on the job. LaSorda, it can be proved, is a patient sort of man. He grew up in Morristown, Pennsylvania, and became a serious baseball fan at an early age. When he was twelve or thirteen, he volunteered for duty as a crossing guard at his parochial school because he knew that the reward for this service was a free trip to a big-league ball game—an event he had yet to witness. The great day came at last, the sun shone, and the party of nuns and junior fuzz repaired to Shibe Park, where the Phillies were playing the Giants. Young Tom LaSorda had a wonderful afternoon, and just before the game ended he and some of his colleagues forehandedly stationed themselves beside a runway under the stands, where they could collect autographs from the players coming off the field. The game ended, the Giants came clattering by, and Tom extended his scorecard to the first hulking, bespiked hero to come in out of the sunshine.

"C'n I have your autograph, please, mister?" he said.

"Outta my way, kid," the Giant said, brushing past the boy.

When Tom LaSorda tells the story now, the shock of this moment is still visible on his face. "I couldn't *believe* it," he says. "Here was the first big-league player I'd ever seen up close—the first one I ever dared speak to—and what he did was shove me up against the wall. I think tears came to my eyes. I watched the guy as he went away toward the clubhouse and I noticed the number on his back—you know, like taking the license of a hit-and-run car. Later on, I looked at my program and got his name. It was Buster Maynard, who was an outfielder with the Giants then. I never forgot it."

Seven or eight years went swiftly by (as they do in instructive, moral tales), during which time Tom LaSorda grew up to become a promising young pitcher in the Dodger organization. In the spring of 1949, he was a star with the Dodger farm team in Greenville, North Carolina, in the Sally League, and took the mound for the opening game of the season at Augusta, Georgia, facing the Augusta Yankees. Tom retired the first two batters, and then studied the third, a beefy right-handed veteran, as he stepped up to the box.

The park loudspeaker made the introduction: "Now coming up to bat for the Yankees, Buster May-narrd, right field!"

LaSorda was transfixed. "I looked in," he says, "and *it was the same man!*"

The first pitch to Maynard nearly removed the button from the top of his cap. The second, behind his knees, inspired a beautiful sudden *entrechat*. The third, under his Adam's apple, confirmed the message, and Maynard threw away his bat and charged the mound like a fighting bull entering the plaza in Seville. The squads spilled out onto the field and separated the two men, and only after a lengthy and disorderly interval was baseball resumed.

After the game, LaSorda was dressing in the visitor's locker room when he was told that he had a caller at the door. It was Buster Maynard, who wore a peaceable but puzzled expression. "Listen, kid," he said to LaSorda, "did I ever meet you before?"

"Not exactly," Tom said.

"Did I bat against you someplace, maybe?"

"Nope."

"Well, why were you tryin' to take my head off out there?"

LaSorda spread his hands wide. "You didn't give me your autograph," he said.

Tom LaSorda tells this story each spring to the new young players who make the Dodger club. "Always give an autograph when somebody asks you," he says gravely. "You never can tell. In baseball, anything can happen."

Content

1. In most of your writing assignments, you are asked to include an explicit thesis statement. In this essay, the thesis is implicit; that is, it is never directly stated but rather implied. In paragraph 5, we are given a sense of Angell's thesis; what do you understand Angell's main point to be?

2. In his essay on sports writing, William Zinsser admires "the humanity" of the best sportswriters and encourages writers to take players "off the sanitized slope of Olympus," out of the world of heroic myth into one with which the reader identifies. Angell consciously destroys the superhuman, heroic image of sports. How? How might this new view affect your response to sports and sports figures?

3. Angell acknowledges that many people find baseball boring for its lack of action: "nothing happens." Even his first story ends in a let-down. After long delays and raised hopes for "perpetually gloomy fans," the player strikes out. Nothing happens. Everybody goes home. What does the choice and placement of this story suggest about the writer's attitude toward baseball and about his intent in this essay?

Stories for a Rainy Afternoon

Technique

1. Angell begins his humorous sketch of baseball with a present-tense narrative that is not in itself humorous and so not part of the stories that follow. What do you think is the purpose of this introductory paragraph?
2. The stories that Angell tells are of isolated events occuring over many years and involving several teams and long-forgotten players. What unifies these several brief sketches, making them integral parts of an essay rather than a series of disjointed recollections?
3. Angell's writing is highly detailed and descriptive: All players are referred to by name; the fans' umbrellas are "brightly colored golf umbrellas"; and after a long rain delay, "Courtney stood in, chomped down on his wad of tobacco, waggled his bat, and glared out at the pitcher." Find two or three other examples of Angell's detailed and descriptive style, and be prepared to discuss how this style contributes to the overall point of the essay.
4. Roger Angell is a widely-read essayist, not a traditional sportswriter, and he knows his sports pieces will be read by many who know or care little about sports. (Some will even be "baseball-haters," as he calls them.) Do you think this essay is enjoyable even for the reader who is not what Angell calls a "true fan"?

Language

1. Angell uses little of the sports lingo that William Zinsser warns against. Instead, he reaches for fresh images: players "running like Jackrabbits," Musial "setting sail" for second base. Find other descriptions that catch your attention, and explain the images they evoke as you read the essay.
2. Angell frequently uses overstatement, the technique of choosing words that are more serious than the topic would ordinarily merit: teams are caught in "calamities undreamed of," or face "epochal disasters," humorous errors become "appalling accidents," Stengel faces "severe adversity." What is the effect of this overstatement?

Vocabulary

confabulations   derricking   caterwauling
explicated   caroms   calamity
melodrama

Writing Suggestions

1. Angell's first paragraph is rich in descriptive language. The events of the brief narrative can be followed even by someone who is not a baseball fan. Write a descriptive sports paragraph, painting a word description of a particular moment in some sport. This need not be a humorous moment. Your aim is to make the reader "see" the event clearly through your choice of detail and your careful ordering of detail and event.

2. To entertain his readers "on a rainy afternoon," Angell has chosen several moments in sport that evoke his memory and tickle his humor. Write a sports anecdote of your own, a story for a rainy afternoon, evoking an enjoyable or humorous memory from your own sports history as a player or spectator.

Unconquerable

Red Smith

Red Smith (1905–1982) was for many years one of America's most widely read and respected sports journalists. He graduated from Notre Dame in 1927 and then went on to become a reporter and sportswriter for the Milwaukee Sentinel, *the* St. Louis Star, *and the* Philadelphia Record; *in 1971 he began a syndicated column for the* New York Times. *Taut, vivid prose and a sense of humanity were the chief characteristics of Smith's writing, as the following essay on Jackie Robinson demonstrates. Through description and reminiscence, this vignette captures Robinson's fierce competitiveness as a baseball player and his remarkable courage as a man.*

In the scene that doesn't fade, the Brooklyn Dodgers are tied with the Phillies in the bottom of the 12th inning. It is 6 p.m. on an October Sunday, but the gloom in Philadelphia's Shibe Park is only partly due to oncoming evening. The Dodgers, champions-elect in August, have frittered away a lead of 13½ games, and there is bitterness in the dusk of this last day of the 1951 baseball season. Two days ago, the New York Giants drew even with Brooklyn in the pennant race. Two hours ago, the numbers went up on the scoreboard: New York 3, Boston 2. The pennant belongs to the Giants unless the Dodgers can snatch it back.

With two out and the bases full of Phillies, Eddie Waitkus smashes a low, malevolent drive toward center field. The ball is a blur passing second base, difficult to follow in the half-light, impossible to catch. Jackie Robinson catches it. He flings himself headlong at right angles to the flight of the ball, for an instant his body is suspended in midair, then somehow the outstretched glove intercepts the ball inches off the ground.

He falls heavily, the crash drives an elbow into his side, he collapses. But the Phillies are out, the score is still tied.

Now it is the 14th inning. It is too dark to play baseball, but the rules forbid turning on lights for a game begun at 2 o'clock. Pee Wee Reese pops up. So does Duke Snider. Robin Roberts throws a ball and a strike to Robinson. Jackie hits the next pitch upstairs in left field for the run that sets up baseball's most memorable playoff.

That was the day that popped into mind when word came yesterday that Jack Roosevelt Robinson had died at 53. Of all the pictures he left upon memory, the one that will always flash back first shows him stretched out full length in the insubstantial twilight, the unconquerable doing the impossible.

The word for Jackie Robinson is "unconquerable." In *The Boys of Summer*, Roger Kahn sums it up: "In two seasons, 1962 and 1965, Maury Wills stole more bases than Robinson did in all of a 10-year career. Ted Williams' lifetime batting average, .344, is two points higher than Robinson's best for any season. Robinson never hit 20 home runs in a year, never batted in 125 runs. Stan Musial consistently scored more often. Having said those things, one has not said much because troops of people who were there believe that in his prime Jackie Robinson was a better ball player than any of the others."

Another picture comes back. Robinson has taken a lead off first base and he crouches, facing the pitcher, feet fairly wide apart, knees bent, hands held well out from his sides to help him balance, teetering on the balls of his feet. Would he be running? His average was 20 stolen bases a year and Bugs Baer wrote that "John McGraw demanded more than that from the baseball writers."

Yet he was the only base-runner of his time who could bring a game to a stop just by getting on base. When he walked to first, all other action ceased. For Robinson, television introduced the split screen so the viewer at home as well as the fan in the park could watch both the runner on first and the pitcher standing irresolute, wishing he didn't have to throw.

Jackie Robinson established the black man's right to play second base. He fought for the black man's right to a place in the white community, and he never lost sight of that goal. After he left baseball, almost everything he did was directed toward that goal. He was involved in the foundation of the Freedom National Banks. He tried to get an insurance company started with black capital and when he died he was head of a construction company building housing for blacks. Years ago a friend, talking of the needs of blacks, said "good schooling comes first."

"No," Jackie said, "housing is the first thing. Unless he's got a home he wants to come back to, it doesn't matter what kind of school he goes to." 10

There was anger in him and when he was a young man he tended to raise his falsetto voice. "But my demands were modest enough," he said, and he spoke the truth. The very last demand he made publicly was delivered in the mildest of terms during the World Series just concluded. There was a ceremony in Cincinnati saluting him for his work in drug addiction and in his response he mentioned a wish that he could look down to third base and see a black manager on the coaching line. 11

Seeing him in Cincinnati recalled the Dylan Thomas line that Roger Kahn borrowed for a title: "I see the boys of summer in their ruin." At 53 Jackie was sick of body, white of hair. He had survived one heart attack, he had diabetes and high blood-pressure and he was going blind as a result of retinal bleeding in spite of efforts to cauterize the ruptured blood vessels with laser beams. With him were his wife Rachel, their son, David, and daughter, Sharon. Everybody was remembering Jack Jr., an addict who beat the heroin habit and died at 24 in an auto accident. 12

"I've lost the sight in one eye," Jackie had told Kahn a day or so earlier, "but they think they can save the other. I've got nothing to complain about." 13

Content

1. Zinsser suggested that great sportswriters are distinguished by "their humanity." It is not surprising, then, that he admires Red Smith, whose writing Zinsser finds "strong enough to carry strong convictions." In what ways is Smith's "humanity" evident in this article?
2. Clearly, Smith admires Robinson for a great deal more than his playing ability. What are the qualities that he believes made Jackie Robinson "unconquerable"?

Technique

1. A narration tells a story, recounts an event. Smith begins his article by narrating the last day of the 1951 baseball season. In what way does this technique contribute to the success of Smith's article?
2. Smith changes from the present to past tense throughout the article in a carefully controlled manner. Note the places in which he uses present tense and those in which he uses past tense. What pattern or patterns emerge? Do you find this technique effective?

Language

1. Zinsser admires Smith's "good English words." Discuss the effect of the following terms: "malevolent drive" (paragraph 2), "frittered away the lead" (paragraph 1), "insubstantial twilight" (paragraph 5). How else might Smith have worded these sentences; what images would be evoked by the alternatives you provide? Which do you prefer, and why?
2. Look up the word "unconquerable" in your dictionary. In what ways does this seem to be an appropriate word to express Smith's memory of Robinson?

Vocabulary

malevolent	insubstantial	cauterize
intercepts	falsetto	

Writing Suggestions

1. Write a paragraph in which you capture, as Smith does in his opening paragraphs, the unique quality of some individual by recounting an event that you believe typifies that person's character.
2. Write an essay in which you describe a sports figure whom you particularly admire, analyzing the personal and athletic traits that make him or her unique. Use clear descriptions of moments in his or her career and evocative images of his character to encourage the reader to share in your response to the athlete.

Language in Science and Technology

6

We could characterize the times in which we live in a number of ways, of course, but the "age of science and technology" may be the most fitting label. Our scientific discoveries—and advances in technology that inevitably spring from such discoveries—more than anything else distinguish our century from all previous human history. Incredibly, individuals born in the first decade of the 1900s—still very much an age of the horse-and-buggy—now find themselves in an era of space travel, supersonic passenger airplanes, heart transplants, artificial hearts, home computers, television satellites, global telephone systems, laser surgery—the list is inexhaustible. Some of these discoveries and inventions represent a fulfillment of timeless human aspirations, others suggest altogether new concepts, while still others—namely nuclear weapons—threaten to obliterate the civilization that science has helped to build.

Not surprisingly, language is one of the many areas influenced by science and technology, if only because the new processes that science defines and the new products technology manufactures require new words. Science and technology steadily pour new words and new meanings for old words into the mainstream of language, as the first paragraph here demonstrates ("satellites," "computers," "supersonic," "laser"). Beyond enriching our vocabulary, science and particularly technology also constantly redefine the media of language, the way words get spoken and written, listened to and read. The very quantity of information and the blinding speed at which it is delivered to us in themselves provide an astonishing contrast to centuries in which the letter, laboriously written and sluggishly delivered, was the primary mode of written communication.

We need not, however, think only in terms of how science affects language, for scientists and technicians often feel compelled to use nontechnical language to try to explain to the layperson what they do and to connect scientific discovery and technological advancement with humanistic concerns. In other words, the meaning of science cannot be defined entirely or expressed solely in the language of science.

The essays in this section, written either by scientists or those who observe them, reflect this desire to place science and technology in the context of all human affairs. In these essays, our century's most renowned scientist discusses the need for a common language among scientists, and a celebrated physician shows how language unifies us biologically. An anthropologist and a student of literature show us that scientists who study the languages of gorillas and computers are ultimately engaged in reaffirming the astounding complexity of human speech and writing. And finally, a contemporary philosopher reveals the extent to which powerful irrational attitudes toward disease persist in this age of advanced medical techniques.

Albert Einstein, the supreme and supremely humane scientist, provides the keynote for the section; the very fact that he should advocate a "common language of science" in what was his second language attests to the genuineness of his commitment. His career as a whole, moreover, demonstrated as well as any other that science is, for better or worse, intertwined with every part of human society, for he was forced to flee Nazi Germany, and his discoveries in physics helped point the way to the creation of atomic weapons, which he deplored. Einstein reminds us that the scientific method, however powerful it is by itself (indeed, *because* it is so powerful), can be destructive if those who use it do not share a common desire for the "welfare and the free development of the talents" of everyone. The "common language" that his title mentions, then, consists chiefly of common goals, a common direction in which scientific thought should propel the human race.

Lewis Thomas, renowned as much for his essays as his significant achievements in medicine, also addresses the issue of a common language. Thomas views the idea of such a language less in terms of common goals, however; in fact, at one point he writes, "If we were ever to put all our brains together to make a common mind the way ants do, it would be an unthinkable thought, way over our heads." In a strictly biological sense, Thomas suggests, humans cannot and probably should not become a single organism, in the manner of an anthill or a beehive. Rather, he acknowledges and celebrates our innate, genetically programmed capacity to understand and generate complex language. This "social talk," as Thomas terms it, distinguishes us from other animals and binds us together globally as does no other force in our lives.

Francine Patterson and Eugene Linden might take exception to, or at least qualify, Thomas' contention that a sophisticated language is the sole property of humans. As their essay shows, scientists are currently engaged in teaching animals to communicate with humans; the narrative "Koko's First Words" details this exploration of non-human use of language. In their essay Patterson and Linden document a substantial sophistication in one gorilla's capacity to use and interpret sign language. Even as scientific debate continues about whether a gorilla's gestures may, in fact, constitute a language like our own, the excitement of the investigations is undeniable. That we are increasingly interested in animal communication shows that we are still hopeful of reducing the destructiveness and insensitivity of our relationship with other animals, and indeed with all of nature. As other scientists have suggested, our interest in animal intelligence may prove there is still hope for our own intelligence.

One could also place Ruth Nelson's essay, "The First Literate Computers?", in the subject area of non-human language, although humans are completely responsible for giving the computer its language and its capacity to understand language. Like the studies of animal languages, the project to make computers literate as Nelson describes it ultimately reaffirms the astounding complexity of human language. As Nelson suggests, "the true subject of artificial intelligence is not computers but man." In their attempts to enable machines to acquire language, scientists learn more and more about the relationship between syntax and meaning, the complexities of translation, and the political and social biases inherent even in a seemingly simple conversation. Once again, therefore, specialized inquiry leads to general considerations.

The last essay in this section—Susan Sontag's "A Rhetoric of Disease"—reveals the persistence of irrational impulses even in an age dominated by the rational scientific method and the mechanisms of technology. Sontag explores the symbolic nature of two diseases: tuberculosis, which fascinated our culture in the nineteenth century, and cancer, which fascinates and terrifies us today.

The irrational responses to these diseases, Sontag shows, reveal and perhaps even determine our attitudes toward death and medicine in general—and they also result in peculiar ways of talking and writing about cancer and cancer patients. Indeed, "the language of cancer" lays bare numerous twentieth-century attitudes toward death, disease, and medicine. Whereas in the first essay Einstein argued that we should not pursue science independently of humanistic goals, Sontag in the concluding piece suggests that the "scientific mind" must still contend with instinctual, impulsive forces in the human psyche.

The Common Language of Science
Albert Einstein

Albert Einstein (1879–1955) was born in Germany and spent the early part of his career in the Swiss patent office in Bern. While working there, he published in 1905 the first of several papers on the theory of relativity, papers that were to revolutionize the science of physics. In 1933, Einstein fled Germany and came to the United States, continuing his research at Princeton University. Aside from Relativity: The Special and General Theory *(1918), Einstein also wrote a more personal book,* The World As I See It *(1934). In the following essay, Einstein provides a brief analysis of how he believes humans acquired a "scientific language." He then goes on to argue that scientists need to connect their work with such values as liberty and the common welfare.*

The first step towards language was to link acoustically or otherwise commutable signs to sense-impressions. Most likely all sociable animals have arrived at this primitive kind of communication—at least to a certain degree. A higher development is reached when further signs are introduced and understood which establish relations between those other signs designating sense-impression. At this stage it is already possible to report somewhat complex series of impressions; we can say that language has come to existence. If language is to lead at all to understanding, there must be rules concerning the relations between the signs on the one hand and on the other hand there must be a stable correspondence between signs and impressions. In their childhood individuals connected by the same language grasp these rules and relations mainly by intuition.

When man becomes conscious of the rules concerning the relations between signs the so-called grammar of language is established.

In an early stage the words may correspond directly to impressions. At a later stage this direct connection is lost insofar as some words convey relations to perceptions only if used in connection with other words (for instance such words as: "is," "or," "thing"). Then word-groups rather than single words refer to perceptions. When language becomes thus partially independent from the background of impressions a greater inner coherence is gained.

Only at this further development where frequent use is made of so-called abstract concepts, language becomes an instrument of reasoning in the true sense of the word. But it is also this development which turns language into a dangerous source of error and deception. Everything depends on the degree to which words and word-combinations correspond to the world of impression.

What is it that brings about such an intimate connection between language and thinking? Is there no thinking without the use of language, namely in concepts and concept-combinations for which words need not necessarily come to mind? Has not everyone of us struggled for words although the connection between "things" was already clear?

We might be inclined to attribute to the act of thinking complete independence from language if the individual formed or were able to form his concepts without the verbal guidance of his environment. Yet most likely the mental shape of an individual, growing up under such conditions, would be very poor. Thus we may conclude that the mental development of the individual and his way of forming concepts depend to a high degree upon language. This makes us realize to what extent the same language means the same mentality. In this sense thinking and language are linked together.

What distinguishes the language of science from language as we ordinarily understand the word? How is it that scientific language is international? What science strives for is an utmost acuteness and clarity of concepts as regards their mutual relation and their correspondence to sensory data. As an illustration let us take the language of Euclidian geometry and Algebra. They manipulate with a small number of independently introduced concepts, respectively symbols, such as the integral number, the straight line, the point, as well as with signs which designate the fundamental operations, that is the connections between those fundamental concepts. This is the basis for the construction, respectively definition of all other statements and concepts. The connection between concepts and statements on the one hand and the sensory data on the other hand is established through acts of counting and measuring whose performance is sufficiently well determined.

The super-national character of scientific concepts and scientific language is due to the fact that they have been set up by the best brains of all countries and all times. In solitude and yet in cooperative effort as regards the final effect they created the spiritual tools for the technical revolutions which have transformed the life of mankind in the last centuries. Their system of concepts have served as a guide in the bewildering chaos of perceptions so that we learned to grasp general truths from particular observations.

What hopes and fears does the scientific method imply for mankind? I do not think that this is the right way to put the question. Whatever this tool in the hand of man will produce depends entirely on the nature of the goals alive in this mankind. Once these goals exist, the scientific method furnishes means to realize them. Yet it cannot furnish the very goals. The scientific method itself would not have led anywhere, it would not even have been born without a passionate striving for clear understanding.

Perfections of means and confusion of goals seem—in my opinion—to characterize our age. If we desire sincerely and passionately the safety, the welfare and the free development of the talents of all men, we shall not be in want of the means to approach such a state. Even if only a small part of mankind strives for such goals, their superiority will prove itself in the long run.

Content

1. Einstein suggests several steps in the development of language. List these steps and be prepared to explain what you understand the differences between each to be.

2. What do you think Einstein means when he says that "language has come to existence" at the point when we can show relationships between impressions?

3. The organization of Einstein's essay suggests that he believes scientific language is the most advanced step in the development of language. How, according to Einstein, does it differ from other forms of language?

4. Einstein says that scientific language has allowed scientists to grasp general truths, that it provides the tools for discovery and accomplishment. What danger, according to Einstein, still remains?
5. What distinction does Einstein draw between "means" and "goals" in paragraph 9? Why is this a significant distinction?

Technique

1. Einstein develops this essay by offering one explanation about how language evolved. Outline the developmental steps he describes and be prepared to discuss whether or not you think this is an effective approach.
2. To what kind of audience do you think Einstein addresses this essay? Fellow scientists? Linguists? Laymen? Cite passages that led you to your conclusion.
3. In this essay, Einstein frequently asks rhetorical questions. Paragraph 4, for instance, consists entirely of rhetorical questions. Look up the term "rhetorical question" in your dictionary, and evaluate the contribution of Einstein's questions to the essay as a whole and to the main point he is making at the end.

Language

1. The title of Einstein's essay is "The Common Language of Science." Look up the word "common" in your dictionary and discuss its significance to the essay. In what way is the language of science "common"?
2. Crucial to Einstein's belief in the importance of scientific language is his point in paragraph 5 that "the same language means the same mentality." Look up the word "mentality" and discuss its meaning in Einstein's context.

Vocabulary

acoustically   abstract   coherence
commutable   perceptions

Writing Suggestions

1. In paragraph 4, Einstein asks a series of questions about the relationship between language and thinking. Write an essay in which you

analyze that relationship in your own life. To what extent, for instance, must you verbalize or write your thoughts before they are meaningful?

2. Write a paragraph in which you substitute a set of pictorial "signs" or "symbols" for all the nouns; then write a paragraph in which you describe either the simplicity or the complexity of such a procedure. How, for example, did it make you "see" nouns in a new way?

3. In the final paragraph, Einstein says that our age is characterized by the perfection of means and confusion of goals. Analyze the meaning of this statement by discussing one scientific development, the "proper" use of which must be determined by the proper goals of the user.

Social Talk

Lewis Thomas

(For biographical information on Lewis Thomas, see page 46.) In "Social Talk," Thomas begins by contrasting humans as social beings with ants and bees, insects that are social to such an extent that their societies form single organisms. The one attribute that binds humans together to this degree, Thomas goes on to argue, is our innate ability to generate and understand sophisticated language.

Not all social animals are social with the same degree of commitment. In some species, the members are so tied to each other and interdependent as to seem the loosely conjoined cells of a tissue. The social insects are like this; they move, and live all their lives, in a mass; a beehive is a spherical animal. In other species, less compulsively social, the members make their homes together, pool resources, travel in packs or schools, and share the food, but any single one can survive solitary, detached from the rest. Others are social only in the sense of being more or less congenial, meeting from time to time in committees, using social gatherings as *ad hoc* occasions for feeding and breeding. Some animals simply nod at each other in passing, never reaching even a first-name relationship.

It is not a simple thing to decide where we fit, for at one time or another in our lives we manage to organize in every imaginable social arrangement. We are as interdependent, especially in our cities, as bees or ants, yet we can detach if we wish and go live alone in the woods, in theory anyway. We feed and look after each other, constructing elaborate systems for this, even including vending machines to dispense ice cream in gas stations, but we also have numerous books to tell us how to live off the land. We cluster in family groups, but we tend, unpredictably, to turn on each other and fight as if we were different species. Collectively, we hanker to accumulate all the information in the universe and distribute it around among ourselves as though it were a kind of essential foodstuff, ant-fashion (the faintest trace of real news in science has the action of apheromone, lifting the hairs of workers in laboratories at the ends of the earth), but each of us also builds a private store of his own secret knowledge and hides it away like untouchable treasure. We have names to label each as self, and we believe without reservation that this system of taxonomy will guarantee the entity, the absolute separateness of each of us, but the mechanism has no discernible function in the center of a crowded city; we are essentially nameless, most of our time.

Nobody wants to think that the rapidly expanding mass of mankind, spreading out over the surface of the earth, blackening the ground, bears any meaningful resemblance to the life of an anthill or a hive. Who would consider for a moment that the more than three billion of us are a sort of stupendous animal when we become linked together? We are not mindless, nor is our day-to-day behavior coded out to the last detail by our genomes, nor do we seem to be engaged together, compulsively, in any single, universal, stereotyped task analogous to the construction of a nest. If we were ever to put all our brains together in fact, to make a common mind the way the ants do, it would be an unthinkable thought, way over our heads.

Social animals tend to keep at a particular thing, generally something huge for their size; they work at it ceaselessly under genetic instructions and genetic compulsion, using it to house the species and protect it, assuring permanence.

There are, to be sure, superficial resemblances in some of the things we do together, like building glass and plastic cities on all the land and farming under the sea, or assembling in armies, or landing samples of ourselves on the moon, or sending memoranda into the next galaxy. We do these together without being quite sure why, but we can stop doing one thing and move to another whenever we like. We are not committed or bound by our genes to stick to one activity forever, like the wasps. Today's behavior is no more fixed than when we tumbled out over Europe to build cathedrals in the twelfth century. At that time we were convinced that it would go on forever, that this was the way to live, but it was not; indeed, most of us have already forgotten what it was all about. Anything we do in this transient, secondary social way, compulsively and with all our energies but only for a brief period of our history, cannot be counted as social behavior in the biological sense. If we can turn it on and off, on whims, it isn't likely that our genes are providing the detailed instructions. Constructing Chartres was good for our minds, but we found that our lives went on, and it is no more likely that we will find survival in Rome plows or laser bombs, or rapid mass transport or a Mars lander, or solar power, or even synthetic protein. We do tend to improvise things like this as we go along, but it is clear that we can pick and choose.

For practical reasons, it would probably be best for us not to be biologically social, in the long run. Not that we have a choice, of course, or even a vote. It would not be good news to learn that we are all roped together intellectually, droning away at some feature-less, genetically driven collective work, building something so immense that we can never see the outlines. It seems especially hard, even perilous, for this to be the burden of a species with the unique attribute of speech, and argument. Leave this kind of life to the insects and birds, and lesser mammals, and fish.

But there is just that one thing. About human speech.

It begins to look, more and more disturbingly, as if the gift of language is the single human trait that marks us all genetically, setting us apart from the rest of life. Language is, like nest-building or hive-making, the universal and biologically specific activity of human beings. We engage in it communally, compulsively, and auto-matically. We cannot be human without it; if we were to be separated from it our minds would die, as surely as bees lost from the hive.

We are born knowing how to use language. The capacity to recognize syntax, to organize and deploy words into intelligible sen-tences, is innate in the human mind. We are programmed to identify patterns and generate grammar. There are invariant and variable structures in speech that are common to all of us. As chicks are endowed with an innate capacity to read information in the shapes of overhanging shadows, telling hawk from other birds, we can identify the meaning of grammar in a string of words, and we are born this way. According to Chomsky, who has examined it as a biologist looks at live tissue, language "must simply be a biological property of the human mind." The universal attributes of language are genetically set; we do not learn them, or make them up as we go along.

We work at this all our lives, and collectively we give it life, but we do not exert the least control over language, not as individuals or committees or academies or governments. Language, once it comes alive, behaves like an active, motile organism. Parts of it are always being changed, by a ceaseless activity to which all of us are committed; new words are invented and inserted, old ones have their meaning altered or abandoned. New ways of stringing words and sentences together come into fashion and vanish again, but the underlying structure simply grows, enriches itself, expands. Individual languages age away and seem to die, but they leave progeny all over the place. Separate languages can exist side by side for centuries without touching each other, maintaining their integrity with the vigor of incompatible tissues. At other times, two languages may come together, fuse, replicate, and give rise to nests of new tongues.

If language is at the core of our social existence, holding us together, housing us in meaning, it may also be safe to say that art and music are functions of the same universal, genetically determined mechanism. These are not bad things to do together. If we are social creatures because of this, and therefore like ants, I for one (or should I say we for one?) do not mind.

Content

1. In this brief essay, Thomas discusses animal and human activity, group and individual behavior, and language. What do you believe Thomas' thesis is? What would you cite to support your answer?
2. In paragraph 2, Thomas describes several contrasting human qualities. For instance, we are interdependent and yet enjoy isolation. Look closely at the other contrasts in the paragraph. What conclusions do you draw from them about where man fits into the scheme of social animals?

3. In paragraph 4, Thomas distinguishes us from the lower animals by saying that our social behavior is not, like that of ants or bees, driven by "genetic instructions and compulsion." What evidence does he give to support this argument?
4. In paragraph 8, where he arrives at the main point of his essay, Thomas suggests that it is "disturbing" to realize that speech is the one genetically compulsive trait we possess. Why do you suppose Thomas finds this realization disturbing?

Technique

1. Thomas does not state his thesis until close to the end of the essay. How does this organizational technique affect your reading of the essay?
2. In the first paragraphs of the essay, Thomas begins minimizing the differences between man and the other social animals. One instance of this is his use of the word "commitment" in reference to insects and other lower animals. Find other examples of this technique, especially in paragraphs 1 and 2, and discuss the way in which they contribute to his final thesis.
3. In paragraphs 3–6, Thomas emphasizes the contrasts between man and the social animals, but in paragraph 7 he shifts to comparisons that lead to the main point of the essay. Discuss the impact of this one-line, two-sentence paragraph as a transition.
4. Given that Thomas offers more speculation and reflection than hard scientific evidence in support of his thesis, what must carry the weight of the argument in this essay?

Language

1. In the first sentence, Thomas says that "not all social animals are social with the same degree of commitment." What is the meaning of the word "commitment" in this context?
2. In paragraph 6, Thomas narrows his use of "social" by preceding it with the word "biological." Given his argument in the preceding paragraphs, what is your understanding of the more precise term "biologically social"?
3. Thomas uses the word "cumpulsive" frequently, in paragraphs 1, 3, 4, and 8. Look up the word in your dictionary and be prepared to discuss its applicability to the human and lower animal worlds as Thomas describes them.

Vocabulary

conjoined	genetic	motile
congenial	compulsion	replicate
ad hoc	innate	stupendous
taxonomy	programmed	

Writing Suggestions

1. Write an essay in which you analyze one of the human contrasts Thomas mentions in paragraph 2, but do so to make a point of your own. You might use some of the examples Thomas suggests early in paragraph 5. Use cause/effect or comparison/contrast as your main developmental method.
2. Write a paragraph describing some human social activity that you feel links us to the lower social animals.
3. Thomas says that "we do not exert the least control over language." After carefully re-reading his section on language, write an essay arguing either for or against this notion, supporting your argument with specific examples from your own observation about language.

Koko's First Words
Francine Patterson and Eugene Linden

Francine Patterson (b. 1947) received her A.B. in Psychology in 1970 from the University of Illinois; in 1979 she received a Ph.D. in Developmental Psychology from Stanford University. From 1972 to the present, she has worked continually on Project Koko, publishing numerous articles on her findings in such magazines as Science, National Geographic, *and* Brain and Language. *She has served for several years as president and research director of the Gorilla Foundation, which she founded in 1976. Eugene Linden (b. 1947) graduated from Yale University in 1969. He has written numerous articles on subjects ranging from fiber optics and wrestling to the wild animal trade. His books include* Apes, Men, and Language, The Alms Race, *and* Affluence and Discontent: The Anatomy of Consumer Societies. *The narrative essay "Koko's First Words" is taken from Patterson's and Linden's book,* The Education of Koko. *The essay recounts the mystery and excitement of the attempt to teach a gorilla human language.*

Koko first began to show signs she understood the significance of the strange gestures she was constantly witnessing as early as the second week of Project Koko. On July 25, before Koko had been taught any signs through molding, the volunteers reported that she made gestures that resembled the *food* and *drink* signs several times during the morning before I arrived. I was reluctant to accept this as significant. Koko was not making the signs spontaneously in my presence, and I had no reason yet to accept that she was learning by observation alone. (In retrospect, I believe that Koko probably did try to make these signs; she has subsequently surprised me often by making signs she has learned only by observation, without any active instruction.) The volunteers continued to report what seemed to be signing attempts, and I began to notice that Koko was starting to use "natural" signs observed in wild gorillas, such as *gimme*, which looks like a beckoning gesture.

Over the next two weeks, Koko continued her spontaneous approximations of signs, but to me they seemed coincidental, random, unintentional. With all her fidgeting, I wondered whether any of our intent was getting through. On August 7, we began a formal routine of active instruction. My assistants and I used every opportunity that arose during the day to teach Koko *food, drink* and *more*. Rather than hand her her bottle as a matter of course, we would first hold it up and let her see it. If she responded by signing *drink*, we'd give her the bottle. If she made no response, we'd sign, *What's this?* If that still elicited no response, we'd mold her hand into the sign for *drink*. I also asked the zoo volunteers to include some signing in their daily caretaking routine when my assistants and I were absent.

Only two days into this training routine Koko said her first word. On August 9, she consistently responded with close approximations of the *food* sign when I offered her tidbits of fruit. Most frequently she put her index finger to her mouth, but she also made the sign correctly—putting all the fingers of one hand, held palm down, to her mouth. As it dawned on me that for the first time she was consistent and deliberate in her signing, I wanted to jump for joy. Finally she seemed to have made the connection between the gesture and the delivery of food, to have discovered that she could direct my behavior with her own.

I praised Koko profusely and seized every chance to get her to sign *food*, showering her with treats in the process. Whenever she reached for some food, I would prompt her by signing *food* and almost every time she responded. I made sure that she realized she was supposed to ask for things by name by pushing her hand away and signing *no* when she did not make the sign. On several occasions Koko signed *food* without any prompting on my part. After her nap I gave Koko another twenty or so opportunities to sign *food*, and she responded incorrectly only toward the end of the afternoon, by which time the stuffed gorilla had no interest in food whatsoever.

I could not wait to share the news of Koko's breakthrough with Ron and my friends in the Psychology Department at Stanford. Koko too seemed to realize that something exciting was occurring. She was agitated all day, and at one point during the afternoon, she put a bucket over her head and ran around wildly.

Although Koko did not immediately go on to ask the names of other objects, she did attempt to extend the use of her new sign to other situations the next day. She repeatedly used the sign as she watched a volunteer removing discarded food while cleaning her (Koko's) room.

Once Koko made the association between her hand gestures and the objects they represented, she quickly learned the words *drink, more, out, dog, come-gimme, up, toothbrush,* and *that*. Barely into the second month of training, she moved from one-word expressions to two-word combinations—somewhat more quickly than Washoe had. Washoe's first reported combination occurred in her tenth month of training, when she signed *Gimme sweet*. Koko, on the other hand, signed *Gimme food* on August 14, 1972, but because the *gimme* sign in this case might have been a natural reaching motion that Koko combined with the sign for food, I couldn't accept her gesture as a legitimate two-word combination. However, before any doubts about Koko's precocity in combining words could arise, she followed up by signing *food drink* eleven days later. She used this to describe her formula, a mixture of cereal and milk. About a month later, Koko said, *Food more,* to ask for more fruit during a teaching session.

In all, during the first two months, Koko used about 16 different combinations, most of which were limited by her small vocabulary to requests for food or drink: *More food, Drink there, More drink more, There mouth, mouth-you there,* and *Drink more food more*. I accepted about one-third as legitimate expressions of semantic relations.

One of the early criticisms of Washoe, later refuted, was that she did not ask questions. By the third month—September—Koko began to ask questions as well, although she would not phrase them the same way chimps did. Washoe, Lucy, and other sign-language-using chimps were taught to make the sign *question*, which is to simply draw a question mark with the forefinger in the air in front of one's body. Instead of this, from the outset Koko spontaneously used eye contact and gestural intonation to phrase questions, a form that is considered legitimate in Ameslan.

I first noticed it on one afternoon in early September. I was blowing on the window and urging Koko to draw in the mist. After I demonstrated, she did. Then she pointed to my mouth and touched it with her index finger while looking into my eyes. I assumed she was asking me to blow again, and I enthusiastically complied. Soon she tried making her own fog by putting her mouth close to the window, opening it, and extending her tongue slightly, almost licking the window. She succeeded in creating a bit of a mist and drew in it with her finger. Later that day she even more closely approximated my fog-making by adding the hah-hah sound I made when blowing on the window.

A week later Koko made a more elaborate request. As a couple with an infant approached the window, Koko pointed to the glass, then to her mouth, then to my mouth, and then to the glass again. She immediately repeated this same sequence and looked into my eyes. Surprised and fascinated by the complexity of her request, I took a few seconds to guess that she wanted to play the fog-blowing game. I huffed a mist and she drew in it. Then Koko again tried to make her own fog by putting her mouth and tongue to the window.

In addition to making requests, Koko began to give an interrogative cast to signed phrases. By cocking her head, raising her eyebrows, and maintaining eye contact, she turned *There food* into a question as she was being carried off to the nursery, and used the same expression to ask *You there?* while pointing to the glass window.

As Koko's language skills developed, so did her physical coordination and mental sophistication. In October, when she was fifteen months old, her motor skills were rapidly improving and her perceptual abilities becoming very sharp. She figured out how to turn on the kitchen faucet to get herself a drink, made serious but uncoordinated attempts to return the spoon to a container of yogurt in order to feed herself, and manipulated four wooden sticks simultaneously in play.

As much as she enjoyed our dexterity exercises, however, she could not be tricked, even by Ron's clever schemes, into contacting objects she feared. Once Ron attached a rubber spider Koko hated to a large plastic bead with a clear fish line. While I worked on the signs *dog* and *baby* with Koko, Ron placed the bead under the door to Koko's room, hiding the spider out of sight around the corner. Koko saw none of the preparations. When she noticed the bead, she went over to it but looked under the door before pulling on it. The spider came into view, and she jumped back. Ron hid the spider again and Koko pulled on the bead twice more, recoiling both times the spider emerged. After this she batted the bead away when it was presented.

This same day Ron distracted Koko during a feeding session by curling his tongue. She watched him intently through the screen mesh partition in her room and started moving her tongue around in her closed mouth. When Ron left, Koko pounded on the screen until he returned to repeat the performance. Later Koko did something simple but somehow very touching. She took me gently by the hand and led me around her room, pausing frequently to adjust the position of our hands.

If Koko's dexterity was improving, there were still significant limitations on her physical capabilities for signing. A gorilla's hands are somewhat different from the average child's. They are bigger, of course, but they are less well organized for precise motor tasks than ours. The thumb is smaller and placed farther down the hand and away from the rest of the fingers than a human's is. Moreover, the gorilla's precise motor control over its hands, while considerable, is less well developed than ours. This means that certain signs are difficult for Koko to form. In these cases either she will adapt the sign herself, or we will invent a variant for her. For instance, *water* is made by touching the finger-spelling of the letter "W" to the signer's lips. Since Koko cannot made a "W" with her hands (her thumb won't reach her little finger), she will touch the side of an extended index finger to her chin. Similarly, *sand* and *purple* are physically impossible for Koko to articulate because of the small size of her thumb.

Until age four, Koko had trouble executing signs made away from the body, which was true of Washoe as well. Perhaps it was because signs made by bringing hands into contact with the body are better grounded or oriented than those made in the air. Both

Koko and Washoe acquired touch signs more rapidly than non-touch signs, although there is no conceptual difference in signs made away from the body. Koko even tried to convert non-touch signs into touch signs by making them on the body rather than in front of it. *Finished*, for instance, is made with both hands out in front of the body, about shoulder width apart. The hands are held vertically, thumbs up and palms facing the body, and shaken. Koko used to make the *finished* sign by shaking her hands against her chest. Similarly, the sign *milk* involves holding one fist out in front of the body and then squeezing, as if milking a cow. Koko knocked her chest with her fist to say *milk*. (Now, however, she articulates both signs properly.)

Another curiosity of Koko's signing, probably also related to her preference for signs that make contact with the body, is her habit of making motion signs (such as *long*) starting close to the trunk of the body and moving away rather than the other way around. This reversal has been noticed in autistic children as well.

Not all of Koko's variations, mistakes, and inabilities stemmed from physical limitations. In trying to sort out physical from intellectual influences on her signing ability, I saw that she often made common "baby" errors. Deaf infants use a form of baby talk which may invert the motion or simplify the form of a sign. When babies are learning a sign, they have to generate the mirror image of what they are looking at. Many babies do not complete this adjustment for some time. The sign *bird* is made by forming the index finger and thumb into a configuration somewhat like a bird's beak and then placing the hand beside the mouth pointing outward. Koko makes this gesture with the fingers pointing toward the mouth.

Another important influence on Koko's growing signing ability was simply her motivation. Both Washoe and Koko quickly learned signs for objects or actions they desired. Washoe picked up *lollipop* without direct instruction, and Koko similarly learned *swing* and *berry* by imitation within minutes. On the other hand, she took months to pick up the sign for egg, a food she dislikes.

Koko was often sloppy in her signing and would elide one sign into another, or reduce a gesture to its barest skeleton, but in this she was not unlike fluent signers in Ameslan. When two fluent signers are talking, they may frequently take some of the same shortcuts that Koko did. Anyone will recognize that this is the case with spoken language as well. Few people clearly enunciate grammatically precise English. In fact it sounds strange when you hear it. Rather, what are called paralinguistic phenomena—such as cadence, intonation, gesticulation, and stock abbreviations—bear a large measure of the communicative burden. A conversation between two people who know each other well can sound like a meaningless series of mumbles and monosyllables.

Koko's vocabulary was growing at about the same pace as Washoe's—one new sign learned each month—for the first year and a half. At the end of eighteen months, Koko had acquired 22 signs, about the same as Washoe, who had acquired 21 in the equivalent period. When she was three years three months, she had emitted 236 words, of which 78 met our criteria for acceptance.

By then Koko was regularly using such words as *love, hot, baby, time, necklace* (which she learned when we had to start using a leash on walks so she wouldn't dart into traffic), *small, blow, wiper* (meaning a cloth or paper towel), *pillow,* and *bread* (acquired when we started feeding her peanut butter sandwiches for non-meat protein). Her progress was heartening, not only because it compared favorably with Washoe's but also because it belied the gorilla's image as intellectually inferior.

Although Koko was constantly producing new surprises in her signing, it was when I reviewed her earlier signing performances that I was most struck by her increasing facility with the language. Our conversations six months into the project, when Koko was one-and-a-half, were definitely rudimentary:*

A hyphen between two signs indicates either that the two words were signed simultaneously (such as *go-there*) or that the sign translates to two different words in English (such as *frown-sad*).

PENNY: Want *up*?
KOKO: *Up.* (I pick Koko up.)
PENNY: *Come* here, Koko.(Koko comes over to me and we return to the nursery from the back storage area. I am holding a rubber man doll Koko wants.)
PENNY: This is a *man.* (I mold her hands to form the sign *man.*)
KOKO: *Food out more.*

---

*In this and other conversations in the book, the human statements are made in both voice and sign language simultaneously, except where otherwise specified. As stated earlier, signed words are always indicated by italics. Thus, in the statement, "*Where* is the *man*?" all four words were spoken, while *where man* was simultaneously signed.

PENNY: *Man* (Again I mold *man*.)
KOKO: *Drink*.
PENNY: *Man*. (Again I mold the sign.)
KOKO: *Out*. (Again I mold the sign. After a few more moldings I hide the man doll under my smock. Koko looks for the doll.)
PENNY: *Where* is the *man? Where?* (Koko brushes dirt off the bottom of my shoe.) *That dirty*.

By age two-and-a-half, Koko's signing was much more frequent and varied. On November 11, 1973, for instance, we had another conversation about going out. This one began with my spinning Koko around as she lay on the counter.

KOKO: *Tickle*. (I sign *tickle* on Koko's hand.)
PENNY: *What* do you *want?*
KOKO: *Out key*.
PENNY: *What?* (Koko turns and looks out the window. I get out my keys.)
KOKO: *Open sweater key*. (The sweater Koko wears on outings is kept in a locked cupboard. I hold up the keys.)
KOKO: *Key*. (I give Koko the keys.)
KOKO: *Key Key*. (She shakes the keys up and down.)
PENNY: *Koko plays with keys*. (As she plays, I bring some cottage cheese.) *Cheese for you. Give me* the *keys, Koko*. (Koko hands me the keys, then pushes me around and climbs onto my back. I carry her around piggyback for a minute, then drop her off at the counter by the cottage cheese.)
PENNY: *Sit here*.
KOKO: *Out nut bean key*.
PENNY: *Cheese*.
KOKO: *Bean*. (I mold the sign *cheese*.)
KOKO: *Open*. (I again mold *cheese*.)
KOKO: *Bean*. (I give up and give her some more cheese.)
KOKO: *More food*.
PENNY: *Want more?*
KOKO: *Out*. (I mold the sign *cheese*, and offer her another spoonful.)
KOKO: *My cheese eat . . . food*.
PENNY: *More?*
KOKO: *More bean . . . white food*.

A year later, at age three-and-one-half, Koko still liked to go out, although by this time her signing had developed to the point where she could be much more explicit in her requests. On this occasion Koko's desire to go out was prompted by the appearance of our adopted cat, KC (for Koko's cat), at the window of the trailer we had recently moved into. I called, "Here, kitty, kitty, kitty," and Koko, hearing this high-pitched chant for the first time, stared at me in apparent surprise, and then climbed onto my back to get a better look at the cat. Koko took my finger and put it on the door.

KOKO: *Do key do key.* (I mold the sign *open.*)
KOKO: *Open.* (I open the door and take her piggyback down the hall to turn down the heat. As I do so I mold *ride.*)
KOKO (as we turn around to go back): *Go there.*

When we returned, Koko tore around the trailer for a minute until I caught her and brought her back to the kitchen. She went to her potty and signed, *Cat cat cat cat.* Then she returned to the window to look at the cat, who was in the grass hunting. She signed, *More there*, took my chin in her hand, pointed to my mouth, and signed, *More more there.* Wondering if she wanted me to repeat the call I made to KC earlier, I signed, *More cat say?* She replied, *Cat.* So I again called, "Here kitty, kitty, kitty," to her apparent delight and satisfaction.

Koko's days at the zoo were not entirely occupied with language training. One memorable diversion was a party we had for Koko on her third birthday. The party began at 6:00 P.M., after Ron and I had spent an hour and a half preparing for the festivities. Naturally, the first thing Koko did was to open her presents. Barbara Hiller had brought her a 3-D viewer with animal pictures; Lee White, a volunteer, brought a wicker bed, a shrunken head, and a plastic snake that slithered down a stick; Ron gave Koko a quart-sized red glass; and I brought a volleyball, binoculars, a toy frog, rings, and a Snoopy piñata filled with nuts, candy and toys. We hung the piñata from the ceiling of the trailer. Koko signed *look* when she took up the binoculars. She looked through them, and then tried to unscrew the eyecaps (Lee had some time earlier given her a fake pair of binoculars that converted into drinking flasks). Failing to detach the eyecaps, Koko put the binoculars around her neck and walked around like a field marshal.

The destruction of the piñata was a wild and wonderful event. After knocking it down with one deft leap, Koko tackled it with hands, feet, and teeth. As the candy and nuts spilled out of a hole she made, Koko was overcome by the sudden deluge of such riches. She stuffed the treats into her mouth in a frenzy, eating candy wrapper and all. When miniature marshmallows fell out of the piñata, however, Koko became cautious and nibbled them in tiny bites.

Koko ate her birthday cake decorously with a spoon, but when she got to the last bite, she temporarily forgot her manners and scooped the cake directly off the plate with her mouth. We let Koko stay up late after the party. She was content to sit quietly in her new wicker bed hugging a stuffed gorilla as Ron and I ate our dinner.

Content

1. Patterson is a psychologist. What do you believe can be learned about human psychology (human behavior) from experiments such as Project Koko?
2. In paragraph 8, the authors note that Patterson accepted about one-third of Koko's word combinations as "legitimate expressions of semantic relations." What do you understand this to mean?
3. In paragraph 19, the authors distinguish between physical and intellectual influences on Koko's signing behavior. Using specific examples from the essay, explain the difference and discuss its significance to Patterson's study.

Technique

1. Patterson is a scientist and her essay describes a scientific experiment, yet it is not written in scientific terms or presented in the format of a scientific paper. What specific characteristics in this essay indicate that Patterson and Linden were writing for a general audience? In what way does this fact add to or detract from the thesis that gorillas can be taught to communicate with humans through sign language?
2. Patterson's and Linden's essay is highly descriptive. Find one or two passages that are particularly vivid and thus allow you to "see" Koko, and be prepared to discuss what makes them effective.

3. Patterson and Linden end their description of Koko's language acquisition with a seemingly unrelated narrative about the gorilla's third birthday party. What effect does this technique have on the essay as a whole?
4. In the essay, there is repeated comparison to Washoe. What is the purpose of this comparison? Is it effective?

Language

1. The title of this essay is "Koko's First Words." To what extent would you argue that Koko is using *words* and has acquired *language*? How do Koko's "words," for example, differ from a dog's bark or a bird's song?
2. In this essay, the authors describe "signing" with Koko. Look up this word as well as the word "Ameslan," and be prepared to explain their significance for Koko's training.
3. Look carefully at the two transcriptions of "conversations" with Koko (paragraph 24 and 25); to what extent do these conversations make sense? Be prepared to support your point of view in class.

Vocabulary

molding	semantic	Ameslan
signing	intonation	elide
precocity		

Writing Suggestions

1. Write a paragraph in which you emulate Patterson's and Linden's attempt to make their readers see Koko clearly. Describe some animal in such a way that the reader will have a sense of knowing the animal as a result of your vivid description.
2. Koko uses "eye contact and gestural intonation" in her conversations with Patterson. Similarly, humans depend heavily on various forms of body language to convey meaning. Choose an active spot on your campus and observe the eye and gestural intonations in conversations you cannot hear; use your observations as the basis for writing an essay in which you analyze the significance of body language in human communication. For example, you might want to classify types of body language, or you might want to compare the body language of different age, sex, or ethnic groups.

3. Write an essay arguing in favor of or against continued funding for studies of animal communication. For instance, are they merely research exercises involving large amounts of precious funds and accomplishing little, or are they significant studies that might lead both to saving endangered species from extinction and to a better understanding of human behavior?

The First Literate Computers?
Ruth Nelson

Ruth Nelson, who graduated from Brown University in 1968, is currently completing a doctoral dissertation on nineteenth-century American literature at Yale University. In addition, Nelson works as a writer and filmscript consultant. Her interest in "literate computers," the subject of the essay that follows, springs from her own involvement with problems of literary interpretation and theories of language. In the following essay, she summarizes one researcher's work in developing a computer that can read and interpret language. She then goes on to demonstrate that one of the merits of such research is the extent to which it illuminates the mysteries of human literacy.

Although computers can perform complex calculations with astonishing rapidity and index vast quantities of data, they have never been able to "understand" human language. At present, any task a computer is asked to do must be spelled out, step by step, in the unambiguous vocabulary of a computer language. A misplaced comma or an overlooked assumption will foul the computation. For anyone who has even a passing acquaintance with computer-programming, the possibility that a machine might learn to understand the ambiguities of plain English is little short of astounding.

Some exciting recent achievements in computer science, however, are now making it possible. The breakthrough is largely the work of Roger Schank, professor of computer science and psychology at Yale University. Schank has designed programs that can translate, summarize, paraphrase, and answer questions about a wide variety of material ranging from simple stories to newspaper articles. While other human-language programs exist, none has the potential scope or flexibility of Schank's. Some, such as Joseph Weizenbaum's famous ELIZA program, which imitates the responses of a Rogerian analyst, are not comprehension programs at all; they only *appear* to duplicate the process of understanding by responding to key words and phrases. Although the performance of Schank's programs remains primitive in comparison to human skills and reasoning powers, they lay the foundation for future progress in the field and may prefigure a revolution in computerized information-processing.

Schank, a young linguist and a computer scientist who sports shoulder-length hair and a beard, likes to illustrate the problems of natural-language comprehension with old comedy routines of Burns and Allen. For example, this sequence:

GRACIE: A truck hit Willy.
GEORGE: What truck?
GRACIE: The truck that didn't have its lights on.
GEORGE: Why didn't it have its lights on?
GRACIE: It didn't have to. It was daytime.
GEORGE: Why didn't the truck driver see Willy?
GRACIE: He didn't know it was Willy.

We laugh because Gracie makes mistakes it would never occur to us to make. Yet these same mistakes would occur to a computer, unless properly programmed. Schank's computer has been taught to avoid common mistakes such as:

INPUT: How could John take the exam?
OUTPUT: He took it with a pen.

INPUT: Now what haven't I added to the cake batter?
OUTPUT: A pound of dog hair and an air filter.

INPUT: How did John die?
OUTPUT: Well, first he was alive.

Schank's research belongs to the fairly recent and highly experimental field of computer science called artificial intelligence. Artificial intelligence, or AI, seeks to duplicate the characteristics of human intelligence. Theoretically, a computer can be taught to imitate any human skill so long as it is given a sufficiently detailed and precise account of human performance. To date, researchers have attempted programs that model simple problem-solving skills, basic motor-visual functions (such as hand-eye coordination), and, of course, natural language comprehension. Surprisingly, the major obstacle confronting them has not been the obstinacy of the computer, but the absence of psychological, linguistic, and neurological theories that adequately describe the simplest acts of human perception. From the start, AI researchers have been forced to investigate long-neglected areas of cognitive psychology and to evolve new theories of human reasoning.

Schank illustrates some of the difficulties by citing the early failures of machine translation. At first, researchers hoped that given two dictionaries and a few rules of grammar, a computer could quickly render one language into another. However, translation of even very simple sentences involved more than a mechanical matching of terms and rearranging of word order. An English sentence such as "It's beautiful" might be equivalent to the French "C'est beau," if "it" referred to an object. But if "it" referred to the weather, the appropriate French equivalent would be "Il fait beau"; literally, "It does beautiful."

The problem, as Schank points out, is that early programmers hoped to sidestep the issue of understanding. Human beings do not match words. They find equivalent expressions for the ideas the words convey. In order to teach computers how to translate, they must first be taught how human beings understand.

Schank received his Ph.D. in linguistics from the University of Texas in 1969. From the beginning, he was dissatisfied with the aims and practices of his chosen field. Chomsky's assumption that man's capacity for language is due to innate grammatical structures encoded in the mind had led, he felt, to an exclusive and misguided preoccupation with syntactic analysis.

While Schank does not deny the existence of some kind of "deep structure" in the brain, the first and foremost goal of a linguist, he believes, is to understand the process of understanding. Whatever the theoretical value of Chomsky's ideas, they had offered little insight into this process. As Chomsky himself admitted, the sentence "Colorless green ideas sleep furiously," while syntactically flawless, is conceptually meaningless. For Chomsky, this example proved that syntax was not dependent upon meaning. Schank's view differs from Chomsky's primarily in the emphasis it places on semantics and on the complex thought processes that permit people to relate the meanings of individual words to one another and to objects and events in their experience of the world. Syntactic cues, such as word order, help to establish the relationships that exist among the ideas that words convey, but these cues, by themselves, do not determine meaning. The difference between "Join me in a cup of coffee" and "Join me in the pool" has nothing to do with syntax and everything to do with the difference between a cup and a pool.

Thus, the chief problem for programmers has been to re-create in the computer an equivalent knowledge of the world. Some have solved this problem by creating programs dealing with a "microworld"—a set of blocks or a chess board—to which the computer can relate the meaning of words. The drawbacks of such an approach, however, are obvious. With a microworld, the computer can be taught to understand simple commands such as "Pick up the block," or "Line up the blocks in a row." But it cannot interpret sentences that do not relate to the block world.

Schank's originality was in devising a method that extends the computer's knowledge of the world to include other kinds of human experiences that cannot be represented by modeling physical relationships. He calls the theory on which his programs are based conceptual dependency theory. Conceptual dependency essentially provides an elaborate system of elementary concepts called "primitives" that correspond to various elements in our experience. There are primitives for time and primitives for place; primitives for different kinds of objects and kinds of actions. There are also rules for governing the possible relationship of these primitives. Computer analysis depends upon relating the individual words to their appropriate primitives or group of primitives in much the same way that human comprehension depends upon relating words to concepts derived from experience.

For example, the computer has a primitive for events that involve movement through space (walking, running, etc.) and another primitive for events that involve an exchange of possessions (giving, receiving, etc.). In order to understand the sentence "John took the plane," the computer must decide, as we must decide, what kind of event the sentence concerns. At first, we may feel the meaning is obvious: clearly John traveled someplace on an airplane—he moved through space. A second look, however, reveals other possible interpretations. It might mean that John took possession of an airplane, a toy airplane, or a woodworking tool. Each interpretation of "took" and "plane" leads to a different meaning—some legitimate, some absurd.

Schank's computer requires a minimum of three programs operating in tandem in order to determine the meaning of simple sentences: a Parser, which categorizes the information according to primitives; an Inferencer, which makes logical connections between the primitives and checks them against other facts in the sentence for inconsistencies; and a Memory, which stores all the information accumulated by the Parser and Inferencer.

Despite its ambiguities, "John took the plane" poses relatively few problems. Like a human being, the Parser would assume that it concerns traveling on an airplane until the Inferencer notifies it of a logical inconsistency. If "John took the plane" is followed by the sentence "He arrived in New York at 10:30," the Inferencer would know its initial assumption was correct; the "arrived" also refers to movement through space and "New York" refers to a destination. However, if "John took the plane" is followed by "Mary grabbed it back. The children fought over the new toy," the Inferencer would demand a reevaluation. In this case, the Inferencer would notice the contradiction between "grabbed," which refers to an exchange of possessions, and "took," which was previously understood as a movement in space. The word "toy" would also help the Inferencer and Parser further identify "plane" as something small enough to be physically seized; a toy airplane, perhaps, rather than a giant 747.

The computer analysis of "John took the plane" dramatizes how much knowledge we need in order to comprehend even the simplest sentence. The more difficult the text, the more information is assumed and the more complex the process of inference. Schank has recently completed two new programs, SAM and PAM, to provide the information and inferential framework needed to solve other common interpretative problems.

Analyzing the content of paragraphs humans understand with ease engages all these programs in a long and tedious series of consultations with one another. But once these programs have done their work, it is easy to see how the conceptual structure they have produced may be used. It may be condensed for the purpose of summary, or expanded for the purpose of paraphrase. Specific items of interest may be readily located in order to answer questions. Finally, a Generator program can take the conceptual structure and turn it into human language. The Generator program can quickly produce a Chinese summary or a Spanish paraphrase of an English story.

For a society drowning in paper, the practical applications of such programs are obvious. We can easily visualize a day when a busy executive could ask the computer for summaries of company reports, or legislators could receive answers to questions concerning articles in various technical fields. For the average individual, these programs promise a time when the vast resources of the computer will be accessible without the need of costly special training.

Many problems must be overcome first, and, given the inherent difficulty of the task, some may never be fully conquered. Despite the sophistication of its programs, Schank's computer can only handle a limited range of materials. Programs currently exist for understanding newspaper articles about automobile accidents, earthquakes, and visiting dignitaries—events that involve a predictable pattern of information. Abstract, figurative, or complexly motivated material is beyond the computer's present capacity.

The analysis of a political speech, for example, would require programs that could handle abstract ideas, such as religion, freedom, and duty, as well as figurative usages such as "Religion is the opiate of the masses." In addition, since politicians rarely say what they mean directly—the President's address to wheat farmers in Kansas may have more to do with Russian détente than American agriculture—the computer would also need complex programs to interpret motives, identify policies, and monitor changing domestic and foreign circumstances.

Schank, in collaboration with social psychologist Robert Abelson, has made a start in this direction with a curious program called POLITICS. POLITICS interprets headlines from the standpoint of a cold war idealogue. It interprets

**Russia Masses Troops
on the Czech Border**

as

RUSSIA MAY ORDER ITS TROOPS
INTO CZECHOSLOVAKIA

Similarly, it interprets

**Russia Sent Massive Arms Shipments
to the MPLA in Angola**

as

RUSSIA WANTS TO CONTROL
ANGOLA THROUGH THE MPLA

POLITICS was not designed for practical use, but rather to demonstrate the ease with which a computer assumes a point of view. Contrary to popular belief, computers will not necessarily be more objective intepreters of written material. Much of the information that computers and people need to understand language is subjective, especially if it concerns human behavior or abstract ideas. Sometimes only a fine line separates fact from opinion or prejudice. Programmers of the future will not only have to give the computer more information, they will have to consider its quality as well.

Present computer design also imposes limitations. Schank's comprehension programs already make a significant demand upon the computer's capacity. And even if computer storage could be expanded to include all the knowledge of an average adult, time would still be a factor. It takes Schank's computer about 10 minutes to understand a brief newspaper account of a car crash. More complicated comprehension programs will require even more time.

Schank is presently at work on a new program called FRUMP, which will minimize some of these difficulties. FRUMP (fast reading, understanding, and memory processor) is a skimming program that operates on SAM-type scripts and can process limited kinds of material very quickly (about three seconds for the car-crash story) by locating significant information and ignoring the rest. Unlike Schank's more complex comprehension programs, FRUMP has a clearly foreseeable future. FRUMP can speedily summarize and transmit all kinds of routine information for business or government. It has already demonstrated its abilty to monitor the UPI wire and will be commercially available beginning this summer.

The future of Schank's other programs and of AI work in general is harder to predict. Technology has advanced so quickly that in a very short time we can expect computers with the speed and capacity necessary for more sophisticated programs. But whether such programs will exist remains a question. Schank himself is confident that within 10 or 15 years he will have programs that can handle political speeches and other kinds of difficult material. Others are less optimistic.

Whether such programs *should* exist poses an even more difficult question. Good information is vital to a free society. Will computers supply more and better information or will they, as the example of the POLITICS programs suggests, provide vast new sources of propaganda and a new means of thought control? In a controversial new book, Computer Power and Human Reason, MIT's Joseph Weizenbaum warns of the risks of placing too much faith in computer intelligence. Weizenbaum became skeptical of artificial intelligence when some people suggested that his ELIZA program could replace practicing clinical psychologists. Computers are not people, he cautions, and we must decide what jobs we are willing to turn over to them and what tasks should remain in human hands. On another and more profound level, he doubts whether the computer can ever serve as an adequate model for human cognitive processes and fears that AI's assumption that people are information-processing machines will diminish our concept of ourselves.

In this debate, Schank has become the most outspoken advocate of continued AI research and program development. The word "computer," he argues, does not mean "infallible." So long as people learn to treat computer-monitored information as they would treat information derived from newspapers and magazines, the benefits of improved accessibility, he believes, far outweigh the disadvantages. He also believes that computers do provide a valid model of human consciousness, one that permits scientists to experiment with broad cognitive theories that cannot be tested in any other way.

Whether or not one agrees with Schank on all these issues, the value of his own work and that of others in AI cannot be denied. The true subject of artificial intelligence is not computers but man. Programming a computer to duplicate human skills has taught us to respect the miracle of human intelligence.

Schank's own work has already contributed greatly to linguistic theory and will soon be felt in all areas that depend upon a theory of language comprehension. His conceptual dependency alone provides an intriguing analysis of semantic structures. In the future, he plans to continue his study of cognitive processes. Someday he hopes to teach his computer to make mistakes—not the mistakes that Gracie makes, but the mistakes that are inevitable in the course of human comprehension. "If you can get a computer to make the same kinds of mistakes people make," Schank says, "you know you are on to something right."

Content

1. In paragraph 1 (and throughout the essay), Nelson points out that such human components of language as intonation, context, and

changed punctuation can trick a computer into misinterpretation. "Let's barbecue father" is considerably different than "Let's barbecue, father," though all of the words are the same. Find other examples of potentially confusing sentences (from the essay and from your own experience). What problems do these examples suggest to you in our attempt to develop literate computers?

2. In the third paragraph, Nelson introduces the central notion that the greatest problem in developing a literate computer is not so much the limits of computers as our own inability to "describe the simplest acts of human perception." Explain the problem as you understand it, using examples from the essay to clarify your explanation.

3. In her concluding paragraphs, Nelson says, "The true subject of artificial intelligence is not computers but man." What is your understanding of this statement?

Technique

1. Nelson's first paragraph reminds us of the supposed limitations of computers, but with the second paragraph, she moves on to an examination of computers that refutes the opening paragraph's assumptions. What word does Nelson use to mark the changed approach, and how effective is the change?

2. Nelson's essay centers on the work of one computer scientist, and she refers to him by name frequently. What else does Nelson do to make Schank's presence in the essay vivid?

3. Explaining the difficulties of teaching a computer to understand human language, Nelson uses many specific examples. Find two or three and discuss how these examples clarify her discussion.

4. What audience is most likely to appreciate Nelson's essay? The general reader? The well-educated layperson? Support your conclusion with details from the essay.

Language

1. In her title, Nelson asks if we are reaching the age of "literate computers." Look up the word "literate" in your dictionary. Do you believe, based on what Nelson's article tells us about new computer-science advances, that computers are becoming literate?

2. In the first sentence, Nelson points out that computers have never

been able to "understand" human language. What do you think this statement means?
3. What, according to Nelson, is artificial intelligence?

Vocabulary

ambiguous	conceptual	idealogue
cognitive	tandem	cognitive
semantics	abstract	syntax
cues		

Writing Suggestions

1. In paragraph 11, Nelson uses the example of "John took the plane" to explain that "the more difficult the text, the more information is assumed and the more complex the process of inference." Write a paragraph or brief essay in which you analyze the difficulties of interpreting another ambiguous sentence, one that you or your classmates think of. Emulating Nelson's technique, discuss the possible meanings and the ways in which we understand the actual meaning of a syntactically ambiguous sentence.

2. Carefully re-read the final five paragraphs of Nelson's essay, which discuss some of the dangers and the advantages of research in artificial intelligence and "literate" computers. Write an essay in which you argue for or against such research. Use specific detail from the essay or from your own experience and knowledge to support your argument.

3. Many education specialists now say that within a few years being computer literate will be as crucial for the university graduate as being literate in English and Math now is. Write an essay in which you analyze the significance of computer literacy for your generation.

A Rhetoric of Disease

Susan Sontag

Susan Sontag (b. 1933) has taught English, philosophy, and religion, and she has written reviews, short stories, novels, and one screenplay—as well as directing a motion picture. For these various endeavors she has received awards from the American Association of University Women, the Rockefeller Foundation, and the Guggenheim Foundation. The following essay is taken from Illness as Metaphor *(1978), a study of figurative language in relation to lethal diseases. She first compares the symbolic significance of tuberculosis in earlier centuries with the symbolic significance of cancer today, then contrasts the physical effects of the two diseases.*

Two diseases have been spectacularly, and similarly, encumbered by the trappings of metaphor: tuberculosis and cancer.

The fantasies inspired by TB in the last century, by cancer now, are responses to a disease thought to be intractable and capricious—that is, a disease not understood—in an era in which medicine's central premise is that all diseases can be cured. Such a disease is, by definition, mysterious. For as long as its cause was not understood and the ministrations of doctors remained so ineffective, TB was thought to be an insidious, implacable theft of a life. Now it is cancer's turn to be the disease that doesn't knock before it enters, cancer that fills the role of an illness experienced as a ruthless, secret invasion—a role it will keep until, one day, its etiology becomes as clear and its treatment as effective as those of TB have become.

Although the way in which disease mystifies is set against a backdrop of new expectations, the disease itself (once TB, cancer today) arouses thoroughly old-fashioned kinds of dread. Any disease that is treated as a mystery and acutely enough feared will be felt to be morally, if not literally, contagious. Thus, a surprisingly large number of people with cancer find themselves being shunned by relatives and friends and are the object of practices of decontamination by members of their household, as if cancer, like TB, were an infectious disease. Contact with someone afflicted with a disease regarded as a mysterious malevolency inevitably feels like a trespass; worse, like the violation of a taboo. The very names of such diseases are felt to have a magic power. In Stendhal's *Armance* (1827), the hero's mother refuses to say "tuberculosis," for fear that pronouncing the word will hasten the course of her son's malady. And Karl Menninger has observed (in *The Vital Balance*) that "the very word 'cancer' is said to kill some patients who would not have succumbed (so quickly) to the malignancy from which they suffer." This observation is offered in support of anti-intellectual pieties and a facile compassion all too triumphant in contemporary medicine and psychiatry. "Patients who consult us because of their suffering and their distress and their disability," he continues, "have every right to resent being plastered with a damning index tab." Dr. Menninger recommends that physicians generally abandon "names" and "labels" ("our function is to help these people, not to further afflict them")—which would mean, in effect, increasing secretiveness and medical paternalism. It is not naming as such that is pejorative or damning, but the name "cancer." As long as a particular disease is treated as an evil, invincible predator, not just a disease, most people with cancer will indeed be demoralized by learning what disease they have. The solution is hardly to stop telling cancer patients the truth, but to rectify the conception of the disease, to de-mythicize it.

When, not so many decades ago, learning that one had TB was tantamount to hearing a sentence of death—as today, in the popular imagination, cancer equals death—it was common to conceal the identity of their disease from tuberculars and, after they died, from their children. Even with patients informed about their disease, doctors and family were reluctant to talk freely. "Verbally I don't learn anything definite," Kafka wrote to a friend in April 1924 from the sanitorium where he died two months later, "since in discussing tuberculosis . . . everybody drops into a shy, evasive, glassy-eyed manner of speech." Conventions of concealment with cancer are even more strenuous. In France and Italy it is still the rule for doctors to communicate a cancer diagnosis to the patient's family but not to the patient; doctors consider that the truth will be intolerable to all but exceptionally mature and intelligent patients. (A leading French oncologist has told me that fewer than a tenth of his patients know they have cancer.) In America—in part because of the doctor's fear of malpractice suits—there is now much more candor with patients, but the country's largest cancer hospital mails routine communications and bills to outpatients in envelopes that do not reveal the sender, on the assumption that the illness may be a secret from their families. Since getting cancer can be a scandal that jeopardizes one's love life, one's chance of promotion, even one's job, patients who know what they have tend to be extremely prudish, if not outright secretive, about their disease. And a federal law, the 1966 Freedom of Information Act, cites "treatment for cancer" in a clause exempting from disclosure matters whose disclosure "would be an unwarranted invasion of personal privacy." It is the only disease mentioned.

All this lying to and by cancer patients is a measure of how much harder it has become in advanced industrial societies to come to terms with death. As death is now an offensively meaningless event, so that disease widely considered a synonym for death is experienced as something to hide. The policy of equivocating about the nature of their disease with cancer patients reflects the conviction that dying people are best spared the news that they are dying, and that the good death is the sudden one, best of all if it happens while we're unconscious or asleep. Yet the modern denial of death does not explain the extent of the lying and the wish to be lied to; it does not touch the deepest dread. Someone who has had a coronary is at least as likely to die of another one within a few years as someone with cancer is likely to die soon from cancer. But no one thinks of concealing the truth from a cardiac patient: there is nothing shameful about a heart attack. Cancer patients are lied to, not just because the disease is (or is thought to be) a death sentence, but because it is felt to be obscene—in the original meaning of the word: ill-omened, abominable, repugnant to the senses. Cardiac disease implies a weakness, trouble, failure that is mechanical; there is no disgrace, nothing of the taboo that once surrounded people afflicted with TB and still surround those who have cancer. The metaphors attached to TB and to cancer imply living processes of a particularly resonant and horrid kind.

Throughout most of their history, the metaphoric uses of TB and cancer crisscross and overlap. The *Oxford English Dictionary* records "consumption" in use as a synonym for pulmonary tuberculosis as early as 1398. (John of Trevisa: "Whan the blode is made thynne, soo folowyth consumpcyon and wastyng.") But the premodern understanding of cancer also invokes the notion of consumption. The OED gives as the early figurative definition of cancer: "Anything that frets, corrodes, corrupts, or consumes slowly and secretly." (Thomas Paynell in 1528: "A canker is a melancolye impostume, eatynge partes of the bodye.") The earliest literal definition of cancer is a growth, lump, or protuberance, and the disease's name—from the Greek *karkinos* and the Latin *cancer*, both meaning crab—was inspired according to Galen, by the resemblance of an external tumor's swollen veins to a crab's legs; not, as many people think, because a metastatic disease crawls or creeps like a crab. But etymology indicates that tuberculosis was also once considered a type of abnormal extrusion: the word tuberculosis—from the Latin *tuberculum*, the diminutive of *tuber*, bump, swelling—means a morbid swelling, protuberance, projection, or growth. Rudolf Virchow, who founded the science of cellular pathology in the 1850s, thought of the tubercle as a tumor.

Thus, from late antiquity until quite recently, tuberculosis was—typologically—cancer. And cancer was described, like TB, as a process in which the body was consumed. The modern conceptions of the two diseases could not be set until the advent of cellular pathology. Only with the microscope was it possible to grasp the distinctiveness of cancer, as a type of cellular activity, and to understand that the disease did not always take the form of an external or even palpable tumor. (Before the mid-nineteenth century, nobody could have identified leukemia as a form of cancer.) And it was not possible definitively to separate cancer from TB until after 1882, when tuberculosis was discovered to be a bacterial infection. Such advances in medical thinking enabled the leading metaphors of the two diseases to become truly distinct and, for the most part, contrasting. The modern fantasy about cancer could then begin to take shape—a fantasy which from the 1920s on would inherit most of the problems dramatized by the fantasies about TB, but with the two diseases and their symptoms conceived in quite different, almost opposing, ways.

TB is understood as a disease of one organ, the lungs, while cancer is understood as a disease that can turn up in any organ and whose outreach is the whole body.

TB is understood as a disease of extreme contrasts: white pallor and red flush, hyperactivity alternating with languidness. The spasmodic course of the disease is illustrated by what is thought of as the prototypical TB symptom, coughing. The sufferer is wracked by coughs, then sinks back, recovers breath, breathes normally; then coughs again. Cancer is a disease of growth (sometimes visible; more characteristically, inside), of abnormal, ultimately lethal growth that is measured, incessant, steady. Although there may be periods in which tumor growth is arrested (remissions), cancer produces no contrasts like the oxymorons of behavior—febrile activity, passionate resignation—thought to be typical of TB. The tubercular is pallid some of the time; the pallor of the cancer patient is unchanging.

TB makes the body transparent. The X-rays which are the standard diagnostic tool permit one, often for the first time, to see one's insides—to become transparent to oneself. While TB is understood to be, from early on, rich in visible symptoms (progressive emaciation, coughing, languidness, fever), and can be suddenly and dramatically revealed (the blood on the handkerchief), in cancer the main symptoms are thought to be, characteristically, invisible—until the last stage, when it is too late. The disease, which is often discovered by chance or though a routine medical checkup, can be far advanced without exhibiting any appreciable symptoms. One has an opaque body that must be taken to a specialist to find out if it contains cancer. What the patient cannot perceive, the specialist will determine by analyzing tissues taken from the body. TB patients may see their X-rays or even possess them: the patients at the sanitorium in *The Magic Mountain* carry theirs around in their breast pockets. Cancer patients don't look at their biopsies.

TB was—still is—thought to produce spells of euphoria, increased appetite, exacerbated sexual desire. Part of the regimen for patients in *The Magic Mountain* is a second breakfast, eaten with gusto. Cancer is thought to cripple vitality, make eating an ordeal, deaden desire. Having TB was imagined to be an aphrodisiac, and to confer extraordinary powers of seduction. Cancer is considered to be desexualizing. But it is characteristic of TB that many of its symptoms are deceptive—liveliness that comes from enervation, rosy cheeks that look like a sign of health but come from fever—and an upsurge of vitality may be a sign of approaching death. (Such gushes of energy will generally be self-destructive, and may be destructive of others: recall the Old West legend of Doc Holliday, the tubercular gunfighter released from moral restraints by the ravages of his disease.) Cancer has only true symptoms.

TB is disintegration, febrilization, dematerialization; it is a disease of liquids—the body turning to phlegm and mucus and sputum and, finally, blood—and of air, of the need for better air. Cancer is degeneration, the body tissues turning to something hard. Alice James, writing in her journal a year before she died from cancer in 1892, speaks of "this unholy granite substance in my breast." But this lump is alive, a fetus with its own will. Novalis, in an entry written around 1798 for his encyclopedia project, defines cancer, along with gangrene, as "full-fledged *parasites*—they grow, are engendered, engender, have their structure, secrete, eat." Cancer is a demonic pregnancy. St. Jerome must have been thinking of a cancer when he wrote: "The one there with his swollen belly is pregnant with his own death" (*"Alius tumenti aqualiculo mortem parturit"*). Though the course of both diseases is emaciating, losing weight from TB is understood very differently from losing weight from cancer. In TB, the person is "consumed," burned up. In cancer, the patient is "invaded" by alien cells, which multiply, causing an atrophy or blockage of bodily functions. The cancer patient "shrivels" (Alice James's word) or "shrinks" (Wilhelm Reich's word).

TB is a disease of time; it speeds up life, highlights it, spiritualizes it. In both English and French, consumption "gallops." Cancer has stages rather than gaits; it is (eventually) "terminal." Cancer works slowly, insidiously; the standard euphemism in obituaries is that someone has "died after a long illness." Every characterization of cancer describes it as slow, and so it was first used metaphorically. "The word of hem crepith as a kankir," Wyclif wrote in 1382 (translating a phrase in II Timothy 2:17); and among the earliest figurative uses of cancer are as a metaphor for "idleness" and "sloth."* Metaphorically, cancer is not so much a disease of time as a disease or pathology of space. Its principal metaphors refer to topography (cancer "spreads" or "proliferates" or is "diffused"; tumors are surgically "excised"), and its most dreaded consequence, short of death, is the mutilation or amputation of part of the body.

TB is often imagined as a disease of poverty and deprivation—of thin garments, thin bodies, unheated rooms, poor hygiene, inadequate food. The poverty may not be as literal as Mimi's garret in *La Bohème*; the tubercular Marguerite Gautier in *La Dame aux camélias* lives in luxury, but inside she is a waif. In contrast, cancer is a disease of middle-class life, a disease associated with affluence, with excess. Rich countries have the highest cancer rates, and the rising incidence of the disease is seen as resulting, in part, from a diet rich in fat and proteins and from the toxic effluvia of the industrial economy that creates affluence. The treatment of TB is identified with the stimulation of appetite, cancer treatment with nausea and the loss of appetite. The undernourished nourishing themselves—alas, to no avail. The overnourished, unable to eat.

The TB patient was thought to be helped, even cured, by a change in environment. There was a notion that TB was a wet disease, a disease of humid and dank cities. The inside of the body became damp ("moisture in the lungs" was a favored locution) and

---

*As cited in the OED, which gives as an early figurative use of "canker": "that pestilent and most infectious canker, idlenesse"—T. Palfreyman, 1564. And of "cancer" (which replaced "canker" around 1700): "Sloth is a Cancer, eating up that Time Princes should cultivate for Things sublime"—Edmund Ken, 1711.

had to be dried out. Doctors advised travel to high, dry places—the mountains, the desert. But no change of surrounding is thought to help the cancer patient. The fight is all inside one's own body. It may be, is increasingly thought to be, something in the environment that has caused the cancer. But once cancer is present, it cannot be reversed or diminished by a move to a better (that is, less carcinogenic) environment.

TB is thought to be relatively painless. Cancer is thought to be, invariably, excruciatingly painful. TB is thought to provide an easy death, while cancer is the spectacularly wretched one. For over a hundred years TB remained the preferred way of giving death a meaning—an edifying, refined disease. Nineteenth-century literature is stocked with descriptions of almost symptomless, unfrightened, beatific deaths from TB, particularly of young people, such as Little Eva in *Uncle Tom's Cabin* and Dombey's son Paul in *Dombey and Son* and Smike in *Nicholas Nickleby*, where Dickens described TB as the "dread disease" which "refines" death

> of its grosser aspect . . . in which the struggle between soul and body is so gradual, quiet, and solemn, and the result so sure, that day by day, and grain by grain, the mortal part wastes and withers away, so that the spirit grows light and sanguine with its lightening load . . .

Contrast these ennobling, placid TB deaths with the ignoble, agonizing cancer deaths of Eugene Gant's father in Thomas Wolfe's *Of Time and the River* and the sister in Bergman's film *Cries and Whispers*. The dying tubercular is pictured as made more beautiful and more soulful; the person dying of cancer is portrayed as robbed of all capacities of self-transcendence, humiliated by fear and agony.

Content

1. In paragraph 3, Sontag says that mysterious diseases such as TB or cancer are "felt to be morally, if not literally, contagious." In what way do we tend to think of cancer as "morally contagious" and of contact with the victim as a "trespass"?
2. In paragraph 5, Sontag suggests that the "modern denial of death" is unique and powerful. Do you believe we are more likely to deny death than in previous ages? Why or why not?

3. In paragraph 8, Sontag begins a lengthy description of society's conceptions of TB and cancer. Are these accurate, medically sound descriptions, or are they metaphorical descriptions? How do you know?

Technique

1. Sontag's thesis is separated into two parts. The first appears in the one-sentence opening paragraph; the second does not appear until the final sentence of paragraph 3. Paraphrase her thesis and discuss the effect of its placement in the essay.
2. The point of Sontag's long contrast of our conceptions of TB and cancer is implied rather than explicitly stated. The final sentence of the essay is a particularly dramatic contrast. What point do you believe Sontag is making with her contrast?
3. To what audience does Sontag address this essay? Support your conclusion with specific details.

Language

1. Look up the word "rhetoric" in your dictionary. Given your understanding of that word, what does Sontag's title tell you about the essay that follows?
2. Sontag spends all of paragraph 8 summarizing the *Oxford English Dictionary* definitions of cancer and TB. Why do you believe this is an important step in her discussion?
3. In the first sentence, Sontag says that TB and cancer have been "encumbered by the trappings of metaphor." Look up the words "encumbered" and "metaphor," and discuss the meaning of Sontag's opening statement.

Vocabulary

encumbered	implacable	oncologist
metaphor	etiology	equivocate
intractable	malevolency	transcendence
capricious	paternalism	oxymoron
pieties	pejorative	febrilization
ministrations	de-mythicize	beatific
insidious		

Writing Suggestions

1. Write an essay in which you describe your own metaphorical image of cancer. Consider, for instance, how your image of this "mysterious," "malevolent" disease differs from your response to heart disease, for example.

2. Sontag points out that with cancer there are numerous "conventions of concealment." Write an essay arguing the pros and cons of complete candor between doctor and patient and/or between the patient and his friends or family. Support your analysis with examples from your own experience or with examples from the essay.

Language and the Arts
7

Beyond the langauge of words, per se, humans have evolved other kinds of languages, other means of communicating emotions, feelings, or ideas for which words, however rich, seem inadequate. The creative artist, in particular, frequently dwells in this realm of nonverbal communication, a realm often more difficult, it seems, for both the creator and the observer. Nevertheless, human beings share the impulse to create objects—a dance, a painting, a symphony—that communicate a vision of life.

The selections in this chapter are drawn from the worlds of photography, film, dance, and theater, and were written by some of the foremost contemporary artists in each field. Whatever their artistic media, however, all the writers represented here explore the complex forces involved in the act of creating—the difficulty of expressing oneself or one's vision through the creative medium—and the challenge to the observer of sharing in the special language, the vision, of the creator.

The first selection in this chapter is not a traditional essay but a grouping of observations by the American artist, Edward Weston, revealing what it is to create and to communicate the creative vision. In selections from his *Daybooks*, photographer Edward Weston says that it is not the artist's role to express and reveal himself through his work; rather the artist must know and reveal to others the object of his work as it is. For Weston, then, the artist is unique because he is a seer and presenter, seeing what others might miss and sharing his insight with them. Weston's own art is unique because his subjects are frequently everyday items rarely associated with art (peppers, squash, egg slicers); but, he says, through his photography he reveals the "mystery of the life force" he sees in the object. Weston's work is a form, then, an articulation of, the artist's unique knowledge. For Weston, the artist's challenge is to communicate the vision, to present the thing as it is, and through this process of revelation to be "the instrument through which inarticulate man speaks."

Weston's observations suggest the difficulty artists face in converting the image in their minds into a work the viewers will comprehend as the artists themselves see it. Filmmaker Ingmar Bergman and choreographer Agnes de Mille both express this challenge. Bergman explains "the complicated birth process" of a film, beginning as a "hazy" split-second impression that leaves behind a mood. The filmmaker's challenge, if he wants to share that vision with the public, is to perform a conjurer's trick, spinning the image into public statement, transforming "rhythms, moods, atmosphere, tensions, sequences, tones, and scents into words and sentences, into an understandable screenplay." De Mille too, working with dance as yet another form of language, describes the exhausting process of finding "the revealing gesture," of turning what both she and Bergman refer to as the "nucleus" of the creation into comprehensible form.

Both de Mille and Bergman, in noting the difficulty of holding the hazy image while achieving clarity of form, long for the exactness of musical notation, which Bergman says allows the artist "to put on paper all the shades and tones of [the] vision." In "How We Listen," however, composer Aaron Copland reminds us that the advantage of notation does not always solve the problem of communication between the audience and the artist. Looking at the language of music from the perspective of the listener rather than the creator, Copland points out three levels of listening: the sensuous (letting ourselves go to the pleasant sound), the expressive (understanding how the composer uses the "sound stuff" to create mood), and the musical (using form, tone, color, and note manipulation). The expressive, Copland says, is the most controversial plane: Listeners are determined to assign a specific meaning to a work (a meaning perhaps directed by the listener's associations). At the other extreme, the composer insists the work "means nothing but the notes themselves," refusing to assign meaning in his desire to give music a life of its own. Copland's essay is an attempt to mediate between the extremes, a recognition that there is meaning in the music, but "no closer than a general concept." We cannot, he says, pin a "word meaning" on a musical composition.

The language of music, like the language of the other art forms discussed thus far in this chapter, seems separate from word-meaning language. Not so for the final essay presented here. In it the renowned French actress Simone Signoret reveals the frustrations she confronted when attempting to play Lady Macbeth on the London stage. Her artistic media, in contrast to the photographer's or the musician's, is language as we commonly know it, albeit the language of seventeenth-century England, Shakespeare's English. As Signoret makes painfully clear, being fluent in English, being a professional actress with years of stage and screen experience, taking two extra months to rehearse and memorize her lines before the final extended formal rehearsals—all this was not sufficient to allow her to master the "rhythms" of Shakespeare's English.

By her own account, Signoret was unable to convey to her audience either the "essence " of Lady Macbeth or a sense of herself as an actress who could "amaze people by the force of her cold determination." Her essay, then, reveals the artists' plight when the chosen artistic medium seems to fail, when the artists are not satisfied that they have successfully communicated their visions to the audience. Yet, as Signoret's tone also reveals, dedicated artists ultimately move beyond that apparent failure because of a firm commitment to the "language" of their art. Whatever their primary artistic medium, however—color, shape, form, gesture, music, acting—the artists represented in this chapter turn as well to traditional language when they explain to careful and interested readers how they attempt, in the words of Edward Weston, to transform "things seen into things known." The selections in this chapter reveal both the artists' and the audiences' struggle to achieve that transformation as they communicate through the several languages of the arts.

Things Seen into Things Unknown
Edward Weston

Edward Weston (1886–1958) was an American photographer famous for his pictures of Mexico and the California Coast, as well as those of commonplace objects. He made significant achievements in both traditional and experimental photography, and along with Ansel Adams and Willard Van Dyck, promoted the principles of "pure photography." "Things Seen into Things Known," which is taken from his Daybooks, explains both the philosophy and the process of his photography. Neither an essay, per se, nor a traditional diary, the following selection seems to strike a balance between the tone and structure of each.

    August 14. My work is always a few jumps ahead of what I say about it! I am simply a means to an end: I cannot, at the time, say why I record a thing in a certain way, nor why I record it at all! Why indeed does one give up material comfort for the sake of an idea,—for "art?" Certainly public applause no longer spurs me on, though I want it, need it for my belly's sake:—I mean applause in the sense of wide fame. An audience is needed, if only a handful, or maybe one person. The artist must function, must fulfill his place as a giver—but maybe I am not an "artist," nor my product "art!"

    This question, an old and hackneyed one was brought up again by a group of "real artists," painters of course, while viewing my recent retrospective exhibit, 1914-31, at Denny-Watrous'. I set about at once to prove by logical deduction that photography could be an art,—or at least an art in the very terms these painters think in, and I proved it very easily to my own satisfaction, though I am sure my logic would not even dent their defense mechanism. Then I suddenly realized I did not care what photography was labeled, that what I was doing had so much more importance, more vitality than their painting, that a great gulf separated their intent and mine. Of course this I have known for years, but have not clearly stated my case in words. These painters, most painters, and the photographers who imitate them, are "expressing themselves": "Art" is considered as a "self-expression." I am no longer trying to "express myself," to impose my own personality on nature, but without prejudice, without falsification, to become identified with nature, to see or *know* things as they are, their very essence, so that what I record is not an *interpretation*—my idea of what nature *should be*—but a *revelation,* a piercing of the smoke screen artificially cast over life by neurosis, into an absolute, impersonal recognition. Art is weakened in degree, according to the amount of personality expressed: to be explicit, according to the warping and twisting of knowledge by inhibitions. Granting we all have inhibitions, economic, sexual,—these must not color our work. The artist is not a petty individual God on a throne, free to exploit and expose his heartaches and bellyaches,—

he is an instrument through which articulate mankind speaks: he may be a prophet who at a needed moment points the way, forming the future, or he may be born at a time when his work is a culmination, a flowering in soil already prepared.

So, when a few years ago I wrote that I was no longer interested in interpretation, but in presentation, I was only stating a half-truth, for after all the commercial photographer, the illustrator of catalogues, also "presents." Then what is the difference between the "presentation" I would make of a cabbage and that made by the commercial man? The latter with matter-of-fact approach sees a cabbage as an unrelated fact, devoid of interest except as a means to sauerkraut. I feel in the same cabbage, all the mystery of life force, I am amazed, emotionally stirred, and by my way of presentation my recognition of the reason for the cabbage form, its significance in relation to all forms, I am able to communicate my experience to others.

This "emotional stirring" is not to be understood as melodrama, nor the vague rhapsodies of a mooning poet counting daisy petals for an answer to his doubts,—but as a great flame of recognition—the significance of facts—wisdom controlling the means (brush, chisel, camera)—and presenting this knowledge in a communicable form.

August 21. These thoughts are continually broken. Last week I feel that I was on the way toward the most clarified statement I have made. Well—to try again—

In discussing "self-expression" with a visitor, she said—"but these prints of yours are different from other workers',—you are expressing your personality."

I will answer by quoting Dora Hagemeyer who wrote in a very clear, understanding way about my exhibit. "But in Carmel, we find him moving beyond the artist. It is here that he has transcended art and become the seer. Seen through his eyes, the concealed flight in the wing of a bird, the sculpture of a bud, are transformed from things *seen* to things *known*."

A "seer" is one who sees with the inner eye and is able to give concrete expression to his knowledge of facts, things,—conveying this intelligent perception, without personal bias, in a direct, clarified form, so that the spectator can participate in the revelation.

The form,—composition, construction—must not be considered as a formula to be learned by rule. It is far more important. It is the most clarified, forceful way the seer (see-er) can command for the presentation and communciation of his experience. It will vary according to the special qualities, the significance of the thing to be presented.

October 24. Since July 11th, over three months ago, I have made no entry in this book. On that date, I casually noted that Merle had in mind a book on my work. It has now gone to press! For these three months I have "lived" this book, literally. Weeks passed, with prints under consideration strewn all over my room. The first dozen or so were easy to select, work that *had* to be included, prints that were epochal in my life. But after these, came the struggle to eliminate from amongst a hundred or more possibilities. To confine myself to the limit of thirty reproductions, lay aside dozens that I wanted to use, was a task which made me question my own decisive ability. Merle raised the number to thirty-six; but even then I wavered between my desires. Probably I will always regret certain omissions.

I have learned much from this struggle. For one thing, my critical faculty towards my work has sharpened. I have always thought that I was severe enough in judging my photographs, but faced with presenting them in a book from which I could never escape, I discovered the word "but"; "this print is fine *but—*" And I have learned something about writing! That it is one thing to jot down thoughts in a daybook; another to present them to an audience,—again, one from which I could not escape! Continually, I would face myself, and say, "Do you really mean this?—Could it be misunderstood?—Have I clearly expressed my meaning?—And how about my technique, my choice of words, their exact relation to my thoughts?—Have I been pedantic?"

I wrote, and destroyed, until I had corns on my bum, bleary eyes, writer's cramp, and a befogged brain. Finally I achieved a clarified concise statement—at least I think so today, and mailed it yesterday.

Sunday morn, Sept 14. —4:30—wide awake with thoughts on my yesterday's negatives: squash—winter squash—marvellous cream white forms—one like a starfish—one a pointed comet sweeping through space—another, fluted like a Greek column: solid, smooth, absolute,—abstract? I am fishing for words to give my feeling for their detached quality—their gesture of complete beauty.

Things Seen into Things Known

So! I am in the same class I rebel against? Comparing a rock to Lincoln's face! No—I am trying to give a *feeling* for these forms in *words*. With the prints before one, they could stand alone in their own significance, any associated thought should come as a matter of course,—of course one can see, must see the startling similarity of forms, the repetitions all through nature. I suppose the layman is amazed and has to exclaim, because he, a non-observer, sees for the first time through the artist. The artist then becomes an interpreter, a go-between.

The glorious new pepper Sonya brought me has kept me keyed up all week and caused me to expose eight negatives:—I'm not satisfied yet! These eight were all from the same viewpoint: rare for me to go through this. I started out with an underexposure—by the time I had developed the light had failed, and though I tripled my time again I undertimed! Again I tried, desperately determined to get it because I could ill afford the time. Giving an exposure of 50 minutes at 5:00 I timed correctly, but during exposure the fire siren shrieked, and promply the fire truck roared by followed by every car in town: the old porch trembled, my wobbly old camera wobbled, the pepper shimmied, and I developed a moving negative. Next morning I went at it again: interruptions came, afternoon came, light weak, prolonged exposures necessary,—result, one negative possible, but possible also to improve upon it.

I tried the light from the opposite side in the next morning light,—brilliant sun through muslin. Better! A reason for my failures. Three negatives made, on a new angle so different as to be another pepper. And more failures, this time sheer thoughtlessness: a background of picture backing was placed too close and came into focus when stopped down which I could not see but should have realized the corrugations plainly show and spoil the feeling. The one exposure from a new angle was perfect. So I have made eight negatives from the same angle and yet must go on. Today it is foggy and I am faced with an entirely new approach.

All this work has been done between moments of greeting tourists, printing, mounting, etc. Small wonder I have failed.

But the pepper is well worth all time, money, effort. If peppers would not wither, I certainly would not have attempted this one when so preoccupied. I must get this one today: it is beginning to show the strain and tonight should grace a salad. It has been suggested that I am a cannibal to eat my models after a masterpiece.

But I rather like the idea that they become part of me, enrich my blood as well as my vision. Last night we finished my now famous squash, and had several of my bananas in a salad.

Content

1. In defining "art" in paragraph 2, Weston distinguishes between *interpretation* and *revelation*. Explain what you think he means by this distinction and how it relates to the topic of "seeing vs. knowing" that he discusses later.
2. How does Weston define "the commercial man" as opposed to "the artist"? Cite specific examples from his journal in your answer.
3. Characterize Weston's attitude toward writing about art. What appears to be his goal in writing about photography? What are his chief fears?

Technique

1. What is the significance of the title? What theme does it suggest?
2. In your view, how successful is Weston at convincing you of his idea of photography? Which of these journal entries communicated his excitement most effectively. Why?
3. How would you characterize the form of these journal entries? Does the form satisfy Weston's own requirements of artistic form ("the most clarified, forceful way the seer can command for the presentation and communication of his experience")? Explain.
4. In your view, how well do Weston's references to specific photographic projects support his general statements about art and the role of artists?

Language

1. Explain what you think Weston means when he writes that he is no longer trying to "express himself" in art? How does he define "self-expression" and what reasons does he give for avoiding it?
2. Compare and contrast Weston's attempt to produce a perfect photograph of an object and his attempt to write a clear statement about his philosophy of art. Does he, for instance, sometimes experience the same frustration at not being able to discover the right form? What similarities and differences between photography and writing does Weston himself suggest?

3. How does Weston explain the difference between recording thoughts in a "daybook" and presenting them in a book that will accompany published photographs?

Vocabulary

revelation   pedantic   rhapsody
explicit   neurosis   corrugation
culmination   inhibition

Writing Suggestions

1. Weston writes, "I have learned something about writing! That it is one thing to jot down thoughts in a Daybook; another to present them to an audience. . .!" Write a paragraph or two about the differences between writing for a personal diary and writing for a wider audience. Include such considerations as form, tone, and conventions of grammar. Support your generalizations with references to your own experience with the two kinds of writing.

2. Write an essay that explains your "philosophy" of the art in which you are most interested—photography, drama, painting, pottery, or the like. As Weston does, try to combine general statements with references to actual artistic projects you have undertaken. You may also want to address the issue of "self-expression," defining it in your own terms.

3. Reproductions of some of Weston's photographs should be readily available in your library; look at some of the photographs carefully, then write a short paper in which you analyze the photographs in some of the terms Weston uses.

Film-making

Ingmar Bergman

Ingmar Bergman (b. 1918), one of the world's most acclaimed film-makers, began his career in 1943 with the screenplay for "Torment." "Smiles of a Summer Night" won a Cannes Film Festival award in 1956. Thereafter, a series of award-winning, critically acclaimed films confirmed his reputation; they include "The Seventh Seal" (1956), "Through A

Glass Darkly" (1961), "Cries and Whispers" (1972), and "Fanny and Alexander" (1983). He is perhaps best known for his use of surrealistic and symbolic techniques. The essay that follows explains the film-making process as Bergman sees it—an unpredictable, evocative, and almost magical form of art. Even as a child, Bergman tells us, he thought of himself as a "conjurer."

During the shooting of The Virgin Spring, we were up in the northern province of Dalarna in May and it was early in the morning, about half past seven. The landscape there is rugged, and our company was working by a little lake in the forest. It was very cold, about 30 degrees, and from time to time a few snowflakes fell through the gray, rain-dimmed sky. The company was dressed in a strange variety of clothing—raincoats, oil slickers, Icelandic sweaters, leather jackets, old blankets, coachmen's coats, medieval robes. Our men had laid out some ninety feet of rusty, buckling rail over the difficult terrain, to dolly the camera on. We were all helping with the equipment—actors, electricians, make-up men, script girl, sound crew—mainly to keep warm. Suddenly someone shouted and pointed toward the sky. Then we saw a crane floating high above the fir trees, and then another, and then several cranes, floating majestically in a circle above us. We all dropped what we were doing and ran to the top of a nearby hill to see the cranes better. We stood there for a long time, until they turned westward and disappeared over the forest. And suddenly I thought: this is what it means to make a movie in Sweden. This is what can happen, this is how we work together with our old equipment and little money, and this is how we can suddenly drop everything for the love of four cranes floating above the tree tops.

My association with film goes back to the world of childhood.

My grandmother had a very large old apartment in Uppsala. I used to sit under the dining-room table there, "listening" to the sunshine which came in through the gigantic windows. The cathedral bells went ding-dong, and the sunlight moved about and "sounded" in a special way. One day, when winter was giving way to spring and I was five years old, a piano was being played in the next apartment. It played waltzes, nothing but waltzes. On the wall hung a large picture of Venice. As the sunlight moved across the picture the water in the canal began to flow, the pigeons flew up from the square, people talked and gesticulated. Bells sounded, not those of

Uppsala Cathedral but from the picture itself. And the piano music also came from that remarkable picture of Venice.

A child who is born and brought up in a vicarage acquires an early familiarity with life and death behind the scenes. Father performed funerals, marriages, baptisms, gave advice and prepared sermons. The devil was an early acquaintance, and in the child's mind there was a need to personify him. This is where my magic lantern came in. It consisted of a small metal box with a carbide lamp—I can still remember the smell of the hot metal—and colored glass slides: Red Riding Hood and the Wolf, and all the others. And the Wolf was the Devil, without horns but with a tail and a gaping red mouth, strangely real yet incomprehensible, a picture of wickedness and temptation on the flowered wall of the nursery.

When I was ten years old I received my first, rattling film projector, with its chimney and lamp. I found it both mystifying and fascinating. The first film I had was nine feet long and brown in color. It showed a girl lying asleep in a meadow, who woke up and stretched out her arms, then disappeared to the right. That was all there was to it. The film was a great success and was projected every night until it broke and could not be mended any more.

This little rickety machine was my first conjuring set. And even today I remind myself with childish excitement that I am really a conjurer, since cinematography is based on deception of the human eyes. I have worked it out that if I see a film which has a running time of one hour, I sit through twenty-seven minutes of complete darkness—the blankness between frames. When I show a film I am guilty of deceit. I use an apparatus which is constructed to take advantage of a certain human weakness, an apparatus with which I can sway my audience in a highly emotional manner—make them laugh, scream with fright, smile, believe in fairy stories, become indignant, feel shocked, charmed, deeply moved or perhaps yawn with boredom. Thus I am either an impostor or, when the audience is willing to be taken in, a conjurer. I perform conjuring tricks with apparatus so expensive and so wonderful that any entertainer in history would have given anything to have it.

A film for me begins with something very vague—a chance remark or a bit of conversation, a hazy but agreeable event unrelated to any particular situation. It can be a few bars of music, a shaft of light across the street. Sometimes in my work at the theater I have envisioned actors made up for yet unplayed roles.

The Living Language

These are split-second impressions that disappear as quickly as they come, yet leave behind a mood—like pleasant dreams. It is a mental state, not an actual story, but one abounding in fertile associations and images. Most of all, it is a brightly colored thread sticking out of the dark sack of the unconscious. If I begin to wind up this thread, and do it carefully, a complete film will emerge.

This primitive nucleus strives to achieve definite form, moving in a way that may be lazy and half asleep at first. Its stirring is accompanied by vibrations and rhythms which are very special and unique to each film. The picture sequences then assume a pattern in accordance with these rhythms, obeying laws born out of and conditioned by my original stimulus.

If that embryonic substance seems to have enough strength to be made into a film, I decide to materialize it. Then comes something very complicated and difficult: the transformation of rhythms, moods, atmosphere, tensions, sequences, tones and scents into words and sentences, into an understandable screenplay.

This is an almost impossible task.

The only thing that can be satisfactorily transferred from that original complex of rhythms and moods is the dialogue, and even dialogue is a sensitive substance which may offer resistance. Written dialogue is like a musical score, almost incomprehensible to the average person. Its interpretation demands a technical knack plus a certain kind of imagination and feeling—qualities which are so often lacking, even among actors. One can write dialogue, but how it should be delivered, its rhythm and tempo, what is to take place between lines—all this must be omitted for practical reasons. Such a detailed script would be unreadable. I try to squeeze instructions as to location, characterization and atmosphere into my screenplays in understandable terms, but the success of this depends on my writing ability and the perceptiveness of the reader, which are not always predictable.

Now we come to essentials, by which I mean montage, rhythm and the relation of one picture to another—the vital third dimension without which the film is merely a dead product from a factory. Here I cannot clearly give a key, as in a musical score, nor a specific idea of the tempo which determines the relationship of the elements involved. It is quite impossible for me to indicate the way in which the film "breathes" and pulsates.

I have often wished for a kind of notation which would enable me to put on paper all the shades and tones of my vision, to record distinctly the inner structure of a film. For when I stand in the artistically devastating atmosphere of the studio, my hands and head full of the trivial and irritating details that go with motion-picture production, it often takes a tremendous effort to remember how I originally saw and thought out this or that sequence, or what was the relation between the scene of four weeks ago and that of today. If I could express myself clearly, in explicit symbols, then this problem would be almost eliminated and I could work with absolute confidence that whenever I liked I could prove the relationship between the part and the whole and put my finger on the rhythm, the continuity of the film.

Thus the script is a very imperfect *technical* basis for a film. And there is another important point in this connection which I should like to mention. Film has nothing to do with literature; the character and substance of the two art forms are usually in conflict. This probably has something to do with the receptive process of the mind. The written word is read and assimilated by a conscious act of the will in alliance with the intellect; little by little it affects the imagination and the emotions. The process is different with a motion picture. When we experience a film, we consciously prime ourselves for illusion. Putting aside will and intellect, we make way for it in our imagination. The sequence of pictures plays directly on our feelings.

Music works in the same fashion; I would say that there is no art form that has so much in common with film as music. Both affect our emotions directly, not via the intellect. And film is mainly rhythm; it is inhalation and exhalation in continuous sequence. Ever since childhood, music has been my great source of recreation and stimulation, and I often experience a film or play musically.

It is mainly because of this difference between film and literature that we should avoid making films out of books. The irrational dimensions of a literary work, the germ of its existence, is often untranslatable into visual terms—and it, in turn, destroys the special, irrational dimension of the film. If, despite this, we wish to translate something literary into film terms, we must make an infinite number of complicated adjustments which often bear little or no fruit in proportion to the effort expended.

I myself have never had any ambition to be an author. I do not want to write novels, short stories, essays, biographies, or even plays for the theater. I only want to make films—films about conditions, tensions, pictures, rhythms and characters which are in one way or another important to me. The motion picture, with its complicated process of birth, is my method of saying what I want to my fellow men. I am a film-maker, not an author.

Thus the writing of the script is a difficult period but a useful one, for it compels me to prove logically the validity of my ideas. In doing this, I am caught in a conflict—a conflict between my need to transmit a complicated situation through visual images, and my desire for absolute clarity. I do not intend my work to be solely for the benefit of myself or the few, but for the entertainment of the general public. The wishes of the public are imperative. But sometimes I risk following my own impulse, and it has been shown that the public can respond with surprising sensitivity to the most unconventional line of development.

When shooting begins, the most important thing is that those who work with me feel a definite contract, that all of us somehow cancel out our conflicts through working together. We must pull in one direction for the sake of the work at hand. Sometimes this leads to dispute, but the more definite and clear the "marching orders," the easier it is to reach the goal which has been set. This is the basis for my conduct as director, and perhaps the explanation of much of the nonsense that has been written about me.

While I cannot let myself be concerned with what people think and say about me personally, I believe that reviewers and critics have every right to interpret my films as they like. I refuse to interpret my work to others, and I cannot tell the critic what to think; each person has the right to understand a film as he sees it. Either he is attracted or repelled. A film is made to create reaction. If the audience does not react one way or another, it is an indifferent work and worthless.

I do not mean by this that I believe in being "different" at any price. A lot has been said about the value of originality, and I find this foolish. Either you are original or you are not. It is completely natural for artists to take from and give to each other, to borrow from and experience one another. In my own life, my great literary experience was Strindberg. There are works of his which can still make my hair stand on end—*The People of Hemsö*, for example.

And it is my dream to produce *Dream Play* some day. Olof Molander's production of it in 1934 was for me a fundamental dramatic experience.

On a personal level, there are many people who have meant a great deal to me. My father and mother were certainly of vital importance, not only in themselves but because they created a world for me to revolt against. In my family there was an atmosphere of hearty wholesomeness which I, a sensitive young plant, scorned and rebelled against. But that strict middle-class home gave me a wall to pound on, something to sharpen myself against. At the same time they taught me a number of values—efficiency, punctuality, a sense of financial responsibility—which may be "bourgeois" but are nevertheless important to the artist. They are part of the process of setting oneself severe standards. Today as a film-maker I am conscientious, hard-working and extremely careful; my films involve good craftsmanship, and my pride is the pride of a good craftsman.

Among the people who have meant something in my professional development is Torsten Hammaren of Gothenburg. I went there from Hälsingborg, where I had been head of the municipal theater for two years. I had no conception of what theater was; Hammaren taught me during the four years I stayed in Gothenburg. Then, when I made my first attempts at film, Alf Sjöberg—who directed *Torment*—taught me a great deal. And there was Lorens Marmstedt, who really taught me film-making from scratch after my first unsuccessful movie. Among other things I learned from Marmstedt is the one unbreakable rule: you must look at your own work very coldly and clearly; you must be a devil to yourself in the screening room when watching the day's rushes. Then there is Herbert Grevenius, one of the few who believed in me as a writer. I had trouble with script-writing, and was reaching out more and more to the drama, to dialogue, as a means of expression. He gave me great encouragement.

Finally, there is Carl Anders Dymling, my producer. He is crazy enough to place more faith in the sense of responsibility of a creative artist than in calculations of profit and loss. I am thus able to work with an integrity that has become the very air I breathe, and one of the main reasons I do not want to work outside of Sweden. The moment I lose this freedom I will cease to be a film-maker, because I have no skill in the art of compromise. My only significance in the world of film lies in the freedom of my creativity.

The Living Language

Today, the ambitious film-maker is obliged to walk a tightrope without a net. He may be a conjurer, but no one conjures the producer, the bank director, or the theater owners when the public refuses to go see a film and lay down the money by which producer, bank director, theater owner and conjurer can live. The conjurer may then be deprived of his magic wand; I would like to be able to measure the amount of talent, initiative and creative ability which has been destroyed by the film industry in its ruthlessly efficient sausage machine. What was play to me once has now become a struggle. Failure, criticism, public indifference all hurt more today than yesterday. The brutality of the industry is undisguised—yet that can be an advantage.

So much for people and the film business. I have been asked, as a clergyman's son, about the role of religion in my thinking and film-making. To me, religious problems are continuously alive. I never cease to concern myself with them; it goes on every hour of every day. Yet this does not take place on the emotional level, but on an intellectual one. Religious emotion, religious sentimentality, is something I got rid of long ago—I hope. The religious problem is an intellectual one to me: the relationship of my mind to my intuition. The result of this conflict is usually some kind of tower of Babel.

Philosophically, there is a book which was a tremendous experience for me: Eiono Kaila's *Psychology of the Personality*. His thesis that man lives strictly according to his needs—negative and positive—was shattering to me, but terribly true. And I built on this ground.

People ask what are my intentions with my films—my aims. It is a difficult and dangerous question, and I usually give an evasive answer: I try to tell the truth about the human condition, the truth as I see it. This answer seems to satisfy everyone, but it is not quite correct. I prefer to describe what I *would like* my aim to be.

There is an old story of how the cathedral of Chartres was struck by lightning and burned to the ground. Then thousands of people came from all points of the compass, like a giant procession of ants, and together they began to rebuild the cathedral on its old site. They worked until the building was completed—master builders, artists, laborers, clowns, noblemen, priests, burghers. But they all remained anonymous, and no one knows to this day who built the cathedral of Chartres.

Regardless of my own beliefs and my own doubts, which are unimportant in this connection, it is my opinion that art lost its basic creative drive the moment it was separated from worship. It severed an umbilical cord and now lives its own sterile life, generating and degenerating itself. In former days the artist remained unknown and his work was to the glory of God. He lived and died without being more or less important than other artisans; "eternal values," "immortality" and "masterpiece" were terms not applicable in his case. The ability to create was a gift. In such a world flourished invulnerable assurance and natural humility.

Today the individual has become the highest form and the greatest bane of artistic creation. The smallest wound or pain of the ego is examined under a microscope as if it were of eternal importance. The artist considers his isolation, his subjectivity, his individualism almost holy. Thus we finally gather in one large pen, where we stand and bleat about our loneliness without listening to each other and without realizing that we are smothering each other to death. The individualists stare into each other's eyes and yet deny the existence of each other. We walk in circles, so limited by our own anxieties that we can no longer distinguish between true and false, between the gangster's whim and the purest ideal.

Thus if I am asked what I would like the general purpose of my films to be, I would reply that I want to be one of the artists in the cathedral on the great plain. I want to make a dragon's head, an angel, a devil—or perhaps a saint—out of stone. It does not matter which; it is a sense of satisfaction that counts. Regardless of whether I believe or not, whether I am a Christian or not, I would play my part in the collective building of the cathedral.

Content

1. Bergman tells us that as a film-maker he thinks of himself as either a "conjurer" or an "impostor." What do you understand him to mean by this? How does he seem to distinguish between these two terms?

2. Bergman says that the idea for a film often begins with "something very vague—a chance remark or a bit of conversation." As a film viewer, to what extent do you value these small impressions, in contrast to the more obvious elements of a film, such as the plot and the characters?

3. Speculate about Bergman's reasons for calling the studio an "artistically devastating atmosphere."
4. Summarize Bergman's reasons for suggesting that we should avoid making films out of books. Do you agree with this point? Why or why not?

Technique

1. Bergman begins his essay with two anecdotes—one about making a film in Sweden, the other about early childhood memories. How do these contribute to our sense of Bergman's attitude toward film-making?
2. Bergman defines film-making in part by comparing it with music and contrasting it with literary works. How effective is this technique in giving us an idea about the nature of film-making? Explain.

Language

1. Review Bergman's reasons for maintaining that the script of a film is "a very imperfect technical basis for a film."
2. According to Bergman, why is dialogue a difficult element in film-making?
3. In your own words, explain what Bergman appears to want to communicate through the art of film-making. In his view, how does it differ from what a literary author tries to communicate?

Vocabulary

medieval	personify
embryonic	gesticulate

Writing Suggestions

1. Write a page or two of a film script, and then write a paragraph in which you assess the difficulties you encountered trying to write in this particular form.
2. Select a book that you have read that was subsequently made into a film. Write an essay in which you compare and contrast the literary

and cinematic versions; you may ultimately want to argue in favor of one version.
3. As a variation of the previous two writing suggestions, write a page or two of a script that adapts a novel you have read. Then write a paragrpah in which you assess the demands that are placed on a script writer who is adapting a novel. What does he or she add? What does he or she leave out?
4. Write a movie review. Evaluate the theme(s), the characters, the acting, the photography, and the action of the film. Pay attention, as well, to the kinds of detail that Bergman writes about, including the notion of the film-maker as a "conjurer"; that is, how easy was it for you to believe in the film? Explain.

To Make Up a Dance

Agnes de Mille

Agnes de Mille began designing dances in the 1950s; since then she has choreographed dozens of ballets and musicals and has won numerous awards for her productions. Her books about dance include Dance to the Piper *(1952),* To A Young Dancer *(1962), and* Speak to Me, Dance with Me *(1974). She has also contributed essays to* Esquire, Vogue, *and* Atlantic Monthly. *The following selection takes us deliberately through the initial process of choreography, from the first fragmentary ideas to the moment when the choreographer meets the dance company.*

By the time I composed *Rodeo* I had crystallized a technique of composing. It was in essentials the same method I had fumbled with in my early pantomimes, but it has routined itself with the subsequent Broadway practice into a true discipline.

To make up a dance, I still need, as I needed then, a pot of tea, walking space, privacy and an idea. When I first visualize the dance, I see the characters moving in color and costume. Before I go into rehearsal, I know what costumes the people wear and generally what color and texture. I also, to a large extent, hear the orchestral effects. Since I can have ideas only under the stress of emotion, I must create artificially an atmosphere which will induce this excitement. I shut myself in a studio and play gramophone music, Bach,

Mozart, Smetana, or almost any folk music in interesting arrangements. At this point I avoid using the score because it could easily become threadbare.

I start sitting with my feet up and drinking pots of strong tea, but as I am taken into the subject I begin to move and before I know it I am walking the length of the studio and acting full out the gestures and scenes. The key dramatic scenes come this way. I never forget a single nuance of them afterwards; I do usually forget dance sequences.

The next step is to find the style of gesture. This is done standing and moving, again behind locked doors and again with a gramophone. Before I find how a character dances, I must know how he walks and stands. If I can discover the basic rhythms of his natural gesture, I will know how to expand them into dance movement.

It takes hours daily of blind instinctive moving and fumbling to find the revealing gesture, and the process goes on for weeks before I am ready to start composing. Nor can I think any of this out sitting down. My body does it for me. It happens. That is why the choreographic process is exhausting. It happens on one's feet after hours of work, and the energy required is roughly the equivalent of writing a novel and winning a tennis match simultaneously. This is the kernel, the nucleus of the dance. All the design develops from this.

Having established a scenario and discovered the style and key steps, I then sit down at my desk and work out the pattern of the dances. If the score is already composed, the dance pattern is naturally suggested by and derived from the pattern of the music. If it remains to be composed as it does in all musical comedies, the choreographer goes it alone. This, of course, is harder. Music has an enormous suggestive power and the design of the composer offers a helpful blueprint.

All I know about dance composition I learned from folk dances. These are trustworthy models because they are the residuum of what has worked; there is no folk dance extant that did not work. I had first become aware of the importance of folk dancing when Dr. Lily Campbell asked me to reconstruct medieval singing games for her class in English Drama. I have studied folk forms since where possible. It must be remembered that outside of Louis Horst's classes in preclassic dance forms, choreography is taught nowhere and there are no texts on the subject. I learned by trial and error as did all my colleagues.

Through practice I have learned to project a whole composition in rough outline mentally and to know exactly how the dancers will look at any given moment moving in counterpoint in as many as five groups. As an aid in concentration, I make detailed diagrams and notes of my own arbitrary invention, intelligible only to me and only for about a week, but they are not comparable in exactness to music notation.

At this point, I am ready, God help me, to enter the rehearsal hall.

I don't believe any choreographer ever overcomes his terror of the waiting company. Imagine a composer facing the New York Philharmonic with his score projected in his head, not a note on paper, and the task before him of teaching the symphony by rote to the waiting men. He could start by whistling the main theme to the first violins.

Well, there they stand, the material of your craft, patient, disciplined, neat and hopeful in their black woolens. They will offer you their bodies for the next several weeks to milk the stuff of your ideas out of their muscles. They will submit to endless experimentation. They will find technique that has never been tried before; they will submerge their personalities and minds to the blindest, feeblest flutterings of yours. They will remember what you forget. They are pinning all the hopes of their past practices and future performings on the state of your brains. There they stand and consider you as you walk into the room. If they know you and are fond of you, it's easier. But at best, it's a soul-challenging moment.

Content

1. From de Mille's point of view, what does a choreographer have to know in order to create a dance? Did any of the background information she provided surprise you? Explain.
2. De Mille emphasizes the process of putting a dance together, but she does not explicitly say what the purpose of dance is or if it indeed has a purpose. Based on your knowledge of ballet or other dance forms, explain what you understand the purpose of dance to be.
3. Characterize de Mille's emotions when she first meets the dancers with whom she will work.
4. What value do folk dances have for de Mille as she choreographs a new dance?

Technique

1. De Mille's essay analyzes the process of choreography. Outline the essay according to the steps of that process and then assess the effectiveness of de Mille's description of the process.
2. De Mille provides several concrete details of her actual working environment. Which of these were most vivid? How did they contribute to your understanding of the choreographic process?
3. In paragraph 10, de Mille contrasts the role of the choreographer with that of a symphony composer. What differences does she seem to want to point out? How helpful was this analogy in explaining the job of a choreographer?

Language

1. De Mille explains the process of choreography without using technical terms. In your view, did this enhance or limit the success of her essay? Explain.
2. De Mille uses the term "dance composition." How is a dance composition similar to a written composition, an essay? Do some of the same principles of organization apply? Explain.
3. According to de Mille, folk dances are "trustworthy models because they are the residuum of what has worked." Look up the words "residuum" and "residue" in your dictionary, and then discuss what you believe she means by "residuum" in this instance.

Vocabulary

choreography	residuum	nucleus
ballet	nuance	

Writing Suggestions

1. Write an essay in which you compare and contrast ballet with the dancing that everyday people do. Pay particular attention to the purpose, style, or history of the two dance forms.
2. Attend a dance class or a rehearsal for a dance performance. Then write an essay, perhaps in the form of a newspaper article, in which

you describe the environment, some of the personalities of dancers and choreographers, and the process of instruction or rehearsal. Your audience should be similar to the one that de Mille seemed to have in mind.

How We Listen
Aaron Copland

Aaron Copland (b. 1900) is one of America's most respected and accomplished composers. His compositions include Billy the Kid *(1938),* Rodeo *(1942), and* Appalachian Spring *(1944). As these titles suggest, Copland has always attempted to blend the complexity of classical music with American folk themes and folk lengends. His essay, "How We Listen," reflects this comprehensive attitude toward music as well. Here Copland classifies several "levels" of listening, applies these to specific pieces of music, and then, in a more persuasive vein, convinces us that we should not simply listen* to *music but listen* for *something in music.*

We all listen to music according to our separate capacities. But, for the sake of analysis, the whole listening process may become clearer if we break it up into its component parts, so to speak. In a certain sense we all listen to music on three separate planes. For lack of a better terminology, one might name these: (1) the sensuous plane, (2) the expressive plane, (3) the sheerly musical plane. The only advantage to be gained from mechanically splitting up the listening process into these hypothetical planes is the clearer view to be had of the way in which we listen.

The simplest way of listening to music is to listen for the sheer pleasure of the musical sound itself. That is the sensuous plane. It is the plane on which we hear music without thinking, without considering it in any way. One turns on the radio while doing something else and absent-mindedly bathes in the sound. A kind of brainless but attractive state of mind is engendered by the mere sound appeal of the music.

You may be sitting in a room reading this book. Imagine one note struck on the piano. Immediately that one note is enough to change the atmosphere of the room—proving that the sound element in music is a powerful and mysterious agent, which it would be foolish to deride or belittle.

The surprising thing is that many people who consider themselves qualified music lovers abuse that plane in listening. They go to concerts in order to lose themselves. They use music as a consolation or an escape. They enter an ideal world where one doesn't have to think of the realities of everyday life. Of course they aren't thinking about the music either. Music allows them to leave it, and they go off to a place to dream, dreaming because of and apropos of the music yet never quite listening to it.

Yes, the sound appeal of music is a potent and primitive force, but you must not allow it to usurp a disproportionate share of your interest. The sensuous plane is an important one, but it does not constitute the whole story.

There is no need to digress further on the sensuous plane. Its appeal to every normal human being is self-evident. There is, however, such a thing as becoming more sensitive to the different kinds of sound stuff as used by various composers. For all composers do not use that sound stuff in the same way. Don't get the idea that the value of music is commensurate with its sensuous appeal or that the loveliest sounding music is made by the greatest composer. If that were so, Ravel would be a greater creator than Beethoven. The point is that the sound element varies with each composer, that his usage of sound forms an integral part of his style and must be taken into account when listening. The reader can see, therefore, that a more conscious approach is valuable even on this primary plane of music listening.

The second plane on which music exists is what I have called the expressive one. Here, immediately, we tread on controversial ground. Composers have a way of shying away from any discussion of music's expressive side. Did not Stravinsky himself proclaim that his music was an "object," a "thing," with a life of its own, and with no other meaning than its own purely musical existence? This intransigent attitude of Stravinsky's may be due to the fact that so many people have tried to read different meanings into so many pieces. Heaven knows it is difficult enough to say precisely what it is that a piece of music means, to say it definitely, to say it finally so that everyone is satisfied with your explanation. But that should not lead one to the other extreme of denying to music the right to be "expressive."

My own belief is that all music has an expressive power, some more and some less, but that all music has a certain meaning behind the notes and that that meaning behind the notes constitutes, after all, what the piece is saying, what the piece is about. This whole problem can be stated quite simply by asking, "Is there a meaning to music?" My answer to that would be, "Yes." And "Can you state in so many words what the meaning is?" My answer to that would be, "No." Therein lies the difficulty.

Simple-minded souls will never be satisfied with the answer to the second of these questions. They always want music to have a meaning, and the more concrete it is the better they like it. The more the music reminds them of a train, a storm, a funeral, or any other familiar conception the more expressive it appears to be to them. This popular idea of music's meaning—stimulated and abetted by the usual run of musical commentator—should be discouraged wherever and whenever it is met. One timid lady once confessed to me that she suspected something seriously lacking in her appreciation of music because of her inability to connect it with anything definite. That is getting the whole thing backward, of course.

Still, the question remains, How close should the intelligent music lover wish to come to pinning a definite meaning to any particular work? No closer than a general concept, I should say. Music expresses, at different moments, serenity or exuberance, regret or triumph, fury or delight. It expresses each of these moods, and many others, in a numberless variety of subtle shadings and differences. It may even express a state of meaning for which there exists no adequate word in any language. In that case, musicians often like to say that it has only a purely musical meaning. They sometimes go farther and say that *all* music has only a purely musical meaning. What they really mean is that no appropriate word can be found to express the music's meaning and that, even if it could, they do not feel the need of finding it.

But whatever the professional musician may hold, most musical novices still search for specific words with which to pin down their musical reactions. That is why they always find Tschaikovsky easier to "understand" than Beethoven. In the first place, it is easier to pin a meaning-word on a Tschaikovsky piece than on a Beethoven one. Much easier. Moreover, with the Russian composer, every time you come back to a piece of his it almost always says the same thing to you, whereas with Beethoven it is often quite difficult to put your finger right on what he is saying. And any musician will tell you that that is why Beethoven is the greater composer. Because music which always says the same thing to you will necessarily soon become dull music, but music whose meaning is slightly different with each hearing has a greater chance of remaining alive.

Listen, if you can, to the forty-eight fugue themes of Bach's *Well Tempered Clavichord*. Listen to each theme, one after another. You will soon realize that each theme mirrors a different world of feeling. You will also soon realize that the more beautiful a theme seems to you the harder it is to find any word that will describe it to your complete satisfaction. Yes, you will certainly know whether it is a gay theme or a sad one. You will be able, in other words, in your own mind, to draw a frame of emotional feeling around your theme. Now study the sad one a little closer. Try to pin down the exact quality of its sadness. Is it pessimistically sad or resignedly sad; is it fatefully sad or smilingly sad?

Let us suppose that you are fortunate and can describe to your own satisfaction in so many words the exact meaning of your chosen theme. There is still no guarantee that anyone else will be satisfied. Nor need they be. The important thing is that each one feel for himself the specific expressive quality of a theme or, similarly, an entire piece of music. And if it is a great work of art, don't expect it to mean exactly the same thing to you each time you return to it.

Themes or pieces need not express only one emotion, of course. Take such a theme as the first main one of the *Ninth Symphony*, for example. It is clearly made up of different elements. It does not say only one thing. Yet anyone hearing it immediately gets a feeling of strength, a feeling of power. It isn't a power that comes simply because the theme is played loudly. It is a power inherent in the theme itself. The extraordinary strength and vigor of the theme results in the listener's receiving an impression that a forceful statement has been made. But one should never try to boil it down to "the fateful hammer of life," etc. That is where the trouble begins. The musician, in his exasperation, says it means nothing but the notes themselves, whereas the nonprofessional is only too anxious to hang on to any explanation that gives him the illusion of getting closer to the music's meaning.

Now, perhaps, the reader will know better what I mean when

I say that music does have an expressive meaning but that we cannot say in so many words what that meaning is.

The third plane on which music exists is the sheerly musical plane. Besides the pleasurable sound of music and the expressive feeling that it gives off, music does exist in terms of the notes themselves and of their manipulation. Most listeners are not sufficiently conscious of this third plane. . . .

Professional musicians, on the other hand, are, if anything, too conscious of the mere notes themselves. They often fall into the error of becoming so engrossed with their arpeggios and staccatos that they forget the deeper aspects of the music they are performing. But from the layman's standpoint, it is not so much a matter of getting over bad habits on the sheerly musical plane as of increasing one's awareness of what is going on, in so far as the notes are concerned.

When the man in the street listens to the "notes themselves" with any degree of concentration, he is most likely to make some mention of the melody. Either he hears a pretty melody or he does not, and he generally lets it go at that. Rhythm is likely to gain his attention next, particularly if it seems exciting. But harmony and tone color are generally taken for granted, if they are thought of consciously at all. As for music's having a definite form of some kind, that idea seems never to have occurred to him.

It is very important for all of us to become more alive to music on its sheerly musical plane. After all, an actual musical material is being used. The intelligent listener must be prepared to increase his awareness of the musical material and what happens to it. He must hear the melodies, the rhythms, the harmonies, the tone colors in a more conscious fashion. But above all he must, in order to follow the line of the composer's thought, know something of the principles of musical form. Listening to all of these elements is listening on the sheerly musical plane.

Let me repeat that I have split up mechanically the three separate planes on which we listen merely for the sake of greater clarity. Actually, we never listen on one or the other of these planes. What we do is to correlate them—listening in all three ways at the same time. It takes no mental effort, for we do it instinctively.

Perhaps an analogy with what happens to us when we visit the theater will make this instinctive correlation clearer. In the theater, you are aware of the actors and actresses, costumes and sets, sounds and movements. All these give one the sense that the theater is a pleasant place to be in. They constitute the sensuous plane in our theatrical reactions.

The expressive plane in the theater would be derived from the feeling that you get from what is happening on the stage. You are moved to pity, excitement, or gayety. It is this general feeling, generated aside from the particular words being spoken, a certain emotional something which exists on the stage, that is analogous to the expressive quality in music.

The plot and plot development is equivalent to our sheerly musical plane. The playwright creates and develops a character in just the same way that a composer creates and develops a theme. According to the degree of your awareness of the way in which the artist in either field handles his material will you become a more intelligent listener.

It is easy enough to see that the theatergoer never is conscious of any of these elements separately. He is aware of them all at the same time. The same is true of music listening. We simultaneously and without thinking listen on all three planes.

In a sense, the ideal listener is both inside and outside the music at the same moment, judging it and enjoying it, wishing it would go one way and watching it go another—almost like the composer at the moment he composes it; because in order to write his music, the composer must also be inside and outside his music, carried away by it and yet coldly critical of it. A subjective and objective attitude is implied in both creating and listening to music.

What the reader should strive for, then, is a more *active* kind of listening. Whether you listen to Mozart or Duke Ellington, you can deepen your understanding of music only by being a more conscious and aware listener—not someone who is just listening, but someone who is listening *for* something.

Content

1. Copland divides the listening process into three components. List these and briefly explain in your own words what you understand them to be.
2. According to Copland, how close should a listener come to pinning a definite meaning to a piece of music? To what extent do you agree with his view? Explain.

3. From Copland's point of view, what is the "ideal listener" like? How close are you to being an ideal listener? Do you value the same things in music that Copland seems to value? Explain.

Technique

1. How satisfactory did you find the categories of listening that Copland sets out at the beginning of his essay? Are they, for instance, sufficiently distinguished from each other from your point of view? Explain.
2. What evidence does Copland provide for his contention that the meaning of a piece of music unaccompanied by words cannot be pinpointed? Did you find his reasoning convincing? Why or why not?
3. Copland emphasizes that he has "mechanically" divided the listening process into three parts and that the process is actually far more instinctive and fluid. In your view, was it necessary for him to qualify his analysis in such a way? Why or why not?
4. Copland draws an analogy between the theater and music. How effective was this comparison in explaining his analysis? In your view, did the analogy come at an appropriate moment in the essay? Why or why not?

Language

1. Based on Copland's observations about music, explain the chief differences between music and written or spoken language. That is, how do these forms of language communicate differently?
2. Music "may even express a state of meaning for which there exists no adequate word in any language," Copland writes. "In that case, musicians often like to say that it has only a purely musical meaning." To what extent do you agree with Copland's observations? Do you think the meaning of a musical piece can always be named in some way? Explain.
3. To deepen our understanding of the "language" of music, Copland suggests, we should be more *active* listeners. Do you agree with this point? To what extent do you consider yourself to be an "active listener"? Explain.

Vocabulary

apropos	inherent	fugue
deride	commensurate	correlation
usurp	engender	

Writing Suggestions

1. Copland suggests that for musical novices the music of Tschaikovsky is easier to understand than the music of Beethoven. Listen to a piece of music by each of these composers and then write a paragraph in which you agree with or take issue with Copland's view.
2. Write an essay in which you explain why you enjoy listening to one particular kind of music rather than another. What does the music mean to you? You may wish to compare and contrast classical music with the kind of music you enjoy more (or less). When did you first learn to enjoy it? Do your friends share your musical taste?
3. Write an essay in which you assess the value of listening to music. Why do you listen to music? Why should others listen to it? As Copland does, try to define the ideal listener.
4. Borrow a recording of a piece of music (without lyrics) that you have not heard before and write a "review" of it. Before writing the review, you may want to decide for yourself to what extent one should attempt to pinpoint the meaning of music. Also, be sure that the reader knows the criteria by which you are evaluating the piece of music.

A Flying Leap into the Unknown
Simone Signoret

Simone Signoret (b. 1921) is the stage name of Simone Kaminker, a German-born French actress who has starred in dozens of films and plays. She appeared in several French films, including "Casque d'Or" and "La Ronde," before becoming an international film star. In 1961 she won an Academy Award as best actress for her role in "Room at the Top." Her American films include "Ship of Fools" and "The Deadly Affair." In the following essay, Signoret turns her attention to the stage in an attempt to play Lady Macbeth. A problem with language, it seems, turned a great Shakespearean tragic role into a comic one.

Sorry, William Shakespeare, I won't do it again.

I don't want to brag, but I think I've probably sweated more blood working on the part of Lady Macbeth than anyone else in the world—which still didn't prevent my stunt from misfiring completely.

In the first place, it wasn't my stunt. The whole thing was amicably cooked up in London in 1966 by friends who wanted to do me a good turn. Alec Guinness wanted to play Macbeth again, which was an event quite sufficient in itself. Sir Alec, the great film star, wanted to return to the classics in a dusted-off, unclassical production. My lords, ladies and gentlemen, Shakespeare lovers the world over: you see this announced in the press, and immediately you book seats at the Royal Court Theatre two months in advance. When, a few days later, my lords, ladies, gents, Shakespeare lovers, etc., read that Lady Macbeth is to be played by Casque d'Or* Alice Aisgill,† you may scratch your heads and wonder why. Nonetheless, you book those precious Royal Court Theatre seats, possibly in the same frame of mind as you'd get tickets for a royal charity ball, in which a trapeze act, to be performed in the flies without a net by a blues singer, is billed.

It still happens to me today that I wake up of a morning and say to myself: "Great! This evening I don't have to play Lady Macbeth!"

An unaccomplished trapeze artist may fall. Some have fallen, and have required years of physical therapy to recover from having tried to prove for one evening that they could spread out from their own branch and, with the speed of light, learn something which someone else had been studying from the cradle on. Many of them don't fall, fortunately. They heave a great sigh of relief as they return to the sawdust of that unfamiliar circus ring.

I've never had the courage to learn tightrope walking or a wild animal act, a magician's routine, how to leap through a flaming hoop, roller skate or ride a bicycle you can take apart. They are definitely not up my alley! So what on earth—or in heaven—possessed me to even begin to suspect that I would be able to play (for a charity ball which was to drag on for a full month of an "exceptional run") Lady Macbeth when I was incapable of reproducing the Shakespearean accents they had every right to expect to hear?

"Nou pahtim cink sans may pah un prron ramphor
Nou nou vim troa milan arrrivan topor"‡

wouldn't sound right to a Frenchman's ear, even if Laurence Olivier made a special trip to Paris to offer us his personal version of Rod-

---
*The film for which Signoret received her first (of three) British "Academy Awards."
†The part played by Signoret in the British film, "Room at the Top."
‡*Nous partîmes cinq cents mais par prompt renfort.*
Nous nous rîmes trois mille en arrivant au port.

rique. But this phenomenon will never happen, I know, because he told me so with much gentleness and humor the day after our opening.

I've probably exaggerated in the example I've just given. It's actually quite tolerable, my little French accent in English; some even find it charming. Only, unfortunately, speaking English quite fluently doesn't mean that you can speak Shakespeare, sing Shakespeare, scan Shakespeare's rhythms—in short, act Shakespeare. Even if someone has invited you to participate in a nonconformist and dusted-off production like that at the Royal Court.

Nevertheless, I took the thing very seriously indeed. I bought six different editions of Macbeth and retired to Autheuil to study my text for two months before rehearsals began. Then there would be two months of rehearsal in London before the opening night of that much heralded series of thirty-one special performances.

Six different editions . . . That was a foreigner's idea to begin with. No Anglo-Saxon actress would ever have taken it into her mind to read and compare all those texts. The only result of doing it was to still further deepen the mysteries that all good Shakespeareans have decided to put aside or ignore or treasure, and for good reason.

In one edition a speech of Lady Macbeth would end with a question mark, in another it would be between quotation marks, and a third would simply end with a period. In all of them, however, it was quite clear that the Macbeths had never had a child, and yet at a certain moment (Act I, Scene 7, if you want real pinpoint precision), Lady M. goes on about this babe from whose boneless gums she would have plucked her nipple! Mystery, mystery! So, having retired to the heart of Normandy, I was trying to solve these riddles. I was having a great time. My friends who innocently dropped in to say hello were lured into a terrible trap from which there was no escape. They were handed one of the six editions and made to listen to me "recite." As there were quite a few difficult lines, it was a little like playing "the game." Every evening during that month of terrifying "exceptional" performances, when it came time to say "Nor place, nor time," the beautiful face of my friend Françoise Arnoul would appear before me, her finger on her wrist watch to remind me of the word "time," which I had such trouble memorizing.

With my lines learned by heart, I appeared at the first reading. I was very proud of my "by heart." Unfortunately, all my bad habits were already locked in place. I thought I had the rhythm right, but

A Flying Leap into the Unknown

it was all wrong. I had done almost everything upside down. It's only today that I fully realize to what extent your pride in trying to take a flying leap into the unknown can make you forget everything that your natural instinct has taught you ever since you began acting.

For two months, day after day, I had slid imperceptibly into the traps waylaying bad actors. If you know all the words and never really think about the reasons that have made your character say what he or she does, you fall into that trap. It was a perfect illustration justifying the phrase already quoted: "Heavens, you must have a marvelous memory."

I don't mean to say that I didn't have ideas about the character of Lady M., nor do I mean to say that I hadn't come to understand her as I read my six different texts. I'd even go so far as to say that I psychoanalyzed her, followed her scent, and took her apart and put her back together again. Only, you see, the important thing was "knowing the lines." There'd be time enough later to find out why she said them.

Our director, William Gatskill, Alec Guinness and the whole cast did everything they could to help me during those two months of rehearsal. They tried to rid me of the bad habits I had firmly contracted while I thought I was preparing myself piously to serve Shakespeare. I've often thought since that they must have been utterly nonplused after that first read-through. Maybe they met in the pub next door and told each other that it would turn out all right; I'd get the hang of that lovely language. After all, there were still two months. . . .

At the end of the first week I thought I had improved. They thought so too; at least that's what they said. It's probably at that moment (when it still wasn't too late) that less kindly people would have politely asked me to go home. It would have been easy to find an excuse for the press and the booking office. There are always those strange viruses that actors catch while waiting in the wings, which prevent them from honoring their contracts. I think I would have been perfectly capable of finding answers to the questions that would have been asked if they had decided to drop me. "No," I would have said, "I'm not capable of doing Lady Macbeth. Please excuse me; anyone can make a mistake."

When these things happen to a beginner, they're cruel. But when they happen to someone who, as they say, has a reputation, they're bitter but you get over them.

But since my friends were kind, if the idea of booting me out had ever crossed their minds, they suppressed it. Or perhaps they got so used to my flaws that they stopped noticing them—or possibly they even liked them? That's what's called a collective aberration. It's the great invisible monster curled up in the dress circle of the empty theater in which one rehearses in a euphoric condition. In order to track down the monster and kill him, often the eye and ear of an outsider is sufficient, but one who has real affection for the cast—a family friend. It has to be someone who isn't afraid of being unpopular when he tells the truth.

"Whoa, there! Stop this massacre, friends! You've goofed badly."

But no one came to stop the massacre while there was still time. Those who saw our last rehearsals probably thought that it was too late to pull the alarm cord. Montand came for two days while there was still time—it was two weeks before opening night. His criticism was pertinent, but I decided to ignore it, sure as I was of my Anglo-Saxon accomplishments.

It was a Lady M. frozen stiff with stage fright but sure that she had been right to persist who made her entry onstage that first night. By the next day she was a poor creature who would have given millions to be elsewhere. With one or two exceptions, the entire press detested the whole production. The critics were cruel to Gatskill, whose nonconformist courage had shocked them. They were not gentle with Alec, whose interpretations had often surprised them. And as far as I was concerned, they were the worst one could dream of. They weren't cruel, they weren't hurtful, they were clearly miserable. They were terribly sorry. They were sorry, they said, because they liked me so much. But honestly . . . ! I was impossible, inaudible, unbearable. Yet some of them must have understood me. They were the ones who said they had suffered intensely listening to me suffer with those words. They had pitied me. But that's generally not the purpose in the mind of an actress lady out to amaze people by the force of her cold determination.

The day after the opening I was faced with thirty evenings, a century, during which I was to appear and be judged every evening, since the theater had been sold clean out since the announcement of the good news of Shakespeare at the Royal Court.

I have said that I would have been given millions to be elsewhere. This is probably the moment for me to point out that Alec and I were paid, during the run of that play, at the popular-theater rate: seven pounds a day. But I know I would have tried to find those millions the next day, and the day after that, and all those thirty days, in order not to have to set foot on that stage in front of all those people who already knew that I wouldn't be able to make it, but who were there because they had reserved their tickets in advance. They were there, and I could see them mouthing my lines along with me, and better than I could. Sometimes, though, there were some Japanese doing "London by Night." I didn't seem to bother them.

The cast was marvelously kind to me. They would see me each evening trembling with fear before my first entrance onstage, letter in hand. That letter, which Lady Macbeth reads to the audience because it's a résumé of the preceding action and a premonition of the crimes to come, should be read with the contained passion and icy-cold calm of a totally resolute woman. That's difficult when the paper is shaking in your hand as though it were a morning newspaper held on a bumpy bus.

On the third evening the last reviews had fallen before mine eyes—or rather on my head—just before I went onstage. There wasn't a reason in the world, I thought, that everyone in the audience hadn't read them too. And so it happened that during my first scene with Alec Guinness, during my third or fourth speech, I suddenly stopped. He caught on and saved me. He slid in, "If we should fail . . ." which comes much later in the scene. He used it to save his friend, who was in the process of drowning, having "dried up." It helped me to go on, and since we were playing to an audience of connoisseurs, they applauded. When the time came for him to repeat "If we should fail," this time in context, they applauded again.

I must have made some improvement during those four weeks. And, as it sometimes happens when the thrashing is unmerciful, we even had our defenders—and our fans.

But still, Will Shakespeare, I swear I'll never do it again.

Content

1. In your own words, summarize Signoret's attitude toward her own performance. In answering this question, consider Signoret's tone and find specific details in the essay to support your answer.

2. Why, according to Signoret, is speaking English (with a "charming accent") and knowing one's lines "by heart" not enough to act Shakespeare? What does the essay suggest to you about the difficulties of becoming proficient in another language?
3. In this essay, Signoret paints a vivid picture of preparing for and then failing in a major role. In what way has this altered or enriched your vision of the actor's work?

Technique

1. Signoret describes her performance in *Macbeth* by using several analogies, including that of a blues singer performing a trapeze act. Find one or two other analogies and discuss how they add to the clarity of her description.
2. Signoret repeats several times that there were to be 31 special performances. Why? How effective is this technique of repetition?
3. What is the effect of Signoret's final sentence?

Language

1. In the opening paragraph, Signoret refers to playing Lady Macbeth as her "stunt." Why do you believe she selected this word, and what image does it convey?
2. Signoret, a native French speaker, writes here of the difficulties of performing a Shakespearean role in English. Yet she demonstrates her proficiency in English by using several colloquialisms such as "not up my alley" and "get the hang of it." Find other examples of colloquial English and discuss their effect on the essay as a whole.
3. What does Signoret mean when she says she thought she was "preparing (herself) piously to serve Shakespeare"? Why would she use the word "serve" here? And why "piously"?

Vocabulary

connoisseurs
piously
nonplused

aberration
euphoric

Writing Suggestions

1. Signoret played games to memorize her lines—thinking of her friend's watch, for instance, to remember the word "time." Think of some memory-assisting "game" you have played to help you learn something, and write a paragraph in which you teach your reader the process.
2. Write an essay describing and evaluating an excellent performance by an actor that you have watched recently. What made the actor succeed? Use specific details and strong analysis to support your evaluation of the performance.
3. Write an essay in which you analyze your reaction to having once tried something that was "not up your alley." Try to be, as Signoret is here, frank in your appraisal of both your performance and your response to the attempt.

Writers on Writing

8

Part One of this reader offers essays that suggest the rich possibilities of language, not just as a way to communicate but also as a subject of discussion. Parts Two through Seven enlarge on these possibilities inasmuch as they include essays that are chiefly about language and its connection with a specific area of our lives—sports, technology, politics, and so on. This last section preserves the intent of the first and subsequent ones, except that here we have focused on writers reflecting on what it means to write and to be writers.

As with the selections throughout the reader, these essays reflect a wide range of experience; thus, the writers here include a highly acclaimed British novelist and feminist writer, a world-famous Welsh poet, a young woman who died before she could realize her dream of becoming a professional writer, a surgeon, an essayist and novelist from California, a scientist, and a distinguished American poet who did not publish his first volume of poems until he was 54.

One likely place to catch a glimpse of writers as they are thinking about writing is in their diaries. Accordingly, we have included entries from the diaries of Virginia Woolf, a famous and accomplished writer, and Anne Frank, who at the time of her entry had no hope of ever having her prose read by anyone and who could only dream of accomplishment and fame.

The excerpt from Woolf's diary reveals more self-doubt and frustration than we might perhaps expect from a writer who has mastered her craft. She records a "guilty intensity" that afflicts her when she reads her own diary, which is "often so ungrammatical, and crying for a word altered. . . ." As Woolf herself points out, however, this "rough and random" style leads to mastery because it provides practice, it allows the mind to stretch and associate freely, and it may even form the basis for a work of art.

The selection from Anne Frank's remarkable diary shows her to have had the same extraordinary capacity for self-criticism that Woolf possessed. "I am the best and sharpest critic of my own work," she announces. Although she begins the entry by expressing the misery and terror of her family's fugitive existence, she quickly turns to the subject of her writing: the pieces she has actually undertaken and the works she hopes to write that will allow her to "go on living after [her] death." In the very act of writing about writing, she unwittingly achieved this immortality, for in a world that sought to obliterate her every opportunity to learn and write—even to survive—her elegant, honest diary is at once a gesture of courage and the work of art she hoped to produce. The perseverance that this entry demonstrates is a triumph of spirit; the record of her courage and aspirations is a triumph of language.

From two diarists, the section proceeds to two poets, the Welshman Dylan Thomas and the American William Stafford. We often think of poets as writers who observe the world more intensely than most others perceive it. In "The Colours of Words," Dylan Thomas reminds us that words themselves are part of the world that poets envision differently. Like Frank's diary entry, Thomas' notes discuss a writer's awakening, except that Thomas reaches back beyond adolescence to his earliest awareness of words. Throughout this piece, he articulates the physical, palpable effect words had on him, regardless of their meaning. "These words were, to me, as notes of bells, the sounds of musical instruments, the noises of wind, sea, and rain, the rattle of milkcarts . . .," he writes. When he became a writer, this relationship to the physical quality of words persisted: "I do not like writing *about* words, because then I often use bad and wrong and stale and woolly words. What I like to do is to treat words as a craftsman does his wood or stone or what-have-you, to hew, carve, mould, coil, polish, and plane them. . . ."

In "Writing," William Stafford reveals himself to be less of a bard than Thomas and more of a patient, meditative poet. This difference, however, by no means diminishes his enthusiasm for the possibilities of language. In fact, "possibility" is the keynote of Stafford's essay: The process of writing he follows is, he tells us, "like fishing." Accepting the linguistic inventiveness with which he thinks we all were born, he allows himself to be completely receptive to the various paths that writing places before him; he is "headlong to discover." Thus, the chief "skill" he cultivates is the capacity to rely on "stray impulses that will, with trust, find occasional patterns that are satisfying." Like Woolf, therefore, Stafford perceives even the opportunities for failure in this process as possibilities for undreamed-of discoveries.

At first glance, Joan Didion's attitude toward writing seems completely contradictory to Woolf's and Stafford's. Early in her essay, "Why I Write," she calls writing "an aggressive, even a hostile act." As her essay develops, however, it reveals notions of writing-as-discovery that are similar to the processes that Woolf and Stafford describe. In college, Didion tells us, she failed at thinking, although we subsequently find out that she failed only at one kind of thinking and succeeded at another—meditating on images. This gift for meditation in turn led her to discover that she was a writer, which she defines as "a person whose most absorbed and passionate hours are spent arranging words on pieces of paper." Mental pictures remain her chief source of inspiration: The image of an actress walking through a Las Vegas casino, for instance, leads to an entire novel. Like Thomas' infatuation with words and like Stafford's "fishing," Didion's obsession with "shimmering images" leads her to discover why she is writing.

Writing is not the profession of the two remaining essayists here, but it is still central to their life's work. Without writing, the surgeon Richard Selzer finds medicine to be incomplete: By writing about his profession he can avoid both the despair and the vanity which too often, he feels, characterize doctors. The zest and exuberance with which he describes the body and its afflictions argue for (and, to a great extent, fulfill) his ideal of the "writing doctor," the person who can make an ailing body whole again with medicine and make the meaning of medicine whole with words.

In some ways, Robert Day's "What is a Scientific Paper?" runs against the grain of the other pieces in this section. Much of the essay concerns the product of writing—"a published report describing original research results"—rather than the process, which Woolf, Frank, Thomas, Stafford, Didion, and Selzer variously define and celebrate. But as Day himself suggests, the form and intent of the scientific paper have, like an organism, evolved through "tradition, editorial practices, scientific ethics, and the interplay of printing and publishing procedures." Further, he stresses the unavoidable fact of virtually every scientist's life: No matter how painstaking and inspired a scientist's work may be, it must ultimately take shape in a report. Thus, writes Day, "a scientist will spend months or years of hard work to secure his data, and then unconcernedly let much of their value be lost because of his lack of interest in the communication process."

Various implicit definitions of "the writer" emerge from these essays, notes, and diary entries. For Woolf and Frank, the writer is completely dedicated, almost obsessively working to perfect the craft and prepare the mind. For Thomas, the writer is one who has fallen in love with words themselves, while Stafford and Didion are somewhat less driven, allowing themselves to be led toward discovery by an image, a phrase, even a stray syllable. For the surgeon, Richard Selzer admits, writing may not be a practical necessity, but only the "writing doctor" can understand the complete significance of medicine for mankind. Similarly, by defining the scientific paper, Robert Day reminds scientists that they are inevitably writers, and that good science, for better or worse, depends upon good writing.

A Writer's Diary

Virginia Woolf

> *Virginia Woolf (1882–1941) was a distinguished British novelist and feminist writer, a member of the famous group of British intellectuals known as the Bloomsbury Group. Woolf's books include* Jacob's Room *(1922),* Mrs. Dalloway *(1925),* To the Lighthouse *(1927), and* A Room of One's Own *(1929). In the following selection from* A Writer's Diary *(1954), she analyzes her own writing habits and speculates about whether a diary might in itself constitute an art form.*

Easter Sunday, April 20th

In the idleness which succeeds any long article, and Defoe is the second leader this month, I got out this diary and read, as one always does read one's own writing, with a kind of guilty intensity. I confess that the rough and random style of it, often so ungrammatical, and crying for a word altered, afflicted me somewhat. I am trying to tell whichever self it is that reads this hereafter that I can write very much better; and take no time over this; and forbid her to let the eye of man behold it. And now I may add my little compliment to the effect that it has a slapdash and vigour and sometimes hits an unexpected bull's eye. But what is more to the point is my belief that the habit of writing thus for my own eye only is good practice. It loosens the ligaments. Never mind the misses and the stumbles. Going at such a pace as I do I must make the most direct and instant shots at my object, and thus have to lay hands on words, choose them and shoot them with no more pause than is needed to put my pen in the ink. I believe that during the past year I can trace some increase of ease in my professional writing which I attribute to my casual half hours after tea. Moreover there looms ahead of me the shadow of some kind of form which a diary might attain to. I might in the course of time learn what it is that one can make of this loose, drifting material of life; finding another use of it than the use I put it to, so much more consciously and scrupulously, in fiction. What sort of diary should I like mine to be? Something loose knit and yet not slovenly, so elastic that it will embrace anything, solemn, slight or beautiful that comes into my mind. I should like it to resemble some deep old desk, or capacious hold-all, in which one flings a mass of odds and ends without looking them through. I should like to come back, after a year or two, and find that the collection had sorted itself and refined itself and coalesced, as such deposits so mysteriously do, into a mould, transparent enough to reflect the light of our life, and yet steady, tranquil compounds with the aloofness of a work of art. The main requisite, I think on re-reading my old volumes, is not to play the part of censor, but to write as the mood comes or of anything whatever; since I was curious to find how I went for things put in haphazard, and found the significance to lie where I never saw it at the time. But looseness quickly becomes slovenly. A little effort is needed to face a character or an incident which needs to be recorded. Nor can one let the pen write without guidance; for fear of becoming slack and untidy like Vernon Lee. Her ligaments are too loose for my taste.

Content

1. In this passage, Woolf does not explicitly reveal the purpose of her diary. Judging from what she writes about the diary here, what do you believe that purpose is?

2. In the opening lines of this paragraph, Woolf says that when she reads her diary entries, she does so with "a kind of guilty intensity." Why do you think re-reading the diary makes her feel this way? In what sense do you think she feels "guilty"?
3. In her opening "apology," Woolf states that she wants to tell "whatever self it is" that reads the diary later that she can write better than this. To whom do you think she is referring? Why?
4. In the end, Woolf seems to favor an approach to the diary that would blend haphazard thoughts with "effort." What do you think she means by this paradoxical combination, and why do you believe she prefers this approach?

Technique

1. Because this passage is a diary entry, we assume that the intended audience is Woolf herself. Re-read the passage carefully; do you believe she had only herself in mind as she wrote this, or do you think there is a broader intended audience? Be prepared to support your conclusion with specific details from the passage.
2. Woolf's discussion of her diary begins with negative comments about her writing. This negativism is soon replaced, however, with speculation about the ideal diary and even with a cautious optimism about her own. How does this developmental pattern affect your reaction to her diary?

Language

1. Woolf's writing in this passage is rich in figurative language. Find and read carefully the following examples: "direct and instant shots at my object," "lay hands" on words . . . and "shoot them." What is the common source of this imagery, and what do you think it suggests about Woolf's attitude toward writing?
2. Find one or two other examples of the figurative language Woolf uses to describe her writing or her diary and discuss their effectiveness as means of communicating her feelings about writing.
3. At the end of this entry, Woolf says that she doesn't want her diary to become "slovenly." Look this word up in your dictionary and discuss what you believe Woolf means by it here.

Vocabulary

slovenly   afflicted   capacious
slapdash   elastic   requisite

Writing Suggestion

1. Virginia Woolf speaks of her reasons for keeping a diary—to find, in part, eventually, what "one can make of this loose, drifting material of life." If you have ever kept a diary, or if you keep a journal now, write an essay analyzing why you write it, what you gain from the process. How does the nature and form of your diary/journal reflect its purpose for you?

I Want to Write
Anne Frank

Anne Frank (1929–1945) lived in hiding in Amsterdam with her parents for over two years before being discovered by the German Gestapo in 1944 and transported to Bergen–Belsen concentration camp near Hanover, where she died. Her diary (Het Achterhus) was first published in 1947 and first translated from the Dutch in 1952. It was made into both a prize-winning play and a motion picture, and it has been translated into 30 languages. Her hiding place on Prinzengracht Canal in Amsterdam has become a museum and a shrine. In the following diary entry, she reflects on her predicament, her dream of becoming a writer, and what writing already means to her: "I can shake off everything if I write; my sorrows disappear, my courage is reborn."

Tuesday, 4 April, 1944

Dear Kitty,

For a long time I haven't had any idea of what I was working for any more; the end of the war is so terribly far away, so unreal, like a fairy tale. If the war isn't over by September I shan't go to school any more, because I don't want to be two years behind. Peter filled my days—nothing but Peter, dreams and thoughts until Saturday, when I felt so utterly miserable; oh, it was terrible. I was holding back my tears all the while I was with Peter, then laughed with Van Daan over lemon punch, was cheerful and excited, but the moment I was alone I knew that I would have to cry my heart out. So, clad in my nightdress, I let myself go and slipped down onto the floor. First I said my long prayer very earnestly, then I cried with my head on my arms, my knees bent up, on the bare floor, completely folded up. One large sob brought me back to earth again, and I quelled my tears because I didn't want them to hear anything in the next room. Then I began trying to talk some courage into myself. I could only say: "I must, I must, I must . . ." Completely stiff from the unnatural position, I fell against the side of the bed and fought on, until I climbed into bed again just before half past ten. It was over!

And now it's all over. I must work, so as not to be a fool, to get on, to become a journalist, because that's what I want! I know that I can write, a couple of my stories are good, my descriptions of the "Secret Annexe" are humorous, there'a lot in my diary that speaks, but—whether I have real talent remains to be seen.

"Eva's Dream" is my best fairy tale, and the queer thing about it is that I don't know where it comes from. Quite a lot of "Cady's Life" is good too, but, on the whole, it's nothing.

I am the best and sharpest critic of my own work. I know myself what is and what is not well written. Anyone who doesn't write doesn't know how wonderful it is; I used to bemoan the fact that I couldn't draw at all, but now I am more than happy that I can at least write. And if I haven't any talent for writing books or newspaper articles, well, then I can always write for myself.

I want to get on; I can't imagine that I would have to lead the same sort of life as Mummy and Mrs. Van Daan and all the women who do their work and are then forgotten. I must have something besides a husband and children, something that I can devote myself to!

I want to go on living even after my death! And therefore I am grateful to God for giving me this gift, this possibility of developing myself and of writing, of expressing all that is in me.

I can shake off everything if I write; my sorrows disappear, my courage is reborn. But, and that is the great question, will I ever be able to write anything great, will I ever become a journalist or a writer? I hope so, oh, I hope so very much, for I can recapture everything when I write, my thoughts, my ideals and my fantasies.

I haven't done anything more to "Cady's Life" for ages; in my mind I know exactly how to go on, but somehow it doesn't flow from my pen. Perhaps I never shall finish it, it may land up in the wastebasket, or the fire . . . that's a horrible idea, but then I think to myself, "At the age of fourteen and with so little experience, how can you write about philosophy?"

So I go on again with fresh courage, I think I shall succeed, because I want to write!

Yours, Anne

Content

1. As revealed in this passage, Frank has several reasons for wanting to write. What are they?
2. Anne Frank wrote her diary when she was 14 years old, hiding from the Nazis with her family and other Jews. This entry reveals both typical adolescent emotions and, paradoxically, surprisingly sophisticated reasoning that suggest her situation and her sensitivity set her apart from the "typical" teenager. Find examples of both levels of expression and discuss how they work together to present a picture of the writer.
3. Although this is not a traditional essay, we can nevertheless identify a theme that unites the many thoughts expressed here. That theme is the need for bravery or, to use Frank's recurring word, "courage." The theme appears frequently, for instance in her determination to quell her tears. Find other examples of Frank's will to be courageous and discuss how they contribute to the tone of the passage.
4. Frank has unusual self-assurance for a 14-year-old. For instance, she believes she is a good writer. Find the sentences that reveal this confidence and discuss why she believes in her writing ability.
5. Even while she clearly takes pride in her writing, Frank can also, like Virginia Woolf, be a severe self-critic. Find examples of her criticism and discuss their effect on your reading of the more self-confident passages.

Technique

1. Frank's diary entry has no organizational pattern of the sort we expect to find in a traditional essay. It is instead stream of consciousness writing; she allows her thoughts to flow freely and she records them as they occur to her. Make a list of the topics that Frank covers, and discuss why, in your opinion, such an approach does or does not make the passage interesting reading.
2. The passage is rich in details that allow the reader to "picture" both the scene and the mood that Frank describes. Find one or two examples of concrete details and discuss their effectiveness.
3. Given Frank's youth and her dramatic, tragic situation, the reader of her diary should be particularly alert to its tone. In your own words, explain what you believe to be the tone of this passage. Be prepared to support your opinion with specific examples from the diary.

Language

1. At the end of the first paragraph, Frank says, "It was over." To what do you believe she is referring? Why?
2. Frank begins paragraph 5 by saying, "I want to get on." What do you believe she means by this statement?

Vocabulary

quelled   clad
bemoan   earnestly

Writing Suggestion

1. Anne Frank calls herself her own "best and sharpest critic." Write a paragraph or a brief essay in which you act as your own best and sharpest critic. Avoid writing what you think an English teacher would think are your strengths and weaknesses. Like Frank, assess your writing according to your own criteria. If you can, refer to specific pieces of writing—term papers, essays, short stories, letters of application.

The Colours of Words

Dylan Thomas

Dylan Thomas (1914–1953) was born and raised in Swansea, Wales, and after finishing school worked for the South Wales Evening Post. *The impact of his first book,* Eighteen Poems *(1934), was immediate and profound. He became known for his powerful, lyrical use of language and for his public reading of poetry. He died, in fact, during a reading tour of American universities. In the following essay, Thomas recounts his first conscious experiences of language and poetry. He also vividly describes his intense response to words and their capacity to express "the common fun of earth."*

You want to know why and how I first began to write poetry, and which poets or kind of poetry I was first moved and influenced by.

To answer the first part of this question, I should say I wanted to write poetry in the beginning because I had fallen in love with words. The first poems I knew were nursery rhymes, and before I could read them for myself I had come to love just the words of them, the words alone. What the words stood for, symbolised, or meant, was of very secondary importance; what mattered was the *sound* of them as I heard them for the first time on the lips of the remote and incomprehensible grown-ups who seemed, for some reason, to be living in my world. And these words were, to me, as the notes of bells, the sounds of musical instruments, the noises of wind, sea, and rain, the rattle of milkcarts, the clopping of hooves on cobbles, the fingering of branches on a window pane, might be to someone, deaf from birth, who has miraculously found his hearing. I did not care what the words said, overmuch, nor what happened to Jack & Jill & the Mother Goose rest of them; I cared for the shapes of sound that their names, and the words describing their actions, made in my ears; I cared for the colours the words cast on my eyes. I realise that I may be, as I think back all that way, romanticising my reactions to the simple and beautiful words of those pure poems; but that is all I can honestly remember, however much time might have falsified my memory. I fell in love—that is the only expression I can think of—at once, and am still at the mercy of words, though sometimes now, knowing a little of their behaviour very well, I think I can influence them slightly and have even learned to beat them now and then, which they appear to enjoy. I tumbled for words at once. And, when I began to read the nursery rhymes for myself, and, later, to read other verses and ballads, I knew that I had discovered the most important things, to me, that could be ever. There they were, seemingly lifeless, made only of black and white, but out of them, out of their own being came love and terror and pity and pain and wonder and all the other vague abstractions that make our ephemeral lives dangerous, great, and bearable. Out of them came the gusts and grunts and hiccups and heehaws of the common fun of the earth; and though what the words meant was, in its own way, often deliciously funny enough, so much funnier seemed to me, at that almost forgotten time, the shape and shade and size and noise of the words as they hummed, strummed, jigged and galloped along. That was the time of innocence; words burst upon me, unencumbered by trivial or portentous association; words were their spring-like selves, fresh with Eden's dew, as they flew out of the air. They made their own original associations as they sprang and shone. The words, "Ride a cockhorse to Banbury Cross," were as haunting to me, who did not know then what a cock-horse was nor cared a damn where Banbury Cross might be, as, much later, were such lines as John Donne's, "Go and catch a falling star, Get with child a mandrake root," which also I could not understand when I first read them. And as I read more and more, and it was not all verse, by any means, my love for the real life of words increased until I knew that I must live *with* them and *in* them, always. I knew, in fact, that I must be a writer of words, and nothing else. The first thing was to feel and know their sound and substance; what I was going to do with those words, what use I was going to make of them, what I was going to *say* through them, would come later. I knew I had to know them most intimately in all their forms and moods, their ups and downs, their chops and changes, their needs and demands (Here, I am afraid, I am beginning to talk too vaguely. I do not like writing *about* words, because then I often use bad and wrong and stale and woolly words. What I like to do is to treat words as a craftsman does his wood or stone or what-have-you, to hew, carve, mould, coil, polish and plane them into patterns, sequences, sculptures, fugues of sound expressing some lyrical impulse, some spiritual doubt or conviction, some dimly-realised truth I must try to reach and realise.) It was when I was very young, and just at school, that, in my father's study, before homework that was never done, I began to know one kind of writing from another, one kind of goodness, one kind of badness. My first, and greatest, liberty was that of being able to read everything and anything I cared to. I read indiscriminately, and with my eyes hanging out. I could never have dreamt that there were such goings-on in the world between the covers of books, such sand-storms, and ice-blasts of words, such slashing of humbug, and humbug too, such staggering peace, such enormous laughter, such and so many blinding bright lights breaking across the just-awaking wits and splashing all over the pages in a million bits and pieces all of which were words, words, words, and each of which was alive forever in its own delight and glory and oddity and light.

Content

1. Thomas begins his explanation of why he was moved to write poetry by saying that as a child he had "fallen in love with words." In your own words, what does Thomas mean by this statement?

2. What do you believe Thomas means when he refers to "the colours the words cast" on his eyes? Do words "cast colours" for you? Think of some possible examples and be prepared to discuss them in class.
3. Toward the end of this passage, Thomas says he does not "like to write *about* words." Why not?

Technique

1. Thomas is clearly in love not only with the sound and color of words but with figurative language as well. He compares his discovery of words, for instance, to "the notes of bells." Find other metaphors Thomas uses to explain his love of words and discuss their effectiveness.
2. Thomas appears to be so delighted with figurative language that he packs metaphor inside metaphor. To describe his love of words, for example, he compares them not just to branches on a window pane but rather to "the fingering of branches on a window pane." How does the use of the figurative word "fingering" add to the richness of the metaphor as a whole?
3. At one point in this passage, Thomas refers to words as "seemingly lifeless." But he is determined to give them extraordinary life in his writing. He says, for instance, that he "fell in love" with words as a child and that now he is "at the mercy of words." What technique is Thomas using here to give life to words? Find other examples of this technique and discuss how Thomas' use of it contributes to the meaning of this selection.

Language

1. Thomas says that "incomprehensible adults" were for some reason living in his world. Look up the word "incomprehensible" in your dictionary. Why do you believe Thomas chose to use this word here? Does its use add anything to Thomas' explanation of his early love for the sound of, rather than the meaning of, words?
2. Thomas loves to play with the sounds, shapes, and colors of words, words that he says "hummed, strummed, jigged and galloped along" in his childhood. How does his playfulness with words add to or distract from the meaning of this passage?

Vocabulary

| symbolized | falsified | vague |
| romanticizing | abstractions | ephemeral |

Writing Suggestion

1. Dylan Thomas says that he is in love with the sound and color of words, and several of the words he plays with in this essay reveal the enjoyment he gets from them. From this selection or from your own observations, choose a word the sound of which delights you, and write a paragraph describing the sensation it gives you apart from its meaning.

Writing

William Stafford

William Stafford (b. 1914) was educated at the University of Kansas and the University of Iowa. He was a conscientious objector during World War II; his first book, Down in My Heart *(1947), concerns these experiences. Stafford has published several volumes of poetry, including* Traveling Through the Dark *(1962) and* A Glass Face in the Rain *(1982). He won the National Book Award for poetry in 1962 and has taught at Lewis and Clark College in Oregon since 1957. In "Writing," Stafford describes the process of writing as he envisions it; in his view, the writer must cultivate receptivity and patience.*

A writer is not so much someone who has something to say as he is someone who has found a process that will bring about new things he would not have thought of if he had not started to say them. That is, he does not draw on a reservoir; instead, he engages in an activity that brings to him a whole succession of unforeseen stories, poems, essays, plays, laws, philosophies, religions, or—but wait!

Back in school, from the first when I began to try to write things, I felt this richness. One thing would lead to another; the world would give and give. Now, after twenty years or so of trying, I live by that certain richness, an idea hard to pin, difficult to say, and perhaps offensive to some. For there are strange implications in it.

One implication is the importance of just plain receptivity. When I write, I like to have an interval before me when I am not likely to be interrupted. For me, this means usually the early morning, before others are awake. I get pen and paper, take a glance out the window (often it is dark out there), and wait. It is like fishing. But

I do not wait very long, for there is always a nibble—and this is where receptivity comes in. To get started I will accept anything that occurs to me. Something always occurs, of course, to any of us. We can't keep from thinking. Maybe I have to settle for an immediate impression: it's cold, or hot, or dark, or bright, or in between! Or—well, the possibilities are endless. If I put down something, that thing will help the next thing come, and I'm off. If I let the process go on, things will occur to me that were not at all in my mind when I started. These things, odd or trivial as they may be, are somehow connected. And if I let them string out, surprising things will happen.

If I let them string out. . . . Along with initial receptivity, then, there is another readiness: I must be willing to fail. If I am to keep on writing, I cannot bother to insist on high standards. I must get into action and not let anything stop me, or even slow me much. By "standards" I do not mean "correctness"—spelling, punctuation, and so on. These details become mechanical for anyone who writes for a while. I am thinking about what many people would consider "important" standards, such matters as social significance, positive values, consistency, etc. I resolutely disregard these. Something better, greater, is happening! I am following a process that leads so wildly and originally into new territory that no judgment can at the moment be made about values, significance, and so on. I am making something new, something that has not been judged before. Later others—and maybe I myself—will make judgments. Now, I am headlong to discover. Any distraction may harm the creating.

So, receptive, careless of failure, I spin out things on the page. And a wonderful freedom comes. If something occurs to me, it is all right to accept it. It has one justification: it occurs to me. No one else can guide me. I must follow my own weak, wandering, diffident impulses.

A strange bonus happens. At times, without my insisting on it, my writings become coherent; the successive elements that occur to me are clearly related. They lead by themselves to new connections. Sometimes the language, even the syllables that happen along, may start a trend. Sometimes the materials alert me to something waiting in my mind, ready for sustained attention. At such times, I allow myself to be eloquent, or intentional, or for great swoops (treacherous! not to be trusted!) reasonable. But I do not insist on any of that; for I know that back of my activity there will be the coherence of my self, and that indulgence of my impulses will bring recurrent patterns and meanings again.

This attitude toward the process of writing creatively suggests a problem for me, in terms of what others say. They talk about "skills" in writing. Without denying that I do have experience, wide reading, automatic orthodoxies and maneuvers of various kinds, I still must insist that I am often baffled about what "skill" has to do with the precious little area of confusion when I do not know what I am going to say and then I find out what I am going to say. That precious interval I am unable to bridge by skill. What can I witness about it? It remains mysterious, just as all of us must feel puzzled about how we are so inventive as to be able to talk along through complexities with our friends, not needing to plan what we are going to say, but never stalled for long in our confident forward progress. Skill? If so, it is the skill we all have, something we must have learned before the age of three or four.

A writer is one who has become accustomed to trusting that grace, or luck, or—skill.

Yet another attitude I find necessary: most of what I write, like most of what I say in casual conversation, will not amount to much. Even I will realize, and even at the time, that it is not negotiable. It will be like practice. In conversation I allow myself random remarks—in fact, as I recall, that is the way I learned to talk—, so in writing I launch many expendable efforts. A result of this free way of writing is that I am not writing for others, mostly; they will not see the product at all unless the activity eventuates in something that later appears to be worthy. My guide is the self, and its adventuring in the language brings about communication.

This process-rather-than-substance view of writing invites a final, dual reflection:

1. Writers may not be special—sensitive or talented in any usual sense. They are simply engaged in sustained use of a language skill we all have. Their "creations" come about through confident reliance on stray impulses that will, with trust, find occasional patterns that are satisfying.

2. But writing itself is one of the great, free human activities. There is scope for individuality, and elation, and discovery, in writing. For the person who follows with trust and forgiveness what occurs to him, the world remains always ready and deep, an inexhaustible environment, with the combined vividness of an actuality

and flexibility of a dream. Working back and forth between experience and thought, writers have more than space and time can offer. They have the whole unexplored realm of human vision.

Content

1. Stafford's first two sentences explicitly state his thesis. Be prepared to discuss what you think Stafford means when he says that a writer is not so much one with something to say as one who has discovered a process.
2. In paragraph 4, Stafford writes that in the early stages of writing he must "be willing to fail" and that he "cannot bother to insist on high standards." According to Stafford, why is this so? Did you find these statements persuasive? Explain.
3. Stafford says that he allows himself to express any thought, however trivial, and to accept any idea that comes to him. He allows himself to be eloquent or "for great swoops (treacherous! not to be trusted!) reasonable." For a writer with Stafford's technique, why do you think being reasonable is not to be trusted, is even treacherous?
4. Stafford concludes his essay by suggesting that for him writing is more a matter of trust than of skill. Has his essay convinced you that this is true? Why or why not?

Technique

1. In part of the essay, Stafford uses process analysis to develop his ideas on writing. Make an outline from the essay, showing the steps that Stafford takes in writing. Look back once again at Stafford's first sentence, where he says that a writer is one who has "found a process," and then decide whether or not process analysis was an effective technique for this essay.
2. In this essay, Stafford uses many incomplete sentences and frequently interrupts himself. Find several examples of this technique. Does it complement or distract from the explanation of his writing process?

Language

1. In paragraph 3, Stafford talks of the importance of "just plain receptivity." Look up the word "receptivity" in your dictionary and explain its meaning in Stafford's essay.

2. To describe the first stages of writing, Stafford uses a fishing metaphor (paragraph 3). Why do you think this is or is not an appropriate metaphor for the process he describes?
3. Stafford says that when he is in the early stages of writing, he cannot bother with "standards." In your own words, what does he mean by this?

Vocabulary

receptivity	standards	treacherous
implications	resolutely	orthodoxies
trivial	diffident	

Writing Suggestion

1. William Stafford says that in free writing, "something always occurs to you." Try some free writing like Stafford suggests, perhaps for ten minutes on several different occasions. Keep the pen moving continuously and let yourself "accept" whatever comes to you. Then write a brief paper analyzing the effectiveness of the process as a means of unlocking your mind and giving you ideas for more formal writing.

Why I Write

Joan Didion

For biographical information on Joan Didion, see page 67. In the following essay, Didion explains what compels her to write and presents some vivid examples of her writing process.

Of course I stole the title for this talk from George Orwell. One reason I stole it was that I like the sound of the words: *Why I Write*. There you have three short unambiguous words that share a sound, and the sound they share is this:

I
I
I

In many ways writing is the act of saying *I*, of imposing oneself upon other people, of saying *listen to me, see it my way, change your* mind. It's an aggressive, even a hostile act. You can disguise its aggressiveness all you want with veils of subordinate clauses and qualifiers and tentative subjectives, with ellipses and evasions—with the whole manner of intimating rather than claiming, of alluding rather than stating—but there's no getting around the fact that setting words on paper is the tactic of a secret bully, an invasion, an imposition of the writer's sensibility on the reader's most private space.

I stole the title not only because the words sounded right but because they seemed to sum up, in a no-nonsense way, all I have to tell you. Like many writers I have only this one "subject," this one "area": the act of writing. I can bring you no reports from any other front. I may have other interests: I am "interested," for example, in marine biology, but I don't flatter myself that you would come out to hear me talk about it. I am not a scholar. I am not in the least an intellectual, which is not to say that when I hear the word "intellectual" I reach for my gun, but only to say that I do not think in abstracts. During the years when I was an undergraduate at Berkeley I tried, with a kind of hopeless late-adolescent energy, to buy some temporary visa into the world of ideas, to forge for myself a mind that could deal with the abstract.

In short I tried to think. I failed. My attention veered inexorably back to the specific, to the tangible, to what was generally considered, by everyone I knew then and for that matter have known since, the peripheral. I would try to contemplate the Hegelian dialectic and would find myself concentrating instead on a flowering pear tree outside my window and the particular way the petal fell on my floor. I would try to read linguistic theory and would find myself wondering instead if the lights were on in the bevatron up the hill. When I say that I was wondering if the lights were on in the bevatron you might immediately suspect, if you deal in ideas at all, that I was registering the bevatron as a political symbol, thinking in shorthand about the military–industrial complex and its role in the university community, but you would be wrong. I was only wondering if the lights were on in the bevatron, and how they looked. A physical fact.

I had trouble graduating from Berkeley, not because of this inability to deal with ideas—I was majoring in English, and I could locate the house-and-garden imagery in *The Portrait of a Lady* as well as the next person, "imagery" being by definition the kind of specific that got my attention—but simply because I had neglected to take a course in Milton. For reasons which now sound baroque I needed a degree by the end of the summer, and the English department finally agreed, if I would come down from Sacramento every Friday and talk about the cosmology of *Paradise Lost*, to certify me proficient in Milton. I did this. Some Fridays I took the Greyhound bus, other Fridays I caught the Southern Pacific's City of San Francisco on the last leg of its transcontinental trip. I can no longer tell you whether Milton put the sun or the earth at the center of his universe in *Paradise Lost*, the central question of at least one century and a topic about which I wrote 10,000 words that summer, but I can still recall the exact rancidity of the butter in the City of San Francisco's dining car, and the way the tinted windows on the Greyhound bus cast the oil refineries around Carquinez Straits into a grayed and obscurely sinister light. In short my attention was always on the periphery, on what I would see and taste and touch, on the butter, and the Greyhound bus. During those years I was traveling on what I knew to be a very shaky passport, forged papers: I knew that I was no legitimate resident in any world of ideas. I knew I couldn't think. All I knew then was what I couldn't do. All I knew then was what I wasn't, and it took me some years to discover what I was.

Which was a writer.

By which I mean not a "good" writer or a "bad" writer but simply a writer, a person whose most absorbed and passionate hours are spent arranging words on pieces of paper. Had my credentials been in order I would never have become a writer. Had I been blessed with even limited access to my own mind there would have been no reason to write. I write entirely to find out what I'm thinking, what I'm looking at, what I see and what it means. What I want and what I fear. Why did the oil refineries around Carquinez Straits seem sinister to me in the summer of 1956? Why have the night lights in the bevatron burned in my mind for twenty years? *What is going on in these pictures in my mind?*

When I talk about pictures in my mind I am talking, quite specifically, about images that shimmer around the edges. There used to be an illustration in every elementary psychology book showing a cat drawing by a patient in varying stages of schizophrenia.

This cat had a shimmer around it. You could see the molecular structure breaking down at the very edges of the cat: the cat became the background and the background the cat, everything interacting, exchanging ions. People on hallucinogens describe the same perception of objects. I'm not a schizophrenic, nor do I take hallucinogens, but certain images do shimmer for me. Look hard enough, and you can't miss the shimmer. It's there. You can't think too much about these pictures that shimmer. You just lie low and let them develop. You stay quiet. You don't talk to many people and you keep your nervous system from shorting out and you try to locate the cat in the shimmer, the grammar in the picture.

Just as I meant "shimmer" literally I mean "grammar" literally. Grammar is a piano I play by ear, since I seem to have been out of school the year the rules were mentioned. All I know about grammar is its infinite power. To shift the structure of a sentence alters the meaning of the sentence, as definitely and inflexibly as the position of a camera alters the meaning of the object photographed. Many people know about camera angles now, but not so many know about sentences. The arrangement of the words matters, and the arrangement you want can be found in the picture in your mind. The picture dictates the arrangement. The picture dictates whether this will be a sentence with or without clauses, a sentence that ends hard or a dying-fall sentence, long or short, active or passive. The picture tells you how to arrange the words and the arrangement of the words tells you, or tells me, what's going on in the picture. *Nota bene:*

It tells you.

You don't tell it.

Let me show you what I mean by pictures in the mind. I began *Play It as It Lays* just as I have begun each of my novels, with no notion of "character" or "plot" or even "incident." I had only two pictures in my mind, more about which later, and a technical intention, which was to write a novel so elliptical and fast that it would be over before you noticed it, a novel so fast that it would scarcely exist on the page at all. About the pictures: the first was of white space. Empty space. This was clearly the picture that dictated the narrative intention of the book—a book in which anything that happened would happen off the page, a "white" book to which the reader would have to bring his or her own bad dreams—and yet this picture told me no "story," suggested no situation. The second picture did. This second picture was of something actually witnessed.

A young woman with long hair and a short white halter dress walks through the casino at the Riviera in Las Vegas at one in the morning. She crosses the casino alone and picks up a house telephone. I watch her because I have heard her paged, and recognize her name: she is a minor actress I see around Los Angeles from time to time, in places like Jax and once in a gynecologist's office in the Beverly Hills Clinic but have never met. I know nothing about her. Who is paging her? Why is she here to be paged? How exactly did she come to this? It was precisely this moment in Las Vegas that made *Play It as It Lays* begin to tell itself to me, but the moment appears in the novel only obliquely, in a chapter which begins:

> Maria made a list of things she would never do. She would never: walk through the Sands or Caesar's alone after midnight. She would never: ball at a party, do S-M unless she wanted to, borrow furs from Abe Lipsey, deal. She would never: carry a Yorkshire in Beverly Hills.

That is the beginning of the chapter and that is also the end of the chapter, which may suggest what I meant by "white space."

I recall having a number of pictures in my mind when I began the novel I just finished, *A Book of Common Prayer*. As a matter of fact one of these pictures was of that bevatron I mentioned, although I would be hard put to tell you a story in which nuclear energy figured. Another was a newspaper photograph of a hijacked 707 burning on the desert in the Middle East. Another was the night view from a room in which I once spent a week with paratyphoid, a hotel room on the Colombian coast. My husband and I seemed to be on the Colombian coast representing the United States of America at a film festival (I recall invoking the name "Jack Valenti" a lot, as if its reiteration could make me well), and it was a bad place to have fever, not only because my indisposition offended our hosts but because every night in this hotel the generator failed. The lights went out. The elevator stopped. My husband would go to the event of the evening and make excuses for me and I would stay alone in this hotel room, in the dark. I remember standing at the window trying to call Bogotá (the telephone seemed to work on the same principle as the generator) and watching the night wind come up and wondering what I was doing eleven degrees off the equator with a fever of 103. The view from that window definitely figures in *A Book of Common Prayer*, as does the burning 707, and yet none of these pictures told me the story I needed.

The picture that did, the picture that shimmered and made these other images coalesce, was the Panama airport at 6 A.M. I was in this airport only once, on a plane to Bogotá that stopped for an hour to refuel, but the way it looked that morning remained superimposed on everything I saw until the day I finished *A Book of Common Prayer*. I lived in that airport for several years. I can still feel the hot air when I step off the plane, can see the heat already rising off the tarmac at 6 A.M. I can feel my skirt damp and wrinkled on my legs. I can feel the asphalt stick to my sandals. I remember the big tail of a Pan American plane floating motionless down at the end of the tarmac. I remember the sound of a slot machine in the waiting room. I could tell you that I remember a particular woman in the airport, an American woman, a *norteamericana*, a thin *norteamericana* about 40 who wore a big square emerald in lieu of a wedding ring, but there was no such woman there.

I put this woman in the airport later. I made this woman up, just as I later made up a country to put the airport in, and a family to run the country. This woman in the airport is neither catching a plane nor meeting one. She is ordering tea in the airport coffee shop. In fact she is not simply "ordering" tea but insisting that the water be boiled, in front of her, for twenty minutes. Why is this woman in this airport? Why is she going nowhere, where has she been? Where did she get that big emerald? What derangement, or disassociation, makes her believe that her will to see the water boiled can possibly prevail?

> She had been going to one airport or another for four months, one could see it, looking at the visas on her passport. All those airports where Charlotte Douglas's passport had been stamped would have looked alike. Sometimes the sign on the tower would say "Bienvenidos" and sometimes the sign on the tower would say "Bienvenue," some places were wet and hot and others dry and hot, but at each of these airports the pastel concrete walls would rust and stain and the swamp off the runway would be littered with the fuselages of cannibalized Fairchild F-227's and the water would need boiling.
> "I knew why Charlotte went to the airport even if Victor did not.
> "I knew about airports."

These lines appear about halfway through *A Book of Common Prayer*, but I wrote them during the second week I worked on the book, long before I had any idea where Charlotte Douglas had been or why she went to airports. Until I wrote these lines I had no character called "Victor" in mind: the necessity for mentioning a name, and the name "Victor," occurred to me as I wrote the sentence. *I knew why Charlotte went to the airport* sounded incomplete. *I knew why Charlotte went to the airport even if Victor did not* carried a little more narrative drive. Most important of all, until I wrote these lines I did not know who "I" was, who was telling the story. I had intended until that moment that the "I" be no more than the voice of the author, a 19th-century omniscient narrator. But there it was:

> "I knew why Charlotte went to the airport even if Victor did not.
> "I knew about airports."

This "I" was the voice of no author in my house. This "I" was someone who not only knew why Charlotte went to the airport but also knew someone called "Victor." Who was Victor? Who was this narrator? Why was this narrator telling me this story? Let me tell you one thing about why writers write: had I known the answer to any of these questions I would never have needed to write a novel. 18

Content

1. In paragraph 2, Didion says that writing is "the act of saying *I*." What do you understand Didion to mean by this statement? Do you agree with her?
2. This essay reveals Didion thinking carefully about her life, her writing, and her world. Yet, in paragraph 4, she tells us that as a college student she tried to think and failed. What do you believe she means by that statement?
3. In paragraph 7, Didion says, "I write entirely to find out what I'm thinking, what I'm looking at, what I see and what it means." Explain this passage, drawing on your own experience as well as on Didion's.
4. The difficult concept of pictures "shimmering" in the mind is central to Didion's discussion of why she writes. Is Didion's explanation clear? Why or why not?
5. The last line of Didion's essay summarizes her thesis. Be prepared to explain its meaning in class, using specific examples from the essay to support and clarify your explanation.

Technique

1. Didion begins her essay with an almost whimsical explanation of her reasons for stealing her title from George Orwell and follows that with a paragraph considerably different in tone. How would you describe the tone of the second paragraph? Did you find the two paragraphs effective as attention-getting devices? Why or why not?
2. Didion uses numerous examples to explain her tendency to deal in the tangible rather than in the abstract. For instance, she says that in college her mind was easily distracted from Hegelian dialectic to a pear tree outside her window. Find two or three other examples and discuss their effectiveness in clarifying her point.
3. Paragraph 6 consists of a one-line sentence fragment. Read this brief "paragraph" in conjunction with those immediately preceding and following it and discuss the purpose it serves.
4. Didion uses an extended example to clarify her belief that the pictures in her mind make her write and choose her story for her. Discuss the ways in which her description of writing *Play It as It Lays* and *A Book of Common Prayer* clarifies her point.

Language

1. Didion calls writing "a hostile act." Look up the word "hostile" in your dictionary and explain why Didion applies it to the act of writing.
2. In paragraph 3, Didion uses a metaphor in stating that writing is her only subject: "I can bring you no reports from any other front," she says. In what ways does this war metaphor complement the point she has been making about writing?
3. Didion says that her mind deals in what most people consider the peripheral. Look up the word "peripheral" and decide why Didion believes that people consider her concerns peripheral.

Vocabulary

aggressive	coalesce	baroque
hostile	intimate	superimpose
abstracts	alluding	bevatron
peripheral	tangible	

Writing Suggestions

1. Didion says she is directed in her writing by the pictures in her mind, which tell her what to write and how to structure the writing. Write an essay describing one of your own "pictures in the mind." What story does it tell you, and how does it suggest what you would need in order to structure your writing to reveal the picture?
2. Didion speaks of grammar's infinite power and notes that to shift the structure of a sentence alters the meaning. Choose a sentence from your own writing; try re-writing it two or three times, each in a different way. Write a paragraph, explaining the way these changes alter the sentence's meaning.

Why a Surgeon Would Write
Richard Selzer

Richard Selzer (b. 1928) received a medical degree from Albany Medical College in 1953 and has had a private practice in general surgery since 1960. In 1975 he won the National Magazine Award from the Columbia University School of Journalism. His books include Rituals of Surgery *(1974) and* Mortal Lessons *(1977). In the following essay, Selzer argues that writing completes and enriches his notion of medicine and saves him from both the vanity and despair that often afflict physicians. The essay is also remarkable for its harrowing depiction of the human body as the surgeon knows it.*

Someone asked me why a surgeon would write. Why, when the shelves are already too full? They sag under the deadweight of books. To add a single adverb is to risk exceeding the strength of the boards. A surgeon should abstain. A surgeon, whose fingers are more at home in the steamy gullies of the body than they are tapping the dry keys of a typewriter. A surgeon, who feels the slow slide of intestines against the back of his hand and is no more alarmed than were a family of snakes taking their comfort from such an indolent rubbing. A surgeon, who palms the human heart as though it were some captured bird.

Why should he write? Is it vanity that urges him? There is glory enough in the knife. Is it for money? One can make too much money. No. It is to search for some meaning in the ritual of surgery, which is at once murderous, painful, healing, and full of love. It is a devilish hard thing to transmit—to find, even. Perhaps if one were to cut out a heart, a lobe of the liver, a single convolution of the brain, and paste it to a page, it would speak with more eloquence than all the words of Balzac. Such a piece would need no literary style, no mass of erudition or history, but in its very shape and feel would tell all the frailty and strength, the despair and nobility of man. What? Publish a heart? A little piece of bone? Preposterous. Still I fear that is what it may require to reveal the truth that lies hidden in the body. Not all the undressing of Rabelais, Chekhov, or even William Carlos Williams have wrested it free, although God knows each one of those doctors made a heroic assault upon it.

I have come to believe that it is the flesh alone that counts. The rest is that with which we distract ourselves when we are not hungry or cold, in pain or ecstasy. In the recesses of the body I search for the philosopher's stone. I know it is there, hidden in the deepest, dampest cul-de-sac. It awaits discovery. To find it would be like the harnessing of fire. It would illuminate the world. Such a quest is not without pain. Who can gaze on so much misery and feel no hurt? Emerson has written that the poet is the only true doctor. I believe him, for the poet, lacking the impediment of speech with which the rest of us are afflicted, gazes, records, diagnoses, and prophesies.

I invited a young diabetic woman to the operating room to amputate her leg. She could not see the great shaggy black ulcer upon her foot and ankle that threatened to encroach upon the rest of her body, for she was blind as well. There upon her foot was a Mississippi Delta brimming with corruption, sending its raw tributaries down between her toes. Gone were all the little web spaces that when fresh and whole are such a delight to loving men. She could not see her wound, but she could feel it. There is no pain like that of the bloodless limb turned rotten and festering. There is neither unguent or anodyne to kill such a pain yet leave intact the body.

For over a year I trimmed away the putrid flesh, cleansed, anointed, and dressed the foot, staving off, delaying. Three times each week, in her darkness, she sat upon my table, rocking back and forth, holding her extended leg by the thigh, gripping it as though it were a rocket that must be steadied lest it explode and scatter her toes about the room. And I would cut away a bit here, a bit there, of the swollen blue leather that was her tissue.

At last we gave up, she and I. We could no longer run ahead of the gangrene. We had not the legs for it. There must be an amputation in order that she might live—and I as well. It was to heal us both that I must take up knife and saw, and cut the leg off. And when I could feel it drop from her body to the table, see the blessed *space* appear between her and that leg, I too would be well.

Now it is the day of the operation. I stand by while the anesthetist administers the drugs, watch as the tense familiar body relaxes into narcosis. I turn then to uncover the leg. There, upon her kneecap, she has drawn, blindly, upside down for me to see, a face; just a circle with two ears, two eyes, a nose, and a smiling upturned mouth. Under it she has printed SMILE, DOCTOR. Minutes later I listen to the sound of the saw, until a little crack at the end tells me it is done.

So, I have learned that man is not ugly, but that he is Beauty itself. There is no other his equal. Are we not all dying, none faster or more slowly than any other? I have become receptive to the possibilities of love (for it is love, this thing that happens in the operating room), and each day I wait, trembling in the busy air. Perhaps today it will come. Perhaps today I will find it, take part in it, this love that blooms in the stoniest desert.

All through literature the doctor is portrayed as a figure of fun. Shaw was splenetic about him; Molière delighted in pricking his pompous medicine men, and well they deserved it. The doctor is ripe for caricature. But I believe that the truly great writing about doctors has not yet been done. I think it must be done *by* a doctor, one who is through with the love affair with his technique, who recognizes that he has played Narcissus, raining kisses on a mirror, and who now, out of the impacted masses of his guilt, has expanded into self-doubt, and finally into the high state of wonderment. Perhaps he will be a nonbeliever who, after a lifetime of grand gestures and mighty deeds, comes upon the knowledge that he has done no more than meddle in the lives of his fellows, and that he has done at least as much harm as good. Yet he may continue to pretend, at least, that there is nothing to fear, that death will not come, so long as people depend on his authority. Later, after his patients have left, he may closet himself in his darkened office, sweating and afraid.

There is a story by Unamuno in which a priest, living in a small Spanish village, is adored by all the people for his piety, kindness, and the majesty with which he celebrates the Mass each Sunday. To them he is already a saint. It is a foregone conclusion, and they speak of him as Saint Immanuel. He helps them with their plowing and planting, tends them when they are sick, confesses them, comforts them in death, and every Sunday, in his rich, trilling voice, transports them to paradise with his chanting. The fact is that Don Immanuel is not so much a saint as a martyr. Long ago his own faith left him. He is an atheist, a good man doomed to suffer the life of a hypocrite, pretending to a faith he does not have. As he raises the chalice of wine, his hands tremble, and a cold sweat pours from him. He cannot stop for he knows that the people need this of him, that their need is greater than his sacrifice. Still . . . still . . . could it be that Don Immanuel's whole life is a kind of prayer, a paean to God?

A writing doctor would treat men and women with equal reverence, for what is the "liberation" of either sex to him who knows the diagrams, the inner geographies of each? I love the solid heft of men as much as I adore the heated capaciousness of women—women in whose penetralia is found the repository of existence. I would have them glory in that. Women are physics and chemistry. They are matter. It is their bodies that tell of the frailty of men. Men have not their cellular, enzymatic wisdom. Man is albuminoid, proteinaceous, laked pearl; woman is yolky, ovoid, rich. Both are exuberant bloody growths. I would use the defects and deformities of each for my sacred purpose of writing, for I know that it is the marred and scarred and faulty that are subject to grace. I would seek the soul in the facts of animal economy and profligacy. Yes, it is the exact location of the soul that I am after. The smell of it is in my nostrils. I have caught glimpses of it in the body diseased. If only I could tell it. Is there no mathematical equation that can guide me? So much pain and pus equals so much truth? It is elusive as the whippoorwill that one hears calling incessantly from out the night window, but which, nesting as it does low in the brush, no one sees. No one but the poet, for he sees what no one else can. He was born with the eye for it.

Once I thought I had it: Ten o'clock one night, the end room off a long corridor in a college infirmary, my last patient of the day, degree of exhaustion suitable for the appearance of a vision, some manifestation. The patient is a young man recently returned from Guatemala, from the excavation of Mayan ruins. His left upper arm wears a gauze dressing which, when removed, reveals a clean punched-out hole the size of a dime. The tissues about the opening are swollen and tense. A thin brownish fluid lips the edge, and now and then a lazy drop of the overflow spills down the arm. An abscess, inadequately drained. I will enlarge the opening to allow better egress of the pus. Nurse, will you get me a scalpel and some. . . ?

What happens next is enough to lay Francis Drake avomit in his cabin. No explorer ever stared in wilder surmise than I into that crater from which there now emerges a narrow gray head whose sole distinguishing feature is a pair of black pincers. The head sits atop a longish flexible neck arching now this way, now that, testing the air. Alternately it folds back upon itself, then advances in new boldness. And all the while, with dreadful rhythmicity, the unspeakable pincers open and close. Abscess? Pus? Never. Here is the lair of a beast at whose malignant purpose I could but guess. A Mayan devil, I think, that would soon burst free to fly about the room, with horrid blanket-wings and iridescent scales, raking, pinching, injecting God knows what acid juice. And even now the irony does not escape me, the irony of my patient as excavator excavated.

With all the ritual deliberation of a high priest I advance a surgical clamp toward the hole. The surgeon's heart is become a bat hanging upside down from his rib cage. The rim achieved—now thrust—and the ratchet of the clap close upon the empty air. The devil has retracted. Evil mocking laughter bangs back and forth in the brain. More stealth. Lying in wait. One must skulk. Minutes pass, perhaps an hour. . . . A faint disturbance in the lake, and once again the thing upraises, farther and farther, hovering. Acrouch, strung, the surgeon is one with his instrument; there is no longer any boundary between its metal and his flesh. They are joined in a single perfect tool of extirpation. It is just for this that he was born. Now—thrust—and clamp—and *yes*. Got him!

Transmitted to the fingers comes the wild thrashing of the creature. Pinned and wriggling, he is mine. I hear the dry brittle scream of the dragon, and a hatred seizes me, but such a detestation as would make of Iago a drooling sucktit. It is the demented hatred of the victor for the vanquished, the warden for his prisoner. It is the hatred of fear. Within the jaws of my hemostat is the whole of the evil of the world, the dark concentrate itself, and I shall kill it. For mankind. And, in so doing, will open the way into a thousand years of perfect peace. Here is Surgeon as Savior indeed.

Tight grip now . . . steady, relentless pull. How it scrabbles to keep its tentacle-hold. With an abrupt moist plop the extraction is complete. There, writhing in the teeth of the clamp, is a dirty gray body, the size and shape of an English walnut. He is hung everywhere with tiny black hooklets. Quickly . . . into the specimen jar of saline . . . the lid screwed tight. Crazily he swims round and round, wiping his slimy head against the glass, then slowly sinks to the bottom, the mass of hooks in frantic agonal wave.

"You are going to be all right," I say to my patient. "We are *all* going to be all right from now on."

The next day I take the jar to the medical school. "That's the larva of the botfly," says a pathologist. "The fly usually bites a cow and deposits its eggs beneath the skin. There, the egg develops into the larval form which, when ready, burrows its way to the outside through the hide and falls to the ground. In time it matures into a fullgrown botfly. This one happened to bite a man. It was about to come out on its own, and, of course, it would have died."

The words *imposter, sorehead, servant of Satan* sprang to my lips. But now he has been joined by other scientists. They nod in agreement. I gaze from one gray eminence to another, and know the mallet-blow of glory pulverized. I tried to save the world, but it didn't work out.

No, it is not the surgeon who is God's darling. He is the victim of vanity. It is the poet who heals with his words, stanches the flow of blood, stills the rattling breath, applies poultice to the scalded flesh.

Did you ask me why a surgeon writes? I think it is because I wish to be a doctor.

Content

1. Selzer's job here, to explain the writing surgeon, is difficult because he must overcome his audience's assumption that the worlds of surgery and writing are far distant from one another. Why, according to Selzer, does a surgeon, at least this surgeon, write?

2. In describing his love of the wounded body, Selzer notes that he will use the defects and deformities of his patients for his "sacred purpose of writing." In your own words, explain your understanding of Selzer's sense of writing as a "sacred" act.

3. In paragraph 20, Selzer unites the poet and the surgeon in his discussion of his search for the human soul. Explain your understanding of the implication that the poet and the surgeon are one.
4. Like Didion, Selzer summarizes his thesis in the final sentence of his essay. Explain the meaning of that sentence.

Technique

1. Selzer, like Thomas and Didion, writes this essay in response to having been asked why he writes. Considering the tone and content of this essay, who do you believe Selzer's audience to be?
2. Selzer's opening paragraph contains a graphic descripiton of the surgeon's job. What is the effect of this startling paragraph on the subject of the essay?
3. Selzer's essay has many questions ("What? Publish a heart? A little piece of bone? Preposterous") and short, terse sentences ("A surgeon should abstain," or "It awaits discovery"). Find other examples of each, and explain what you believe to be the effect of these stylistic techniques on Selzer's discussion of writing surgeons.
4. In paragraphs 4–7, Selzer gives an extended, graphic description of the trials of a young woman with gangrene and of his own trials in treating her. What role does this description play in the essay as a whole?

Language

1. In Selzer's profession, he deals with cold, harsh realities of life and death. Yet he describes the act of surgery in abstract terms—such as, "I search for the philosopher's stone"—that contrast sharply with his factual descriptions of the act. Find other examples of his abstract philosophical response to the concrete act of surgery, and discuss the role they play in this essay.
2. In paragraph 9, Selzer says that a doctor is one who "has played Narcissus, raining kisses on a mirror." Look up "Narcissus" in your dictionary, and explain the meaning of this passage.

Vocabulary

indolent	splenetic	capaciousness
ungent	caricature	penetralia
anodyne	paean	repository
Narcissus		

Writing Suggestion

1. Choosing the academic discipline with which you are most familiar (or a profession other than medicine), write an essay in which you address the issue "Why a _____ Would Write." Using Selzer's essay as a model, include vivid details to capture the flavor of the discipline or profession.

What is a Scientific Paper?

Robert Day

Robert Day (b. 1924) has served on the Council of Biology Editors and the Publications Board of the American Society for Microbiology. The following selection is from his widely read book, How to Write and Publish a Scientific Paper *(1979). Day defines the scientific paper, including its history and its purposes, then argues compellingly for the importance of the writing process to the scientist.*

A scientific paper is a written and published report describing original research results. That short definition must be qualified, however, by noting that a scientific paper must be written in a certain way and it must be published in a certain way, the way being defined by three centuries of developing tradition, editorial practice, scientific ethics, and the interplay of printing and publishing procedures.

To properly define "scientific paper," we must define the operative mechanism whereby a scientific paper is created, namely, valid publication. Abstracts, theses, conference reports, and many other types of literature are published, but such publications do not normally meet the test of valid publication. Further, even if a manuscript meets all of the other tests, it is not validly published if it is published in the wrong place. That is, a relatively poor research report, but one that meets the tests, is validly published if accepted and published in the right place (a primary journal, usually), whereas a superbly prepared research report is not validly published if published in the wrong place. Most of the government report literature and conference literature, as well as house organs and other ephemeral publications, do not qualify as primary literature.

Many people have struggled with the definition of "valid publication," from which is derived the definition of "scientific paper." The Council of Biology Editors (CBE), the principal professional organization (in biology, at least) dealing with such problems, arrived at the following definition:

> An acceptable primary scientific publication must be the first disclosure containing sufficient information to enable peers (1) to assess observations, (2) to repeat experiments, and (3) to evaluate intellectual processes; moreover, it must be susceptible to sensory perception, essentially permanent, available to the scientific community without restriction, and available for regular screening by one or more of the major recognized secondary services (e.g., currently *Biological Abstracts, Chemical Abstracts, Index Medicus, Excerpta Medica, Bibliography of Agriculture*, etc., in the United States and similar facilities in other countries).

At first reading, it might seem that the above definition is excessively complex, or at least verbose. But those of us who had a hand in drafting it weighed each word carefully, and we doubt that an acceptable definition could be provided in appreciably fewer words. Because it is important that students, authors, editors, and all others concerned understand what a scientific paper is and what it is not, let us work our way through this definition to see what it really means.

"An acceptable primary scientific publication" starts out as the defined substantive, but this gives way to "the first disclosure," the rest of the definition defining "first disclosure." Certainly, first disclosure of new research data often takes place via oral presentation at a scientific meeting. But, the thrust of the CBE statement is that disclosure is more than disgorgement by the author; effective first disclosure is accomplished *only* when the disclosure is in a form in which peers of the author can (either now or in the future) readily assimilate that which is disclosed.

Thus, sufficient information must be presented so that potential users of the data can (i) assess observations, (ii) repeat experiments, and (iii) evaluate intellectual processes. (Are the author's conclusions justified by the data?) Then, the disclosure must be "susceptible to sensory perception." This may seem an awkward phrase, because in normal practice it simply means publication; however, this definition provides for disclosure not just in terms of visual materials (printed journals, microfilm, microfiche) but also perhaps in nonprint, nonvisual forms. For example, "publication" in the form of audio cassettes, if that publication met the other tests provided in the definition, would constitute effective publication. In the future, it is quite possible that first disclosure will be entry into a computer data base.

Regardless of the form of publication, that form must be essentially permanent, must be made available to the scientific community without restriction, and must be made available to the information retrieval system (*Biological Abstracts, Chemical Abstracts, Index Medicus, Science Citation Index,* etc.). Thus, publications such as newsletters and house organs, many of which are of value for their news or other features, cannot serve as repositories for scientific knowledge.

To restate the CBE definition in simpler but not more accurate terms, a scientific paper is (i) the first publication of original research results, (ii) in a form whereby peers of the author can repeat the experiments and test the conclusions, and (iii) in a journal or other source document which is readily available within the scientific community. Or, as DeBakey said it, "the contents of an article shall be *new, important and comprehensible.*"

I have belabored this question of definition for two very good reasons. First, the entire community of science has long labored with an inefficient, costly system of scientific communication precisely because it (authors, editors, publishers) has been unable or unwilling to define primary publication. As a result, much of the literature is buried in meeting abstracts, obscure conference reports, government publications, or in books or journals of miniscule circulation.

Other papers, in the same or slightly altered form, are published twice or more often; occasionally, this is the result of poor ethics on the part of the author, but more often it is the lack of definition as to which conference reports, books, and compilations are (or should be) primary publications and which are not. Redundancy and confusion result.

Second, a scientific paper is, by definition, a particular kind of document containing certain specified kinds of information. A scientific paper "demands exactly the same qualities of thought as are needed for the rest of science: logic, clarity, and precision." Therefore, if the graduate student or the budding scientist (and even some of those scientists who have already published many papers) can fully grasp the significance of this definition, his writing task should be a good deal easier. Confusion results from an amorphous task.

The easy task is the one in which you know exactly what must be done and in exactly what order it must be done.

Without equivocation, I say that a scientific paper is primarily an exercise in organization. A scientific paper is, or should be, highly stylized, with distinctive and clearly evident component parts. Each scientific paper should have, in proper order, its Introduction, Materials and Methods, Results, and Discussion. Any other order will pose hurdles for the reader and probably the writer. "Good organization is the key to good writing."

This prescribed order is one that I have taught and recommended for many years. Until recently, however, there have been several somewhat different systems of organization that were preferred by some journals and some editors. The tendency toward uniformity has increased since 1972, when the order cited above was prescribed as a standard.

This order is so eminently logical that, increasingly, it is used for many other types of expository writing. Whether one is writing an article about chemistry, archeology, economics, or crime in the streets, an effective way to proceed is to answer these four questions, in order: (i) What was the problem? Your answer is the *Introduction*. (ii) How did you study the problem? Your answer is the *Materials and Methods*. (iii) What did you find? Your answer is the *Results*. (iv) What do these findings mean? Your answer is the *Discussion*.

The well-written scientific paper should report its original data in an organized fashion and in appropriate language. In the chapters that follow, I examine each aspect of that organization, while commenting on language along the way.

In short, I take the position that the preparation of a scientific paper has almost nothing to do with writing, per se. It is a question of *organization*. A scientific paper is not "literature." The preparer of a scientific paper is not really an "author" in the literary sense. In fact, I go so far as to say that, if the ingredients are properly organized, the paper will virtually write itself.

Some of my old-fashioned colleagues think that scientific papers should be literature, that the style and flair of an author should be clearly evident, and that variations in style encourage the interest of the reader. I disagree. I think scientists should indeed be interested in reading literature, and perhaps even in writing literature, but the communication of research results is a more prosaic procedure. As Booth put it, "Grandiloquence has no place in scientific writing."

Today, the average scientist, to keep up in his field, must examine the data reported in hundreds or even thousands of papers. Therefore, it seems obvious to me that scientists and, of course, editors must demand a system of reporting data that is uniform, concise, and readily understandable.

I once heard it said: "A scientific paper is not designed to be read. It is designed to be published." Although this was said in jest, there is much truth to it. And, actually, if the paper is designed to be published, it will also be in a prescribed form that can be read, or at least its contents can be grasped quickly and easily by the reader.

In addition to organization, the second principal ingredient of a scientific paper should be appropriate language within that organization. In this book, I keep emphasizing proper use of English, because it is in this area that most scientists have trouble.

If scientific knowledge is at least as important as any other knowledge, then it must be communicated effectively, clearly, in words of certain meaning. The scientist, to succeed in this endeavor, must therefore be literate. David B. Truman, when he was Dean of Columbia College, said it well: "In the complexities of contemporary existence the specialist who is trained but uneducated, technically skilled but culturally incompetent, is a menace."

Although it is recognized that the ultimate goal of scientific research is publication, it has always been amazing to me that so many scientists neglect the responsibilities involved. A scientist will spend months or years of hard work to secure his data, and then unconcernedly let much of their value be lost because of his lack of interest in the communication process. The same scientist who will overcome tremendous obstacles to carry out a measurement to the fourth decimal place will be in deep slumber while his secretary is casually changing his micrograms per milliliter to milligrams per milliliter and while the printer slips in an occasional pound per barrel.

Language need not be difficult. In scientific writing, we say: "The best English is that which gives the sense in the fewest short words" (a dictum printed for some years in the "Instructions to

Authors" of the *Journal of Bacteriology*). Literary tricks, metaphors and the like, divert attention from the message to the style. They should be used rarely, if at all, in scientific writing. Justin Leonard, assistant conservation director of Michigan, once said: "The Ph.D. in science can make journal editors quite happy with plain, unadorned, eighth-grade level composition" (*Bio-Science*, September 1966).

At this point, we have defined a scientific paper, which was the intent of this chapter. Before we proceed, however, it may be helpful to add a few related definitions.

Let us preserve "scientific paper" as the term for an original research report. How should this be distinguished from research reports that are not original, or not scientific, or somehow fail to qualify as scientific papers? Let us look at several specific terms: "review paper," "conference report," and "meeting abstract."

A review paper may review almost anything, most typically the recent work in a defined subject area or the work of a particular individual or group. Thus, the review paper is designed to summarize, analyze, or synthesize information that *has already been published* (research reports in primary journals). Although much or all of the material in a review paper has previously been published, the spectre of dual publication does not normally arise because the review nature of the work is usually obvious (often in the title of the publication, such as *Microbiological Reviews*, *Annual Review of Biochemistry*, etc.).

A conference report is a paper published in a book or journal as part of the proceeding of a symposium, national or international congress, workshop, round table, or the like. Rarely, such conferences are designed for the presentations of original data, and the resultant proceedings (book or journal) qualifies as primary publication. More often, such conference presentations are basically review papers, presenting reviews of the recent work of particular scientists or recent work in particular laboratories. Some of the material reported at some conferences (especially the exciting ones) is mainly in the form of preliminary reports, in which new, original data are reported, often accompanied by interesting speculation. But, usually, these preliminary reports do not qualify, nor are they intended to qualify, as scientific papers. Later, often much later, such work is validly published in a primary journal; by this time, the loose ends have been tied down, all essential experimental details are recorded (so that a competent worker could repeat the experiments), and the speculations are now recorded as conclusions.

Therefore, the vast conference literature that appears in print normally is not *primary*. If original data are presented in such contributions, the data can and should be published (or republished) in an archival (primary) journal. Otherwise, the information may be effectively lost. If publication in a primary journal follows publication in a conference report, there may be copyright and permission problems affecting portions of the work, but the more fundamental problem of dual publication normally does not and should not arise.

Meeting abstracts, like conference proceedings, are of several widely varying types. Conceptually, however, they are similar to conference reports in that they can and often do contain original information. They are not primary publications, nor should publication of an abstract be considered as a bar to later publication of the full report.

In the past, there has been little confusion regarding the typical one-paragraph abstracts published in part of the program or distributed along with the program of a national meeting or international congress. It was usually understood that the papers presented at these meetings would later be submitted for publication in primary journals. More recently, however, there has been a strong trend towards extended abstracts (or "synoptics"). Because it is very expensive to publish all of the full papers presented at a large meeting, such as a major international congress, and because such publication is still not a substitute for the valid publication offered by the primary journal, the movement to extended abstracts makes a great deal of sense. The extended abstract can supply virtually as much information as a full paper; basically, what it lacks is the experimental detail. However, precisely because it lacks experimental detail, it cannot qualify as a scientific paper.

Those of us who are involved with publishing these materials see the importance of careful definition of the different types of papers. More and more publishers, conference organizers, and individual scientists are beginning to agree on these basic definitions. General acceptance of such definitions will greatly clarify both primary and secondary communication of scientific information.

I have tried to answer the question "What is a scientific paper?" Perhaps a better answer, certainly a more succinct one, was provided by the wag who described a drug as "any substance which, when injected into a laboratory rat, produces a scientific paper."

Content

1. In your own words, explain Day's definition of a "scientific paper;" consider such things as purpose, audience, structure, and, in particular, the relationship that Day draws between the writing of a scientific paper and its publication.
2. The type of writing discussed in this essay differs significantly from the writing discussed in other selections in this chapter. In what ways would you say it differs?
3. Although Day's article does not explicitly discuss why he writes (as the other articles in this section did), it does imply his purpose. What do you believe it is?
4. Speaking of scientific writing, Day notes that "Confusion results from an amorphous task. The easy task is the one in which you know exactly what must be done and in exactly what order it must be done." How do you believe some of the other writers in this section, William Stafford for instance, would respond to this approach to writing? Why?
5. In paragraph 12, Day says that a scientific paper is "primarily an exercise in organization." Explain the organizational pattern he suggests, and discuss what you understand Day to mean by this statement.

Technique

1. Day organizes his essay by defining what a scientific paper is and is not. How effective do you find this technique in supporting his argument that there must be uniformity in scientific writing and publishing?
2. Day's audience is the scientific community, the "students, authors, editors" whom he feels need to be able to understand what a scientific paper is and is not. How do you think his sense of that audience affects the tone of his delivery?

Language

1. In paragraph 17, in comparing scientific to literary writing, Day says of the former that it is a "more prosaic procedure." Look the word "prosaic" up in your dictionary, and explain your understanding of his meaning.

2. One of Day's goals in scientific writing is "uniformity." Look the word up and explain why you think uniformity is a requisite of this specialized form of writing but not of the other writing you've read about in this section.
3. Day uses many terms that reflect his scientific background: assess, disclosure, screening, primary. Find other examples and decide if you feel these terms are appropriate to his discussion or if they distract from it.

Vocabulary

substantive	assess	amorphous
disclosure	prosaic	abstract
disgorgement	belabored	
equivocation	grandiloquence	

Writing Suggestion

1. Robert Day's essay is quite different from the other essays in this section. He writes in a different style and to a different audience, and his concerns are unlike those of the other writers in this section. Write an essay in which you contrast Day's essay with any other selection in the chapter, considering such points as tone, style, diction, and purpose.

Copyrights and Acknowledgments

MAN THE TALKER   From *Word Play: What Happens When People Talk* by Peter Farb. Copyright © 1973 by Peter Farb. Reprinted by permission of Alfred A. Knopf, Inc.

THE WORM IN THE BRAIN   Copyright © 1979 by Richard Mitchell. By permission of Little, Brown and Company.

THE HYSTERIA ABOUT WORDS   Reprinted by permission of The National Observer, © Dow Jones & Company, Inc. 1963. All rights reserved.

A GROWING WEALTH OF WORDS   © 1981 Saturday Review Magazine Co. Reprinted by permission.

HUMPTY DUMPTY   Reprinted from *Alice in Wonderland* by Lewis Carroll, A Norton Critical Edition, Edited by Donald J. Gray, by permission of W.W. Norton & Company, Inc. Copyright © 1971 by W.W. Norton & Company, Inc.

NOTES ON PUNCTUATION   From *The Medusa and the Snail* by Lewis Thomas. Copyright © 1974, 1975, 1976, 1977, 1978, 1979 by Lewis Thomas. Reprinted by permission of Viking Penguin Inc.

DOCTORTALK   Reprinted by permission of *The New Republic*, © 1979, The New Republic, Inc.

RYBERNIAN   From *Family Matters*, Copyright © 1982 by Burton Bernstein. Reprinted by permission of Summit Books, a Simon & Schuster division of Gulf & Western Corporation. This article originally appeared in *The New Yorker*.

ON GOING HOME   From *Slouching Towards Bethlehem* by Joan Didion. Copyright © 1967, 1968 by Joan Didion. Reprinted by permission of Farrar, Straus and Giroux, Inc.

A VISIT TO MY AUNT   From " 'How Are You?' 'I Am Fine, Thank You, And You?' " by Maxine Hong Kingston, in *The State of the Language*, Leonard Michaels and Christopher Ricks, eds. Reprinted by permission of the University of California Press.

Copyrights and Acknowledgments

SEXISM IN THE LANGUAGE OF MARRIAGE   From *Sexism in Language*, © 1977 by NCTE. Reprinted with the permission of the National Council of Teachers of English, Urbana, Ill.

LYING WELL IS THE BEST REVENGE   Reprinted from *Psychology Today Magazine*. Copyright © 1982, Ziff-Davis Publishing Company.

LETTER FROM BIRMINGHAM JAIL   From *Why We Can't Wait* by Martin Luther King, Jr. Copyright © 1963 by Martin Luther King, Jr. By permission of Harper & Row, Publishers, Inc.

THE SECOND GOD   From *The Second God* by Tony Schwartz. Copyright © 1981 by Tony Schwartz. Reprinted by permission of Random House, Inc.

PORNO-VIOLENCE   From *Mauve Gloves & Madmen, Clutter & Vine* by Tom Wolfe. Copyright © 1967, 1976 by Tom Wolfe. Reprinted by permission of Farrar, Straus and Giroux, Inc.

WHERE HAVE THE CHILDREN GONE?   Copyright © 1982, by Newsweek, Inc. All rights reserved. Reprinted by permission.

AN EPITAPH FOR SATURDAY REVIEW—AND CULTURE TOO   Reprinted by permission of *The Los Angeles Times*. Copyright 1982. This first appeared in *The Los Angeles Times*.

AS THE LINGO LANGUISHES   Copyright © 1980 by M.F.K. Fisher. From *The State of the Language*, edited by Leonard Michaels and Christopher Ricks, published by University of California Press.

IT'S NATURAL! IT'S ORGANIC! OR IS IT?   Copyright 1980 by Consumers Union of United States, Inc., Mount Vernon, NY 10550. Reprinted by permission from *Consumer Reports*, July 1980.

WHY I'M NOT BORED   November 30, 1974—in *Before My Eyes* by Stanley Kauffmann. Copyright © 1974 by Stanley Kauffmann. By permission of Harper & Row, Publishers, Inc.

POLITICS AND THE ENGLISH LANGUAGE   Copyright 1946 by Sonia Brownell Orwell; renewed 1974 by Sonia Orwell. Reprinted from *Shooting an Elephant and Other Essays* by George Orwell by permission of Harcourt Brace Jovanovich, Inc.

THE INDISPENSABLE OPPOSITION   Used with permission of the President and Fellows of Harvard College. Originally printed in the *Atlantic Monthly*, August 1939.

CONFUSION WORSE CONFOUNDED   Copyright © 1977 by *Harper's Magazine*. All rights reserved. Reprinted from the April 1977 issue by special permission.

THE POLITICAL VOCABULARY OF HOMOSEXUALITY   © 1980 by Edmund White. Reprinted by permission of the author.

ARIA   From *The Hunger of Memory* by Richard Rodriguez. Copyright © 1982 by Richard Rodriguez. Reprinted by permission of David R. Godine, Publisher, Boston.

FOUL PLAY: SPORTS METAPHORS AS PUBLIC DOUBLESPEAK   Copyright © 1976 by NCTE. Reprinted with the permission of the National Council of Teachers of English, Urbana, Ill.

Copyrights and Acknowledgments

YOU COULD LOOK IT UP   From *Casey*, Copyright © 1967 by Joseph Durso. Reprinted by permission of the author.

HYPERBOLE'S CHILD   Reprinted by permission of A. Bartlett Giamatti. Originally appeared in *Harper's Magazine*.

SPORTS   Copyright © 1980 by William K. Zinsser. Reprinted by permission of the author.

STORIES FOR A RAINY AFTERNOON   From *Five Seasons* by Roger Angell. Copyright © 1972, 1973, 1974, 1975, 1976, 1977 by Roger Angell. Reprinted by permission of SIMON & SCHUSTER, a Division of Gulf & Western Corporation.

UNCONQUERABLE   Copyright © 1974 by Walter W. Smith. Reprinted by permission of TIMES BOOKS/The New York Times Book Co., Inc. from *Strawberries in the Wintertime: The Sporting World of Red Smith*.

THE COMMON LANGUAGE OF SCIENCE   From *Out of My Later Years* by Albert Einstein, published by Philosophical Library, 1950. Reprinted by permission of the publisher.

SOCIAL TALK   From *The Lives of a Cell* by Lewis Thomas. Copyright © 1972 by the *New England Journal of Medicine*. Copyright © 1974 by Lewis Thomas. Reprinted by permission of Viking Penguin Inc.

KOKO'S FIRST WORDS   From *The Education of Koko* by Francine Patterson and Eugene Linden. Copyright © 1981 by Francine Patterson and Eugene Linden. Reprinted by permission of Holt, Rinehart and Winston, Publishers.

THE FIRST LITERATE COMPUTERS?   Reprinted from *Psychology Today Magazine*. Copyright © 1978, Ziff-Davis Publishing Company.

A RHETORIC OF DISEASE   From *Illness as Metaphor* by Susan Sontag. Copyright © 1977, 1978 by Susan Sontag. Reprinted by permission of Farrar, Straus and Giroux, Inc.

THINGS SEEN INTO THINGS KNOWN   From *Daybooks* by Edward Weston. Quotations by Edward Weston © 1981, Arizona Board of Regents, Center for Creative Photography.

FILM-MAKING   From *Four Screen Plays of Ingmar Bergman*, Copyright © 1960 by Ingmar Bergman. Reprinted by permission of SIMON & SCHUSTER, a Division of Gulf & Western Corporation.

TO MAKE UP A DANCE   From *Dance to the Piper* by Agnes de Mille. Reprinted by permission of Harold Ober Associates Incorporated. Copyright © 1951, 1952 by Agnes de Mille. Copyright renewed 1979, 1980 by Agnes de Mille.

HOW WE LISTEN   From *What to Listen for in Music* by Aaron Copland. Copyright © 1957. Reprinted by permission of McGraw-Hill Book Company.

A FLYING LEAP INTO THE UNKNOWN   From *Nostalgia Isn't What It Used to Be* by Simone Signoret. Copyright © 1976 by Editions du Seuil. English translation copyright © 1978 by Harper & Row, Publishers, Inc.

A WRITER'S DIARY   From *A Writer's Diary* by Virginia Woolf, copyright © 1953, 1954 by Leonard Woolf; renewed 1981, 1982 by Quentin Bell and Angelica Garnett. Reprinted by permission of Harcourt Brace Jovanovich, Inc.

I WANT TO WRITE   Excerpt from *The Diary of a Young Girl* by Anne Frank. Copyright © 1952 by Otto H. Frank. Reprinted by permission of Doubleday & Company, Inc.

THE COLOURS OF WORDS   Reprinted by permission of Harold Ober Associates Incorporated. Copyright © 1961 by the Trustees for the Copyrights of Dylan Thomas.

WRITING   From "A Way of Writing" by William Stafford. Reprinted by permission of *Field* Magazine.

WHY I WRITE   Reprinted by permission of Wallace & Sheil Agency, Inc. Copyright © 1976 by Joan Didion. Article first appeared in *The New York Times Book Review*.

WHY A SURGEON WOULD WRITE   From *Mortal Lessons*, Copyright © 1974, 1975, 1976 by Richard Selzer. Reprinted by permission of SIMON & SCHUSTER, a Division of Gulf & Western Corporation.

WHAT IS A SCIENTIFIC PAPER?   Reproduced with permission from R.A. Day's *How to Write and Publish a Scientific Paper*, ISI Press, Philadelphia, 1979 (© Robert A. Day).

```
A 3
B 4
C 5
D 6
E 7
F 8
G 9
H 0
I  1
J  2
```